# Digital
# Certificates

# Digital
# Certificates
## Applied Internet Security

Jalal Feghhi
Jalil Feghhi
Peter Williams

**ADDISON–WESLEY**

**An Imprint of Addison Wesley Longman, Inc.**
Reading, Massachusetts · Harlow, England · Menlo Park, California
Berkeley, California · Don Mills, Ontario · Sydney
Bonn · Amsterdam · Tokyo · Mexico City

Many of the designations used by manufacturers and sellers to distinguish their products are claimed as trademarks. Where those designations appear in this book, and Addison Wesley Longman, Inc., was aware of a trademark claim, the designations have been printed in initial capital letters or all capital letters.

The authors and publisher have taken care in preparation of this book, but make no expressed or implied warranty of any kind and assume no responsibility for errors or omissions. No liability is assumed for incidental or consequential damages in connection with or arising out of the use of the information or programs contained herein.

The publisher offers discounts of this book when ordered in quantity for special sales. For more information, please contact:

Corporate, Government, and Special Sales
Addison Wesley Longman, Inc.
One Jacob Way
Reading, Massachusetts 01867
Tel: (781) 944-3700

*Library of Congress Cataloging-in-Publication Data*

Feghhi, Jalal.
   Digital certificates : applied Internet security / Jalal Feghhi, Jalil Feghhi,
Peter Williams.
      p.  cm.
   Includes index.
   ISBN 0-201-30980-7
   1. Internet (Computer network) — Security measures. 2. Data
encryption (Computer science) 3. Computer security. I. Feghhi,
Jalil, 1960– . II. Williams, Peter, 1937– . III. Title.
TK5105.875.I57F44 1998
005.8—dc21                                                          98–22330
                                                                          CIP

Text printed on recycled paper.

ISBN 0-201-30980-7
1 2 3 4 5 6 7 8 9—MA—0302010099
*First printing, September 1998*

*We dedicate this thoughtful work to our families, Paula, Niloufar, Ebrahim, Samar, Kathy, and Jessica; our parents; Adna; our fond memory of Hassan, Audrey, and Frank; our friends; and all the readers who use it to promote a fun, friendly, and multicultural Internet.*

# CONTENTS

# Foreword

Only 10 years ago, security technology was entirely the province of the national security agencies, with minimal systems activity in industry or academia. Of course there was cryptographic activity elsewhere, but the concept of open secure systems or of interoperability were hardly considered. Several advances have come together to change this situation. The speed of computers has made software solutions for many cryptographic algorithms practicable. The growth of the Internet has made communications between different communities much more feasible—and has led to large-scale use by industry and commerce. On the one hand, this has led to the growth of electronic commerce; on the other hand, it has led to increasing vulnerability of commercial systems. These developments have a need for security technology to allow sensitive transactions, to prevent unauthorized access to sensitive information, and to protect sensitive infrastructure.

The increase in the need for security products has had a number of contradictory ramifications. The national security authorities have tried to prevent too widespread an adoption of strong cryptographic protection—partly by inhibiting standardization and partly by legislative action. At the same time, privacy concerns have led some countries to require strong protection by law—and even mandated that the protection be certified in various ways. Commerce has become concerned that they may be debarred from their own information by disgruntled employers, and law enforcement *employees?* authorities are concerned that they could be hampered in their work. This has led to a number of requirements for a much more manageable and verifiable security infrastructure with specification of many new facilities. Examples are the need to verify the security services provided, to provide key recovery, and to provide flexible facilities. It has also led to a huge demand for industrial-strength security products.

The first generation of security activities to address the requirements resulting from this were very amateurish. These traits were common in most of the early security activities of the late 1980s and early 1990s. For example, the authors and I had such activities in mobile X.400, PEM, and X.509 v1 certificates and security pilots. It is only in the last few years that one of us has started to put together well-designed, high-quality, integrated open security services. It has become clear that many more management activities were required than had been anticipated. It is necessary to have a structured approach to the provision of the necessary components and provision of security services. Moreover, it is not possible to look at the needs of security services by themselves. For example, the attempts to mandate specific electronic mail systems or types of directories because of their security potential have failed; security services must be integrated into the services people wish to use. Even now many systems are closed; they work well if a security domain uses services from one supplier or domain; cross-certification or interoperability between suppliers or across different classes of application fail.

This book addresses some of the countercurrents just mentioned. It considers the range of components needed for complete systems. It gives a current account of many of the relevant systems that have been developed. It discusses many of the choices that must be made for those wanting to install systems. In this it provides a welcome contrast to the specific products from manufacturers. In fact, the in-depth discussion of what can be provided in security systems on the Internet allows the reader to be much more searching in an analysis of the suitability of such products. This may, in turn, influence suppliers to provide more of the services that the market, and the users, really need.

I welcome this book. It will occupy an important place in my bookcase for many years.

*Peter T. Kirstein*
*Professor of Computer Communications Systems*
*and Director of Research*
*Computer Science Department*
*University College, London*

# Preface

Public-key cryptography and digital certificates are relative newcomers on the Internet scene, although they have been around for many years in closed commercial and financial networks and military systems. In this book, we concentrate on the aspects of these technologies that target the Internet culture and address the needs of Internet consumers.

Internet consumers have already begun to reap the benefits of digital certificates. They can use popular e-mail products to send and receive secure e-mail, connect to secure Web sites to purchase goods or obtain services, and allow downloaded Java applets or ActiveX controls to run on their computers after verifying the origin of the downloaded code.

Systems engineers have traditionally faced many challenges when incorporating security technologies into consumer systems. They usually add protection mechanisms late in the design process, and they can never quite get rid of all the outstanding security issues—the maze of twisty paths and interconnections between protector and protectee seem simply endless. *The basic trick to managing the unmanageable seems to be to exploit trust.* But, to rely upon such a vague concept to solve engineering problems, we also need an infrastructure that addresses assurance, confidence, liability, insurance, agreements, and accreditation.

However, do trust and the supporting infrastructure enable individuals and corporations to conduct monetary transactions on the Internet? How can we implement the required notion of trust in this global, open network?

In this book, we argue that digital certificates are destined to enable secure electronic commerce on the Internet. The technological liberation introduced by public-key cryptography allows the public component of key pairs to be shared openly, thus creating a basic infrastructure for trust-based security. Packaged in internationally standardized message formats, public keys can be signed and certified to form identity certificates by anyone who wishes to be a certificate-issuing authority.

By using the corresponding personal, private component of the key pair, you can establish your identity to Web sites to purchase goods, obtain services, or just say "Hi! It's me!" to the world in a digitally signed e-mail message. The mathematical relationship between the public and private parts of a key pair enables anyone to ascertain your identity by verifying that you are indeed in the possession of your private key, merely by using your public key. Now, if consumers trust popular, branded certificate-issuing authorities to assure the *quality* of this kind of key certification, we are well on the way to establishing trust and facilitating commerce on the Internet. We have addressed the hard problem of identifying and authenticating arbitrary, willing parties with standards corporations and society required to embrace electronic commerce.

We would like to invite you to share our passion and take the plunge into the once-so-secret world of cryptography and keys and help build the Internet public-key infrastructure. We encourage you to begin obtaining or issuing certificates and to use them for experimentation, business, or to reduce the cost of using more expensive trusted networking technologies. By using certificate-based security systems, deploying prototype services, coming to grips with the basic building blocks of certificate-issuing systems, and sharing the learning process with others, we will collectively build another layer of net relationships, this time fashioning the Internet's trust networks.

By reinventing a world founded on trust instead of fear of dominance, not only do we all win additional safety and security, but the resulting infrastructure will expand commercial and technological opportunities and horizons. In creating a mass medium, however, we need to be careful not to undermine precisely what made the Internet so appealing to ordinary people when we deploy a common security infrastructure. We need to ensure the Internet can still represent the individual, even when it protects institutions. Step forward, digital certificates.

## Intended Readers, Reading Strategies, and Distinctive Treatment

We have written the book with three groups of readers in mind:

- Users who require a technical perspective on mass-market public-key security applications

- Programmers and designers of certificate-based security solutions

- Senior managers charged with fielding or buying certification authority systems and services

Although we have taken pains to present our discussion in a logical fashion that would permit a sequential reading of the book, you may prefer to take your own route through the chapters.

By exploiting the skills of each author, we have sought to combine an experienced system designer's objective view of actual mass-market system and security technologies, a wizard developer's presentation of the reality of programming and customizing certificate-issuing systems for local needs, and many years of experience in designing and implementing standards-based, certificate-based security systems. We trust that the combination of our backgrounds and skills will enable you to satisfy your reading goals.

## About This Book

This book addresses issues concerning the scale and diversity of an increasingly prosperous but as yet rather unsecure Internet. It explains how digital certificates establish trust for the Internet and how trust enables applications to operate safely, as intended by their original designers. We have selected topics that range from introducing the fundamentals of security and digital certificates to providing coverage of advanced material on certification practice statements and computer security management. Often, we introduce a concept early on and revisit it later in the book, each time analyzing and explaining it from a different perspective.

We leave it to other books to address these matters and other topics, such as certificate revocation, security policy, and systems for nonrepudiation. One book in particular is an excellent companion to this one: *Secure Computing—Threats and Safeguards* (McGraw-Hill, 1997), written by Rita C. Summers. This book contains a digest of much of the available published research in the area of secure computing, and it is especially relevant to the advanced topics of this book covered in Part IV.

## Content of the Book

The book is composed of six parts and four appendices. The first three parts cover the fundamentals of security, cryptography, and digital certificates; certificate-based security applications that address threats to Internet consumers; and vendors that supply public-key–based products and services. Part IV presents advanced material aimed at users and operators interested in the world of commercial-grade public key infrastructure.

Parts V and VI begin a practical journey to round out the ideas presented in the earlier parts of the book. They provide deployment projects to help a programmer or system administrator obtain hands-on experience with the application of digital certificates to enable Web server and client authentication. These parts also demonstrate how to set up a local certificate-issuing system that outsources key management using VeriSign OnSite, and how to program Microsoft Certificate Server to issue certificates using a variety of languages (Java, Visual Basic, C++) and the open X.509 certificate formats. You can refer to the part descriptions that we have provided for each part of the book to find out more information about the material covered in each part.

The four appendices contain material from other sources. Appendix A, from RSA Laboratories, explains the language of certificate notation (ASN.1). Appendix B, from Microsoft, provides a summary of certificate extension formats supported in many of the commonly available certificate-using products. Finally, Appendix C provides a summary of VeriSign Certification Practice Statement, and Appendix D contains VeriSign's perspective on the economics of outsourcing key management.

## Software Used in This Book

Change is happening fast in the field of digital certificates, and commercial vendors are rapidly deploying new public-key–based security products in the marketplace. This fast rate of change posed a difficult question for us: How much vendor-specific material should we include to present a technological perspective on mass-market public-key security applications without jeopardizing the useful lifespan of this book?

Because this book is about the applied aspects of public-key technology as well as its theory, we decided to provide a rather detailed exposition of some relevant vendor-specific products that were new to the marketplace at the time we were writing this book. However, we limited our coverage of products for which there is already a reasonable amount of documentation. By carefully limiting the number of vendor-specific technologies and providing a considerable amount of essential, basic material, we believe we have written a book that will serve as a fundamental guide to digital certificates.

We have used the following vendor-specific technologies in this book. To explain the fundamentals of trust-based software management, we have used Netscape Communicator 4.04 and Microsoft Internet Explorer 4.0 browsers. To illustrate how to send and receive secure e-mail, we have used Netscape Messenger and Microsoft Outlook Express, which come bundled with the browsers. We have used sample Web pages from the VeriSign public site to illustrate the steps required to obtain certificates and to set up a local certificate-issuing system that outsources key management to VeriSign. Finally, we have used Microsoft Internet Information Server 4.0 to illustrate server and client authentication, and we have developed the practical projects of Part VI with Microsoft Certificate Server 1.0 running on Windows NT Server 4.0.

## Getting in Touch

For updates to this book, check out the Web page http://www.awl.com/cseng/titles/0-201-30980-7.

# Acknowledgments

First, we would like to acknowledge many unnamed people who have worked within the standards communities to define and lay out the possibility of a collective security infrastructure for open networks. According to Douglas Steedman,[1] the primary forces included Hoyt Kesterson, Sharon Boeyen, and Al Grimstad, who worked on or contributed to the original X.500 Directory, upon which so much of this work is founded. Seminal work in digital certificates in the open Internet space is largely due to Steve Kent and John Linn, their supporters and founders, and a small cast of several hundred active security newsgroup participants. Without their persistence in arguing for such a clearly workable technology as digital certificates in the Internet Engineering Task Force, we probably would not be where we are today. We would also like to acknowledge the outreach programs of various government agencies such as NIST, the National Security Agency and Department of Defense, the U.K. Defense Research Agency, and the R&D and pilot programs of the European Commission.

Policy management ideas have fundamentally affected commercial certificate-based security systems, taking them from pure specifications to viable businesses that solve real security problems. We will not even attempt to list those from the legal, banking, and accounting professions who ensured that this vital topic became a part of the technical infrastructure, but we do recognize their fundamental contribution.

Many people contributed to this book by reviewing parts or all of the manuscript: Russell Nelson from Crynwr Software; Sigmund Handelman from IBM's T.J. Watson Research Center; Theodore S. Barassi from CertCo, LLC; Dave Crocker from Brandenburg Consulting; William James from The James Gang; Norman Weinstein; Tim Matthews from RSA Data Security; and Warwick Ford from VeriSign. We would especially like to thank Arn Schaeffer from VeriSign who meticulously read the entire manuscript during his vacation.

The publishing of this book would not have been possible without Addison Wesley Longman. Karen Gettman and Mary Hart worked with us from start to finish. John Fuller and Jason Jones helped with electronic production of the book. Maureen Hurley acted as the production editor. The marketing team at Addison

---

1. Chair of the CCITT Directory group and author of *X.500—The directory standards and its application*, Technology Appraisals Ltd.

Wesley Longman included Tracy Russ, Marketing Manager; Katherine Kwack, Marketing Specialist; Deborah King, Publicist; and Laura Potter, Marketing Assistant. Finally, we would like to acknowledge all the hard work that Karen Tongish put into copyediting the manuscript.

Finally, we would like to recognize the following organizations for giving us permission to use their material in this book: Ed Gerck, ITU, Microsoft Corp., Network Associates, Inc., RSA Data Securities, Inc., U.S. Army, Naval Computer and Telecommunications Command, and VeriSign Inc. We would also like to acknowledge VeriSign and @Home as the companies that employed the authors at the time we were writing the manuscript. The ideas presented in this book, however, are our own and not necessarily those of our employers.

# Part I

# Security, Cryptography, and Digital Certificates

In January 1997 when one of the authors of this book went to work for VeriSign, an Internet security company, some people thought that he worked as a security guard, and others thought he worked for a company that traded securities on Wall Street. "No, I work for a company that enables secure communications over the Internet," he said. Over the past 2 years, however, people have been using the Internet to conduct commerce or browse for information. As a result, they have become more aware of the security issues related to the Internet.

So, what is Internet security? Why do we need it? How can we use it to build applications that communicate securely over the Internet? Chapter 1 addresses these questions. You should read this chapter to understand that there are threats lurking out there in the Internet and that there are security services available to safeguard your assets. You should also begin to understand how applications communicate with one another over a network and how communications can be secured.

But what is the foundation of secure communications? When applications communicate over the Internet, there are no guards to watch the flow of packets, no way to prevent eavesdroppers from sniffing the network, and no way to keep intruders from tampering with your communications. In Chapter 2, you will learn that the foundation of Internet communications security is mathematics. Everything boils down to mathematics, and mathematics of ciphers alone dictates how secure your communications really are. After you read Chapter 2, you should understand what secret keys are, what public and private keys are, and what you can do with these mathematical keys.

The term *digital certificates* is part of the title of this book, so it is about time we started talking about certificates. Chapter 3 teaches you what these binary large objects are, what information they contain, and who issues them. You should also understand that when you obtain a digital certificate, you have a public and a private key, you keep your private key to yourself, and you ask a certification authority to certify your public key as your own.

Chapter

# 1

# Security and the Internet

All Internet communications are inherently unsecure and subject to eavesdropping and tampering. Any Internet communication might be hostile, intended to steal sensitive information from a user's computer, destroy files, or cripple a computer system. A rogue server in the Internet can trick unwary users into revealing sensitive information. A dishonest user may masquerade as an authorized user of a system in order to carry out fraudulent activities. Internet security issues are numerous.

This chapter provides a framework for discussing and analyzing these issues and aims to establish the problem space that digital certificates and Internet security seek to address. We will begin with an abstract model of communication and computation over the Internet. We will continue by developing the notions of threats, assets, safeguards, attacks, policies, and services, and will discuss mechanisms used to formalize the treatment of such issues. We will then provide a high-level model for open-systems communications, describe the ISO Reference model and the TCP/IP Internet model of communications, and conclude by interrelating many of the disparate concepts presented in this chapter.

## Why Security in the Internet?

Computing over the Internet has two significant characteristics: distributed processing and open communications. Figure 1-1 illustrates an abstract model for this computation, in which two local environments are connected to each other by the Internet. The local environment can be as simple as a standalone PC, or it can consist of a number of heterogeneous workstations connected over a local area network (LAN). The processing of a task may be distributed between the two local environments, which communicate with each other via the Internet. All communications via the Internet are *open* and, unless protected, are subject to eavesdropping or tampering.

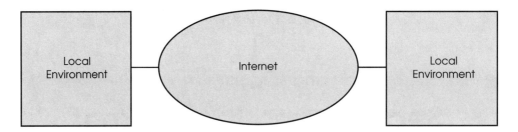

**Figure 1-1**   An abstract model for computing over the Internet.

The Internet model of computation poses a number of security issues. To better appreciate the impact of these issues, let's assume that the local environments in Figure 1-1 represent a Web browser and a Web server. Here are the security issues:

- **Eavesdropping**   All messages between the browser and the server can be intercepted by an eavesdropper. If messages are encrypted, the eavesdropper may attempt to decrypt them and recover the original messages.

- **Tampering**   All messages between the browser and the server are subject to malicious alterations. The objective might be to effect a desired behavior on the server or the browser or to disrupt the communication link.

- **Unsecure server**   The server or the host computer may be broken into by an enemy to steal sensitive information, such as credit card numbers.

- **Denial of service**   The server is subject to threats intended to disrupt its operation. A disrupted server may become unavailable for use by authorized users.

- **Downloadable code**   Code can be downloaded from a server to a browser and executed locally on the browser's host computer. The downloaded code may attempt to improperly access and transfer sensitive information to the server.

- **Unsecure browser**   A buggy browser can be attacked by an intruder in an attempt to steal sensitive information.

- **Impersonation and masquerading**   An impostor can impersonate an authorized user to a server and carry out improper activities, such as transferring funds. Similarly, a rogue server may masquerade as an authentic server to trick a user into releasing confidential information to unauthorized parties.

Society's increasing dependence on computers and the Internet compound these security issues and provide opportunities for pernicious attacks. The ultimate goal of security is to minimize the vulnerabilities of computer resources and assets against threats and to discourage attacks by keeping the cost of breaking into a system very high compared to any potential gain in doing so.

## Threats, Safeguards, and Attacks

A **threat** is a person, a computer program, a natural disaster, an accident, or even an idea that poses some danger to an asset. An **asset** is anything of value. A threat might be intentional, such as deliberately breaking into a system, or accidental, such as spilling coffee on a computer. Threats can come from people outside an organization, or they can come from disgruntled employees inside. Threats may be active, such as disrupting the operation of a Web server, or passive, such as quietly eavesdropping on communications between two parties. In the rest of this section, we analyze threats in detail and identify ways to protect assets from threats. Refer to [FORD97], [RUSS91], [SUMM97], and [X800] for a similar treatment of this material.

### Intentional versus Accidental Threats

Much more information is lost through accidental mishaps than through intentional malice. Accidental threats can take a variety of forms. For example, a privileged user can change the read protection on a confidential file, a user can delete a needed file or spill a soft drink on a keyboard, or an untrained system administrator can misconfigure a firewall. Accidental threats cannot always be prevented. The extent of their damage, however, can be minimized by instituting and following proper security procedures. We categorize natural threats, such as fires, earthquakes, floods, tornadoes, or power failures, as accidental threats.

Intentional threats are deliberately instigated by attackers in an attempt to compromise the security of a system for financial gain, industrial espionage, or some other motive. Most of the research in the area of information, physical, and personnel security has been geared toward identifying and thwarting such threats. All the threats listed in the "Active versus Passive Threats" section of this chapter are considered intentional threats.

### Insider versus Outsider Threats

It is estimated that about 80 percent of system penetrations are carried out by authorized insiders who violate their access privileges to perform unauthorized functions. The motivations behind insider threats vary widely. A disgruntled employee might be trying to take revenge by disrupting a service or may be attempting to steal and sell sensitive information. A greedy employee may be bribed or blackmailed into revealing a password or might intentionally not arm a security alarm system when leaving the office for the day. Not all insider threats are intentional, however. An employee may not be aware of a new security procedure or may forget to shred sensitive printed documents.

Outsider threats are carried out by outside enemies who do not have any authorized access privileges. They may use a home PC and a modem to penetrate a computer that is connected to the Internet, or they may disguise themselves as maintenance personnel to gain access to a building. Serious threats can be realized when an outsider threat is combined with an insider threat.

## Active versus Passive Threats

Passive threats constitute dangers that do not interfere with the overall operation of a system or change its state, even though they might compromise its integrity by accessing privileged information. Communications monitoring is the most prominent passive threat, in which an eavesdropper quietly listens to the communication between two parties without disrupting it. Tapping a telephone wire or sniffing packets from a network are common methods of monitoring a communication. In an open network such as the Internet, it is usually very difficult to detect communications monitoring, and it is impossible to prevent it.

An active threat goes beyond passively monitoring a communication link—it actually disrupts the operation of a system or actively attempts to access privileged information. The following are active threats:

- **Authorization violation**  A person misuses authorization privileges to perform unauthorized functions. This type of threat is usually posed by insiders, but it may also be employed by outsiders who use a penetrated employee's account to gain unauthorized access to the more privileged parts of a system.

- **Communications tampering**  This type of threat interferes with the communications between two or more parties by modifying their messages, inserting spurious messages, deleting part or all of their messages, or replaying them. Communications tampering may even take the form of duping a user into revealing sensitive information to a rogue server.

- **Denial of service**  Authorized access to services, resources, or information is deliberately hampered. This type of threat may be accomplished by suppressing traffic or generating extra traffic. For example, a Web server might be flooded with packets to disrupt its intended service. The denial-of-service threat might be targeted at all users of a system or a particular user. An attacker might, for example, suppress all messages directed to a security logging service to disrupt its function.

- **Man-in-the-middle**  This is a threat caused by an attacker who intercepts all of the communications between two parties, fooling them into thinking that they are communicating with each other, while they are actually communicating with the attacker.

- **Masquerade**  An impostor pretends to be an authorized entity to gain access privileges, or an authorized user might impersonate another authorized user in order to gain extra access privileges. Masquerade attacks are typically carried out in combination with other kinds of active attacks, such as a replay attack, to penetrate a system's defenses.

- **Replay**  An enemy repeats a message or part of a message to produce an unauthorized effect. The enemy may, for instance, capture and replay a sequence of authentication messages in order to masquerade as a legitimate user.

- **Repudiation**  A party involved in or witness to a communication later denies being involved in or a witness to it.

- **Spoofing**  The spoofing threat is a ruse that causes a legitimate user to release sensitive information to an impostor or carry out an action that violates system security. A rogue server, for example, may dupe users into believing that they are communicating with an authentic server and steal their credit card numbers.

- **System penetration**  An impostor gains access to a system either by masquerading as an authorized user or exploiting system weaknesses. The impostor usually first penetrates a nonprivileged or less secure computer and then uses the penetrated system to launch attacks against more privileged computers.

- **Trojan horse**  A Trojan horse is a computer program that disguises itself as a legitimate application in order to carry out improper actions. A good example of a Trojan horse is a rogue login program that writes a user's login and password to a file before actually logging in the user. The file can be later visited by an insider or mailed to an outsider to launch a system penetration attack.

## Safeguards and Attacks

**Safeguards** are physical controls, mechanisms, measures, and policies put in place to prevent threats from being realized or to reduce the impact of a realized threat. A safeguard against communications monitoring, for example, is to encrypt messages before transmitting them across an open network. A system is usually penetrated at its weakest point, so to be effective safeguards must address all areas of security, including computer security, communications security, personnel security, and physical security. For example, encryption is an effective safeguard against passive eavesdropping, but it is useless if the system has no physical security restrictions.

Certain security services provide safeguards against threats to computer and communications security. They provide defense against impostors masquerading as authorized users, authorization violation, eavesdropping, communication tampering, and repudiation. We will discuss these services in detail in the "Information Security Services" section later in this chapter.

An attack is a realization of a threat. Attacks result from vulnerabilities, which are weaknesses in a safeguard or the absence of a safeguard. Security measures usually increase the cost of a system and make it harder to use. Threat assessment is the process of identifying specific threats against which a system requires protection. A system is usually vulnerable in many ways, but an attacker may not be able to exploit all of them.

## Security Policies

A security policy, from an abstract perspective, states the security-related considerations that are, or are not, permitted during the operation of a system. A top-level security policy sets forth considerations that are integral to the secure operation of a system without necessarily providing implementation details on how the desired results should be achieved. A security policy usually goes through an iterative process of refinement based on the specifics of the system to which it will be applied. The resulting policy restates the general considerations in more precise terms drawn directly from the security requirements of the system.

An asset usually has a security policy even though one might not be explicitly defined. You might, for example, back up important files on your home computer on a regular basis. Similarly, you may have decided to disable Java or JavaScript inside your browser or use PKZIP to encrypt sensitive files. As the value of your assets increases, it becomes more important for you to define appropriate security policies and enforce them.

Many threats to computer and communications security involve breaches of authorization. Specifying authorized and unauthorized behavior, therefore, is an important part of a security policy. Policies can be considered identity-based or rule-based depending on how authorization considerations are stated.

### Identity-Based Policies

Identity-based security policies specify authorization criteria based on specific, unique attributes to provide access on a need-to-know basis. A common way to implement these policies is through **access control lists** (ACLs), which essentially list all the entities who are authorized to access a resource. An ACL is considered a part of a resource, and a system must check its ACL before it allows access to that resource. Digital certificates provide another identity-based access-control mechanism (see Chapter 6).

## Rule-Based Policies

A rule-based security policy uses a set of rules and (usually) labels to determine the authorization requirements of a system. Every person, process, and piece of data has a security label. For example, a document may be labeled *unclassified, confidential, secret,* or *top secret.* A person has a clearance label, depending on his or her level of trustworthiness. A rule-based security policy sets forth the appropriate labels, clearance levels, and rules governing authorized access. A rule might specify, for example, that top secret documents can be accessed only by those with the highest clearance level. Unlike an ACL, a rule is not managed as part of a resource. A more sophisticated use of labels and rules is employed by the Department of Defense (DoD) to implement its security polices.

# Information Security

A security policy formalizes the proper and improper uses of a system, the possible threats against the system, and safeguards to protect assets from the threats. Perhaps the most important asset of a system is the information it contains. Many of the threats we have outlined in this chapter have the ultimate objective of improperly accessing information.

**Information security** is the discipline of ensuring that information is not revealed to unauthorized people, information is not tampered with, and authorized people are not impeded from accessing computer resources. Computer security and communications security are two divisions of information security. **Computer security** deals with securing data stored on a computer, whereas **communications security** addresses the protection of data while it is in transit from one system to another.

It is critical to keep in mind that information security must be used in conjunction with other security disciplines to provide a completely secure system. It would be pointless, for example, to protect sensitive data while it is in transit from one computer to another if the computers themselves are not physically secure and can be freely accessed. Some security disciplines relevant to information security are the following (we will revisit this topic in Part IV):

- **Administrative security** Administrative security includes tasks such as working with management to define a security policy, performing risk analysis, planning for disasters, monitoring employees, assigning security profiles for user accounts, and doing backups.

- **Media security** Media security ensures that sensitive printed material is shredded when it is no longer needed, sensitive information is reproduced in a controlled manner, and backup tapes containing sensitive information are properly disposed of if they are not needed.

- **Physical security**   Physical security protects computers, disks, backup tapes, computer rooms, and buildings.

- **Personnel security**   This area of security deals with informing employees of security policies, identifying and controlling sensitive positions, and screening employees.

## Information Security Services

Information security formalizes six security services that have paramount importance to this book, namely, **authentication, authorization, confidentiality, integrity, nonrepudiation,** and **availability.** These six services can safeguard assets from threats to the security of information. They should be used in conjunction with other security disciplines to ensure an overall secure system. The rest of this section will provide an introductory overview of each of these services and briefly mention how to implement each one. For the authentication service, however, we will cover the various implementation methods in much greater detail. See [FORD97] and [X800] for more information about information security technologies.

### Security Services versus Mechanisms

We make a very clear distinction between a security service and a security mechanism. A **security service** is a quality of a system present to satisfy a security policy. A **security mechanism** is a concrete procedure used to actually implement such a quality. A security service identifies *what* is needed, whereas a security mechanism describes *how* to achieve it.

To better understand this distinction, consider a confidentiality service, which protects data from unauthorized access. One way to implement this service is through the encipherment mechanism, which encrypts data to hide it from unauthorized people. Sometimes more than one security mechanism implements a security service. For example, both ACLs and policy labels implement the authorization service.

### Authentication

Authentication provides assurance for the claimed identity of a user—it verifies that you are who you claim you are. A **claimant** is a person, computer program, or device whose identity is being verified; a **principal** is the actual owner of an identity. **Credentials** are the evidence a claimant presents to establish its identity as a principal. The authentication service provides safeguards against man-in-the-middle, masquerade, and spoofing threats.

Two types of authentication are entity authentication and data origin authentication. In **entity authentication,** a user claims to be a legitimate principal of a system; the authentication service provides assurance to prove or refute the claimed identity. **Data origin authentication** provides evidence that a piece of data, such as an e-mail message, in fact originated from a principal. Entity authentication may be unilateral or mutual. In **unilateral entity authentication,** only one of the parties involved in a communications authenticates itself, whereas in **mutual entity authentication** both parties must authenticate themselves. When a Web browser connects to a secure socket layer (SSL)-enabled Web server, for example, it always unilaterally authenticates the server; the server may optionally perform a mutual authentication of the browser. Mutual authentication plays an important role in preventing spoofing attacks, in which a rogue server dupes a client into revealing sensitive information or a rogue client improperly accesses a server's information.

The authentication service is especially important to the secure operation of a system. A system usually first authenticates an entity when it attempts to establish communications. The identity of the entity is then used to determine its access privileges or to achieve nonrepudiation. During an authentication protocol, two parties usually agree on a shared secret, which is used to provide confidentiality and integrity.

Authentication mechanisms are mainly based on three paradigms: something you know, something you have, and something you are. In the **something-you-know** paradigm, a claimant presents knowledge of something, such as a password or a personal identification number (PIN). In the **something-you-have** approach, a claimant demonstrates the possession of something, such as a physical key, a badge, an automatic teller machine (ATM) card, or a private key stored in a file or on a smart card. The **something-you-are** paradigm is based on some immutable, verifiable trait of a claimant, such as voice, fingerprint, or retina pattern.

Because any of these techniques alone may not provide sufficient identity assurance, a **multifactor authentication system** may be used. Such a system requires a claimant to present more than one kind of evidence to prove its identity. An ATM, for example, requires a person to demonstrate both the knowledge of a PIN and the possession of a card in order to gain access to his account.

## Passwords and PINs—Something You Know

Passwords are the most widely used mechanism to authenticate a person. In this model, a claimant proves its identity by demonstrating the knowledge of a pass phrase, which is a string of letters and numbers. Passwords are used in almost all authentication schemes to some degree.

Passwords have proven to be one of the major vulnerabilities of authentication systems and are at the root of many security compromises. Perhaps their greatest shortcoming is that people tend to choose passwords that are easy to memorize and, consequently, easy to guess. For a password to be memorizable, it should contain, on average, a vowel in every third character, its characters must be case insensitive, and it should not contain digits or any special characters, such as punctuation marks. Under these conditions, one character of a password contains only 2 bits of random information [KAUF95]. A typical 8-character password has, therefore, only 16 bits of random data, making it vulnerable to an off-line password guessing attack, in which every candidate password is exhaustively tried until the correct password is recovered. Password-based authentication systems are, in general, subject to the following kinds of attacks:

- An eavesdropper might learn a password if it is transmitted unencrypted in an open network.

- An intruder penetrates a computer system and reads the password file.

- An attacker easily guesses a poorly chosen password.

- An attacker cracks a password by exhaustively trying all the words in a dictionary.

- An impostor dupes an inexperienced user into revealing a password, sees a PIN when it is entered on a keyboard, or finds the password on a receipt in a trash can.

- An impostor monitors an encrypted password when it is transmitted and then replays it to impersonate a legitimate user.

## Tokens—Something You Have

A claimant can provide evidence for its identity by demonstrating the possession of a token. A **token** is a physical object—it can be a physical key, a driver's license, an ATM card, an employee badge, a hand-held electronic device, or a smart card (refer to [DREI98] for detailed information about smart cards and their applications). Tokens are usually used in conjunction with passwords to provide a higher degree of assurance about the identity of a claimant. In a two-factor authentication system, a principal must demonstrate both the knowledge of a password and the possession of a token before it can gain access to the system. The password is usually used to unlock the token and make it accessible to the authentication system. See http://www.securitydynamics.com/solutions/products/2factor_index.html for a demonstration of a two-factor authentication system.

Tokens come in a variety of physical forms.[1] Depending on their interface, tokens can be distinguished as human-interface tokens, smart cards, or PCMCIA cards. **Human-interface tokens** provide a digital display screen and possibly a keypad to interface with human users. A user typically reads the displayed number and manually enters it into an authentication system. Because humans must manually transfer data between themselves and authentication systems, human-interface tokens have a very low bandwidth interface. Shortly we will discuss a type of token that generates one-time passwords.

A **smart card** is a credit card-sized token that contains a microprocessor, memory to store programs and data, and six electrical contacts that are used to interface with a card reader. The smart-card reader provides electrical power to the processor and interfaces with it using a low-speed character-based protocol. A smart card usually contains a secret value, such as a secret number or a digital signature private key (private keys are covered in Chapter 2). After inserting a smart card into a card reader, a user must typically enter a PIN to unlock the card and allow an authentication system to verify the identity of the smart card holder. Smart cards have a much higher bandwidth than human-interface cards, but they are still limited to the low-speed interface protocol and the limited processing power of the microchip. Because smart cards require special-purpose card readers, it will be a few years before their use becomes pervasive in authentication systems. Netscape and Microsoft have recently added support for smart cards to their browsers. The VeriSign OnSite LRA service, described in Chapter 10, takes advantage of these modern browsers to issue certificates on smart cards in order to authenticate local registration authority (LRA) administrators (VeriSign ships smart card readers to LRA administrators as a part of its service offering).

A **PCMCIA card** is a token designed to interface with standard multipin sockets typically found on laptops. PCMCIA cards can have much greater processing power and interface bandwidth than smart cards.

Token-based authentication systems can use a variety of schemes to verify the identity of a claimant. In the rest of this section we will explore three such schemes:

- **Synchronous one-time password tokens**

  Security Dynamics (http://www.securitydynamics.com) makes a human-interface token called SecureID that displays a code that changes every minute. The code is calculated by hashing together the current time of day and a secret

---

1. The classification of tokens and some of the material in this section have been derived from the work of Warwick Ford and Michael Baum [FORD97].

value, which is permanently stored in the token. To authenticate oneself, a user must enter a preassigned PIN and the code that is currently being displayed by SecureID into the authentication system. The system retrieves the user's secret value based on the entered PIN, finds the hash of the secret value and the current time of day, compares the result with the code entered by the user, and authenticates the user if they match. The clocks on the one-time password token and the authentication system must be synchronized for this scheme to work.

- **Challenge-response tokens**

  In a challenge-response scheme, the authentication system challenges a claimant with a random number. The claimant enters the challenge into his or her token, which produces a response. The response is calculated by hashing together the challenge and a permanently stored secret value, or it may be calculated by encrypting the challenge under the stored secret value. The authentication system performs a similar calculation and verifies the identity of the claimant if the results match. Typically, the user must enter a PIN to unlock the token. It is possible to bypass the manual entry of the challenge and the response by using a smart card.

- **Digital signature smart cards**

  A smart card can hold the private key and the necessary logic to perform digital signature computations. An authentication system engages in a authentication protocol with the smart card and verifies the identity of a user if the computed digital signature is verified. Digital signatures are discussed in Chapter 2.

## Biometrics—Something You Are

Biometrics provides assurance for a claimant's identity based on measurable physiological, behavioral, and morphological human characteristics. Biometrics are usually used in combination with other authentication paradigms to provide a greater level of assurance for a claimant's identity. An authentication system for entering a building, for example, might require employees to press their thumbs on a glass plate, slide their badges through a slot, and enter a PIN. The following is a list of biometric devices in decreasing order of effectiveness:

- **Retina pattern**   The device probes the unique patterns of blood vessels in a person's retinal tissue to ascertain his or her identity.

- **Fingerprint**   The device uses the unique patterns of a person's fingerprint to verify his or her identity.

- **Handprint**   The device examines the unique geometric measurements of a person's hand to determine his or her identity.

- **Voice pattern**   The device exploits the unique vocal, acoustic, phonetic, or linguistic patterns of a person's voice to verify his or her identity.

- **Keystroke pattern**   The device measures the unique rhythm of a person's typing to ascertain his or her identity.

- **Signature**   The device examines the unique patterns and characteristics of a person's handwritten signature to determine his or her identity.

## Authentication Protocols

The strength of an authentication system depends largely on the capabilities of its supporting infrastructure to store a long cryptographic key and perform cryptographic operations. Humans have neither of these capabilities. Unless the infrastructure supplements these qualities for human users, an authentication system must ultimately rely on a short password to verify the identities of the users. Telephones and dumb terminals are examples of infrastructures that do not have these capabilities.

If a human has access to a smart device, such as a computer or smart card, however, the authenticating system can engage in a more elaborate authentication protocol with the device to verify a claimant's identity. These protocols can leverage complex cryptographic operations and use long cryptographic keys to thwart many kinds of communications-based attacks.

- **Challenge-response protocols**

  A challenge-response protocol allows a claimant to authenticate itself to a system by demonstrating its knowledge of a secret cryptographic value without requiring the claimant to reveal the secret. The authenticating system presents the claimant with a randomly generated number called a **challenge.** The claimant inputs the challenge and the secret to a cryptographic function to calculate a **response.** The system verifies the identity of the claimant if the response is the expected value. Because the challenge is a random number, the challenge-response protocol provides an effective safeguard against replay attacks.

- **Transformed password protocols**

  In this protocol, a claimant processes its password through a hash function and sends the result to an authentication system. The system compares the hash with its own stored value for the correct hash and verifies the claimant's identity if the two values are the same. If the system stores passwords instead of their hashes, it has to calculate the hash of the password before carrying out the comparison. The transformed password protocol prevents passwords from being revealed to eavesdroppers, but it is vulnerable to replay attacks.

- **One-time password protocols**

  The one-time password protocol is an improvement over the transformed password protocol to guard against replay attacks that are combined with eavesdropping. This protocol requires a claimant and an authenticating system to share a small secret number $n$. The claimant hashes its password $n$ times to create a **one-time password** and sends it to the system, which also hashes its own stored copy of the password $n$ times and authenticates the claimant if the two results match. Upon a successful authentication, both parties decrement $n$. An intruder cannot launch a replay attack because the next one-time password will be different, and it cannot be determined from previous ones. In this protocol, it is necessary to change a user's password and reset $n$ when $n$ reaches zero. The S/KEY system is a commercial product from Bellcore (http://www.bellcore.com) that uses one-time passwords for authentication.

- **Digital certificate protocols**

  Digital certificate protocols are a variant of challenge-response protocols in which the secret cryptographic value is a private key and the authenticating system uses the public key corresponding to the private key to verify a response. Digital certificates, private keys, and public keys are covered in detail in Chapter 2.

## Authorization

Authorization, also referred to as access control service, guards against improper, unauthorized access to data or a computer resource—authorization establishes what a user is allowed to do. The term *access* refers to reading data, writing data, executing a program, or using a hardware resource such as a printer. A security system often needs to authenticate a user before it can determine his or her access privileges. The authorization service safeguards assets from system penetration and authorization violation threats.

Access control lists and policy labels are two common mechanisms used to implement the authorization service.

## Confidentiality

Confidentiality, also known as secrecy, ensures that data is not revealed or disclosed to unauthorized people. Data might be stored in a computer, or it might be in transit from one computer to another across a network. The confidentiality service safeguards data against the threat of communications monitoring.

Confidentiality can be end-to-end or link-by-link, depending on which network layer protection is imposed upon. In **end-to-end confidentiality,** data remains protected during the entire communication process, from the moment it leaves a source until it reaches its destination across a network. With **link-by-link confidentiality,** data is protected just before it is physically transmitted; confidentiality becomes part of the communication process and is often invisible to an end user. When link-by-link encrypted data moves through a number of network nodes, each node removes the protection envelope and then reprotects the data based on new parameters. On each node, therefore, data becomes unprotected and exposed.

Confidentiality is not limited to protecting data. Information can leak in other ways. For example, an eavesdropper may be able to monitor the number and size of data packets transmitted from a source to a destination even though the payloads of data packets are protected. **Traffic-flow confidentiality** protects against information leakage by protecting the routing headers of data packets. Link-by-link confidentiality provides traffic-flow confidentiality, whereas end-to-end confidentiality does not.

When protecting data, sometimes it becomes necessary to protect certain fields of data differently than other fields. The Secure Electronic Commerce (SET) protocol for e-commerce, for example, protects a customer's credit card number in such a way that a merchant cannot see the credit card number, but the acquiring bank can access the number and charge the customer. **Selective-field confidentiality** addresses such protection requirements.

Encryption is a common mechanism to implement the confidentiality service. Encryption mangles data into an apparently unintelligible form to prevent unauthorized access. Encryption techniques are discussed at length in Chapter 2.

## Integrity

Integrity protects against improper modifications to messages, duplication of messages, insertion of superfluous messages in message sequences, deletion of part or all of messages in a sequence, or reordering of parts of a message sequence. Data integrity also guards against improper creation of messages or replay of old messages. The integrity service is an effective safeguard against communications tampering and replay threats.

Data integrity is of paramount importance, and sometimes it is more important than confidentiality. The financial community, for example, has for a long time been protecting interbank electronic fund transfers with data integrity services without providing confidentiality.

A variety of cryptographic mechanisms are used to implement data integrity, such as encryption and hash functions. Chapter 2 provides detailed coverage of these techniques.

## Nonrepudiation

Nonrepudiation services prevent a party involved in a communication from later falsely denying having participated in all or part of the communication. A party may attempt to repudiate its involvement to cheat another party, or, perhaps due to a system failure, it mistakenly disputes its involvement. A party may dispute the content of a transaction that has occurred, the transaction time, or the identity of the other party. A nonrepudiation service gathers strong evidence during a communication that can be used to resolve such disagreements and counter the repudiation attack. Refer to [FORD97] for comprehensive coverage of nonrepudiation.

Nonrepudiation of origin and nonrepudiation of delivery are two primary types of nonrepudiation services. **Nonrepudiation of origin** gathers evidence to prove the identity of the originator of a message, the content of the message and, optionally, the origination time and date of the message. Nonrepudiation of origin protects the recipient of a message by preventing the originator from later falsely denying having originated the message or disputing the content or origination time of the message.

**Nonrepudiation of delivery** gathers evidence to verify identity of the recipient of a message, the content of the message, and, optionally, the delivery time and date of the message. Nonrepudiation of delivery protects the originator of a message by preventing the recipient from later falsely denying having received the message or disputing the content or delivery time of the message.

Encryption, digital signatures, and arbitrated signatures (notary) are the primary mechanisms used to implement nonrepudiation service. Encryption and digital signatures are discussed at length in Chapter 2.

## Availability

Availability ensures that a computer system, data, and hardware and software resources are available to authorized users without any impediment or disruption. A secure, available computer system must also recover quickly and completely if a disaster occurs. The availability service safeguards computers against denial-of-service threats. Two fundamental methods to achieve availability are prudent system administration and robust system design. We will discuss some of these techniques in Chapter 13.

## Models for Computer Communications

In order to understand how to secure data while in transit, it is critical to understand how data transfers from a source computer to a destination computer across a network. Complex data communication systems use a set of cooperative protocols, called a **protocol suite** or **protocol family,** to transfer data across a network. Figure 1-2 illustrates a conceptual model for data transfer between two application programs connected over a network.

Protocols are stacked on top of each other to create a protocol family. Each layer of protocol handles one part of the overall data transfer task and provides a service

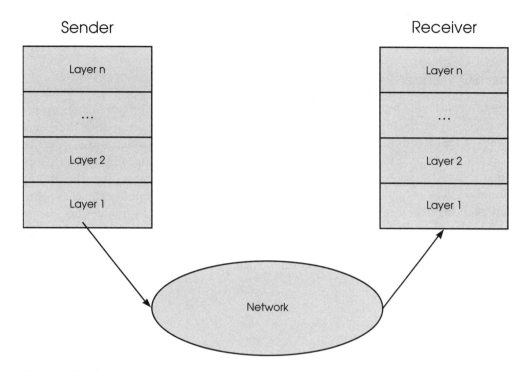

**Figure 1-2**   A conceptual layering model for computer communications.

to the protocol layer above it. A message sent by the originating application travels down through the protocol stack on the source computer, transmits across the network, goes up through the protocol stack on the destination computer, and reaches the target application.

Each layer of the source computer communicates with the corresponding layer of the destination computer. As the message goes down the protocol stack, each layer adds a header containing additional information and delivers the message to the layer below it. As the message goes up the protocol stack on the destination computer, each layer reads and strips off its own header and delivers the message to the layer above it. Each layer at the destination receives exactly the same message sent by the corresponding layer at the source.

The decision to break down the overall data communications task into a family of protocols is not arbitrary. The failures that can arise during data communication are numerous and overwhelming, and it would be impossible to design a single protocol that could deal with all of them. How many layers should be in a protocol family? This decision is arbitrary. In the rest of this section, we will present two concrete communication models with different layering ideas. Chapter 11 discusses the notion of policy in communication models further.

## The ISO 7-Layer Reference Model

The International Organization for Standardization (ISO) has proposed a Reference Model of Open System Interconnection (OSI), referred to as the ISO Reference Model or OSI Reference Model, in an attempt to standardize computer networking. Because the overall task was too big to be handled by a single committee, ISO divided the task into seven subtasks and assigned each to a committee. Each subcommittee was responsible for the design of one protocol layer under the constraint that each layer had to use the services of the lower layer and provide a service to the higher layer. Figure 1-3 shows the seven layers in the ISO Reference Model. Although actual networks seldom fit neatly into this 7-layer model, the ISO model provides a reference framework, common terminology, and useful concepts for all open communication systems.

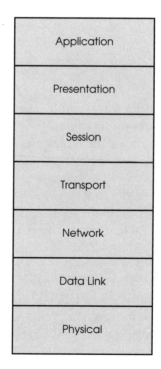

**Figure 1-3**   The ISO 7-layer Reference Model for computer communications.

- **Physical layer**   Layer 1 transmits an unstructured stream of bits across a physical link.

- **Data link layer**   Layer 2 organizes the physical layer's bits into frames and delivers them to specified hardware addresses across a single link.

- **Network layer**   Layer 3 determines routing and forwards packets across a network of multiple links.

- **Transport layer**   Layer 4 provides end-to-end reliable data transfer. It inserts sequence numbers in packets, holds packets until they can be delivered in order, and retransmits lost packets.

- **Session layer**   Layer 5 provides additional services on top of the transport layer services. ISO considered the remote terminal access problem so important that it assigned an entire layer to handle it. Most network architectures do not have this layer.

- **Presentation layer**   Layer 6 includes functions such as compressing data or converting images into bit streams that many applications need when using the network.

- **Application layer**   Layer 7 covers end-user application programs such as e-mail, FTP, login, and so on.

## The TCP/IP Internet 4-Layer Model

The TCP/IP model is designed around a simpler 4-level layering scheme, as shown in Figure 1-4. It is possible to describe the four layers of TCP/IP in terms of the

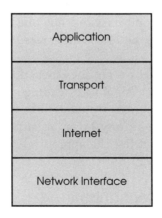

**Figure 1-4**   The TCP/IP 4-layer model for computer communications.

seven layers of the ISO Reference Model, but the analogy is somewhat strained and might obscure the structure of the TCP/IP model.

- **Network interface layer**   Layer 1 accepts Internet protocol (IP) datagrams and forwards them over a specific network. This layer is also referred to as the **data link** layer.

- **Internet layer**   Layer 2 takes a packet from the transport layer, encapsulates it in an IP datagram, fills in the datagram header, and passes the datagram to the network interface layer.

- **Transport layer**   Layer 3 provides end-to-end communication from one application program to another. The transport layer divides the stream of data into packets and passes them to the Internet layer.

- **Application layer**   Layer 4 enables application programs to access services available on a TCP/IP network.

## The OSI Security Architecture (X.800)

The OSI Security Architecture, commonly referred to as **X.800,** is a supplement to the ISO Reference Model principles to ensure secure data transfer between open systems [X800]. The ISO-recommended security measures address only the data transfer aspects of security in open systems. To be effective, these measures must be used in conjunction with other security measures, such as physical security and personnel security, to provide an overall secure system.

Many of the concepts and principles that we have developed in this chapter culminate in this section. We deliberately postponed the treatment of X.800 until now to first familiarize you with the security issues relevant to open networks, threats, safeguards, security services and mechanisms, and the ISO Reference Model. We intend for this section to interrelate the disparate concepts presented earlier and provide a frame of reference.

The OSI Security Architecture outlines measures that can be used to secure data in a communicating open system by providing appropriate security services in each layer. An application program, in addition to providing its own security services, can exploit any service in any layer to satisfy a security policy. The OSI Security Architecture also identifies the appropriate security mechanisms that can be used to implement a service.

### Security Services and Mechanisms

A security service is provided by a layer of a communication open system to ensure the security of data transfers. Each layer of the ISO Reference Model may provide an appropriate security service using an appropriate security mechanism to satisfy a security policy. In practice, the OSI services and mechanisms are used in conjunction with non-OSI services and mechanisms to achieve an overall secure system. Table 1-1 lists the OSI-recommended security services and appropriate mechanisms for implementing them.

## Security Services and Layers

Each layer of an open system may provide a particular security service or exploit an appropriate security service provided in a lower layer. An open system may use security services in more than one layer to provide an overall secure system according to a security policy. An application program can leverage the security services provided within the different layers of the open system in addition to providing its own services and mechanisms, some of which may already exist in lower layers. Table 1-2 lists the OSI-recommended services and the appropriate layers for providing them.

# Summary

Computing over the Internet has two significant characteristics: distributed processing and open communications. Because potential attackers have access to all the communications in an open network, computing over the Internet is inherently unsecure and subject to a number of threats.

A threat is a person, a computer program, a natural disaster, an accident, or even an idea that poses some danger to an asset. An asset is anything of value. Authorization violation, system penetration, spoofing, eavesdropping, and tampering are examples of threats to the security of open communicating systems.

An attack is an actual realization of a threat. Attacks result from vulnerabilities, which are weaknesses in a safeguard or the absence of a safeguard. Security measures usually increase the cost of a system and make it harder to use. Safeguards are physical controls, mechanisms, measures, and policies put in place to prevent attacks or to reduce the impact of an attack.

A security policy states the security-related considerations that are and are not permitted during the operation of a system. Policies can be identity-based or rule-based, depending on how the authorization considerations are stated.

Information security is the discipline of ensuring that information is not revealed to unauthorized people, information is not tampered with, and authorized people are not impeded from accessing computer resources. Information security services are authentication, authorization (access control service), confidentiality (secrecy), integrity, nonrepudiation, and availability.

A security service is a quality of a system that is present to satisfy a security policy. A security mechanism is a concrete procedure used to implement such a

**Table 1-1**  Relationship between Security Services and Mechanisms

| Mechanism / Service | Encipher-ment | Digital signature | Access control | Data integrity | Authenti-cation exchange | Traffic padding | Routing control | Notari-zation |
|---|---|---|---|---|---|---|---|---|
| Peer entity authentication | Y | Y | — | — | Y | — | — | — |
| Data origin authentication | Y | Y | — | — | — | — | — | — |
| Access control service | — | — | Y | — | — | — | — | — |
| Connection confidentiality | Y | — | — | — | — | — | Y | — |
| Connectionless confidentiality | Y | — | — | — | — | — | Y | — |
| Selective field confidentiality | Y | — | — | — | — | — | — | — |
| Traffic flow confidentiality | Y | — | — | — | — | Y | Y | — |
| Connection integrity with recovery | Y | — | — | — | — | — | Y | — |
| Connection integrity without recovery | Y | — | — | — | — | — | Y | — |
| Selective field connection integrity | Y | — | — | — | — | — | Y | — |
| Connectionless integrity | Y | Y | — | — | — | — | Y | — |
| Selective field connectionless integrity | Y | Y | — | — | — | — | Y | — |
| Nonrepu-diation origin | — | Y | — | Y | — | — | — | — |
| Nonrepu-diation delivery | — | Y | — | Y | — | — | — | Y |

**Table 1-2** Relationship between Security Services and Layers

| Layer / Service | 1 | 2 | 3 | 4 | 5 | 6 | 7 |
|---|---|---|---|---|---|---|---|
| Peer entity authentication | — | — | Y | Y | — | — | Y |
| Data origin authentication | — | — | Y | Y | — | — | Y |
| Access control service | — | — | Y | Y | — | — | Y |
| Connection confidentiality | Y | Y | Y | Y | — | Y | Y |
| Connectionless confidentiality | — | Y | Y | Y | — | Y | Y |
| Selective field confidentiality | — | — | — | — | — | Y | Y |
| Traffic flow confidentiality | Y | — | Y | — | — | — | Y |
| Connection integrity with recovery | — | — | — | Y | — | — | Y |
| Connection integrity without recovery | — | — | Y | Y | — | — | Y |
| Selective field connection integrity | — | — | — | — | — | — | Y |
| Connectionless integrity | — | — | Y | Y | — | — | Y |
| Selective field connectionless integrity | — | — | — | — | — | — | Y |
| Nonrepudiation origin | — | — | — | — | — | — | Y |
| Nonrepudiation delivery | — | — | — | — | — | — | Y |

quality. A security service identifies what is needed, whereas a security mechanism describes how to achieve it.

The OSI Security Architecture (X.800) is a supplement to the ISO Reference Model principles to ensure secure data transfer between open systems. X.800 outlines measures that can be used to secure data in a communicating open system by providing appropriate security services in each layer. An application program can exploit any service in any layer to satisfy a security policy in addition to providing its own security services.

# References

[DREI98]   Dreifus, H., and T. Monk. *Smart Cards: A Guide to Building and Managing Smart Card Applications,* John Wiley & Sons, New York, 1998.

[FORD97]   Ford, W., and M. Baum. *Secure Electronic Commerce: Building the Infrastructure for Digital Signatures and Encryption*, Prentice-Hall, Englewood Cliffs, NJ, 1997.

[KAUF95]   Kaufman, C., R. Perlman, and M. Speciner. *Network Security PRIVATE Communications in a PUBLIC World*, Prentice Hall, Englewood Cliffs, NJ, 1995.

[RUSS91]   Russell, D. and G.T. Gangemi. *Computer Security Basics*, O'Reilly & Associates, Sebastopol, California, 1997.

[SUMM97]   Summers, R. *Secure Computing: Threats and Safeguards*, McGraw-Hill, New York, 1997.

[X800]   *Security Architecture for Open Systems Interconnection for CCITT Applications (Recommendation X.800)*, CCITT, Geneva, 1991.

# Chapter
# 2
# Cryptography

**Cryptography** is the science of making the cost of improperly acquiring or altering data greater than the potential value gained. The value of information usually drops with time, and cryptography makes the time required to obtain data in unauthorized ways long enough to decrease its value well below the money spent on obtaining it. This chapter presents a variety of cryptographic techniques that can be used to protect data against improper access or modification. It also describes methods for ascertaining the origin of data and preventing repudiation.

This chapter provides a rather comprehensive overview of cryptography (see [KAUF95] or [SCHN96] for books entirely dedicated to this subject). It covers secret-key cryptosystems, discusses public-key technologies with emphasis on RSA, DSS, and Diffie-Hellman, explains digital certificates, and reviews a variety of schemes that can be used to securely communicate over insecure channels. This chapter also examines different types of attacks on cryptographically secured data and analyzes the role of cryptographic keys in thwarting them.

## Cryptosystems

Cryptography provides techniques for mangling a message into an apparently unintelligible form and then recovering it from the mangled form, as illustrated in Figure 2-1. The original message is called the **plaintext** or the **cleartext,** and the unintelligible message is referred to as **ciphertext.** The mangling step is called **encryption** or **encipherment;** the demangling step is called **decryption** or **decipherment.** The mathematical function that identifies the encryption or decryption steps is termed the **cryptographic algorithm,** or simply the **cipher.**

**Figure 2-1** Encryption and decryption of a message.

The earliest documented application of cryptography is the famous Caesar cipher, in which each letter of a plaintext is replaced by the letter that shows up three positions later in the alphabet. For example, *A* becomes *D*, *B* becomes *E*, and *W* becomes *Z*. Note that in this cipher the letters must wrap around from *Z* to *A*; hence *X* maps to *A*, *Y* maps to *B*, and *Z* maps to *C*. The Caesar cipher, therefore, encrypts the plaintext *CAT* to the ciphertext *FDW* and decrypts the ciphertext *GRJ* to the plaintext *DOG*. The decryption is performed by replacing each ciphertext letter by the letter that comes three positions earlier in the alphabet and wrapping around from *A* to *Z*. The UNIX ROT13 command is a variation of Caesar cipher in which each letter is replaced by the letter that appears 13 positions later in the alphabet.

The Caesar cipher is obviously not a very secure algorithm. Anyone who obtains a ciphertext and knows it is a Caesar cipher can effortlessly recover the original plaintext. A more complicated cryptographic system is **monoalphabetic cipher,** which maps a plaintext character into an arbitrary character of the alphabet. The mapping is not fixed—a plaintext maps to different ciphertexts depending on the exact pairings of the characters. For instance, the plaintext *MOON* becomes *KPPT* if *M* is mapped to *K*, *O* to *P*, and *N* to *T*; *MOON* becomes *LSSD* if *M* is mapped to *L*, *O* to *S*, and *N* to *D*. In the English alphabet, there are 26! (26! is $26 \times 25 \times 24... \times 2 \times 1$), or approximately $4 \times 10^{26}$, possible pairings of letters. If it takes 1 nanosecond ($10^{-9}$ second) to try each pairing, it will take roughly 10 thousand million years to break a monoalphabetic cipher by a brute-force attack. It turns out, however, that by using statistical analysis of a language and determining the letters and letter sequences that are more likely to appear than others, it is relatively easy to break a monoalphabetic cipher.

A **cryptosystem** is a collection of cryptographic algorithms, cryptographic keys, and all possible plaintexts and their corresponding ciphertexts. In the monoalphabetic cipher cryptosystem, for example, the cryptographic algorithm is the replacement of each plaintext letter with a different letter from the alphabet and the key is any pairings of plaintext and ciphertext letters.

## Cryptographic Algorithms

All cryptosystems are based on only three cryptographic algorithms: secret key, public key, and message digest. **Message-digest algorithms** map variable-length plaintext into fixed-length ciphertext. They do not have any keys, and it is computationally infeasible to recover the original plaintext from the ciphertext. Message-digest algorithms are usually used to convert large messages into representative messages of a smaller, more manageable size.

**Secret-key algorithms** encrypt plaintext messages to ciphertexts that are usually the same size. They use one secret key, and it is not feasible to decrypt a ciphertext without the knowledge of the key. Secret-key algorithms are commonly used for bulk encryption. **Public-key algorithms** are similar to secret-key algorithms with the major exception that they use two keys, one public and one private. These algorithms are frequently used to distribute secret keys. Cryptographic algorithms are discussed in more detail later in this chapter.

### Published Algorithms versus Secret Algorithms

One might assume that cryptographic algorithms should be kept secret to improve the security of cryptosystems. This is a false assumption. Secret cryptographic algorithms that are implemented in software can be disassembled to reverse-engineer the algorithm. The RC4 secret-key algorithm, which is a trade secret of RSA Data Security Inc. (RSADSI), was reverse-engineered and anonymously posted to USENet in 1994. The RC2 algorithm, another trade secret of RSADSI, was disassembled and anonymously published to USENet in 1996. Although the hardware-based implementations of secret algorithms are less prone to such attacks, it is only a matter of time and money to buy or steal the hardware and recover the algorithm—or bribe its designer to reveal the algorithm.

A cryptographic algorithm should be published and subjected to public scrutiny in order to uncover any possible weaknesses. One can gain confidence in the security of an algorithm only after other cryptographers have analyzed it for a sufficiently long time and have failed to break it or demonstrate any weaknesses. In fact, some of the best cryptographic algorithms currently in use have evolved as the result of repeated improvements to fix possible attacks discovered by other researchers. The MD5 message-digest function, for example, was derived from its predecessor, MD4, after Boer and Bosselaers found weaknesses in a version of MD4 that used two rounds of processing instead of three [DENB92]. This finding made Ron Rivest, the designer of MD4, sufficiently nervous to strengthen MD4 and create MD5.

Lack of public scrutiny by other researchers is another pitfall of secret algorithms. This argument may not hold if a secret algorithm is designed by an organization such as the National Security Agency (NSA), which has the best cryptographers in the world and can conduct extensive internal reviews. Most other organizations, however, do not have this advantage; they should publish their algorithms and enhance them through peer reviews.

## Keys

A **key** is a mathematical value that determines how a plaintext message is encrypted to produce a ciphertext, and its possession is required to decrypt the ciphertext and recover the original message. A key has a corresponding **key length,** which is the number of bits, or sometimes bytes, in the key. The **key space** of a key is the collection of all the mathematical values that have the same length as the key. A 2-bit key, for example, has four values in its key space: {"00", "01", "10", and "11"}.

In general, a key of length $n$ generates a key space of $2^n$ distinct values. In this book, we use the term **key material** as a synonym for **key.**

Where does the security of a cryptosystem reside if its algorithms are publicly known? It has been postulated in the cryptographic community that the security of a cryptosystem should rest entirely within its key and that an attacker knows its algorithms and has access to all of its ciphertexts [KAHN67]. The security of a cryptosystem can then be measured based on the size of its key space and the available computational power. We will revisit this issue later in the Key Length section.

## Breaking a Cryptosystem

Recall that the security of a cryptosystem must reside entirely with its key and that we must assume an adversary has complete knowledge of its cryptographic algorithms and can intercept all the ciphertexts. **Cryptanalysis** is the procedures, processes, and methods employed to decipher ciphertexts for which the key is unknown. A **cryptanalyst** is someone who uses cryptanalysis to recover the plaintext associated with some ciphertext without having the knowledge of the key.

Given that cryptanalysts have access to a variety of methods to crack a system and can assemble a massive amount of computing power, how do cryptographers know that their systems are secure? If a cryptographic algorithm is published and many cryptanalysts have attempted to break it for many years without any success, then it can be assumed that the cipher is secure. Note that there might be researchers who find it more profitable to make fraudulent use of any weaknesses they find with commercial ciphers than to publish their results. We, however, assume that there are enough smart, professional researchers who publish their findings.

Cryptanalysts employ a variety of techniques to break cryptosystems with varying degrees of success. They may be able to totally break the system and recover the key, or they might just deduce some information about the ciphertext. Their work, however, is hampered by the computational difficulty of the problem. We explain these ideas further in the remainder of this section.

### Different Levels of Breaks

A cryptanalyst may break a cryptosystem with various degrees of severity, ranging from deciphering some bits of information about a ciphertext to recovering the key [KNUD94]. The lowest level of break is called **information deduction,** in which the cryptanalyst may obtain some bits of the key or some information about the plaintext. In **instance deduction,** the analyst finds the entire plaintext corresponding to an intercepted ciphertext. The analyst may achieve **global deduction** and devise another cryptographic algorithm that decrypts a ciphertext to the same plaintext that would be obtained by the original algorithm. Finally, in a **total break,** the analyst successfully recovers the key and can decrypt any encrypted messages.

## Computational Difficulty

Most cryptosystems are only **computationally secure,** meaning that with enough processing power and data storage disks one can eventually break the system. *Eventually* might be many times more than the age of the universe, but in theory, these systems can be broken. Advances in computer technology reduce the computational difficulty of breaking a cryptosystem, whereas increasing key lengths makes it more difficult. A cryptosystem is **unconditionally secure** if no amount of computing power or ciphertext can ever crack the cipher. In theory, there is simply not enough information available to decipher an encrypted message even if an infinite amount of resources is available. **One-time pads** [KAHN67] are the only unconditionally secure cryptosystems (one-time pads are briefly discussed in the Stream Ciphers section later in this chapter).

## Cryptanalytic Attacks

In this section we discuss mathematical attacks against cryptosystems wherein the cryptanalyst has some sample ciphertexts and perhaps the corresponding plaintexts, and he wants to decrypt another ciphertext, or worse, recover the key. Note, however, that a cryptosystem will be attacked at its weakest link, and the nature of the attack may not be mathematical. An adversary may use bribery or torture to obtain a secret key or the plaintext associated with a ciphertext message. The adversary might recover the key from back-up media or a discarded computer disk; he may find the shredded plaintext in a dumpster and piece together the shreds to recover the message. The analysis of such attacks is beyond the scope of this book.

### *Ciphertext Only*

In a **ciphertext-only attack,** a cryptanalyst intercepts some ciphertext and wishes to obtain the corresponding plaintext or recover the key. One way to obtain the plaintext message is to launch a **brute-force attack,** in which the analyst tries each possible key of the key space until the ciphertext decrypts to some meaningful message. In some circumstances, it may be possible to try only a subset of the key space. If the secret key is the hash of a pass phrase, for example, it may be possible to launch a **dictionary attack** and try only the common words of a language.

To identify the correct key, it is important to recognize when the ciphertext message is successfully decrypted. Incorrect keys almost always decrypt a (long enough) ciphertext message to gibberish; hence, any key that decrypts the ciphertext to an intelligible plaintext is probably the correct key. It is essential to have enough ciphertext messages available to launch a successful ciphertext-only attack. A very small amount of ciphertext may decrypt to different meaningful messages under different keys, making it impossible to determine the correct key unless contextual information is also available.

### Known Plaintext

In a **known-plaintext attack,** the cryptanalyst has access to a ciphertext message and its corresponding plaintext message. The pair of ciphertext and plaintext messages is extremely valuable; it may allow the analyst to narrow down the key space or obtain statistics that can subsequently be used to deduce some information about another ciphertext message.

It is not uncommon for a cryptanalyst to acquire a pair of ciphertext and plaintext messages. E-mail applications, for example, place standard headers at the beginning of each message, which provide an analyst with known plaintext.

### Chosen Plaintext

The **chosen-plaintext attack** is a kind of known plaintext attack in which the cryptanalyst can select the plaintext. By choosing the plaintext, the analyst can avoid duplicating data and may be able to target an attack toward the weaker points of an algorithm.

Although it might seem rather surprising, obtaining a plaintext and its corresponding ciphertext is not very difficult. In the Battle of Midway in World War II, for example, Americans determined the Japanese code word for *Midway* by reporting over a clear radio channel that their water purifier had broken down. Then they decrypted Japanese traffic and looked for a report of a broken water purifier. It worked.[1]

A cryptosystem must gracefully withstand ciphertext-only attacks because it must be assumed that attackers can intercept and analyze the ciphertexts. Some cryptosystems can thwart ciphertext-only attacks but are vulnerable to plaintext-only attacks. Others can resist the first two attacks but are vulnerable to the chosen-plaintext attacks. A good cryptosystem must withstand all three kinds of attacks.

## Secret-Key Cryptography

**Secret-key cryptography** uses a **secret key** to encrypt a message into ciphertext and the same key to decrypt the ciphertext into the original message. Secret-key cryptography is also referred to as **symmetric cryptography** or **conventional cryp-**

---

1. We thank Dave Crocker, one of the reviewers of this book, for providing the story of Midway.

**tography;** the secret key is also known as the **session key, content-encryption key,** or **bulk-encryption key.** Due to its relative efficiency, secret-key cryptography is most commonly used for the bulk encryption of data.

Figure 2-2 illustrates two parties, Alice and Bob, who use secret-key cryptography to protect their messages from eavesdroppers. Alice enciphers her message with a secret key using a cryptographic algorithm in encryption mode and transmits the ciphertext to Bob. Bob, who knows the secret key, deciphers the ciphertext with the same cryptographic algorithm in decryption mode and recovers the original plaintext message. Eavesdroppers can intercept the ciphertext message, but they cannot successfully decrypt it without the knowledge of the secret key.

It is essential for Alice and Bob to agree on a shared secret key or for Alice to somehow inform Bob of the key before Bob can start decrypting messages. Alice can run an advertisement in *The New York Times* to inform Bob of the key. She can tell him the key over the telephone, or she can meet him at the San Diego Zoo and slip the key in his back pocket. The problem with most of these kinds of methods is that an attacker has an opportunity to steal the key and then eavesdrop on private messages between Alice and Bob. Passing the key in a crowded place may not have this shortcoming, but it has too much overhead because secret keys must be exchanged often to reduce the amount of ciphertext available in ciphertext or known-plaintext attacks. **Key distribution centers** (KDC) have been proposed and used to solve the secret key exchange problem with symmetric algorithms. These centers, however, suffer from a lack of scalability and require a considerable amount of work to administer the center.

As we will show later, public-key cryptography and digital certificates solve the key exchange problem. The Secure Sockets Layer (SSL) protocol, commonly used to create authenticated and encrypted channels on the Internet, uses digital certificates to negotiate a secret key between a Web browser and a Web server. The Secure Multipurpose Internet Mail Exchange (S/MIME) protocol, which provides secure e-mail over insecure channels, uses digital certificates to securely transmit the secret key from the sender of a message to its recipients. S/MIME is covered at length in Chapter 5.

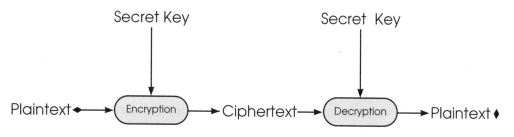

**Figure 2-2** Encryption and decryption using a secret key.

**Table 2-1**  Secret-Key Algorithms

| Algorithm Name | Mode | Key Length (bits) |
|---|---|---|
| Blowfish | Block cipher | Variable up to 448 |
| DES | Block cipher | 56 |
| IDEA | Block cipher | 128 |
| RC2 | Block cipher | Variable from 1 up to 2048 |
| RC4 | Stream cipher | Variable from 1 up to 2048 |
| RC5 | Block cipher | Variable from 1 up to 2048 |
| Triple DES | Block cipher | 56 (112 effective) |

There are a significant number of secret-key algorithms. They employ different techniques to mangle input data, differ in terms of their vulnerability to attacks, have various degrees of efficiency for encryption and decryption, and employ different key lengths. Table 2-1 lists some common secret-key ciphers.

## Stream and Block Ciphers

Two basic categories of symmetric ciphers are block ciphers and stream ciphers. Block ciphers operate on chunks, or blocks, of data, whereas stream ciphers usually operate on data one bit at a time.

### Block Ciphers

**Block ciphers** take a fixed-size block of plaintext, usually 64 bits, and produce a fixed-size block of ciphertext, usually the same size as the input block. The length of the key may be 56, such as for DES, 128, such as for IDEA, or some other value. The block size must be long enough to prevent known-plaintext attacks and short enough to avoid complications and implementation inefficiencies.

Blocks of 64 bits seem to be the right size. With a block size of 8, there are only 256 different 8-bit input blocks, which must be mapped to one of the 256 possible 8-bit output blocks. If a cryptanalyst has access to a few ciphertext and plaintext messages, he can determine a rather large proportion of the $2^8$ mappings and launch pernicious known-plaintext attacks against the algorithm. With 64-bit blocks, there are $2^{64}$ distinct mappings; even a moderate number of ciphertext and plaintext messages reveals only a small proportion of the mappings. Furthermore, the storage requirements for a table with $2^{64}$ entries and the speed of algorithms required to search such a table make known-plaintext attacks computationally costly.

The mapping from an input block to an output block must be one-to-one to make the algorithm reversible. If more than one input block is mapped to one output block, the algorithm can encrypt, but it cannot decrypt—it simply is not possible to identify the actual input block from which the output block resulted.

It is essential for the mapping from an input block to an output block to appear random. In a random mapping, a single change to one bit of an input block should have a 50% probability of flipping every bit of the corresponding output block. In other words, two input blocks that are exactly the same except for one bit should map to two entirely different, uncorrelated output blocks. The random mapping is derived from the secret key, and the only computationally feasible way to reverse the mapping is the knowledge of the key. In the Substitution and Permutation section, we will describe two basic methods to derive random mappings.

### Stream Ciphers

**Stream ciphers** operate over one bit (sometimes one 8-bit byte or one 32-bit word) of input data at a time. **One-time pads** [KAHN67] are stream ciphers that perform an XOR (exclusive-or) of one bit of an input stream with one randomly generated bit to get one bit of the output stream. The sequence of the random bits constitutes the session key, or the **pad,** which is the same size as the input and output streams. To recover the original plaintext, the ciphertext must be XORed with the same pad. One-time pads are unconditionally secure (no amount of computing power can ever break them) and are used for ultra-secure applications.

## Substitution and Permutation

Symmetric ciphers perform a number of substitutions and permutations on a plaintext message to derive the ciphertext. **Substitution** replaces an input value with any of the possible output values. The Caesar cipher, for example, always substitutes a plaintext character with the character three positions on the right to create a ciphertext character. Although more complicated than the Caesar cipher, the monoalphabetic cipher performs a substitution of a plaintext letter with an arbitrary letter of the alphabet. In a block cipher of size $k,$ an input block can be substituted by any of the possible $2^k$ output blocks.

**Permutation** is a special kind of substitution in which the bits of an input block are rearranged to produce a ciphertext block. For example, the ciphertext block *0110* is a permutation of plaintext block *1010*. Permutation preserves the statistics (number of 0s and 1s) of an input block because every bit of input ends up somewhere in the output block.

## Schemes for Encrypting Large Messages in Block Ciphers

If your message does not happen to be exactly 64 bits, or whatever the chosen block size is, you cannot use a block cipher to encrypt it. Most messages are longer than

64 bits, and you need an **encryption scheme** to encrypt the entire message. In this section, we present a brief overview of such schemes; [DES81] provides a more detailed analysis.

The most obvious thing to do is to break up the message into 64-bit blocks, padding the last block if necessary, and encrypt each block. To recover the message, the ciphertext is broken into 64-bit chunks, and each chunk is decrypted. This scheme is called **electronic code book** (ECB).

ECB is vulnerable to ciphertext-only attacks because two identical blocks of input map to the same output block. As a result, ECB is rarely used to encrypt messages. **Cipher block chaining** (CBC) circumvents this weakness by XORing a plaintext block with the ciphertext of the previous block prior to encryption. Because the first block does not have a preceding block, an **initialization vector** (IV) is used to modify the first block. CBC is a common scheme to encrypt messages.

The **output feedback mode** (OFB) uses the session key to create a large pseudorandom stream (pad), which is XORed with the plaintext message to produce the ciphertext. OFB provides an advantage over CBC by allowing the pseudorandom pad to be created independently of the plaintext message. When the message arrives, it can be efficiently XORed with the pad and transmitted. The receiver can precompute the pad and decipher the message as it is being received. The OFB scheme is very similar to one-time pads except that the pad is pseudorandom instead of random. The pseudorandomness of the pad makes OFB computationally secure as opposed to unconditionally secure one-time pads.

A variant of OFB, **cipher feedback mode** (CFB) is another encryption scheme for large messages. It detects message tampering better than OFB does, but it does not allow a substantial amount of pad to be generated ahead of time.

## Public-Key Cryptography

**Public-key cryptography** was invented by Whitfield Diffie and Martin Hellman in 1975 [DIFF76b], although rumor has it that the National Security Agency (NSA) had discovered the same concepts as early as 1966. It involves the use of two distinct keys, one public and one private. The **private key** is kept secret and must never be divulged; the **public key** is not secret and can be freely shared with anyone. Because public-key cryptography employs two distinct keys, it is also referred to as **asymmetric cryptography.** Even though the private key is kept secret, we never refer to it as a "secret key" to avoid confusion with secret keys used in secret-key cryptography.

A public key and its corresponding private key are mathematically related, but it is computationally infeasible to derive the private key from the public key. A public key and its associated private key are commonly called a **key pair.** Due to their mathematical relationship, a message that is encrypted with a public key can be decrypted with its corresponding private key; a message that is encrypted with a private key can be decrypted with its corresponding public key.

Figure 2-3 illustrates how Alice applies public-key cryptography to send a confidential message to Bob. Alice uses Bob's public key to encrypt her message, and transmits the ciphertext message to Bob. Bob uses his private key to decrypt the ciphertext and recover the original message. Eve, an eavesdropper, can intercept the ciphertext message, but she cannot decrypt it because she does not have Bob's private key.

How does Alice obtain Bob's public key? Bob can publish his public key in *The New York Times*, or he can simply call Alice and give it to her over the phone. Note that, unlike secret keys, public keys are public and can be freely advertised. It is essential, however, that Trudy, an intruder, cannot dupe Alice into using her public key instead of Bob's. If she succeeds, she can impersonate Bob to Alice and use her private key to decipher messages intended for Bob. In Chapter 3, we will show how certification authorities and digital certificates can provide a secure, scaleable way to publish public keys.

Public-key algorithms are about 100 to 1000 times slower than secret-key algorithms. As a result, they are rarely used to encrypt a large amount of data. These algorithms are commonly used in the initial phase of communication to authenticate two parties to each other and set up secret keys for bulk encryption. The use of a public-key algorithm in conjunction with a secret-key algorithm results in **hybrid cryptosystems.**

What happens if Alice uses her private key to encrypt her message and sends the encrypted message to Bob? Bob can use Alice's public key to decrypt the message and read it. Eve, who also has Alice's public key (remember, public keys are publicly known), can also decrypt the message and read it. Alice, therefore, cannot use her private key to send confidential messages.

Is there any reason, you might ask, to encrypt a message with a private key? Because Bob could use Alice's public key to decrypt her message to something intelligible, he can assume that the message actually came from Alice. Trudy, the intruder, can use her private key to send an encrypted message to Bob in an attempt

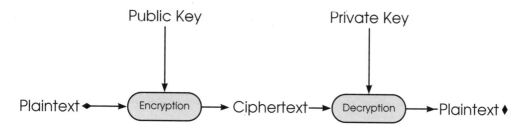

**Figure 2-3** Encryption and decryption using a private and public key pair.

**Table 2-2**  Common Public-Key Algorithms

| Algorithm | Type | Mathematical Foundation |
|---|---|---|
| DSA | Digital signature | Discrete logarithm |
| El Gamal | Digital signature | Discrete logarithm |
| RSA | Confidentiality, digital signature, key exchange | Factorization |
| Diffie-Hellman | Key exchange | Discrete logarithm |

to impersonate Alice. When Bob tries to decrypt the message with Alice's public key, however, he sees gibberish in the plaintext message and realizes that something is wrong. To impersonate Alice, Trudy must have Alice's private key, and Alice has been careful not to reveal her private key.

Encryption of a message with a private key creates a digital signature over the message. Decryption of a digital signature with a public key to verify the identity of the person who generated the signature is called **signature verification.** Digital signatures are discussed in detail in the Digital Signatures section.

A public-key algorithm is **reversible** if it can be used for both confidentiality (encryption) and digital signatures; it is **irreversible** if it can only be used for digital signatures. With an irreversible public-key algorithm, the private key can encrypt plaintext, but it cannot decrypt ciphertext. Yet another category of public-key algorithms that can neither perform encryption nor generate digital signatures is called **key exchange algorithms** because they can be used only to securely negotiate a secret key between two parties. Note that reversible algorithms can also be used for key exchange, whereas irreversible algorithms cannot. Key exchange is also referred to as **key establishment** or **key agreement.**

Public-key algorithms also vary based on the mathematical relationship between the public key and the private key. Table 2-2 lists a number of common public-key algorithms. In the rest of this section, we will explore some of these algorithms and discuss their underlying mathematical foundation. We will also present two public-key schemes.

## RSA

**RSA,** named after its creators, Rivest, Shamir, and Adleman, is the most popular public-key algorithm. RSA can be used for confidentiality, digital signatures, and key exchange. The key length is variable, usually between 512 and 2048. Longer keys increase the computational security of the algorithm, but they decrease the efficiency and produce more ciphertext. The plaintext block can be any size, but it must be smaller than the key length. The ciphertext block is the same size as the key.

The public key in RSA has the form $<e, n>$, where $e$ and $n$ are called the **exponent** and **modulus,** respectively. The key length is the number of bits in $n$, that is, it has the same length as $n$. The modulus $n$ is obtained by multiplying two large primes $p$ and $q$, which are usually chosen at random and are kept secret. The private key has the form $<d, n>$, where $d$ is the multiplicative inverse of $e$ modulo $(p - 1)(q - 1)$. Modular arithmetic is described briefly in the Discrete Logarithm section.

It is easy to calculate $d$ based on the knowledge of $p$ and $q$; it is computationally infeasible to calculate $d$ without $p$ and $q$ for large values of $n$. Because $p$ and $q$ are kept secret, an attacker must attempt to factor $n$ to retrieve $p$ and $q$ in order to derive $d$. Factoring very large numbers, however, is a hard problem and is not computationally feasible. Therefore, the difficulty of breaking RSA is no more than factoring large numbers. So far, no one has been able to find any better way to break RSA other than to factor $n$ (at least no one has published a way!). Consequently, we can assume that, for the time being, breaking RSA is as difficult as factoring large numbers. As computer technology and factorization algorithms advance, the RSA keys must become longer to withstand factorization.[2]

To send an encrypted message from Alice to Bob, Alice calculates $c = m^e$ modulo $n$, where $m$ is the plaintext, $c$ is the ciphertext, and $<e, n>$ is Bob's public key. Bob decrypts the message by calculating $c^d$ modulo $n = (m^e)^d$ modulo $n = m^{ed}$ modulo $n = m$, where $<d, n>$ is Bob's private key. Remember that $d$ is chosen to be the multiplicative inverse of $e$ modulo $n$, so $m^{ed}$ equals $m$. If Alice wants to send a signed message to Bob, she uses her private key to calculate $c = m^d$ modulo $n$, and Bob can verify the signature by performing $c^e$ modulo $n = (m^d)^e$ modulo $n = m^{de}$ modulo $n = m$, where $<e, n>$ is Alice's public key.

Two popular values for the exponent $e$ of the $<e, n>$ public key are 3 and 65,537. These values of $e$ increase the efficiency of encryption and signature verification steps. Randomly chosen 512-bit exponents on the average require about 768 multiplies. Choosing 65,537 for the exponent reduces the number of multiplies to 17, whereas 3 requires only 3 multiplies and optimizes the performance [KAUF95]. RSA does not show any weaknesses for these fixed values of $e$, provided that well-devised public-key cryptography schemes are followed. We will present two such schemes in the Public-Key Cryptography Schemes section.

## Diffie-Hellman

The **Diffie-Hellman** key agreement algorithm enables two parties who have no prior knowledge of one another to exchange messages in public and agree on a

---

2. Advances in computer technology and CPU speed may actually favor the use of stronger cryptography and longer keys more than it favors factorization. Such advances enable a cryptosystem to use longer keys without performance degradation, while attackers cannot leverage the improved CPU speed to offset longer keys.

shared secret key. The algorithm does not provide any capability for confidentiality or digital signatures; it is typically used in conjunction with a secret-key algorithm in a hybrid cryptosystem. The Diffie-Hellman algorithm predates RSA and is the oldest known public-key system still in use. It was invented by Whitfield Diffie and Martin Hellman and published in 1976 [DIFF76b].

Consider two parties, Alice and Bob, who have no prior information about each other. They are communicating on-line on an unsecured channel to establish a shared secret key. Alice picks a large prime, $p$, and a generator, $g$ $(g < p)$ and sends them to Bob. Alice then chooses a large random private key, $d_A$, and calculates a corresponding public key $e_A = g^{d_A}$ modulo $p$. Similarly, Bob picks $d_B$ and $e_B = g^{d_B}$ modulo $p$. Alice and Bob exchange their public keys $e_A$ and $e_B$, and proceed to compute a shared secret key as follows. Alice computes $s_A = e_B{}^{d_A} = (g^{d_B})^{d_A} = g^{d_B d_A}$ modulo $p$; Bob computes $s_B = e_A{}^{d_B} = (g^{d_A})^{d_B} = g^{d_A d_B} = g^{d_B d_A} = s_A$ modulo $p$. In this last step of the algorithm, Alice and Bob have successfully negotiated a common secret key.

Eve, the eavesdropper, can intercept $g, p, e_A$, and $e_B$, but she cannot compute the shared secret unless she can calculate the discrete logarithm of one of the public keys to recover the corresponding private key. Because calculating a discrete logarithm is a computationally hard problem, the Diffie-Hellman algorithm can withstand such passive attacks.

However, the intruder Trudy, who launches active attacks, can do damage. She can cut off Bob from the communication and impersonate him to Alice. Alice has no way of authenticating Bob through the Diffie-Hellman algorithm and must take the risk of establishing a shared secret with an impostor. Trudy can then do far more damage. She can impersonate Alice to Bob and set up a shared secret with him as well as establishing a shared secret with Alice. When Alice sends an encrypted message intended for Bob, Trudy intercepts it, decrypts the encrypted message, encrypts the original message with her shared secret with Bob, and sends it to Bob. Similarly, when Bob sends a response intended for Alice, he recovers the message and then uses his shared secret with Alice to forward the message to her. Alice and Bob will never know that Trudy has been listening to their private conversation. Although it resists passive attacks, the Diffie-Hellman algorithm is vulnerable to active, man-in-the-middle attacks.

### Menezes-Qu-Vanstone Discrete Logarithm Algorithm

The Menezes-Qu-Vanstone (MQV) discrete logarithm algorithm is a variant of Diffie-Hellman in which each party contributes two public-private key pairs instead of one. Each party uses its own two key pairs, the other party's two public keys, and some common parameters to agree on a shared secret key.

The MQV discrete logarithm algorithm is optimized for the case when each party provides an authenticated, permanent key pair and a transient (one-time) key pair. Authenticated key pairs provide a mechanism for the two parties to ascertain the identity of one another through the agreement on a common shared secret.

## Digital Signature Algorithm

**Digital Signature Standard** (DSS) is a standard issued by the U.S. National Institute of Standards and Technology (NIST) for generating signatures over messages. It proposes the **Digital Signature Algorithm** (DSA), which was published as a Federal Information Processing Standard (FIPS) in 1994 [DSS94]. DSA can only sign messages; it cannot provide confidentiality or key establishment. DSA is based on El Gamal signatures, but its performance is tuned for smart cards. El Gamal signatures [ELGA85] use the same kind of keys as Diffie-Hellman. We will revisit this subject later in the Digital Signatures section.

## Mathematical Foundations

Almost all the public-key cryptographic algorithms are based on one of the following mathematical techniques: integer factorization, discrete logarithm, and elliptic curve discrete logarithm. In this section we will provide an introductory overview of each of these techniques.

### Integer Factorization

A positive integer is a **prime number** if and only if it is evenly divisible by exactly two positive integers, 1 and itself. The prime numbers are 2, 3, 5, 7, 11, 13, 17, 19, 23, . . . A **nonprime number** greater than 1 can always be written as a product of smaller prime numbers, known as its **prime factors. Factoring** a number refers to finding all of its prime factors. For example, the prime factors of 6 are 2 and 3, and the prime factors of 7429 are 17, 19, and 23. Factoring a small number is easy, but it quickly becomes more and more difficult as the size of a number increases. Many algorithms have been devised to factor large numbers; see [LENS93] for a good discussion of the number field sieve, which is currently the fastest factoring algorithm for numbers longer than 110 digits, and [BRES89] for a general discussion of factoring algorithms.

Public-key cryptosystems based on integer factorization, such as RSA, rely on the fact that multiplying large prime numbers is computationally easy but that factoring a large number into its prime factors is computationally very difficult. The knowledge of the prime factors can be kept secret and used to derive the private key, while the number resulting from multiplying the prime factors can be made public and used as a basis for the public key. If the cryptosystem does not have any weaknesses, deriving the private key from the public key and breaking the system requires factoring, which is computationally infeasible for large numbers.

### Discrete Logarithm

In **arithmetic modulo $n$** ($n > 0$), two integers are equivalent if they have the same remainder when divided by $n$. The **remainder** of an integer $m$ divided by $n$ is the smallest nonnegative integer that differs from $m$ by a multiple of $n$. The numbers 6, –4, and 16 all have the same remainder, 6, when divided by 10, and, therefore, are equivalent in arithmetic modulo 10. **Modular exponentiation** $a^x$ modulo $n$ is the exponentiation in arithmetic modulo $n$. For example, $3^4$ modulo 10 is 81 modulo 10, which is equivalent to 1 modulo 10. **Discrete logarithm,** which is the inverse arithmetic operation of modular exponentiation, is the problem of finding $x$ where $a^x = b$ modulo $n$. For instance, if $11^x = 1$ modulo 10, then $x$ equals 2.

Public-key cryptosystems based on discrete logarithm rely on the fact that modular exponentiation is a computationally easy problem, and discrete logarithm is a computationally hard problem. In the Diffie-Hellman algorithm, for example, an entity selects a random secret $d$ and sends $e = g^d$ modulo $p$ in an unsecure channel to another party. An eavesdropper, who intercepts $e$ and knows $g$ and $p$, cannot solve the discrete logarithm problem for $d$. [LAMA91] provides a good discussion of calculating discrete logarithms in prime number fields.

### Elliptic Curve Discrete Logarithm

The **elliptic curve discrete logarithm** problem is a computationally harder variant of the discrete logarithm problem. Elliptic curve cryptosystems can, therefore, use smaller key sizes to provide the same level of computational security as discrete logarithm systems. Shorter key sizes generally increase the performance of a public-key cryptosystem and reduce the amount of ciphertext. Elliptic curves have been studied for a number of years and have been implemented in some commercial systems. A good discussion of elliptic curve cryptosystems in presented in [KOBL87].

## Public-Key Cryptography Schemes

Care must be taken when public-key cryptography is used in practice. Consider this: Alice (who is Bob's full-service stock broker) needs to give Bob a tip on a very lucrative stock deal involving the ACME Corporation. She encrypts the message *ACME* with Bob's public key and sends the encrypted message to Bob. Eve, who also knows about a hot stock but does not know which one, intercepts the ciphertext. Eve is desperate to crack the code and buy the same stock, but she does not have Bob's private key. She may attempt to factor Bob's public key to derive his private key, but by the time she has factored the large number, the stock market will be at a record 1,000,000—too late for Eve to buy.

Is there anything Eve can do? Yes. Although she does not have Bob's private key, she has his public key. She can prepare a list of all the tradable stocks, encrypt each stock with Bob's public key, and compare the result with the intercepted ciphertext. When she comes across ACME, she finds out that ACME encrypts to the same ciphertext that Alice sent Bob. Eve now knows the content of the message even though she does not have Bob's private key.

Alice can foil Eve's attempt by including a random number in her message. Now, Eve must prepare a list of all random numbers in addition to the list of stocks. For sufficiently large random numbers, the task ahead of Eve becomes computationally infeasible. Alice is now back in square one. She needs Bob's private key to decrypt the message, but Bob, being a good investor, has been careful not to reveal it. Bob's encryption software, however, must be able to detect the presence of the random number in the message and display only the word *ACME* to him. How would the software ascertain that?

A number of public-key cryptographic schemes are carefully designed to foil common attacks against public-key cryptosystems and provide interoperability between different applications. We will present an introductory overview of two such schemes in this section.

### *Public-Key Cryptographic Standards*

**Public-key cryptographic standards** (PKCS) was developed in 1991 by RSA Laboratories in collaboration with representatives from Apple, Digital, Lotus, Microsoft, the Massachusetts Institute of Technology, Northern Telecom, Novell, and Sun. Since its conception, PKCS has become the basis for many formal standards and is implemented in a variety of commercial applications.

PKCS addresses the pitfalls of public-key cryptography, such as encryption of guessable messages, encryption of short messages when RSA public exponent ($e$) is 3, and sending messages to multiple recipients when $e$ is 3. PKCS provides standards for RSA encryption, Diffie-Hellman key agreement, password-based encryption, extended-certificate syntax, cryptographic message syntax, private-key information syntax, certification request syntax, selected attributes, cryptographic token interface, and personal information exchange syntax.

PKCS is actually a collection of 12 papers on PKCS, PKCS#1 through PKCS#12. Additionally, PKCS provides two supplementary documents, "An Overview of the PKCS Standards" and "A Layman's Guide to a Subset of ASN.1, BER, and DER." We will revisit PKCS standards in Chapter 7. The CD-ROM contains the PKCS papers.

### *IEEE P1363 Standard for Public-Key Cryptography*

The purpose of the IEEE P1363 standard is to broaden the treatment of public-key technology, bring together all the different aspects of this technology under one common framework, promote interoperability, and provide a basis for securing all kinds of digital data. P1363 is currently under development, and the first version is expected to be ready for balloting in 1998.

P1363 brings together a diverse set of areas, such as management of hybrid cryptosystems, key agreement for secret-key systems using public-key systems (e.g., DES with RSA or Diffie-Hellman), authentication of hash values, and encryption and authentication of messages in hybrid systems. P1363 also covers the generation and representation of keys and parameters in hybrid systems and hardware support for public-key schemes.

P1363 identifies three different categories of public-key cryptographic algorithms based on their underlying mathematical foundation: discrete logarithm, elliptic curves, and integer factorization. For each category, it presents a number of different algorithms and schemes. Additionally, P1363 discusses a number of auxiliary functions, such as hash functions, and provides a variety of informative appendices. Refer to http://grouper.ieee.org/groups/1363/index.html for a detailed discussion of P1363.

## Message-Digest Algorithms

A **message-digest algorithm** takes a variable-length message as input and produces a fixed-length digest as output. The fixed-length output is called the **message digest,** a **digest,** or a **hash.** A message-digest algorithm is also referred to as a **one-way hash algorithm,** or simply a **hash algorithm.**

A message-digest algorithm must have three properties in order to be cryptographically secure. First, it must not be feasible to determine the input message based on its digest. In other words, the mapping from a message to its digest is a one-way function and cannot be reversed. Second, it must not be possible to find an arbitrary message that has a particular, desired digest. Third, it should be computationally infeasible to find two messages that have the same digest. Other properties of well-designed message algorithms are that the mapping from a message to a digest appears to be random, and that flipping even one bit of the message results in an entirely new, uncorrelated digest.

It is critical that message-digest algorithms be cryptographically secure. Suppose Alice, who is Bob's secretary, is capable of finding two messages that have the same digest. One of the messages contains the minutes of a recent meeting that Bob had with his staff; the other message instructs the payroll department to give Alice a hefty raise. Alice forwards the first genuine message to Bob, who reads the message and digitally signs its digest. Alice can now dupe the payroll into believing that Bob has signed her pay raise letter and get herself a nice raise.

If the fixed-length output of a message digest has $m$ bits, it will take approximately $2^m$ messages to find a message with a desired digest, and $2^{m/2}$ messages to find two messages that have the same digest. Message-digest functions must therefore have outputs of at least 128 bits because, given the current state of the art, it is computationally infeasible to search $2^{64}$ messages. Table 2-3 lists some well-known message-digest functions and the size of their outputs. **MD5** from RSADSI is a frequently used algorithm, but it is being slowly phased out due to some theoretical weaknesses. Perhaps the most secure message-digest algorithm

**Table 2-3** Some Common Message Digest Algorithms

| Message-Digest Algorithm | Digest Length (bits) |
|---|---|
| MD2 | 128 |
| MD4 | 128 |
| MD5 | 128 |
| SHA | 160 |
| SHA-1 | 160 |

is the U.S. government's **Secure Hash Algorithm** (SHA-1), which generates a 160-bit output.

## Message Authentication Codes

A **message authentication code** (MAC) is a fixed-length data item that is sent together with a message to ascertain the message origination and integrity. MACs are very useful for providing authentication and integrity without confidentiality. A message authentication code is also referred to as a **message integrity code** (MIC).

Secret-key, public-key, and hash algorithms can be used as a basis for MACs. A common way to generate MACs employs a secret-key symmetric block cipher in the CBC mode. The financial community has been using this approach for a long time to protect interbank electronic fund transfers. A cryptographic hash function can also be used to hash together a message and a secret code to produce a MAC. The receiver of the message, who shares the secret code with the sender, calculates the hash of the transmitted message together with its secret code to obtain another MAC. If the two MACs are the same, the receiver can conclude that the message has come from someone who knew the secret, and that the message has not been tampered with while in transit. This is called a **keyed hash function,** and the corresponding MAC is referred to as **hashed message authentication code** (HMAC). The use of HMACs for protecting Internet communications at the network layer is growing. MACs based on public-key cryptography provide nonrepudiation as well as authentication and integrity, as explained in the next section.

## Digital Signatures

A **digital signature** is a data item that vouches for the origin and integrity of a message. The originator of a message uses a **signing key** to sign the message and sends the message and its digital signature to a recipient. The recipient uses a **verification**

**key** to verify the origin of the message and that it has not been tampered with while in transit.

It is extremely valuable if the signing key is distinct from the verification key. The verifier of a message can then verify its authenticity without forcing the signer to reveal the signing key. By keeping the signing key a secret, the signer ensures that the verifier can verify the signature but cannot forge it. Because it is not feasible to forge a party's signature without the possession of its signing key, the signer of a message cannot later repudiate the fact that it has signed the message. This property of distinct signing and verification keys is extremely important, and it provides a way to implement nonrepudiation, which was discussed in Chapter 1.

We saw that a message authentication code can be also used to verify the authenticity of a message. There is, however, an important distinction between digital signatures and MACs. To verify a MAC, the recipient of the message must share with the sender the secret that produced the MAC. As a result, the sender can always repudiate the fact that it sent the message on the grounds that the receiver could have also produced the same MAC.

We now show how public-key cryptography provides a foundation for digital signatures. Alice calculates the digest of her message and uses her private key to encrypt (sign) it, as shown in Figure 2-4. She transmits her message and its signed digest to Bob. Bob decrypts the signature using Alice's public key, computes the digest of the message, and compares the two values. The message is authentic if they are equal. Trudy, who wants to impersonate Alice, cannot generate the same signature because she does not have Alice's private key. If she decides to tamper with the message while it is in transit, the tampered message will hash to a different value than the original one, and Bob will detect that. Alice will find it difficult to repudiate the fact that she sent the message because the digest of the message is signed by her private key. However, Alice can argue that her private key had been compromised and used by someone else to sign the message.

Signing a message instead of its digest, although possible, has a number of shortcomings. First, signing an entire message and sending it along with the message doubles the bandwidth requirements. Second, public-key operations are generally slow, and encrypting an entire message instead of its digest impacts performance. Third, a cryptanalyst can use the plaintext message and its corresponding ciphertext to launch a known-plaintext attack against the cryptosystem.

## RSA Digital Signatures

RSA public-key technology can be used as a basis to generate digital signatures. RSA digital signatures were the de facto industry standard until NIST proposed DSS on August 30, 1991. RSA has been subjected to an intense public scrutiny for a long time, and we can assume that RSA-based digital signatures are computa-

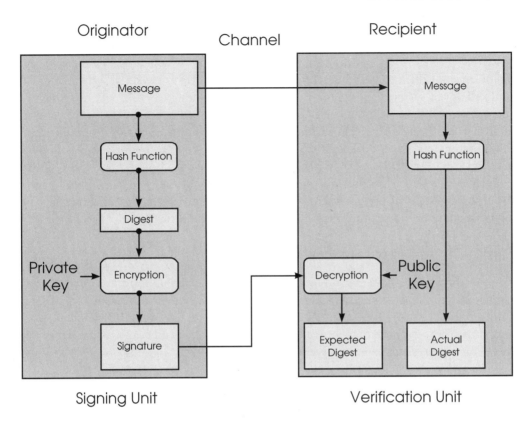

**Figure 2-4** Digital signature generation and verification.

tionally secure. RSA is controlled by RSADSI in the United States and is subject to licensing agreements.

## DSS Digital Signatures

DSS is the proposed NIST standard for digital signatures (see the Digital Signature Algorithm section for a brief overview of DSS and DSA). DSS digital signatures operate in a manner similar to RSA signatures. The signing unit hashes the message and transmits the message and the signed hash; the verification unit verifies the authenticity of the message based on the transmitted signed hash and the sender's public key. DSS permits only keys between 512 and 1024 bits, although DSA does not limit the size of the key. NIST recommends using DSS's sister hash function SHA-1, but it can work with any hash function. Under the surface, however, DSS uses a variant of El Gamal signatures for signing and verification.

The decision by NIST to employ El Gamal signatures instead of standardizing on RSA casued a flurry of debate among cryptographers. The security of DSA is based on the difficulty of taking discrete logarithms, whereas RSA relies on the computational difficulty of factoring large numbers. DSA can only sign messages, while RSA can encrypt and sign. Because U.S. laws severely restrict the export of encryption software, it is easier to distribute software (or hardware) implementations of DSA than RSA. RSA (with $e = 3$) can verify signatures about one hundred times faster than DSA. For signature generation, DSA can be slightly more efficient than RSA, making DSA more appealing for smart cards. The RSA and DSA digital signature schemes are essentially equivalent, and the decision to use one instead of the other depends on factors such as export restrictions, licensing, and usage. It is likely that these two standards will continue to compete in the near future.

## Elliptic Curve Digital Signatures

Elliptic curve cryptosystems can also be used as a foundation for digital signatures. With relatively shorter key sizes, elliptic curves can provide the same degree of computational security as RSA or DSA. As a result, elliptic curve digital signature systems have better performance over their counterparts and are a very attractive choice for smart cards, which have low processing power.

The IEEE P1363 Working Group is currently developing a standard for digital signatures based on elliptic curves. The proposed algorithm is called the **Elliptic Curve Digital Signature algorithm** (ECDSA), which is a variant of DSA. Refer to [MENE93] for detailed information on elliptic curve public-key cryptosystems.

## Blinded Signatures

So far in the presentation of digital signatures, the signer of a message has been the same entity that produced the message. There are circumstances, however, in which a trusted party signs messages presented by other parties. Such signed messages are the digital counterparts of notarized documents, although the legislation governing them is still being defined. Because it is presented by actual messages, the signing party can examine messages prior to signing and find out about their contents.

It will be advantageous to be able to present a document for signing to a party without revealing its content. Consider Alice, who has discovered a new chemical formula and wants to register it with Bob, who works for a registration agency. Alice, however, does not want to reveal her new formula. She wants Bob to sign her patent application, but she does not want him to be able to determine the formula.

Alice can obtain a **blind signature** from Bob as follows. She multiplies her message by a **blinding factor,** which is a randomly generated number. She then sends the blinded message to Bob, who signs it and returns the signed blinded message to Alice. Alice divides Bob's signature by the blinding factor and obtains Bob's signature on the actual message. Bob, on the other hand, does not know the blinding factor and cannot figure out what he just signed. David Chaum invented the concept of blind signatures and holds a number of patents in this area [CHAU83].

## Random Numbers

Random numbers are usually required to generate cryptographic keys, initialization vectors, or challenges. A **pseudorandom number generator** uses a deterministic algorithm to generate a sequence of pseudorandom numbers based on a **seed.** Because it completely determines the generated sequence, the seed must not be predictable. A good way to find an unpredictable seed is to hash together all the available sources of randomness, such as timing of keystrokes, system load, mouse motions, disk seek times, and so on. A seed picked from a very small space or one whose value is the hash of the current time are examples of poorly chosen seeds. A **random number generator,** on the other hand, truly generates unpredictable numbers. Finding a truly random source is usually difficult and might require special hardware.

A cryptosystem with very secure cryptographic algorithms and very secure schemes can be extremely unsecure if it relies on random numbers that can be guessed. In September 1995, a team of researchers at the University of California at Berkeley discovered that the UNIX version of Netscape Navigator seeded its pseudorandom number generator with the computer's time-of-day clock, the Navigator's process number, and other guessable information (http://www.cs.berkeley.edu/~iang/press). Even worse, the same team discovered that they could patch the Navigator's pseudorandom number generator so it would always use the same seed. These flaws compromised the security of the Netscape Navigator and allowed the team to attack it at its weakest point.

## Key Length

To break a cryptosystem that does not have any known weaknesses, an attacker must try each possible key from the key space until a known ciphertext is decrypted to some recognizable plaintext. This is a brute-force attack to recover the key. An 8-bit key has a key space of $2^8$ (256) different possible keys. On the average, it takes only half of this space, or $2^7$ (128), to recover the key in a brute-force attack. Any low-end personal computer can try all the keys in a matter of seconds and recover an 8-bit key; we must use larger keys if we want to have more secure cryptosystems.

The secret-key DES algorithm employs a key size of 56, which generates a key space of $2^{56}$ different keys. If a computer can try one thousand million keys a second, it takes approximately 2 years to recover a DES key. DES can prevent individual attackers and perhaps very small organizations from cracking your code, but it provides little protection against larger organizations or governments, who can afford to spend millions of dollars on computational power and break DES in a matter of seconds.

For all practical purposes, the 56-bit DES algorithm has been cracked. Refer to http://www.rsa.com/pressbox/html/980226.html for a discussion of how a team of enthusiasts used the Internet to link tens of thousands of computers to break a DES code in 39 days.

RC4, a secret-key algorithm used for bulk encryption, can use a key size of up to 2048. Assuming a 128-bit key and a computer capable of trying one thousand million keys a second, it would take $10^{22}$ years to break 128-bit RC4. The universe is $10^{10}$ years old, and not even the largest governments can assemble enough computing power to break 128-bit RC4 in a brute-force attack.

Why not always use long keys, say, 1024-bit long, to be on the safe side? There are a couple of issues with long keys. First, many countries impose restrictions on the strength of cryptographic systems that can be used commercially or exported to other countries. For example, with a few exceptions, the U.S. government restricts the export of encryption software to 40 bits. Second, some cryptographic algorithms cannot take advantage of longer keys; DES, for example, uses only 56-bit keys and cannot exploit longer keys. These algorithms can be modified to leverage longer keys, but, as we have already mentioned, the revisions must be published and analyzed for years to discover any new vulnerabilities. Finally, long keys may make cryptographic algorithms less efficient and increase the amount of ciphertext and bandwidth required, making the overall system less useable.

What is the right-size key? It depends. Remember that the goal of cryptography is to make the value of encrypted information less than the money spent to decrypt it. If you are sending your credit card number on an unsecure network, such as the Internet, a 56-bit DES encryption might be sufficient. An individual attacker would not have the resources required to break the encryption code and recover your card number. An organized crime ring may be able to break the code and make fraudulent use of your credit card, but the expenditure required to crack the code is probably greater than the credit limit on your card (the mobster would have a tough time presenting a profitable business model to his board). To an intelligence agency, the value of knowing your credit card number may be zero, so it would not justify any expenditure to crack the code. On the other hand, if you are a spy and want to transmit the name of a new contact to your base via the Internet, there would be enough value in cracking your code for the intelligence agency to justify spending millions of dollars.

Computing power doubles every 14 months, or goes up by a factor of 10 every 5 years. Ten years from now, a determined individual attacker may be able to break a DES-encrypted credit card number easily. Fortunately, the value of information usually decreases over time, and it becomes less profitable for attackers to crack old code. To determine the required strength of encryption, you need to determine the length of time over which your data should be kept private and the value of the data over time. If at any time the value of data becomes greater than the cost of launching a brute-force attack, your code may be broken (remember that the value of data means different things to different people). In the following sections we discuss possible choices for secret-key and public-key key lengths.

## Secret-Key Key Length

A secret key must be large enough to prevent a brute-force attack, which tries each possible key of the key space to find the key that correctly decrypts some ciphertext to a meaningful plaintext. Table 2-4 shows average times needed to search half the key spaces spanned by secret keys with different lengths based on an attacker's available computer power, as shown in Table 2-5. The worst-case scenarios in Table 2-4 are twice as long. Every bit added to the key, that is, increasing the length by one, doubles the size of the key space so it takes an attacker twice as long to crack the code. How long should your keys be? The answer depends on how valuable your data is, how much the value of your data varies with time, how long the data should

**Table 2-4**  Average Time Needed to Break a Secret-Key Cryptosystem Based on 1997 Technology

| Key Length (bits) | Individual Attacker | Small Group | Academic Network | Large Company | Military Intelligence Agency |
|---|---|---|---|---|---|
| 40 | Weeks | Days | Hours | Milliseconds | Microseconds |
| 56 | Centuries | Decades | Years | Hours | Seconds |
| 64 | Millennia | Centuries | Decades | Days | Minutes |
| 80 | Infeasible | Infeasible | Infeasible | Centuries | Centuries |
| 128 | Infeasible | Infeasible | Infeasible | Infeasible | Millennia |

**Table 2-5**  Attacker's Capability

| Attacker | Computer Resources | Keys/Second |
|---|---|---|
| Individual attacker | One high-end desktop machine and software | $2^{17}-2^{24}$ |
| Small group | 16 high-end machines and software | $2^{21}-2^{24}$ |
| Academic network | 256 high-end machines and software | $2^{25}-2^{28}$ |
| Large company | $1,000,000 hardware budget | $2^{43}$ |
| Military intelligence agency | $1,000,000 hardware budget and advanced technology | $2^{55}$ |

be kept secret, and who your adversary is. If you are a military commander and want to transmit to your pilot the name of the city to bomb, the value of the message is very high and your adversary is a government. The value of your message, however, is worthless after the attack. In this case, you need at least a 80-bit key. If you are the president of Coca-Cola and want to ensure that your secret ingredients remain secret for decades, you should use at least a 128-bit key.

## Public-Key Key Length

The nature of brute-force attacks against public-key algorithms differs from that of secret-key algorithms, in which every possible key of a key space is tried until the correct one is found. A brute-force attack targets the underlying mathematical problem of a public-key algorithm and attempts to recover a private key based on the knowledge of a public key. The attack involves factoring very large numbers or taking discrete logarithms in very large finite fields.

As we explained in the Mathematical Foundations section, these mathematical problems are considered to be hard and computationally infeasible to solve for very large numbers. Table 2-6 presents the strength of public-key algorithms relative to secret-key algorithms; it can be used in conjunction with Tables 2-4 and 2-5 to determine a suitable length for a public key.

# Engineering and Development Issues

To manufacture successful Internet security products, developers need to ensure that their designs interoperate with other products that conform to the important industry standards. Cryptographic systems have a particular requirement for uni-

**Table 2-6**  Relative Strength of Secret Keys versus Public Keys

| Secret Key (bits) | Public Key (bits) Integer Factorization / Discrete Logarithm | Public Key (bits) Elliptic Curve |
|---|---|---|
| 40 | 274 | 57 |
| 56 | 384 | 80 |
| 64 | 512 | 106 |
| 80 | 768 | 132 |
| 96 | 1024 | 160 |
| 112 | 1792 | 185 |
| 120 | 2048 | 211 |
| 128 | 2304 | 237 |

form standards adoption. By definition, these systems will fail to exchange user-provided information if they do not use the same cryptographic keys, parameters, formats, algorithms, and so on.

A number of factors should influence engineering and manufacturing decisions, including U.S. government export laws and regulations; commercial licensing of underlying intellectual property; practices concerning single, dual, or multiple keys and algorithms per individual; and the topic of mandatory private-key escrow (or key recovery). Beyond these issues, a large wide spectrum of cryptopolitics and civil libertarian issues abound for which there are many arenas for public debate.

In the rest of this chapter we consider the effect of some of the more vital factors upon the practice of building applications that rely upon cryptosystems for security.

## United States Government Export Controls

U.S. government export regulations affect the commercial engineering and implementation of the algorithms described earlier in this chapter perhaps more than any other design factor. The goals of the export control program are to regulate the global interoperability of systems that use strong cryptography, channel approved usage of cryptographically enhanced communications, and enforce distribution regimes limiting public access to products affording the individual actual confidentiality of personal communications.

U.S. export control policy dominates the Internet's global landscape in the area of cryptographic systems. To be fair, one might characterize the overt political objective as denying inappropriate hostile use of information secrecy to rogue countries and terrorists. Your favorite Internet newsgroup for exchanging paranoid theories will provide you with a wealth of possible covert goals.

In addition to conventional politics, an oft-cited national security goal also aims to preserve intelligence-gathering capability through analysis of intercepted communications passing over telecommunications and broadcast networks. Unfortunately, the targets of such surveillance practices can buy protection equipment in the commercial market just like ordinary citizens. As a consequence, policies have tended to minimize for *all* parties the privacy benefits of strong cryptography, regardless of their intent. Civil libertarians certainly have an uphill political battle just to maintain traditional individual rights and freedoms in areas where cryptography is entering daily life.

Considering the cryptography embedded in Internet applications, practical commercial engineering must inevitably accommodate the prevailing export policy, given that the Internet is a worldwide phenomenon. However, the regulations are sufficiently flexible to allow particular users and/or patterns of usage to offer higher levels of protection, providing that the mechanisms to ensure such constraints are enforced. For example, a control mechanism may allow one user of Netscape Navigator to exchange data under the RC4 cipher, but only 40 bits of the 128-bit RC4 key are likely to be nominally secret. On the other hand, the same user using the same tool may be allowed to export a wholly secret 128-bit key when communicating with a registered bank.

As we will see in Chapter 14, digitally signed public keys (or digital certificates) issued to particular users can enable deployed systems to dynamically enforce preset rules governing authorized usage of the cryptographic features of mass-market products. By contrast, costly traditional approaches require companies to manufacture different versions of a security product, each with its own embedded cryptography for each authorized use. The use of digital certificates to control cryptography may well remove the main political objection delaying the generalized deployment of strong cryptography. However, this centralized capability—which dynamically and remotely enforces prescribed individual behavior and controls the capabilities of a technology—can be used for good and evil purposes with equal ease.

## Commercial Licensing Issues

Commercial patent-licensing practices concerning the legal use of public-key cryptography on the Internet have been traditionally difficult to apply, for nefarious political and commercial reasons. Similarly, trade-secret protections have affected access to commonly used secret-key ciphers. The impact of intellectual property licensing issues has delayed the generalized availability of protected communications based on strong cryptography. The underlying (U.S.) patents for major public-key cryptosystems (the MIT patent on RSA, Diffie-Hellman, Merkle-Hellman, and the Digital Signature algorithms) are set to expire in a couple of years or have already expired, or automatic, no-cost licenses are becoming available. However, a new set of system, process, and hardware patents are being filed, and they often seek to exploit innovations and inventions used to create an easy-to-use key management infrastructure.

Basic, cost-free cryptography is already available. Unencumbered Diffie-Hellman and DSA algorithms come as a part of all modern Windows systems, for example. Windows developers may use the common secret-key ciphers such as RC2, triple-DES, and RC4 via stable platform APIs. RSA-based certificate issuing (see Chapter 3 and Part VI) is part of all modern Windows NT Server systems, and it is slated to transparently operate at the heart of each instance of NT 5. Java programming language provides a security package to handle certificates and keys, as described in Chapter 3. Similar cryptographic toolkits are delivered when one installs modern Web browsers, as discussed in Part II.

Although the patent and intellectual property issues that have bedeviled the software industry are fast passing into obscurity, they are being replaced by new commercial and political issues that seek to control how cryptography is applied.

Perhaps the safest tack for developers is to use the cryptographic solutions provided by major branded platforms, such as Java or Windows. Lawyers are likely to have already trodden the intellectual property path on one's behalf and to have gauged the political moods.

Although many of the intellectual property issues have centered around free commercial access to cryptographic software, one should be aware that both the developer and user industry is rapidly turning to specialized cryptographic hardware. This makes much of the traditional intellectual property debate moot. Microsoft Internet Explorer's use of RSA to perform SSL client authentication (see Chapters 6 and 15) can already use smart cards featuring embedded key management from such companies as Sclumberger. Similarly, Netscape Suitespot Web servers can interact with PCMCIA cryptoperipherals organized in racks of networked card readers, from such companies as Litronic. High-performance cryptohardware for business systems is emerging from traditional sources such as IBM.

Many of these devices feature intellectual property in the techniques they use to protect private keys and the means they employ during the manufacturing process to ensure trustworthy onboard processing of sensitive data. These factors, together with system and process patents, are likely to dominate the security industry's internal dealings in the coming generation of cryptoproducts and applications. Inevitably, the associated costs will be passed on to the consumer.

## Single-Key, Dual-Key, Multiple Public-Keys per Individual

The design of security systems often relies upon the secrecy properties of keys and ciphertext. The effectiveness of that secrecy critically depends upon how keys are managed and used. Reuse of a key in a stream cipher can have disastrous consequences. After ten years, an RSA key once considered impossible to factor became vulnerable. Clearly, the management of keys needs to be tied to the semantics of the intended mechanism that enciphering facilitates (see the discussion of X.800 in Chapter 1). A key for formally signing one's last will and testament may be different from a signing key used to authenticate oneself to one's computer login process, for example. Compromise of the latter may result in the loss of some data; compromise of the former may disinherit one's chosen heirs.

A debate rages over the prudence of separating two particular types of long term public-key key pairs: those used for signing and those that can encrypt. Some argue that an almost magical property of the reversible RSA algorithm that enables one key to perform both functions should be denied so that these functions can be independently managed according to the distinct risks faced by each. Others argue that such functions must be separated so that governments may legislate third-party escrow of the politically sensitive encryption key, while individuals maintain exclusive control of—and accountability for—their personal signing keys. Others claim that the "debate to separate" is an artifact of the way export regulations are constructed; separation makes it easier to pass export muster because keys used for encryption can be restricted to a smaller size than keys used for document signing.

The debate over the number of keys and who controls them is not restricted to public-key cryptography or even to purely cryptographic matters. The issue of the key agreement mechanism versus the key transport mechanism shows how important it is for protocol designers to understand how key management affects the effectiveness of security protocols.

With the Diffie-Hellman key-agreement algorithm, a secret is uniquely shared between two parties during each party's computation of the relevant mathematics. With RSA's facility for key transport one party must select the secret and transport a key to the other. An observable secret generator or secret storage facility at one party compromises the other party. A compromised RSA key may compromise all previous communication sessions secured using the same key, similarly. These issues are not limited to RSA, however. With DSA signing, reuse of a random number used during document signing can lead to leakage of the signing key to an attacker, with obvious potential for consequences for disruption and fraud.

Although many have tried to reduce the debate on how many keys the average consumer should have to a choice of one or two (i.e., separate signing and encryption mechanisms), the issue is more complex. Currently deployed mass-market systems employ single-key RSA designs on the whole, but the momentum for addressing key function separation by deploying multiple-key and multialgorithm applications is growing, for legitimate risk management reasons. One can only hope that the management complexity thereby introduced does not undermine the effectiveness and ease-of-use of current single-key, single-algorithm deployments in long-established military and commercial security systems.

## Key Escrow and Key Recovery

Intelligence gathering relies upon access to plaintext information, covertly decrypting ciphertext as required, and scanning the world's telecommunications in general. Law enforcement relies upon investigative access to potential evidence of wrongdoing. In the Information Age, access to information by intelligence and investigative agencies is undoubtedly hampered by a culture that embraces indecipherable ciphertext.

As the earlier section on export established, traditional approaches to managing the information access problem have focused on controlling the standards for general interworking. Internet products providers have been induced to either keep key sizes small or constrain the purposes for which key sizes may be larger. Furthermore, international or intergovernmental agreements such as International Traffic in Arms Regulation (ITAR) and Coordinating Committee on Multilateral Export Controls (COCOM) have ensured that commercial plug-and-play cryptography remains an undelivered promise. Such practices deny the ability of a U.K. user to substitute locally manufactured strong U.K. cryptomodules into a U.S. crypto-using product.

With the adoption of hardware cryptoperipheral support into commercial products and the general social requirement for strong cryptography, new approaches are being advocated to control government and corporate access to data. Essentially, they all boil down to one simple idea: You give away the keys to governments and your employer before or as you use them.

For our purposes, it is important to understand how the social influence of key recovery impacts the engineering of products that use cryptographic modules. Platforms such as Windows enable administrators to deliver cryptomodules capable of key recovery to users, which function identically to pristine designs except that privacy may be compromised as a result. An application designer may henceforth allow for the need to notify users of a friendly application of the risks to a private communication that government or corporate access may entail from use of a particular secure system installation. One system of local laws may require consumers to be notified of risks; another may allow certain parties (perhaps under court order) to be targeted into releasing incriminating information on supposedly secure lines.

The practice of creating and using cryptomodules demands significant engineering and production design skill above and beyond merely understanding the ideal properties of the mathematics. Real-world cryptographers must know the intended environment of use and know the threats to which the communication is exposed. In commercial systems, application designers need to accommodate prevailing government policy and simultaneously navigate the difficult seas of ethics, tortuous liability, personal freedoms, and society's well-being.

## Summary

A cryptosystem is a collection of cryptographic algorithms, keys, all the possible plaintexts, and all the associated ciphertexts. The security of a cryptosystem should reside entirely with its keys, and we must assume that an adversary knows the details of the algorithms and can intercept all the ciphertexts. It is therefore much better to publish an algorithm and subject it to public scrutiny to uncover any possible weaknesses. If a cryptographic algorithm is published and many cryptanalysts have attempted to break it for many years without success, it can be assumed that the algorithm is secure.

There are three types of cryptographic algorithms: message digest, secret key, and public key. Message-digest algorithms produce a fixed-length output from a variable-length input message. Secret-key algorithms use a secret key for encryption and decryption; they have relatively fast implementations and are used for bulk encryption. Public-key algorithms use a pair of public and private keys and are about 100 to 1000 times slower than secret-key algorithms. They are used primarily for exchanging secret keys or generating digital signatures.

Cryptanalysts launch ciphertext-only, known-plaintext, and chosen-plaintext attacks against a cryptosystem to deduce information about ciphertexts or recover its keys. Almost all cryptosystems are only computationally secure; that is, they can be broken by trying every possible key of the key space and determining the correct key. The amount of time or computing power to break a system, however, might be prohibitive. Advances in computer algorithms and hardware design decrease the required resources to break a cryptosystem. Increasing the size of a key by one bit doubles the size of the keyspace and makes it twice as hard.

A number of factors will influence developers making practical engineering and manufacturing decisions. They include U.S. government export laws and regulations, commercial licensing of underlying intellectual property, practices concerning single, dual, or multiple keys and algorithms per individual, and the topic of mandatory private key escrow.

# References

[BRES89]    Bressoud, D.M. *Factorization and Primality Testing,* Springer-Verlag, New York, 1989.

[CHAU83]    Chaum, D. "Blind Signatures for Untraceable Payments," *Advances in Cryptology: Proceedings of Crypto '82,* 1983, pp. 199–203.

[DENB92]    Den Boer, B., and A. Bosselaers. "An Attack on the Last Two Rounds of MD4," *Advances in Cryptology—Crypto '91 Proceedings,* 1992, pp. 194–203.

[DES81]    *DES Modes of Operation.* FIPS PUB 81, National Bureau of Standards, U.S. Department of Commerce, Washington, DC, 1981.

[DIFF76b]    Diffie, W., and M.E. Hellman. "New directions in cryptography," *IEEE Transactions on Information Theory,* 22(6), 1976, pp. 644–654.

[DSS94]    *Digital Signature Standard (DSS).* FIPS PUB 186, U.S. Department of Commerce, Washington, DC, 1994.

[ELGA85]    Elgamal, T. "A public key cryptosystem and a signature scheme based on discrete logarithms," *IEEE Transactions on Information Theory,* 31, 1985, pp. 469–472.

[KAHN67]    Kahn, D. *The Codebreakers: The Story of Secret Writing,* Macmillan Publishing Co., New York, 1967.

[KAUF95]   Kaufman, C., R. Perlman. and M. Speciner. *Network Security PRIVATE Communications in a PUBLIC World,* Prentice Hall, Inc., Englewood Cliffs, NJ, 1995.

[KNUD94]   Knudsen, L.R. "Block Ciphers—Analysis, Design, Applications," Ph.D. dissertation, Denmark: Aarhus University, 1994.

[KOBL87]   Koblitz, N. "Elliptic Curve Cryptosystems," *Mathematics of Computation,* 48(177), 1987, pp. 203–209.

[LAMA91]   LaMacchia, B.A., and A.M. Odlyzko. "Computation of Discrete Logarithms in Prime Fields," *Designs, Codes, and Cryptography*, 1, 1991, pp. 46–62.

[LENS93]   Lenstra, A.K., and H.W. Lenstra, Jr., eds., *Lecture Notes in Mathematics 1554: The Development of the Number Field Sieve,* Springer-Verlag, New York, 1993.

[MENE93]   Menezes, A. *Elliptic Curve Public Key Cryptosystem,* Kluwer Academic Publishers, Boston, 1993.

[SCHN96]   Schneier, B. *Applied Cryptography: Protocols, Algorithms, and Source Code in C,* John Wiley & Sons, New York, 1996.

Chapter

# 3

# Digital Certificates, Certification Authorities, and Public-Key Infrastructures

What is a digital certificate, and why do you need one? Generally speaking, a digital certificate serves as a driver's license in the digital world. When you want to access your bank account to transfer funds or access your company's network to download your e-mails, you may be required to have a certificate and be prepared to prove that you possess the private key that mathematically relates to the public key certified in the certificate. But digital certificates are more than just driver's licenses. They also enable you to verify the authenticity of software downloaded via the Internet (Chapter 4), send digitally signed or encrypted e-mail (Chapter 5), control access to resources (Chapter 6), implement nonrepudiation (Chapter 1), and more.

This chapter lays the groundwork for digital certificates. It discusses what they are, their standard formats, who issues them, why we may trust them, and infrastructures required to support them. We could not possibly cover all the material relating to digital certificates in one chapter. This chapter gets you started, and as you read this book, you will learn more about them.

## Digital Certificates

A **public-key certificate** is a binding between an entity's public key and one or more attributes relating to its identity. The entity can be a person, a hardware device such as a router, or a software process. The public-key certificate provides assurance that the public key belongs to the identified entity and that the entity possesses the corresponding private key. A public-key certificate is loosely called a **digital certificate, digital ID,** or simply a **certificate;** the entity identified in a certificate is commonly referred to as the **certificate subject.** If the certificate subject is a legal entity, such as a person, it is often referred to as a **subscriber**. In this chapter, we use the terms *subject* and *subscriber* interchangeably. Figure 3-1 shows a graphical representation of a certificate (we will explain the certificate attributes shown in this figure later in this chapter).

A digital certificate has, generally speaking, the same purpose as an identification card, such as a driver's license.[1] A driver's license binds the photograph of a person to personal information about the person, such as name, address, and gender. It provides assurance to a bank teller, for example, that the person cashing a check is in fact the same person whose name appears on the check.[2]

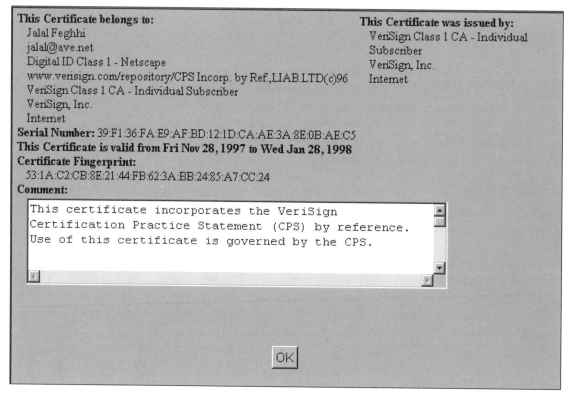

**Figure 3-1**    A digital certificate.

---

1. Digital certificates may be used to represent many types of subscriber attributes relating to identity, such as creditworthiness or authority. While these are purpose-specific identity attributes, they implicate legal issues that may not be consistent with the identification card analogy.

2. Digital certificates have many other uses in addition to serving as authentication cards. As we will discuss throughout this book, they can be used to encode authorization privileges, exchange secret keys, and implement nonrepudiation.

Digital certificates are not generally very useful in large communities if individuals issue their own certificates. How much trust can a bank teller have in a person's identification card if people are free to issue their own driver's licenses? The Department of Motor Vehicles (DMV) regulates the issuance of driver's licenses and ensures that an individual presents correct personal information when applying for a license. Similarly, trusted third-party certification authorities (CAs) confirm the identities of their subscribers and issue digital certificates.

It is critical to be able to verify that a certification authority has issued a certificate or to detect a forged certificate in order to establish trust in digital certificates. Forged certificates allow an attacker to bind his public key to another individual's identity and masquerade as that individual to carry out fraudulent activities. The DMV prevents forgery by incorporating a variety of physical features in a driver's license, such as holograms, the manner a photograph is printed on the license, and lamination. The equipment required to issue a driver's license is expensive and difficult to obtain, thus making it difficult to forge a driver's license. A digital certificate, on the other hand, is a chunk of binary data. The software to create a digital certificate is not complex and is becoming increasingly available. The Java programming language and Microsoft's CryptoAPI embedded in Windows, for example, include features that create digital certificates.

How can forgery of digital certificates be prevented? A certification authority, after authenticating the identity of a subject, digitally signs the certificate, thereby incorporating its signature into the certificate. The certification authority calculates the digital signature by computing the message digest of the certificate and encrypting it with its private key. An attacker cannot forge a certification authority's certificate because he does not know the certification authority's private key and cannot generate the correct digital signature. Furthermore, if an attacker makes any changes to a genuine certificate, the message digest of the certificate changes and no longer matches the certificate authority's signature.

Digital certificates provide a cryptographic mechanism for implementing authentication; they also enable a secure, scaleable way to distribute public keys in large communities. We will explore these properties in the remainder of this section.

## Cryptographic Authentication

In Chapter 1, we introduced the authentication service and emphasized that authentication is perhaps the most essential of all information security services. We also discussed three different paradigms (something you know, something you have, and something you are) to provide assurance of a person's identity, and presented various mechanisms to implement authentication.

A digital certificate provides a way to implement authentication. A user can authenticate herself to a system by presenting her certificate, which binds her public key to her identity, and then proving that she is in possession of the private key that corresponds to the certified public key. A private key is a long mathematical value that cannot be memorized. It is commonly stored in a file, optionally encrypted by a password, or in a hardware token, such as a smart card. The user can prove that she possesses the correct private key by presenting the file that contains the private key or by inserting her smart card in a reader.

Typically, the file that contains the private key is protected by a password, and, similarly, the smart card is protected by a PIN. To authenticate herself, the user has to prove that she knows the correct password or PIN in addition to possessing the private key, thus providing further evidence of her identity. In these cases, a digital certificate serves as a two-factor authentication mechanism (see Chapter 1).

The authentication system engages in a cryptographic protocol with the smart card to verify that the private key possessed by her is in fact the correct private key, which mathematically relates to the certified public key in her certificate. Because the protocol involves cryptographic operations and long cryptographic keys, digital certificate technology provides a stronger authentication mechanism than mechanisms based on short, memorizable passwords.

It is essential to understand that the level of trust that a certificate provides in a user's identity depends on how trustworthy the certification authority is perceived to be. An authenticating system, after verifying a user's private key, develops trust in the identity of the user because it trusts the issuing certification authority. In essence, the certification authority is vouching for the identity of the user.

## Secure, Scaleable Key Distribution

How can a person obtain the public key of another person? Let's assume Alice and Bob are friends, and Alice needs Bob's public key. Alice and Bob can arrange a meeting, and Bob can give Alice a floppy disk containing his public key. Because Alice knows Bob, she trusts that the public key belongs to Bob. Alice can then copy Bob's public key to her computer, or she can just keep it on the disk. It is critical for Alice to securely store Bob's public key at all times and to prevent Trudy, an intruder, from replacing Bob's public key with her own. If Trudy manages to replace the public key, she can masquerade as Bob and dupe Alice into believing that she is communicating with Bob when she is actually communicating with Trudy.

Such a key distribution method might work well for a small community of users who can trust each other. With the growth of electronic commerce and secure e-mail on the Internet, however, there is an ever-increasing need for persons who do not know each other and are geographically dispersed to exchange public keys. Manual distribution of keys simply does not scale to the Internet.

Digital certificates provide an alternative, scaleable model in which trusted third-party certification authorities authenticate persons and certify their public keys. A person can then find another person's public key by obtaining his certificate from a trusted certification authority and verifying the CA's signature. This model of public-key distribution is scaleable because a rather small number of CAs can authenticate a large number of users in a community. Retrieving an individual's public key in this manner is in a sense similar to dialing a (trusted) phone number, such as Directory Assistance, and asking for an individual's phone number.

Digital certificates can be transmitted via unsecure channels and stored in unsecure mediums. Any changes made to a certificate while it is in transit can be detected because the issuing certification authority's signature no longer verifies. Similarly, any changes made to a certificate while it is in storage can be detected. Certificates are *usually* not confidential and do not contain sensitive information. As a result, certificates can be stored in unsecure repositories and freely transported across the Internet.

## Client-Centric Processing

A digital certificate is an open data structure, and it can contain domain-specific knowledge. Client software can determine the authenticity of a certificate and then use the domain-specific information encoded in the certificate to tune its behavior. A certificate may contain all the necessary control information needed to guide the processing of client software, obviating or minimizing the need for the client to rely on a server for its function.

An example will help us to explain this concept. Let's assume that future ATMs will use digital certificates to authenticate customers. A bank issues certificates for its members, and, depending on the member, encodes different control information in the certificates. The bank might issue a certificate entitling premium members to withdraw up to a thousand dollars from an ATM, whereas the limit might be three hundred dollars for ordinary members. When dispensing cash, an ATM can enforce the business logic of the bank and dispense higher amounts of cash to premium customers. The ATM does not need to contact a central server to obtain the cash limit for a customer—it can do the processing locally based on a certificate's control information.

Client-centric processing property of certificates is significant and can be leveraged to build systems that scale better and are less vulnerable to failures. A variety of control information can be encoded in a certificate, such as security privileges, access privileges to use resources, and so on. In Chapter 10, we will demonstrate the use of certificates to implement access control in VeriSign's OnSite LRA service.

# X.509 Digital Certificates

In the preceding section, we presented digital certificates from a rather abstract perspective and identified a public key, a subject's identity, and a certification authority's signature as the main components of a certificate.

In this section, we present a standardized, more elaborate format for certificates. We require a more elaborate format because a certificate might contain more data than a subject's public key and identity. A certificate for secure e-mail, for example, contains a subject's e-mail address in addition to the public key. Furthermore, a certificate needs to be an extensible data structure and customizable to meet the requirements of various certificate-using environments. A financial environment, for example, may need to extend a certificate to encode data about a credit card holder, such as credit card number and credit limit.

We require a standardized format to allow certificate-using applications to interoperate with certificates issued by third-party certification authorities. End users do not get locked into procuring certificates from a particular certification authority, and software developers can write generic code that works with all certificates regardless of their issuers.

The X.509 is an International Telecommunication Union–Telecommunication Standardization Sector (ITU-T) and ISO/International Electrotechnical Commission (IEC) certificate format standard, first published in 1988 as part of the X.500 Directory recommendations. The X.509 version 1 (v1) format was extended in 1993 to incorporate two new fields to support directory access control, resulting in the version 2 (v2) format. Experience gained in attempting to deploy Internet Privacy Enhanced Mail (PEM) based on X.509 v1 in 1993 revealed the deficiency of X.509 v1 and v2 as an open, extensible format. As a result, X.509 v2 was revised to allow for additional extension fields. X.509 version 3 (v3) was released in June 1996.

ISO/IEC and ANSI X9 have also defined standard extension fields for X.509 v3, such as those for conveying additional subject identification information, key attribute information, and policy information. We will discuss extension fields and explore some specific standard fields in a later section.

Figure 3-2 illustrates the X.509 v3 certificate format. An X.509 v3 certificate encompasses a set of basic, predefined fields and zero or more extension fields. We shall discuss these fields in the next two sections.

## X.509 Basic Certificate Fields

In this section we discuss the basic elements of the X.509 v3 certificate format. These elements are the same for the X.509 v2 certificate format.

**Version**    The version field contains the version number of the encoded certificate. The current legal values are 1, 2, and 3.

**Certificate serial number**    This field is an integer assigned by the certification authority. Each certificate issued by a given CA must have a unique serial number.

**Signature algorithm identifier**    This field identifies the algorithm, such as RSA or DSA, used by a CA to digitally sign the certificate.

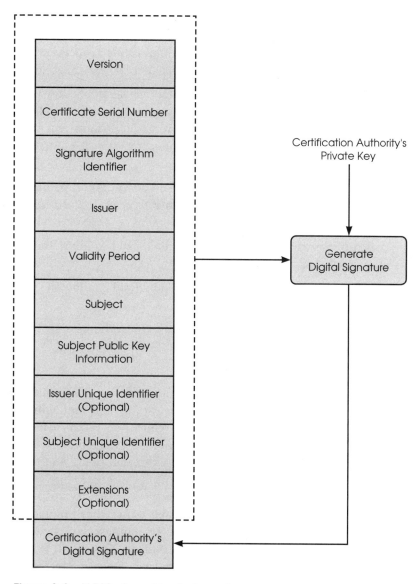

**Figure 3-2**   X.509 v3 certificate format.

**Issuer name**   The issuer field identifies the certification authority who has signed and issued the certificate.

**Validity period**   This field is the time interval during which the certificate remains valid, and the CA is obliged to maintain information about the status of the certificate. The validity field consists of a start date, the date on which the certificate becomes valid, and an end date, the date after which the certificate ceases to be valid. Note that a CA may elect to maintain status information for a longer period. VeriSign, for example, maintains revocation information about a certificate even after the validity period of the certificate ends.

**Subject name**    This field identifies the entity whose public key is certified in the subject public key information field. The subject name must be unique for each subject entity certified by a given certification authority. A CA, however, may issue more than one certificate with the same subject name for the same subject entity.

**Subject public key information**    This field contains the public key material (public key and parameters) and the identifier of the algorithm with which the key is used.

**Issuer unique identifier**    This is an optional field to allow the reuse of issuer names over time.

**Subject unique identifier**    This is an optional field to allow the reuse of subject names over time.

**Extensions**    We will discuss the extensions field in the next section.

## X.509 Extension Fields

The X.509 v3 extensions provide a way to associate additional information for subjects, public keys, managing the certification hierarchy, and managing certificate revocation list distribution. (Certification hierarchies and certification revocation lists are discussed later in this chapter.) The X.509 v3 extension also enables communities and organizations to define their own extension fields and encode information specific to their needs in a certificate.

An extension field has three parts: extension type, criticality indicator, and extension value. The **extension type** is an object identifier that provides semantics and type information (such as a text string, date, or complex data structure) for an extension value. The **extension value** subfield contains the actual value of an extension field, which is described by the extension type. Only one instance of a particular extension field may appear in a given certificate.

The **criticality indicator** is a flag that instructs a certificate-using application whether it is safe to ignore an extension field if it does not recognize the extension type. When processing a certificate, an application can safely ignore a **noncritical extension** field if it does not recognize the extension type. On the other hand, it should reject a certificate that contains a **critical extension** it does not recognize.

The criticality indicator provides a way to implement certificate-using applications that operate safely with certificates and evolve as new extensions are introduced. Noncritical extensions promote evolution of an application as it is gradually extended to respond to new extension fields. Critical extensions ensure the safe operation of an application with certificates that require special handling, especially for security concerns. Critical extensions, in general, may create interpretability problems and should be avoided unless the safe operation of an application becomes a concern.

ITU and ISO/IEC have developed and published a set of standard extensions in an amendment to the X.509 v3 standard [AMEN95]. In the rest of this section, we will discuss some of the extensions that are pertinent to this book.

**Basic constraints** The basic constraints field indicates whether the subject of the certificate is a CA and the maximum allowable depth of a certification path through that CA. Certification paths are discussed in a later section.

**Certificate policy** This field contains the policy under which the CA has issued the certificate and the intended purpose of the certificate.

**Key usage** The key usage field restricts the purpose of the certified public key in the certificate. The various usages of a public key are **digital signature, nonrepudiation, key encipherment, data encipherment, key agreement, certificate signing, CRL signing, encipherment-only,** and **decipherment-only.** This field is useful when it is desirable to constrain the use of a public key that can be used for more than one operation. For example, it might be desirable to restrict an RSA public key to digital signing operations and disable its use for all other purposes (see the Single-Key, Dual-Key, Multiple Public-Keys per Individual section in Chapter 2). The key usage extension field is commonly marked as critical, denoting that the issuing CA limits the certificate and the certified key to the indicated purpose. The use of the key for any other purpose would violate the CA's policy, and a certificate-using application or a user could not legally rely on the certificate for such unauthorized usages.

## X.509 Profiles

As with many ISO telecommunications standards, X.509 was designed as a general framework. It specifies a solution to a very general problem (authentication in distributed systems) and is implementation-independent. Regional or industry workshops are expected to "profile" and augment the specified options, refining the toolkit of options to satisfy local requirements.

For the Internet environment, a principle forum for specifying such a profile is the Internet Engineering Task Force (IETF). For example, the IETF's Public Key Infrastructure (PKIX) working group, which includes representatives from defense contractors, U.S. government security agencies, large commercial security industry players, and a few users, has a rule that specifies that all subjects must be named using X.500 hierarchical naming conventions—even though X.509 mandates no such requirement. Other rules specify conformance conditions that link the contents of certificates to required management system protocols. Versions of the profile series have attempted to require CAs to offer centralized key generation services, for example. As with all such self-regulated forums, these profiling efforts reflect a mixture of governmental, social, and commercial bias and user interests. Chapter 7 contrasts some of the ongoing profiling efforts in various forums that are fashioning industry standards.

**Certificate profiles** regulate the content of certificate extensions. They can specify new extension fields where additional controls are required for particular work environments. It is the ability to select fields from those provided by X.509 and specify their meaning in particular application contexts, such as secure e-mail or trusted software download (see Chapter 4 for a discussion on trusted software), that entitles X.509 to serve as the basis of a large-scale, diverse public-key infrastructure.

As an example, the current draft of the PKIX profile assigns to the standard X.509 key usage field meanings that state the type of security mechanism a signing key may facilitate when signing trusted software or general e-mail. It states that a key that authenticates the origin of trusted software has a public key certificate that contains a key usage extension for which only the digital signature bit may be set. A similar e-mail message can be signed in a nonrepudiation form if the public key certificate contains a key usage flag indicating that signing can occur with nonrepudiation.

However, such semantic prescriptions are somewhat imprecise and a little confusing in terms of their security models. For example, if a piece of software is packaged as an e-mail enclosure and signed, the signature can have nonrepudiation status. A standard that says that when packaged as itself, trusted software signing *cannot* be considered nonreputable, but when packaged as a signed e-mail enclosure it *can* provide nonrepudiation, needs more work. This example highlights the difficulty of writing coherent profiles that address broad swaths of security infrastructure. The general-purpose PKIX profile makes a number of design choices aimed at maximizing compatibility and interworking between competitively marketed first-generation products.

In one particular aspect PKIX inherits a long-standing IETF activity in the area of certificate policy (see Chapter 11). It takes great pains to tailor the generic ISO mechanism for policy specification to instrument Certification Practice Statements (CPS are discussed in a later section). These statements attempt to assign legal meanings to signatures by formalizing the models and practices of trusted third parties, signers, and users. These ideas institute a world in which one party can *accredit* the operations of another and thereby indicate a measure of trust to certificate users. When certificates are issued by CAs acting as trusted third parties (versus mere intranet or extranet certificate issuers), such notions are critical for electronic commerce, which requires legally recognized public trust. (See the discussion of the impact of certificates on electronic commerce in Chapter 12.)

At the heart of any X.509 profile lies the topic of authentication, and the related notions of naming and choosing appropriate name forms for the various classes of objects being identified. By convention, the core underlying name form used by X.509 is the **Distinguished Name** (DN). A DN is just a list of specific names, with a title on each to indicate to which attribute of the subject it refers. For example, the name *<country=GB; surname=Williams>* is a simple two-element name indicating that the party is from Great Britain and the surname is Williams. X.509 enables anyone to invent any attribute to describe any type of object (not just people). The name form is an open-ended construct that enables almost any system of naming to be established, global or local.

Profiles tailor the authentication model of X.509 to specific environments. Profiles themselves can be subprofiled, forming a hierarchy of definitions that allows industry to agree on the specific interpretation of the bits in the X.509 message. As we will see when we discuss aspects of authentication in more detail in Part IV, a very simple data structure relating a name to a key becomes the critical piece of a very complex puzzle when applied to electronic commerce in general.

## Encoding of Certificates

The X.509 certificate format is specified in a notation system called **Abstract Syntax One** (ASN.1). One can apply the **Distinguished Encoding Rules** (DER) to a certificate specified in ASN.1 format to produce a series of octets suitable for transmission over real networks. A detailed discussion of ASN.1 and its system of encoding rules is provided in Chapter 7 and Appendix A.

When DER-encoded, the certificate data structure fields are reduced to a set of lists of more fundamental field elements, where each list element contains either a primitive type or another list. ISO defines encoding rules for standard types such as integers, strings, and lists. In summary, each encoding rule takes the form of a triplet of byte-sets of the form (tag, length, value). The **tag** bytes describe the type with a predefined number. The **length** encodes the length of the value field, and the **value** is a formatted set of octets that represents the element. For example, let's assume the serial number of a certificate has an integer value of 127. This element is wire-encoded as the octets (02 01 7F). The 02 is the tag number for integers assigned by ISO. The value field has a length of 1 byte, and that value is the number hexadecimal 7F, which is 127 decimal. From these conventions, certificate data can be serialized to a file and then signed.

Being a binary value, it is often difficult to handle a certificate value using common tools such as word processors. Consequently, a **base-64 encoding** of the octets is often used. This convention simply enables octets to be reduced to ASCII characters more suitable for transmission by older e-mail programs and for editing in programs that can deal only with human-readable text. Essentially, the technique takes each 18 bits of data and uses 24 bits to represent the same value. The redundancy enables the characters chosen for representation to be limited to those commonly used in text-processing software. The reverse process is of course necessary before the certificate is usable.

Because one piece of base-64 content looks much like another, headers are often used to indicate that the value corresponds to a certificate. One may see a —*BEGIN CERTIFICATE*... header or —*END CERTIFICATE*... footer. In other programs, MIME headers are used similarly, where the base-64 data is preceded by headers such as *application/x-x509-user-cert*.

## Programming Certificates

The detailed formats and encoding of certificates are no longer of concern to users or developers. Designers can concentrate on the requirements and interpretation of fields in profiling efforts and leave the programming to the major platforms of the computing industry. By way of introduction to the practice of writing programs that actually handle certificates, we provide a short discussion of two of the major certificate-using platforms aimed at developers: Microsoft's CryptoAPI programming and Sun Microsystems' Java platform.

### *CryptoAPI*

CryptoAPI is Microsoft's response to the industry call for platforms to standardize cryptographic and key management programming for Win32 applications. The Microsoft Developer Network Web site is an excellent source of information concerning all of Microsoft's programming platforms. It is currently available on-line at http://premium.microsoft.com/msdn/library. One can simply search for *CryptoAPI* to locate a wealth of material on certificates and Microsoft software and sample code.

The simplest way to access and manage low-level cryptographic functions is to link the dynamic link library (DLL) advapi.dll. This DLL provides applications with a standard API through which cryptography can be accessed. It enables many different **Cryptographic Service Providers** (CSPs) to reside on a user's machine, each tailored to specific features and protection qualities. Microsoft supplies a default CSP implemented in software, which provides most of the functionality that general-purpose cryptography users will probably ever need. Similar CSPs provide implementations of other algorithms. The higher-level certificate and secure messaging features of CryptoAPI are provided by crypt32.dll. These libraries and APIs are documented and supported in the Microsoft Platform Software Developer's Kit (SDK), available on the Microsoft Developer's Network (MSDN) Web site. Sample code is available to sign and encrypt files, generate keys, and handle certificate data structures.

A major CryptoAPI data structure is the certificate information object. For ordinary programming purposes, the data structure is handled at the API level as a conventional C structure:

```
typedef struct _CERT_INFO {

    DWORD dwVersion;

    CRYPT_INTEGER_BLOB SerialNumber;

    CRYPT_ALGORITHM_IDENTIFIER

    SignatureAlgorithm;

    CERT_NAME_BLOB Issuer;

    FILETIME NotBefore;

    FILETIME NotAfter;

    CERT_NAME_BLOB Subject;

    CERT_PUBLIC_KEY_INFO SubjectPublicKeyInfo;

    CRYPT_BIT_BLOB IssuerUniqueId;

    CRYPT_BIT_BLOB SubjectUniqueId;

    DWORD cExtension;

    PCERT_EXTENSION rgExtension;

} CERT_INFO, *PCERT_INFO
```

There is probably no better introduction to CryptoAPI programming than to read the Microsoft-annotated sample code. The code fragment at sdkdoc/mancerts_8e05.htm, which generates a signed certificate request, demonstrates many important techniques. One must populate and encode fields, initialize and use appropriate signing keys, and invoke the cryptographic service provider, such as a smart card or the RSA software cryptography. The Common Object Model (COM) and CryptoAPI architecture ensures that developers can easily evolve their products as the underlying interworking standards, formats, and profiles become stable and enter mainstream use.

### *JavaSoft Certificate Programming*

JavaSoft has standardized a package in the Java Developer's Kit (JDK1.1) that is roughly equivalent to CryptoAPI in functionality and features. Much of the foregoing discussion relating to CryptoAPI applies to the JavaSoft security packages, and we do not repeat the same architectural discussion. In this section, we concentrate on the java.security package and discuss its interfaces.

The java.security package consists of five interfaces: Certificate, Key, Principal, PrivateKey, and PublicKey. A dozen supporting classes specify the behavior of signing functions acting in support of certificate-based security protocols and procedures. The Certificate object specified in the Java packages is independent of technical standards because it complies with X.509, Pretty Good Privacy (PGP), and other standard formats.

By default, only the DSA implementation of a security provider for signing is part of every conforming Java installation. An RSA provider, which is rather more useful, can be obtained from a number of sources, such as http://www.baltimore.ie/jcrypto.htm. When using the Win32 Virtual Machine for Java, Java programmers can access CryptoAPI through the J/Direct technology.

As a added-value feature to the baseline JavaSoft security package, Microsoft has designed and implemented a comprehensive permissions package called com.ms.security (http://www.microsoft.com/java/sdk/20/packages/security/default.htm), which may be used in tandem with CryptoAPI to control access to cryptographic and other component services according to system policy specifications. As we will see in Chapter 4, certificates are beginning to play a significant role in ensuring computer system integrity and in the loading and execution of code.

The Java model of certificates in JDK1.1 emphasizes the system integrity of signature and certificate technology over the electronic commerce potential. Java developers will inevitably prefer the Java classes, whereas Windows programmers may directly use CryptoAPI. Whichever method is used, the result is the same to users because both implement the same certificate standard; X.509 certificates are independent of programming models.

## Certificate Revocation Lists (CRLs)

An X.509 certificate has a validity period, which typically lasts from a few months to a few years, during which a certificate-using application may rely on the certificate. A certificate is intended to be valid during its entire scheduled validity period. After a certificate's validity period ends, it expires and becomes invalid; it may no longer be safe for an application to rely on an expired certificate. During the validity period of a certificate, the issuing certification authority maintains information about the status of the certificate and provides this information to a certificate-using application.

**Revocation status** is the most prominent information a CA maintains about the status of a certificate. Revocation status indicates that the scheduled validity period of a certificate has been prematurely terminated and that a certificate-using system should not rely on it. Reliance on a **revoked certificate** is potentially unsafe, and it may conflict with the issuing CA's policy.

A CA may revoke a certificate for a variety of reasons, such as a compromise of the subject's private key, a compromise of the issuing CA's private key, or a change in the subject's affiliation. A compromise of the subject's private key renders encipherment and digital signature mechanisms unsafe and should be reported to the issuing CA. If a CA's private key is compromised, all the certificates issued by the CA after the compromise has taken place are potentially unreliable and must be revoked. A change of the affiliation of the subject with the issuing CA, such as termination of employment, is also grounds for the subject's employer to request a revocation from the CA. Although not as common, a CA may unilaterally revoke a subscriber's certificate if the subscriber uses the certificate in a manner that violates the CA's established policies. See Chapter 4 for the recounting of a real case in which VeriSign unilaterally revoked a subscriber's certificate.

**Certificate revocation lists** (CRLs) are a mechanism that a CA uses to publish and disseminate information about revoked certificates to certificate-using applications. A CRL is a data structure, digitally signed by the issuing CA, that contains the date and time of the CRL publication, the name of the issuing CA, and the serial numbers of all the revoked certificates that have not yet expired. When relying on a certificate, a certificate-using application should obtain the most recent CRL issued by the issuing CA and ensure that the certificate serial number is not listed in the CRL.

How often should CRLs be updated? The frequency is determined by the issuing CA; it may be hourly, daily, weekly, or longer. Frequent updates of CRLs increase the likelihood for a certificate-using system to detect and reject a revoked certificate. Frequent updates, however, put more demands on the supporting infrastructure and bandwidth required for disseminating CRLs. In general, high-valued transactions, such as e-commerce transactions over a particular amount or secure e-mail messages in the Department of Defense, require short intervals between updates; low-valued transactions, such as casual secure e-mail messages, tolerate longer update intervals. A CA must issue CRLs according to its scheduled updates even if it has not revoked any certificates since the last update. A variety of methods exist to propagate CRL information to certificate-using systems. In the rest of this section, we will explore three such methods.

## Polling for CRLs

A certificate-using application can access a CA and poll for the latest CRL. Similar to certificates, CRLs can be stored in unsecure data repositories and can be communicated via unsecure communication channels because they are digitally signed by the issuing CA. Tampering with a CRL changes its message digest, causing its digital signature not to verify. With the polling method, the application needs to know the next scheduled update of the CRL to determine whether it should access the CA and download the latest CRL. The next scheduled update can be conveniently kept in the CRL data structure.

Disseminating revocation information through polling for CRLs imposes a period of unsafe operation for a certificate-using application. During this period, the application may rely on a certificate that has been recently revoked by the issuing CA, but the revocation status will not be available until the next scheduled update. The period between CRL updates can be kept short, perhaps even an hour, but some applications cannot tolerate even such short delays in revocation information.

## Pushing CRLs

A CA can push CRLs to certificate-using applications as soon as it revokes a certificate. In this broadcast approach, revocation information reaches applications without the time-granularity delay inherent in the polling method.

A number of problems hamper the use of the push technology in practice [FORD98]. First, the broadcasting infrastructure must ensure that the pushed revocation information reaches its certificate-using applications. If an intruder manages to delete the information while it is in transit, an application operates unsafely because it cannot detect such deletions. Second, pushing revocation data to a large number of destinations can overwhelm a network, especially if certificate revocation happens frequently. One way to lower the bandwidth requirements is to push only critical revocations, such as private-key compromises. Finally, in a large, unstructured community, determining which applications require pushed revocation information and the required broadcasting infrastructure is an issue.

## On-Line Status Checking

A certificate-using application can execute an on-line query with a CA to determine the revocation status of a certificate. On-line status checking has a number of advantages. It avoids the time-granularity delay of the poll method without incurring the overhead of pushing a massive amount of data to a large number of destinations. Furthermore, it does not require a central management system to determine all the appropriate certificate-using systems because client applications initiate the on-line queries.

On-line status checking, however, requires the CA to operate a trusted data repository server that is available at all times. Furthermore, because the server must digitally sign the result of each on-line query, the processing resources required to run the server could be costly.

# X.509 CRLs

The X.509 CRL format is an ITU-T and ISO/IEC standard, first published in 1988 as version 1 (v1). The X.509 v1 CRL was subsequently modified to allow for extension fields, resulting in X.509 version 2 (v2) CRL format. Figure 3-3 illustrates the X.509 v2 CRL format, which includes a set of basic, predefined fields, zero or more entry extension fields, and zero or more extension fields. We will discuss these fields in the next three sections.

## X.509 Basic CRL Fields

In this section we discuss the basic fields of an X.509 v2 CRL format. These fields are the same for X.509 v1 CRL format.

**Version** The version field should specify version 2 if any extension fields are present. If neither CRL entry extensions nor CRL extensions are present, this field is omitted.

**Signature** This field contains the algorithm identifier of the algorithm used to sign the CRL.

**Issuer name** This field contains the name of the entity that issued and signed the CRL.

**This update** This field indicates the date and time of issue of this CRL.

**Next update** This field indicates the date and time of issue of next CRL. If the CRL update schedule is known to all certificate-using systems, this field may be omitted. It is recommended, however, to include this field at all times. Note that the next CRL could be issued prior to the indicated date, but it will not be issued after the indicated date.

**User certificate** This field contains the certificate serial number of a re-voked certificate.

**Revocation date** This field indicates the effective date of a revocation.

## X.509 CRL Entry Extensions Fields

ANSI X9, ISO/IEC, and ITU have defined a set of standard entry extensions for X.509 v2 CRLs. Communities and organizations can also define their own private entry extensions and encode information specific to their needs in CRLs. X.509 v2 CRL entry extension fields have the same subfields as X.509 v3 certificates. CRL entry extension fields should be designated as noncritical.

The **reason code** identifies one of the following reasons for the certificate revocation: unspecified, key compromise, CA compromise, affiliation changed, superseded, cessation of operation, certificate hold, and remove from CRL. **Key compromise** refers to a detected or suspected compromise of a subject's private key. **CA compromise** is a detected or suspected compromise of the issuing CA. **Affiliation changed**

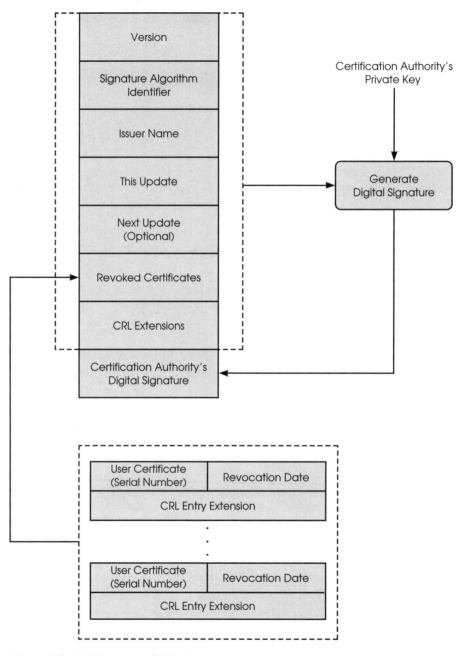

**Figure 3-3** X.509 version 2 CRL format.

means a change in the subject's name or other information about the subject, such as employment termination, has occurred. **Superseded** indicates that the certificate has been replaced, whereas **cessation of operation** means the certificate is no longer valid for its original purpose. **Certificate hold** indicates that the certificate has been temporarily suspended. The reason code **remove from CRL** implies that the certificate must be removed from a previous base CRL.

## X.509 CRL Extensions Fields

ANSI X9, ISO/IEC, and ITU have also defined a set of standard extensions for X.509 v2 CRLs with the same subfields as X.509 v3 certificates. Communities are free to define their own private extensions. Refer to [AMEN96] for a detailed discussion of these extension fields.

# Certification Authorities

In the preceding sections, we discussed digital certificates, CRLs, the X.509 certificate format, and the X.509 CRL format. We explained that a certificate contains a subject's public key and its identification information bound together by the issuing CA's digital certificate. We explored the consequences of a CA's signature on a certificate and highlighted its roles in allowing a certificate-using system to verify the authenticity of the certificate and distributing certificates through unsecure channels.

In this section, we turn our attention to certification authorities. A **certification authority** (CA) is a trusted organization that accepts certificate applications from entities, authenticates applications, issues certificates, and maintains status information about certificates.

A CA may provide a **Certification Practice Statement** (CPS) that clearly states its policies and practices with regard to issuance and maintenance of certificates.[3] Furthermore, a CPS may contain information about the liabilities of a CA toward systems relying on its certificates, and the obligations of its subscribers

---

3. Ted Barassi, one of the reviewers of this book from CertCo, LLC, believes near-to-mid-term market trends suggest that the emerging public-key infrastructure (PKI) is developing within the confines of private relationships, where individuals and entities are participating in an agreed-upon system. These private systems have rules, bylaws, governing contracts, and other mechanisms, which make meaningless the CPS as a standalone—or content-defined—document. The credit card associations' implementation of the Secure Electronic Transaction (SET) protocols is a perfect example of a privately ruled system using PKI. The PKIX implementation of a CPS is likely to be meaningless to the players in a private system, where the applicable rules of engagement, including everything they need to know about the CA and the services it will perform, have already been agreed upon. The trust and information about the CA, assumed necessary by the PKIX CPS, are unnecessary to the private system participant who takes security and informational comfort from the elaborate private rules infrastructure.

toward the CA. A CPS may take the form of a declaration by the CA of the details of its trustworthy system and the practices it employs in its operations and in support of a certificate, or it may be a statute or regulation applicable to the CA that covers similar material. It may also be part of the contract between the CA and the subscriber. A CPS may also include multiple documents, a combination of public law, private contract, and/or declaration.[4] We defer detailed coverage of CPS to Chapter 11.

## Certificate Enrollment

A user typically fills out an application form and submits it to a CA to register for a certificate. The information that the applicant needs to provide largely depends on the class of the certificate and the particular CA; it must, however, include the user's public key and some identification information. In some situations, such as an employer applying on the behalf of a new employee, an applicant may not directly fill out an application form.

Generation of a public-private key pair, secure transfer of the public key to a CA, and secure transfer of the private key to a subscriber are crucial steps during certificate registration. The subscriber can generate the key pair in a local system, securely store the private key, and send the public key along with the application to the CA. The secure storage of the private key can be accomplished by encrypting it with a password or keeping it in a tamper-proof hardware token, such as a smart card. A smart card may be able to generate the key pair itself, provide the public key to external applications, and securely keep the private key. A private key generated in a smart card may never leave the confines of the card—it is generated, stored, and destroyed with the card.

Alternatively, a central system, potentially associated with a CA, can generate the key pair. The central system must then forward the public key to the CA and securely transfer the private key to the subscriber. The subscriber must still take appropriate measures to protect the private key.

---

4. Ted Barassi, one of the reviewers of this book from CertCo, LLC, believes the theory of incorporating the CPS into the certificate seems unlikely to be legally persuasive unless the relying party is required to view and accept the CPS before relying upon the certificate. The legally binding nature of the CPS is subject to many defenses. The relying party can claim that it did not know that it should have looked at the CPS, that the CPS was too large to digest, that it tried to view the CPS but the document—Web site—was not available, or any number of other defenses that will be hard for the CA to overcome. Even in instances where the relying party views and perhaps even agrees in some fashion to the terms of the CPS, it may still be viewed as a contract of adhesion. The legal implications of the CPS are the subject of much ongoing public debate. See the American Bar Association Section of Science and Technology Information Security Committee, Guidelines, Section 1.8, Comment 1.8.1.

The particular requirements of a certificate-using system may dictate the method of key-pair generation. Generating the key pair in the subscriber's local system obviates the need to securely transfer the private key from a central system, and it is required if the private key must not leave the system in which it will be used. Signature private keys typically have this requirement. A central system may have access to more expensive equipment for key-pair generation and create higher-quality key pairs. Furthermore, the central system can back up the private key in addition to delivering it to the subscriber's system. If a private key is lost, perhaps due to a hardware failure or an accidental deletion, messages encrypted with that key can no longer be decrypted and are lost. An encryption private key, therefore, needs to be backed up.

## Subject Authentication

A certification authority must confirm the information a subject has provided in the certificate application prior to binding the subject's public key to its identity. The confirmation process is crucial. If an impostor manages to obtain a certificate that binds his public key to another person's identity, he can masquerade as that person and carry out fraudulent activities.

The measures a CA undertakes to confirm the validity of a subject's identity depend on the level of assurance the subject's certificate purports to provide. A CA may issue different classes of certificates and employ different confirmation measures for each class.

A CA may confirm the identity of a subject if the subject can present valid personal information, such as name, address, phone number, or social security number. The CA can confirm the validity of such personal information with a third-party consumer database, which contains and maintains personal information about a population of subjects. The level of assurance that such identity confirmation measures provide is limited to the degree of difficulty an impostor has in acquiring such personal information.

A CA may require a subject to physically appear in its office and present an appropriate identification card, such as a driver's license, birth certificate, or a passport. Personal presence provides a higher level of assurance about a subject's identity, but it is limited to the degree of difficulty an impostor has in forging such identification cards.

### Local Registration Authorities

If a CA is managing a large, geographically dispersed population, requiring a subject to physically appear at the CA location might be impractical. In such cases, the CA may use **local registration authorities** (LRAs), who provide direct physical contacts with subjects. We will discuss LRAs at length in Chapter 10 and present VeriSign's Onsite, a commercially available LRA service.

## Certificate Generation

After a CA receives and validates a certificate registration or receives a request from an LRA, it generates a corresponding certificate and signs the certificate with its signing private key. The CA then forwards the certificate to the subscriber or to the LRA. Optionally, the CA may back up the certificate or submit it to a certificate repository for distribution.

## Certificate Distribution

A CA may provide a certificate distribution service for a certificate-using system to access and obtain a subscriber's certificate. A person may, for example, use this service to look up another person's certificate, download the certificate into an e-mail application, and send a secure e-mail to that person. A CA can distribute certificates via a variety of methods, such as a directory server or e-mail.

The X.500, Lightweight Directory Access Protocol (LDAP), or proprietary directory servers are viable alternatives for distributing certificates via directory servers. X.500 directories provide a way to disseminate a variety of information, including public certificates, to remote systems; the complexity of implementing X.500 directory servers and client-side applications, however, has hampered their widespread use in the Internet community.

The LDAP is another standard for disseminating information on the Internet. LDAP is a trimmed-down version of X.500 and results in client-side applications that are much easier to implement. As a result, LDAP is rapidly gaining popularity.

## Certificate Revocation

We have already discussed the notion of revocation and explained that the scheduled validity period of a certificate may be prematurely terminated. A certificate revocation request typically originates from a subscriber or an LRA. It is essential that the issuing CA validates the origin and authenticity of a revocation request prior to revoking a certificate. The CA might, for example, require a subscriber to present a challenge phrase, which the CA had given to the subscriber during certificate registration or delivery. A CA should maintain status information about a certificate during its validity period, and provide revocation information to certificate-using systems.

A CA issues periodic CRLs to maintain status information about certificates until they expire. Alternatively, the CA may operate an on-line status-checking server, as was explained in the On-Line Status Checking section. Note that a CA is not required to issue CRLs if it provides other ways to disseminate revocation information.

## Data Repositories

The underlying threat assumptions of the original X.509 standard have evolved since they were first introduced by ISO. Today, there exists a formal notion of a **repository** where certificates and revocation status information such as CRLs are *officially* stored. The official designation of a database as a repository is intended to signal that the operation of the facility is reliable and trustworthy. For example, availablity will be high; the records system will be tamperproof, should legal reliance be made on any representation made using certificate-related identification; the data will be archived for 30 years.

A notion exists that a new breed of security operator will emerge into the security infrastructure charged with the responsibilities to operate the repository on behalf of CAs who may not themselves be capable of maintaining a database at the required level of service. Much as many Web sites allow a professional Web farm to serve their documents, where such providers often have high-speed networks and fault-tolerant operational capability, smaller CAs may contract with a repository provider to perform the official elements of certificate publication processes.

In the state of Utah, officials have established laws and programs to promote and encourage such businesses. If the public CA is a modernization of the service bureau for remote key management processing, an X.509 repository is the modernization of the associated data warehouse. It is possible that through statutory regulation, legally valid digitally signed transactions may require that only *registered* repositories be used by CAs issuing certificates intended to sign contracts and other legal agreements or filings. Before being accepted as a repository subscriber, terms and conditions will surely be imposed, requiring the CA to abide by policies and practices and be subject to audit.

# Public-Key Infrastructures

The widespread adaptation of public-key technology requires a **public-key infrastructure** (PKI) that defines a set of agreed-upon standards, certification authorities, structures between multiple certification authorities, methods to discover and validate certification paths, operational protocols, management protocols, interoperable tools, and supporting legislation. Operational protocols address the requirements to deliver certificates and CRLs to certificate-using systems. Management protocols address requirements for on-line or off-line interactions between different components of two PKI components (e.g., between a CA and a certificate-using system or between two CAs). Management protocols include provisions for registration, initialization, certification, revocation, and key-pair recovery (see Chapter 10 for a discussion of two such protocols).

In the preceding sections, we presented X.509 standards for certificate formats and CRLs, CAs, and some of the management functions, such as certificate generation, distribution, and revocation. In the final section of this chapter, we focus on structures between multiple certification authorities, certification path discovery, and certification path validation.

## Structures between Multiple Certification Authorities

A structure between multiple CAs provides one or more certification paths between a subscriber and a certificate-using application. A **certification path** (or **certification chain**) is a sequence of one or more connected nodes between the subscriber and a root CA. A **root certification authority** is an authority that the certificate-using application trusts and has securely imported and stored its public key. See Figure 3-4 for a list of root CAs in Netscape Navigator. A certificate path indicates how a certificate-using application develops trust in a subscriber's certificate.

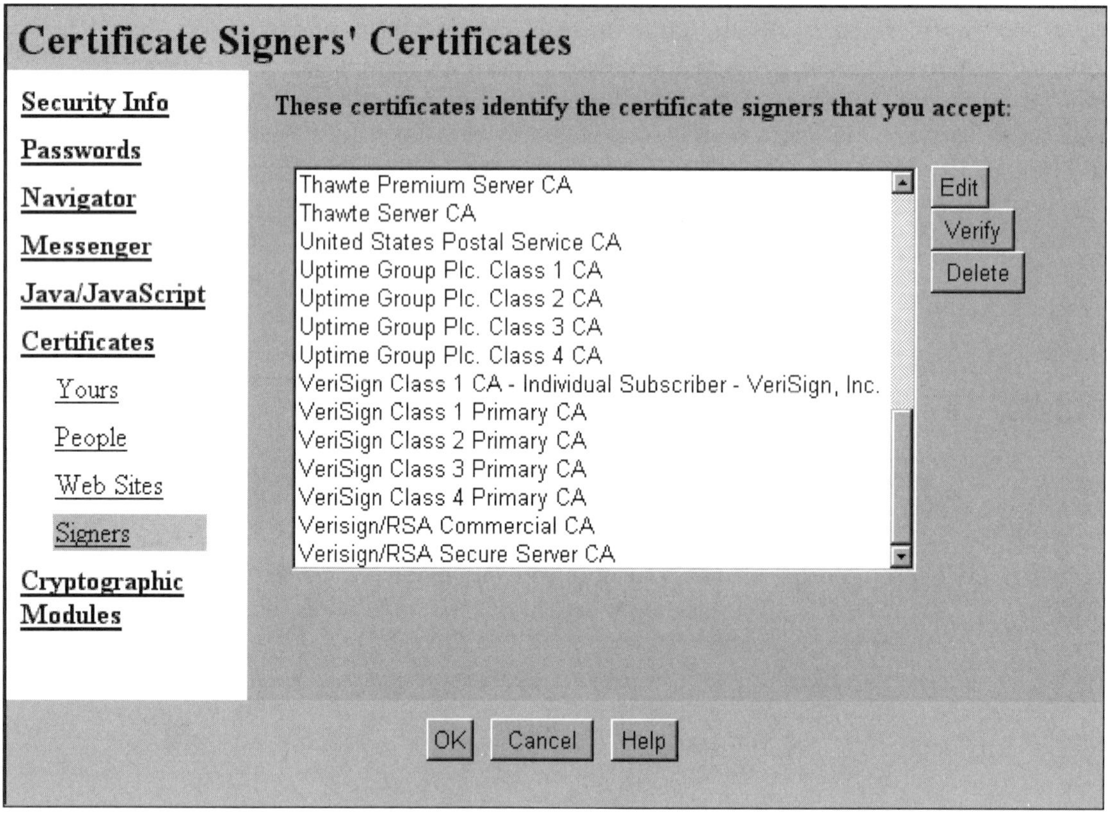

**Figure 3-4**    A sample list of root CAs in Netscape Navigator.

A large-scale deployment of public-key systems must support multiple CAs and the relationships between them. The structures of such relationships vary largely, depending on the community of users, nature of certificate-using applications, geographic scope of the deployment, and other requirements. The structure of CAs required to support a well-organized military unit, for example, may vary from the structure for managing a large community of users who want to exchange secure e-mail messages. In the rest of this section, we will discuss two such structures.

### Top-Down Hierarchical Structure

Figure 3-5 illustrates a top-down hierarchical structure between a number of CAs and a population of subscribers. In this figure, circles represent subscribers, and ellipses denote CAs. An arrow between two CAs means that the source, or superior, CA has

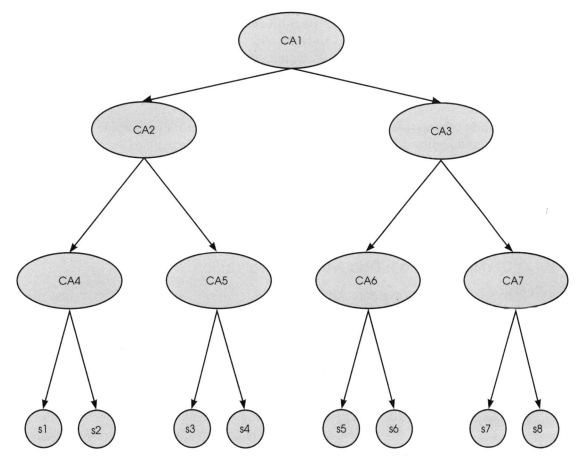

**Figure 3-5** A top-down hierarchical structure.

certified the destination, or subordinate, CA to issue certificates. An arrow between a CA and a subscriber means that the CA has certified the public key of the subscriber.

Let's investigate the certification paths between the subscriber *s1* and another arbitrary subscriber in Figure 3-5. Because *CA4* has issued *s1* a certificate, *s1* most likely trusts *CA4* and considers it a root CA. The certification path between *s1* and *s2* involves only the node *s2*. If *s1* needs to trust *s3*, it must also consider *CA2* as a root CA; the certification path between *s3* and *s1* consists of *s3* and *CA5*. Finally, the certification path between *s5* and *s1* includes *s5*, *CA6*, and *CA3*, provided that *s1* considers *CA1* as a root CA.

A top-down tree structure naturally models organizations that have a hierarchical arrangement and trust flows from top of the hierarchy toward the bottom, as in the command structure in the Department of Defense.

### *Forest of Top-Down Hierarchies*

In a top-down hierarchical structure, all subscribers are required to trust the top-level CA before a subscriber can trust another arbitrary subscriber. This requirement may be natural in well-structured communities, but it is not practical for a global deployment of public-key systems for the Internet community.

It would be unrealistic to expect the Internet population to all trust a central, all-encompassing CA. Instead, the trust in the Internet community is developing as **islands of trust,** in which each community, based on its geographic location, culture, and application-specific requirements, trusts a particular CA.

The practical way to connect these islands of trust is for each root, central CA to cross-certify other root, central CAs. As Figure 3-6 illustrates, the resulting forest of top-down hierarchies allows a certification path between any two arbitrary subscribers. This interconnection between different CAs supports the large-scale deployment of public-key applications, such as secure e-mail.

## Certification Path Discovery and Validation

A certificate-using system needs to obtain a certification path between a subscriber and a root CA before it can evaluate the level of trust in the subscriber's certificate. **Certificate path discovery** is the general problem of determining a certification path between two arbitrary subscribers in an arbitrary structure of interconnections between different CAs.

The certificate path discovery problem has a varying degree of difficulty. In one extreme, both the subscriber and the certificate-using system trust the same CA, in which case the certification path involves only one node, the subscriber's certificate. Depending on the application, a subscriber may be in a better position to determine the certification path and can send all the required certificates along with its own

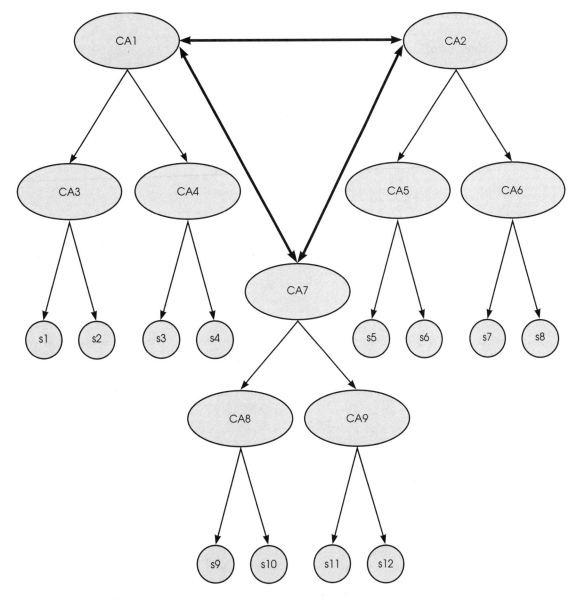

**Figure 3-6**    Another top-down hierarchical structure.

certificate. In the other extreme, the certificate-using system must solve a complex graph theory problem to determine a suitable certification path.

**Certification path validation** is the problem of verifying the binding between the subscriber name and subscriber public key based on a certification path. In the following, we present an algorithm for validating a certification path. Note that the algorithm is intended to demonstrate the main ideas and omits many details.

- Verify that each certificate in the path is signed by the subscriber's public key of the next certificate in the path. If the certificate is the last one in the path, it must be verified by the public key of a root CA.

- None of the certificates in the path is expired.

- None of the certificates in the path is revoked.

- The critical exertions of each certificate are recognized and processed.

## Summary

A public-key certificate binds an entity's public key to its identity. The public-key certificate provides assurance that the public key belongs to the identified entity and that the entity possesses the private key corresponding to the public key. A CA, after authenticating the identity of a subject, digitally signs the certificate and incorporates its signature as a part of the certificate. Digital certificates can be transmitted in unsecure channels and stored in unsecure mediums. Any changes made to a certificate while it is in transit or in storage can be detected because the issuing CA's signature no longer verifies. The X.509 version 3 (v3) is an ITU-T and ISO/IEC certificate format standard published in June 1996.

A certificate is intended to be valid during its entire scheduled validity period; after a certificate's validity period ends, the certificate expires and becomes invalid. A CA may, however, revoke a certificate and prematurely terminate its scheduled validity period. Reliance on a revoked certificate is potentially unsafe, and it may conflict with the issuing CA's policy. CAs use certificate revocation lists (CRLs) to publish and disseminate information about revoked certificates to certificate-using applications. The X.509 CRL format is an ITU-T and ISO/IEC standard, first published in 1988 as version 1 (v1) and subsequently modified to provide provisions for extension fields, resulting in X.509 version 2 (v2) CRL format.

A CA is a trusted organization that accepts certificate applications from entities, authenticates the authenticity of applications, issues certificates, and maintains status information about certificates. A public-key infrastructure (PKI) defines a set of agreed-upon standards, certification authorities, structures between multiple certification authorities, methods to discover and validate certification paths, operational protocols, management protocols, interoperable tools, and supporting legislation.

## References

[AMEN95]   ISO/IEC JTC1/SC 21, Amendment 1 to ISO/IEC 9594-8:1995, *Information Technology—Open Systems Interconnection—The Directory: Authentication Framework, AMENDMENT 1: Certificate Extensions.*

[AMEN96]   ISO/IEC JTC1/SC 21, *Draft Amendments DAM 4 to ISO/IEC 9594-2, DAM 2 to ISO/IEC 9594-6, DAM 1 to ISO/IEC 9594-7, and DAM 1 to ISO/IEC 9594-8 on Certificate Extensions*, 1 December, 1996.

[FORD97]   Ford, W., and M. Baum. *Secure Electronic Commerce: Building the Infrastructure for Digital Signatures and Encryption,* Prentice-Hall, Englewood Cliffs, NJ, 1997.

# Part II

# Applied Internet Security

You now have your digital certificate, but what can you do with it? Are there any applications out on the Internet that use certificates? Yes. There are some very useful applications, and, as the clock ticks, more and more applications are leveraging public-key technology and certificates to address the security issues of open networks.

If you use a browser to surf the Web, you should read Chapter 4 to understand the dangers out there when you visit potentially malicious Web sites and learn how you can protect the valuable information stored in your computer. Make sure you understand what virtual shrink-wrapped software, trusted vendors, and trust-based software management are all about.

If you have access to the Internet, you must be sending and receiving e-mail! Wouldn't it be nice if you could encrypt your e-mail messages to prevent your parents, employer, or anybody else from reading your e-mail? Wouldn't it be nice if the person who receives e-mail from you could be reasonably certain that it has come from you, not an impostor? The good news is that, if you are using a modern browser, you already have access to an e-mail tool that can send encrypted or digitally signed e-mail messages. Chapter 5 discusses S/MIME technology and shows you how to use Netscape's Messenger or Microsoft's Outlook Express to send and receive secure e-mail.

If you have a Web server, you can also use digital certificates to control access to the resources on your server. Read Chapter 6 to find out how to secure your Web server communications and how firewalls and proxy servers use digital certificates to help filter out potentially hostile downloaded code before it ever reaches your computer. You may also want to read Part V, which delves into the details of Web server and client authentication administration.

Chapter 7 is a bonus chapter. What is the nature of the underlying technology that provides all these benefits? How are industry groups ensuring that the open standards used by all vendors are geared for market needs? Chapter 7 presents a technical viewpoint of the security technologies that are at the heart of the evolving security infrastructure. It will help you understand some of the pitfalls to look out for when buying or customizing security technology.

# $\underline{4}$

# Browser Security and Trust-Based Software Management

You have just installed your favorite browser and are ready to surf the Web. Do you know what dangers are lurking on the Internet? Do you know the threats that rogue Web sites with malicious content pose to you? Do you know how to protect yourself?

This chapter is all about teaching you what you need to know to protect yourself. As a bonus, you will learn how digital certificates help implement virtual shrink-wrapped software on the Web, and what trust-based software management is all about.

## Downloaded Web Content

By now most people understand that Web surfing involves a bidirectional information exchange. When you visit a Web site, content is downloaded from the site into your browser, and you may leave behind personal information at the site, such as your name, address, or credit card number.

The Web sites that provide content are intranets, extranets, and the Internet. The Internet includes commercial sites such as on-line catalogs, shareware, and freeware sites such as http://download.com, nonprofit sites, or individual user sites. The content served by these sites includes active content and documents implying commitments. **Active content** is executable code, such as Java, JavaScript, ActiveX, VBScript, plug-ins, and standalone applications, that downloads into a browser and runs on your computer. **Documents implying commitments** are materials that involve a certain level of accountability on the part of their publishers, such as price lists, press releases, stock market quotes, or political statements.

The World Wide Web has changed the notion of buying shrink-wrapped software from a trusted neighborhood store. People download potentially unsafe content from sites across the world. Rogue sites on the Internet serve content as well as reputable sites; by the time reliable content from a reputable site reaches you it may already be contaminated by a virus. There is no tractability or accountability in the conventional model of downloading content from the Internet.

Web surfing is not like watching television. After you leave a site, downloaded content may continue to run on your computer, potentially carrying out improper activities. The personal information you leave behind in a site may jeopardize your privacy or be accessed by a dishonest employee to charge your credit card. The World Wide Web has indeed shifted the security problem from protecting a server from hostile clients to protecting a client from malicious servers.

## Threats of Downloaded Content

In this section, we discuss the threats of Web content in more detail for each of the two categories of downloaded content.

### Threats of Active Content

The World Wide Web started out with static content—you could only view a page in a browser or fill out a form and submit it to a server. There was no sophisticated animation, fancy graphics, client-side logic, or Java duke juggling balls. There was also no use of a client's computing resources except for downloading and displaying pages.

The static nature of Web content changed when Netscape endorsed Sun Microsystems' Java language and announced its intention to support Java in its browser. Java is a full-blown programming language that comes with a standard set of class libraries, including a windowing toolkit. A Web page could then embed Java applets, which would download into a Java-enabled browser and execute on a client computer, using its hardware and software resources. Java applets and Java-enabled browsers transformed the boring, static content of the Web into dynamic, interactive content. Soon afterwards, vendors supported ActiveX, JavaScript, and VBScript in addition to Java in their browsers.

The presence of active content in the Web poses a number of security threats. Once downloaded, active content can potentially have the same access privileges to your computer as software installed from a floppy disk or a CD-ROM. Hostile active content can find and send out sensitive information stored in the computer, damage files, disable the computer, or annoy you. Table 4-1 lists security threats of active content to your computer [BANK95].

**File system**   In this type of threat, active content reads files containing confidential information, deletes files, or modifies them, perhaps with the intention of using modified system files to launch future system break-ins. Active content can reformat an entire file system or make it unavailable for use.

**Table 4-1** Threats of Active Content to a Client

| Client Resource | Confidentiality | Integrity | Availability |
|---|---|---|---|
| File system | Yes | Yes | Yes |
| Network | Yes | — | Yes |
| User environment | Yes | Yes | — |
| Process control | — | — | Yes |
| System calls | Yes | Yes | Yes |
| Output devices | — | — | Yes |
| Input devices | Yes | — | Yes |
| Random memory | Yes | Yes | Yes |

**Network** Active content on one machine within an intranet can break into other machines on the same network by establishing network connections. Active content uses a network connection to an outside server to transfer out confidential information. Excessive use of network ports may preclude other legitimate programs from accessing network resources.

**User environment** A browser holds sensitive information, such as the history of sites that you have visited. Active content can access and send out this information or modify the environment settings.

**Process control** Active content can create too many processes, making computer resources unavailable for other legitimate programs.

**System calls** Active content can use operating system calls to carry out a variety of improper actions.

**Output devices** Active content can pop up too many windows on the computer screen to annoy you or exhaust system resources. You may have no choice but to kill the browser to get rid of all the windows.

**Input devices** You may not be able to use the mouse or the keyboard to interact with a program because active content has disabled them.

**Random memory** Active contents can allocate too much memory, thus limiting the amount of available memory for other legitimate programs.

## Threats of Content Implying Commitments

Web content need not be active to be a threat. Suppose you are a small investor and buy a large number of shares of a company based on news that you received from a news agency over the Internet. The news later turns out to be inaccurate, and you lose a large sum of money. Can you take legal recourse against the news agency? Given the current model of information distribution on the Internet, the news agency can deny sending such news or argue that the news was modified while in transit, and you may find it difficult to prove otherwise.

Do you consider it a threat if your 10-year-old daughter accesses pornographic material on the Internet or receives unsolicited indecent pictures from a Web site? How could you ensure that the sites she visits meet certain standards of decency? Launched in October 1996 by the World Wide Web Consortium (W3C), the **Digital Signature Initiative** (DSig) http://www.w3.org/DSig uses digital signatures, certificates, and metadata technologies to provide a comprehensive solution to the basic problem of helping users decide what to trust on the Web. The ultimate goal of the DSig project is to provide a way to implement the following statement: *signer believes statement about information resource.*

## Sandboxing

One way to manage the threats posed by active content is to completely isolate all the sensitive, potentially unsafe functions of a programming language. A browser can then define a security policy that defines authorized and unauthorized access to all such sensitive functions. Active content written in such a programming language must gain permission from the module enforcing the security policy before it can run a sensitive function to completion and access a resource. The security policy essentially creates a **sandbox,** which controls access to sensitive resources.

The Java programming language is quite notable for its sandbox approach toward warding off the threats of applets downloaded into browsers from the Internet. Java defines a SecurityManager class, which identifies a number of access-control methods called by various methods in the Java system libraries before they perform any potentially unsafe operations. Table 4-2 lists the majority of SecurityManager methods. It is constructive to point out that Java effectively sandboxes most of the threats we outlined in the preceding section.

The SecurityManager methods listed in Table 4-2 all have the naming convention CheckXXX( ), where XXX identifies a resource. If a calling function is not permitted to access a resource, the corresponding CheckXXX( ) method throws a security exception to prevent the unauthorized access. All the Java system library methods must call the appropriate CheckXXX( ) methods before they access a system resource. The canRead ( ) method of the File class, for example, invokes the checkRead( ), as shown here:

**Table 4-2** Java SecurityManager Methods

| Method | Description |
| --- | --- |
| checkAccept( ) | Throws an exception if the calling thread is not permitted to accept a socket connection from the specified host and port number. |
| checkConnect( ) | Throws an exception if the calling thread is not allowed to open a socket connection to the specified host and port number. |
| checkDelete( ) | Throws an exception if the calling thread is not allowed to delete the specified file. |
| checkExec( ) | Throws an exception if the calling thread is not allowed to create a subprocess. |
| checkExit( ) | Throws an exception if the calling thread is not allowed to cause the Java Virtual Machine to halt with the specified status code. |
| checkLink( ) | Throws an exception if the calling thread is not allowed to dynamic link the library code specified by the string argument file. |
| checkListen( ) | Throws an exception if the calling thread is not allowed to wait for a connection request on the specified local port number. |
| checkMulticast( ) | Tests if current execution context is allowed to use (join/leave/send/receive) IP multicast. |
| checkPrintJobAccess( ) | Tests if a client can initiate a print job request. |
| checkPropertiesAccess( ) | Throws an exception if the calling thread is not allowed to access or modify the system properties. |
| checkRead( ) | Throws an exception if the calling thread is not allowed to read the file specified by the string argument. |
| checkSystemClipboardAccess( ) | Tests if a client can get access to the system clipboard. |
| checkTopLevelWindow( ) | Returns false if the calling thread is not trusted to bring up the top-level window indicated by the window argument. |
| checkWrite( ) | Throws an exception if the calling thread is not allowed to write to the file specified by the string argument. |

```
/**
    * Tests if the application can read from the specified file.
    *
    * @return     true if the file specified by this object exists
    *             and the application can read the file;
    *             false otherwise.
    * @exception  SecurityException if a security manager exists, its
    *             checkRead method is called with the pathname
    *             of this File to see if the application is
    *             allowed read access to the file.
    * @see        java.lang.SecurityManager#checkRead(java.lang.String)
    * @since      JDK1.0
    */
public boolean canRead() {
SecurityManager security = System.getSecurityManager();
if (security != null) {
   security.checkRead(path);
}

   return canRead0();
}
```

A browser can subclass SecurityManager and implement each of the CheckXXX
( ) methods according to its security policy. How does the browser determine the
trustworthiness of a piece of Java code and grant or deny it access to a resource?

The browser *may* measure the trustworthiness of Java code based on its origin.
Java applets or applications loaded from the local file system are considered trustworthy and have full access to all the system resources. Java applets loaded over a network are untrustworthy; their access to system resources is severely limited, and they
can work only within the Java sandbox. For such applets, all the CheckXXX( ) methods of the SecurityManager class throw a security exception. Netscape Navigator 3.x
uses this approach to implement its security policy for Java active content.

## Trusted Vendors and Shrink-Wrapped Content

The original model of downloading content from the Web has changed the notion of
buying shrink-wrapped software from a neighborhood store. The notion of the

neighborhood store has given way to hundreds of thousands of Web sites that either sell software over the Internet or have active content in their Web pages. There is no guarantee about the origin of downloaded software and no way to ensure that the software has not been tampered with while in transit over the Internet.

The sandbox model does safeguard sensitive computer resources from the threats of malicious Java applets, but it does so at the expense of severely constraining their capabilities. An applet confined to a sandbox cannot read from local files or write to a file; it cannot establish any network connections except to the originating computer that served the applet. A sandboxed applet is not capable of doing many interesting things that we usually associate with executable code. Can you imagine a word processing applet that could function within a sandbox?

In this section, we discuss code signing technology based on digital signatures that enables software vendors to provide **virtual shrink-wraps** for software programs they release via the Web. This technology provides a way to ascertain the publisher of a software and verify that the software has not been tampered with while being downloaded over a network. Because you can verify the origin and authenticity of active content, you can make an informed decision whether to allow the downloaded code to run on your computer based on the level of trust you have in the software publisher. In particular, you can trust downloaded Java applets and allow them to freely access sensitive computer resources. After familiarizing you with the underpinnings of code signing, we will introduce Authenticode, a specific model for implementing code signing.

## Code Signing

**Code signing** uses digital signatures to provide a reliable software distribution model over open, unsecure networks and enable trust-based management of downloaded software. To better understand code signing, we first explain how a software publisher signs its code and how a browser handles signed code. Later, we will analyze all the salient aspects of code signing.

A **software publisher** first obtains a digital certificate that is valid for signing. Recall from Chapter 3 that a certificate contains a subject name and a public key bound together by a CA's signature, and that the CA can limit the use of the public key for encryption, signing, nonrepudiation, and so on. The publisher may obtain the certificate from an independent CA, which might issue special types of certificates for code signing. Later in this section, we will discuss the ramifications of the type of the certificate used for signing. The publisher signs its code by taking the message digest (hash) of the code and using its private key to encrypt the digest, thus generating a digital signature over the code. The private key used in signing corresponds to the public key that is certified in the software publisher's digital certificate. The publisher augments the code with the digital signature and its certificate in a data structure and releases the structure to its Web site.

When a browser downloads signed code, it verifies the digital signature to ensure that the downloaded code has not been tampered with while in transit. The browser verifies the signature by extracting the public key from the publisher's certificate, decrypting the signature, and comparing the result with the actual message digest, which the browser calculates by hashing the downloaded code. If the code has been tampered with either at the publisher's site or during the download, the decrypted digital signature does not match the actual message digest. The browser can then take any appropriate action. For example, it can refuse to execute the code and warn you about a potential attack. See Chapter 2 for more information on generating and verifying digital signatures.

If the two values match, the browser proceeds to discover and verify a trust path between the submitted publisher's certificate and a preinstalled, root CA. (Refer to Chapter 3 for details on certification path discovery and validation.) The browser can take a suitable action if it cannot verify the publisher's certificate. It can, for example, warn you that the CA who issued the certificate is unknown and ask if you want to trust the certificate.

The browser may take a wide range of actions if it verifies the downloaded signed code. It may automatically execute the code or display the publisher's certificate and get your permission to run the code. We will discuss how a browser exploits signed code in conjunction with its security policy to implement the security requirements of active Web content.

### *Accountability*

Code signing binds a piece of software to the identity of the vendor who published it. A malicious (signed) program downloaded in a browser can be traced back to its publisher, who *may* be held accountable and be subject to litigation. Note that it is very difficult to hold a vendor accountable for unsigned code because the vendor can claim it did not publish the code or argue that the code was tampered with during the download.

The degree to which a consumer of malicious signed code can litigate against a vendor depends on the supporting legal structure, the type of certificate the vendor used to sign the code, and a number of other factors. On June 17, 1997, Fred McLain released an ActiveX control called Exploder Control to http://www.halcyon.com/mclain/ActiveX/welcome.html. When downloaded to a computer that has a power conservation BIOS, Exploder Control shuts down Windows 95 and turns the computer off. Later, McLain obtained an Individual Software Publisher Digital ID from VeriSign, signed his control, and posted it to his public Web site. McLain was soon to lose his certificate. Because he violated his contractual agreements associated with his software publisher certificate when he used it to sign malicious code, VeriSign unilaterally revoked his certificate. McLain's Exploder Control, however, incited a flurry of controversy about the effectiveness of code signing. See Microsoft's views on this controversy at http://www.microsoft.com/security/seccon.htm.

## Authenticity

Code signing provides assurance of authenticity about software downloaded over a network because you can determine the origin of the software and ascertain its integrity. Furthermore, a publisher cannot later deny that it published signed software because its signature appears on the software. (Refer to Chapters 1 and 2 for details on nonrepudiation.)

In essence, code-signed software published on the Internet is analogous to shrink-wrapped software sold in stores. You can download signed code, view the publisher's certificate, and then assume the same level of trust in the quality of the code as you would assume if you had bought shrink-wrapped software from the same publisher in a neighborhood store.

## Binding the Software Publisher to a Policy

You may litigate against a software publisher who signs malicious code. The degree to which you can pursue legal recourse or criminal charges can be strengthened if the publisher uses a special **software publisher certificate** that binds the publisher to a policy. The publisher agrees to abide by the policy as a part of applying for and receiving a publisher certificate from a CA.

The policy may obligate the publisher to refrain from distributing malicious code, check software for viruses before signing, or follow practices to maintain prevailing industry standards. A publisher who knowingly distributes harmful signed code using a software publisher certificate violates its contractual agreement with the issuing CA in addition to breaking other laws relating to releasing viruses in the Internet. The policy therefore acts as a strong deterrent to publishing harmful code.

It is conceivable that there may be different types of software publisher certificates, each providing a different level of assurance about the quality of signed code. A publisher must practice the highest standards of software engineering to qualify for a very high-level certificate, whereas any publisher who pledges not to distribute harmful code might qualify for a lower level certificate. Users of signed code or corporate administrators could then define in their security policies the minimum permitted level of certification for signed code and configure their browsers not to download any signed code that violates their policies.

## Certification Authority Infrastructure

Software publisher certificates might provide various levels of software quality assurances. There also might be a number of CAs who process certificate applications, validate information submitted by applicants, and issue certificates.

A certification authority infrastructure is required to support the requirements of publishing software on the Internet [MICR96c]. An umbrella organization, such as W3C or an industry-specific policy or standards body, would define policies for software publishers and set forth practice requirements for participating CAs. CAs would then certify software publishers or work with local registration authorities (LRAs) to receive approved certificate requests (refer to Chapter 10 to learn more about LRAs). The endorsement of the software industry of such an infrastructure will be critical to its success.

## Microsoft Authenticode 1.0

Earlier, we attempted to explain the fundamental principles of code signing without discussing a specific model for code signing. We discussed how code signing is analogous to buying shrink-wrapped software from a neighborhood store and provides assurance of accountability and authenticity. We also elaborated on the significance of binding a software publisher to a policy and presented a model for a certification authority infrastructure. In this section, we cement the code signing principles by exploring a concrete model for code signing.

Introduced in August 1996, Microsoft Authenticode 1.0 [MICR96a, MICR96b] establishes mechanisms and a supporting infrastructure based on public-key cryptography, X.509 certificates, and the PKCS #7 standard to provide a means for end users and corporations to develop some level of trust in code downloaded from the Internet. Microsoft has been promoting its Authenticode technology as an open industry standard. To accomplish this goal, Microsoft has submitted the Authenticode proposal to W3C, embraced industry standards (X.509 certificates, PKCS #7 format), and sought the participation of other software industry members and standards bodies. Furthermore, Microsoft has published its specifications to promote cross-platform developments.

Authenticode 1.0 can sign standalone executables (.exe files), cabinet files (.cab files), ActiveX controls (.ocx files), and Java classes (.class files). To enhance the security of signed code, it uses 1024-bit RSA keys to generate digital signatures. Note that the use of 1024-bit keys does not impose any export restrictions because the key is used for *signing,* not encryption.

### *Commercial versus Individual Software Publishers*

Authenticode distinguishes between commercial and individual software publishers. **Commercial software publishers** are sole proprietors, partnerships, corporations, or other organizations that develop and market software as a business. **Individual software publishers** are shareware developers, freeware developers, or nonprofit organizations.

What is the value of distinguishing between commercial and individual software publishers? Code signed with a commercial software publisher certificate may be more trustworthy than code signed with an individual publisher certificate because a commercial business typically employs better standards and practices for developing software. A corporation's security policy can permit its employees to run code signed with a commercial certificate only. An individual user, on the other hand, may run both commercial-grade and individual-grade code. A corporate administrator or an end user can configure a browser to enforce an established security policy and automatically ignore code based on the certificate used to sign it.

## Qualifying for a Software Publisher Certificate

A software publisher must meet the following criteria to qualify for a software publisher certificate.

### Identification

A commercial or an individual software publisher must submit its name, address, and other information that provide proof of identity either as a commercial business or an individual. Figure 4-1 shows the required identification information.

### The Pledge

Commercial or individual software publishers must pledge that they will not distribute software that they know, or should have known, contains viruses or might be harmful to a user's computer. The pledge also obligates publishers to employ prevailing industry standards practices, such as checking code for viruses before signing, to ensure that they are not distributing malicious code.

The pledge that a publisher takes to qualify for a publisher certificate serves as an additional deterrent to distributing harmful code. A publisher may break a law by releasing harmful code and may face litigation by the issuing CA for breaking the pledge and contractual agreements.

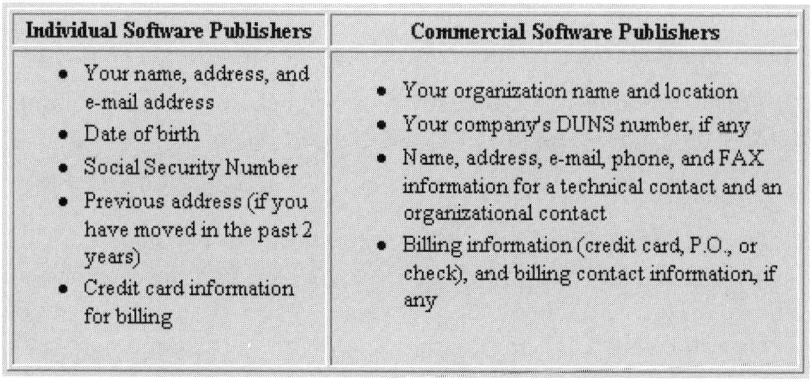

| Individual Software Publishers | Commercial Software Publishers |
|---|---|
| • Your name, address, and e-mail address<br>• Date of birth<br>• Social Security Number<br>• Previous address (if you have moved in the past 2 years)<br>• Credit card information for billing | • Your organization name and location<br>• Your company's DUNS number, if any<br>• Name, address, e-mail, phone, and FAX information for a technical contact and an organizational contact<br>• Billing information (credit card, P.O., or check), and billing contact information, if any |

**Figure 4-1**    Information required to apply for a software publisher certificate.

### *Private Key Protection*

It is highly recommended that commercial software publishers generate and store their private keys in dedicated hardware devices, such as PCMCIA cards.

## *Walking Through the Code-Signing Process with Authenticode*

In this section, we introduce the steps involved in code-signing, from applying for a certificate to signing code. We explain the steps by enrolling for a certificate from VeriSign, which was the first commercial CA to offer commercial and individual software publisher certificates.

### *Publisher Applies for a Software Publisher Certificate*

You can apply for a commercial or an individual software publisher to a CA using a Web browser. Figure 4-2 illustrates the VeriSign Web interface at http://digitalid.verisign.com/ms_pick.htm, which provides enrollment forms for a Class 2 individual software publisher Digital ID for $20.00 and a Class 3 commercial software publisher for $400.00. (These are the prices as this book went to press and are subject to change. We are providing pricing information here to give you a ballpark price.) Before you submit your application, you must agree to the VeriSign Digital ID Subscriber Agreement, which sets forth terms and policies regarding code signing.

During enrollment, a software program in the browser or a hardware device generates a public-private key pair (hardware devices are not currently supported). The browser submits the public key along with the information in the enrollment page to VeriSign, while the private key is either kept in the hardware device or written out to a file if a software program generated the key pair. The browser prompts you for a password to encrypt the private key before saving it in order to minimize the risk of unauthorized access to the private key. It is highly recommended that you save the private key on removable media, such as a floppy disk, to further minimize the risk of unauthorized access.

### *CA Confirms the Publisher's Identity and Approves the Certificate*

VeriSign confirms the identity of an individual applicant by cross-checking the submitted identity information against a consumer database, such as Equifax.

### *Publisher Picks Up the Certificate*

VeriSign informs you via e-mail that it has approved your certificate. The e-mail includes a personal identification number (PIN), which you have to use to pick up your certificate. Figure 4-3 shows the Web page used to pick up the certificate.

After you enter your PIN and submit the form, VeriSign generates an X.509 v3 software publishing certificate, displays its contents in a Web page, and allows you to install it on your computer. Figure 4-4 shows this Web page. Note that the

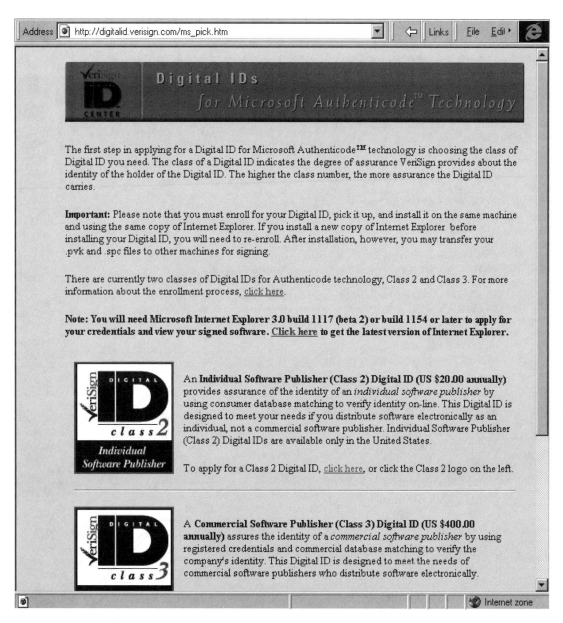

The first step in applying for a Digital ID for Microsoft Authenticode™ technology is choosing the class of Digital ID you need. The class of a Digital ID indicates the degree of assurance VeriSign provides about the identity of the holder of the Digital ID. The higher the class number, the more assurance the Digital ID carries.

**Important:** Please note that you must enroll for your Digital ID, pick it up, and install it on the same machine and using the same copy of Internet Explorer. If you install a new copy of Internet Explorer before installing your Digital ID, you will need to re-enroll. After installation, however, you may transfer your .pvk and .spc files to other machines for signing.

There are currently two classes of Digital IDs for Authenticode technology, Class 2 and Class 3. For more information about the enrollment process, click here.

**Note: You will need Microsoft Internet Explorer 3.0 build 1117 (beta 2) or build 1154 or later to apply for your credentials and view your signed software. Click here to get the latest version of Internet Explorer.**

An **Individual Software Publisher (Class 2) Digital ID (US $20.00 annually)** provides assurance of the identity of an *individual software publisher* by using consumer database matching to verify identity on-line. This Digital ID is designed to meet your needs if you distribute software electronically as an individual, not a commercial software publisher. Individual Software Publisher (Class 2) Digital IDs are available only in the United States.

To apply for a Class 2 Digital ID, click here, or click the Class 2 logo on the left.

A **Commercial Software Publisher (Class 3) Digital ID (US $400.00 annually)** assures the identity of a *commercial software publisher* by using registered credentials and commercial database matching to verify the company's identity. This Digital ID is designed to meet the needs of commercial software publishers who distribute software electronically.

**Figure 4-2**    VeriSign Web interface to apply for a software publisher certificate.

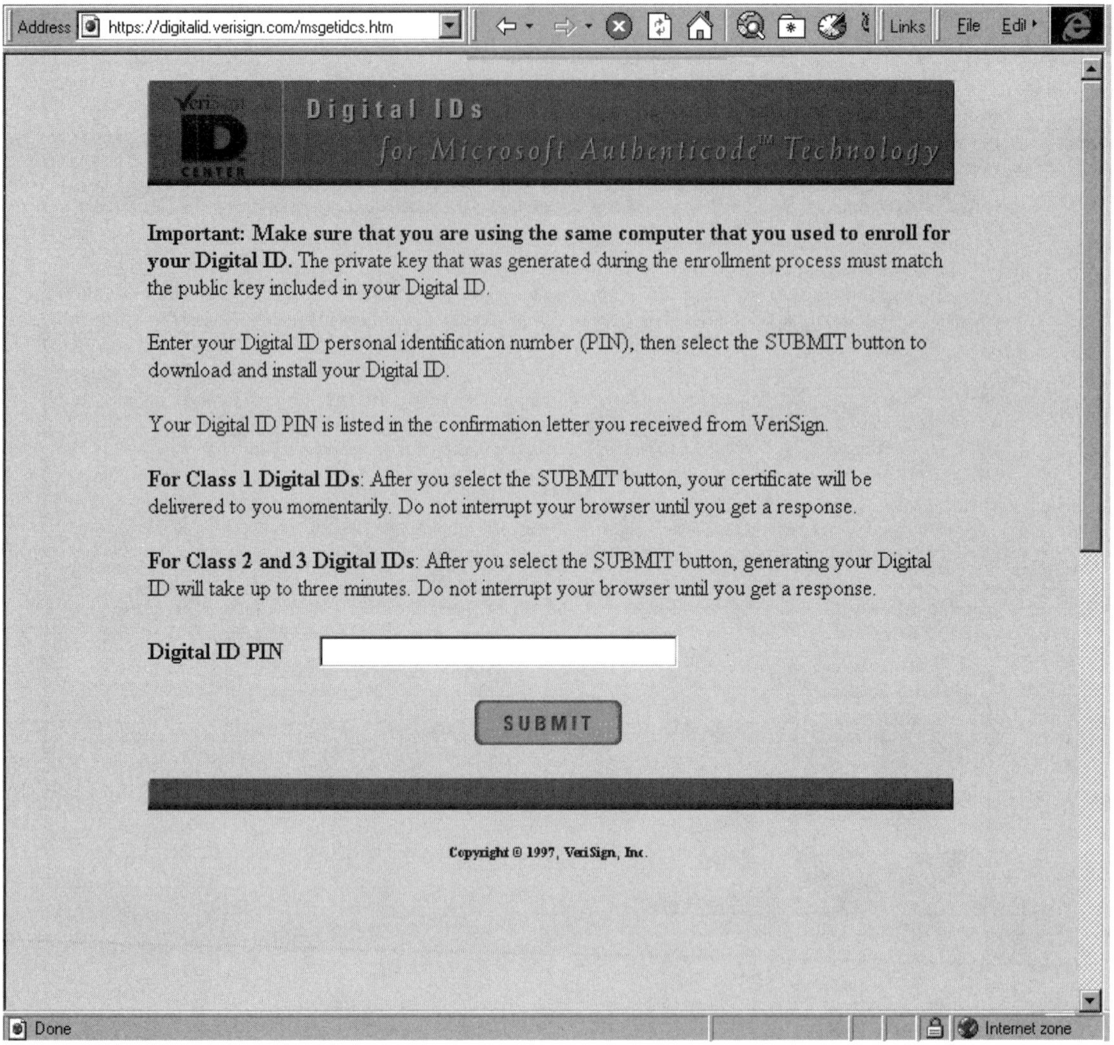

**Figure 4-3** VeriSign Web interface to pick up a software publisher certificate.

unstructured field, which contains the home address, has been intentionally erased for confidentiality reasons. After you install the certificate, you must verify that it contains correct information and ensure that the public-private key pair form a valid key pair.

### *Publisher Distributes Signed Code*

You are now ready to sign your code. Microsoft provides code-signing tools in the ActiveX SDK, which is freely available at http://www.microsoft.com/workshop/

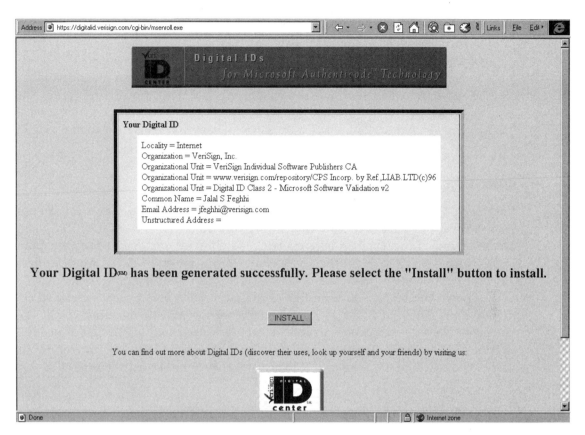

**Figure 4-4**    VeriSign Web interface to view and install a software publisher certificate.

prog/sdk. You can use the utilities in the toolkit to sign your code, include information about yourself or your code, or verify signed code. Code signing should take about five minutes. Consult the code-signing documentation in the ActiveX SDK for information on using these utilities.

Code must be final before you sign it—any changes or patches require redoing the entire code-signing process because they invalidate the already calculated digital signature. You may decide to make code-signing the last step of your release management process (e.g., building, testing, virus checking, and code signing).

## Lifting the Sandbox Barrier

In the Sandboxing section, we posed the question of how the browser would determine the trustworthiness of a piece of Java code and grant or deny it access to a resource. We then pointed out that Netscape Navigator 3.x permits Java code loaded from a local file system to have unrestricted access to sensitive resources while confining downloaded Java code to the sandbox.

Microsoft Internet Explorer (IE) 3.x provides a slight improvement. IE 3.x recognizes code signed with Authenticode, and its security policy can lift the sandbox barrier for downloaded signed Java applets. In other words, IE 3.x can grant the same level of trust to downloaded signed applets as Java code loaded from a local file system. We will explain how IE 3.x controls trust in downloaded signed code in the following section.

## Internet Explorer 3.x and Trusted Vendors

Internet Explorer 3.x recognizes code signed using Authenticode. It can discard unsigned code, run unsigned code with permission from the user, automatically run unsigned code, run signed code from a trusted publisher, or run code from any publisher with a software publisher certificate from a trusted CA. IE was the first browser to implement the notion of a trusted software vendor in the Web.

IE pops up a dialog box to get the user's permission before running signed active content. The dialog box shows the publisher's certificate, whether or not the publisher is a commercial organization or an individual, and the CA that issued the certificate. The dialog box also contains links that provide more information about the signed code and the issuing CA. Figure 4-5 shows the security options of IE 3.x,

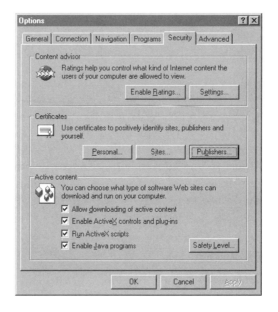

**Figure 4-5**   Security options in Internet Explorer 3.0.

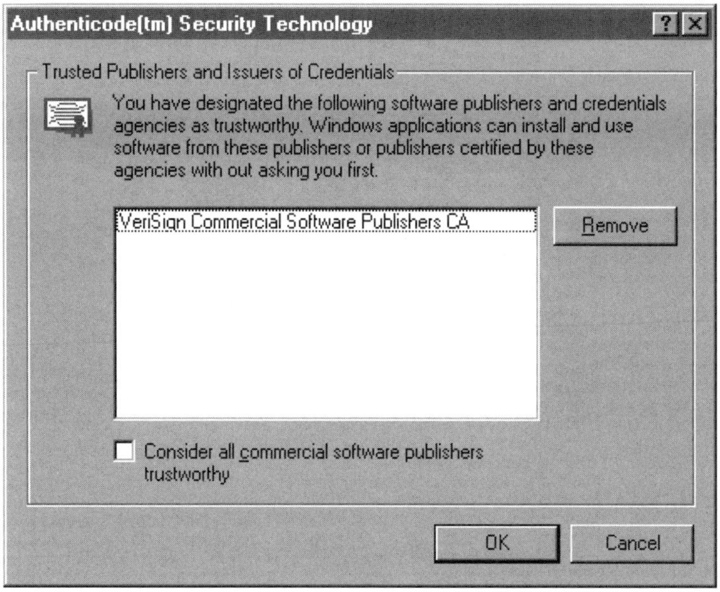

**Figure 4-6**   The default list of trusted CAs in Internet Explorer 3.0 for issuing software publisher certificates.

and Figure 4-6 displays the list of root CAs that IE recognizes as trustworthy agencies to issue software publisher certificates.

### Trusted Vendors

IE 3.x provides two important capabilities to support trusted vendors. First, you can designate the publisher as a trusted vendor, instructing IE to automatically run signed code from this publisher in the future. Second, you can instruct IE to automatically run signed code from any publisher who has received a certificate from the issuing CA.

A corporate administrator can use the Microsoft Internet Explorer Administrator's Kit (IEAK) to specify a list of trusted vendors for all end user browsers, thus enforcing corporate-wide security procedures. Furthermore, a firewall operator can implement filters to accept signed code from certain trusted vendors, ensuring that code from untrusted vendors never reaches end users' computers. See Chapter 6 for a discussion of firewalls that filter downloaded code based on their publishers.

### Safety Levels

IE 3.x also introduced the notion of safety levels, which control how the browser deals with unsigned code. IE 3.x provides three safety levels: high, medium, and low, as shown in Figure 4-7. A high safety level indicates that the browser should

**Figure 4-7** Safety levels in Internet Explorer 3.0.

discard any code that is unsigned, whereas medium means that the browser should obtain the user's permission before running the code. A low safety level instructs the browser to automatically run any unsigned code.

A corporate administrator can use IEAK to preconfigure the safety level to control the downloading of unsigned code throughout a company. For example, the administrator can set the level to high to ensure that unsigned code is never downloaded to users' computers. It is instructive to point out that the word *unsafe* in Figure 4-7 is misleading and should have been *unsigned*. Signed code is not necessarily safe code (recall the discussion on Exploder Control).

## Trust-Based Software Management

The bottom line is that some Web sites have high-quality active content, and others pose a security threat to your computer. It would be impossible to try to regulate the content of the Internet. If you want to surf the Web, you have to accept this fact. If you want to be absolutely sure that downloaded code never damages your computer, you have to unplug your computer from the Internet. But there is another way. Instead of trying to avoid risk, you can manage it.

Trust-based software management is all about managing risk. You manage risk by having absolute trust in some sites, no trust in other sites, and some trust in everything else. You let active content from absolutely trusted sites have free reign over your computer, and prevent active content from untrustworthy sites from being downloaded to your computer at all. You are willing to give active content from sites in the gray area restricted access to your computer.

This scheme does not work with Authenticode 1.0 and version 3.x browsers, which give you a binary choice of either accepting or rejecting code based on its signer. You would need a technology that supports intermediate levels of trust as well as the binary choice—you need to have decision-making control over the whole spectrum of trust. Furthermore, you need an environment that allows you to group Web sites together and assign trust levels to the group—tackling each Web site on the Internet simply does not scale. In the rest of this section, we will familiarize you with Netscape Object Signing and Microsoft Authenticode 2.0 technologies and show you how they help you manage the risks of surfing the Web. Refer to [BLAZ96] and [CHU97] for more information on trust-based software management.

## Object Signing and Netscape Communicator 4.0

Netscape introduced its object signing strategy with its fourth generation browser, Communicator 4.x. **Object signing** [NETS97a] addresses the distribution of reliable content over the Internet by identifying the publisher of signed content, ensuring the integrity of downloaded signed content, and automatically updating signed software components. Furthermore, it provides a mechanism for downloading signed Java or JavaScript programs to step out of the sandbox and request access privileges to sensitive computer resources.

Object signing exploits the same underlying techniques as Authenticode to achieve its goals. It uses public-key cryptography, X.509 certificates, digital signatures, and PKCS standards to sign an object. Communicator recognizes a downloaded signed object, identifies the publisher who signed the object, and verifies the signature to ensure that the object has not been tampered with at the Web site after it was digitally signed or during the transit.

Netscape refers to its technology as *object signing* instead of *code signing* to convey the fact that its technology can sign any kind of file and to distinguish itself from Microsoft's Authenticode. Furthermore, Netscape refers to certificates required for signing as *object signing certificates* as opposed to *software publisher certificates*. Netscape, however, supports the distinction between individual and commercial signing certificates. You can obtain Netscape object signing certificates at http://digitalid.verisign.com/nos_pick.htm.

## *Trust Management*

Communicator provides trust-based management of downloaded active content using digital certificates. Currently, the management is limited to providing fine-grained access control only for Java and JavaScript programs. You can maintain a list of Java or JavaScript software publishers in Communicator. For each publisher, you can explicitly define the kinds of access privileges that you are willing to grant indefinitely, those you will grant during a session until you quit the browser, and those you want to deny. The fine-grained access control creates a continuum of vendors, from completely trustworthy to somewhat trustworthy to untrustworthy.

Code downloaded from a completely trustworthy vendor has automatic access to all computer resources—it is not confined to the sandbox. Code downloaded from a somewhat trustworthy vendor has automatic access only to some designated resources. It can, for example, read from a file, but it cannot modify any files without obtaining your permission first. Finally, code originating from an untrustworthy vendor is automatically forbidden to perform any potentially unsafe operation—it is treated like unsigned code and is confined to the sandbox.

In addition to a continuum of trustworthy vendors, Communicator supports a temporal scope, in which the granting of an access privilege to a vendor is either effective during a session or persists indefinitely until it is reclaimed. Communicator does not extend this temporal scoping to denying of an access privilege, however.

When signed code requests a privilege, Communicator uses the certificate to sign the code to look up the list of vendors it maintains. If it finds a matching vendor, it determines whether you have previously granted or denied this vendor the requested privilege. Communicator automatically grants the privilege if you have granted the privilege; if you have previously refused the requested privilege, Communicator automatically denies the privilege. Finally, if you have not previously granted or denied the requested privilege or if it cannot find a matching vendor, Communicator brings up a dialog box and asks you for a decision.

Let's solidify the material presented so far with actual screen shots from Communicator running a signed applet that needs to step out of the sandbox. Figure 4-8 illustrates the **Security Info** dialog box, which pops up if you click on the **Security** icon inside Communicator. You can view the list of all the root CAs authorized to issue certificates by clicking the **Signers,** as shown in Figure 4-9. If Communicator encounters code signed by a object signing certificate that is not issued by a root CA or does not chain up to a root CA, it consults you to determine the trustworthiness of the unknown CA.

Figure 4-10 illustrates the current list of vendors for which you have already established a level of trust or a lack of trust. This list is currently empty, indicating that Communicator will consult with you before it grants or denies a privilege to a signed code. Let's now run the signed applet available at http://developer.netscape.com/

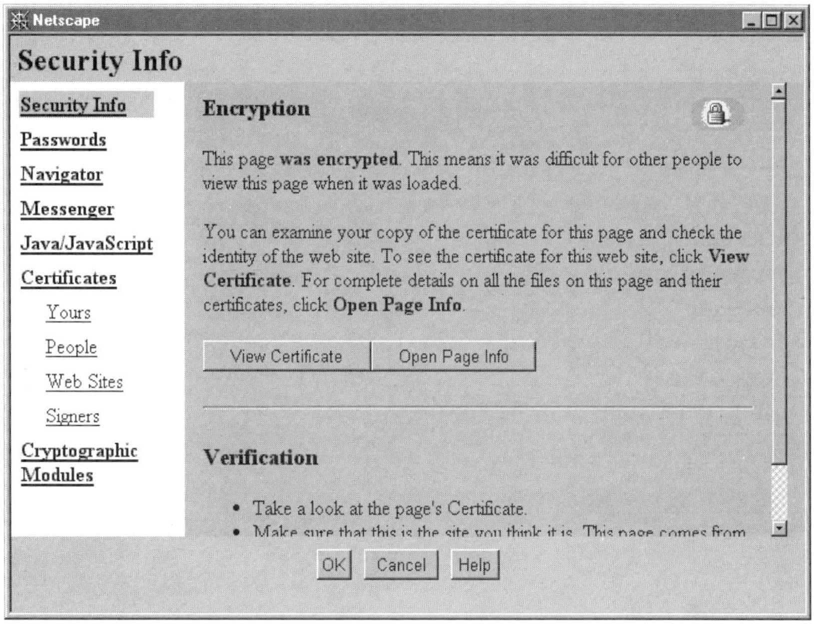

**Figure 4-8**   Communicator Security Info dialog box.

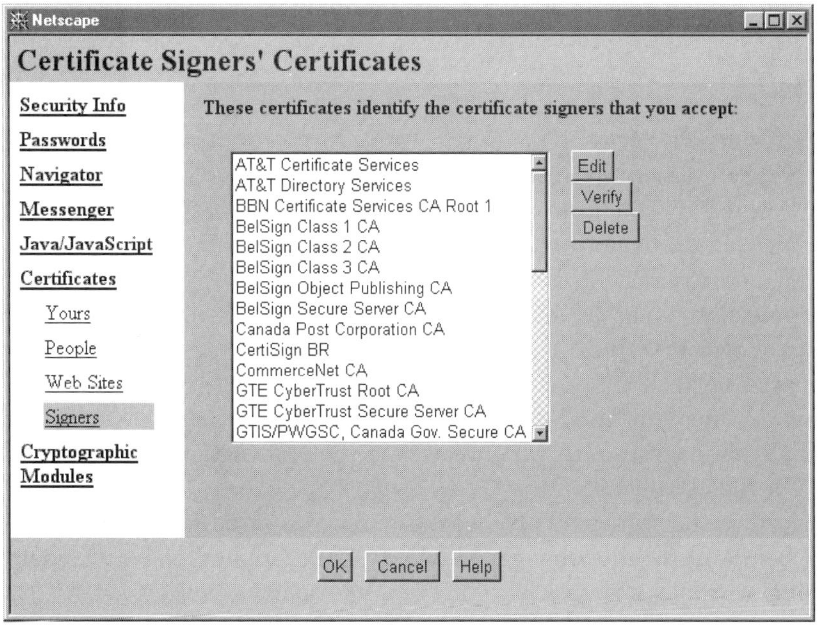

**Figure 4-9**   List of default root CAs in Communicator 4.0.

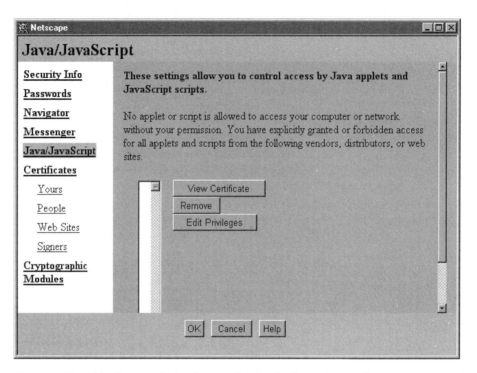

**Figure 4-10**   List of currently trusted and untrusted vendors in Communicator 4.0.

software/signedobj/filesecdemo/FileSecDemo.html, shown in Figure 4-11. This applet requests the privilege to read from a local file; if granted, it opens a dialog box, allows you to specify the file, and displays the contents of the file. Note that this simple applet would not have worked in the previous generation of Netscape browsers due to sandbox restrictions.

If you click on the the **View Local File** button, Communicator pops up the dialog box shown in Figure 4-12 to determine whether you consider the publisher of the signed applet trustworthy to read a local file. Figure 4-13 displays the object signing certificate of the publisher. The certificate clearly shows the name of publisher, the name of the CA who has issued the certificate, and the date the validity period of the certificate ends.

Based on the requested privilege, Communicator assesses the degree of risk you might be taking by allowing signed code to run. Communicator considers the risk of granting an applet access to local files high, as shown in Figure 4-12. The risk level categories are high, medium, and low. The effectiveness of these risk categories in guiding a user's decision is questionable because your view of risk might differ from

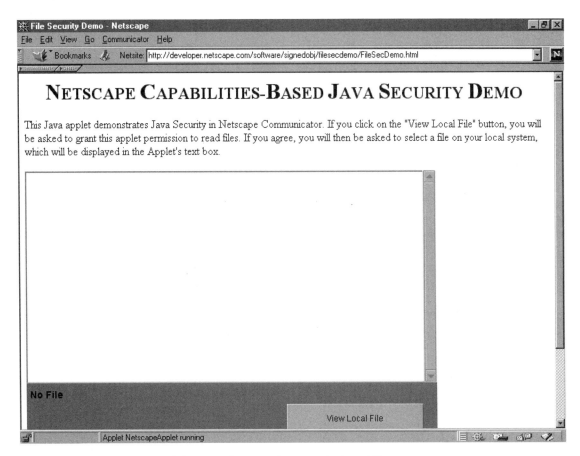

**Figure 4-11**     A signed applet requesting read access to local files.

Netscape's. You should therefore carefully read the privileges that signed code is requesting before granting them.

Let's grant the applet the requested privilege. The applet brings up a dialog box to capture the name of a local file and successfully reads its contents (if you are actually trying the applet, use a notepad file with a .txt extension). Figure 4-14 shows that Alec B Plumb, the publisher of the applet, is now added to the list of vendors, and Figure 4-15 illustrates that Alec B Plumb is permitted only to read local files. Note that the granted privilege lasts during the current session and ends when you quit the browser. If you run the applet again during the same session, Communicator automatically allows the applet to read local files and does not ask your permission again.

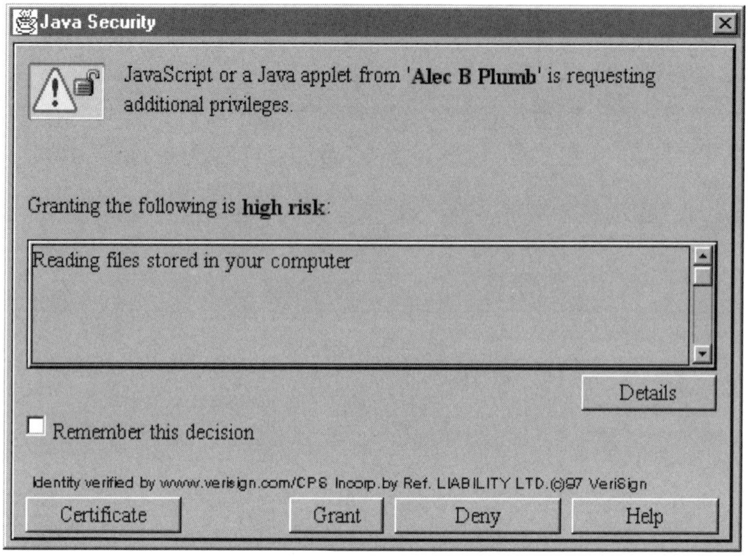

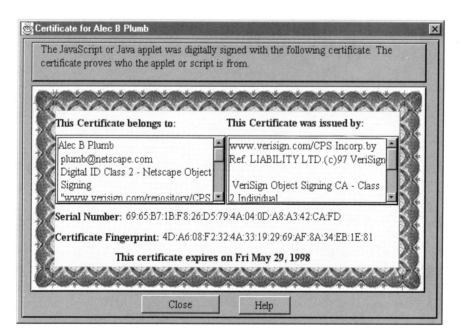

**Figure 4-12**    A security dialog box asking user for granting or denial of read-access privilege.

**Figure 4-13**    Object signing certificate used to sign the applet.

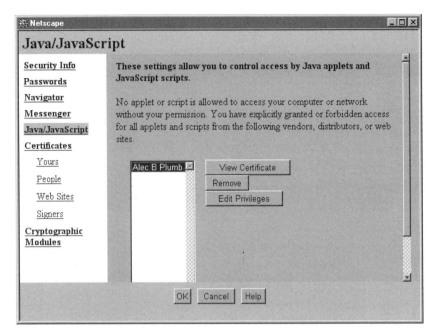

**Figure 4-14**   List of trusted and untrusted vendors after running the signed applet.

**Figure 4-15**   Alec B Plumb has session read-access privilege.

Figure 4-16 shows what happens if you check the **Remember this decision** box when you grant access to the applet. In this case, Communicator will always automatically grant the read-access privilege to the applet, even after you quit the browser. If you deny the requested privilege, the applet fails to read from a local file, as shown in Figure 4-17. Checking the **Remember this decision** box instructs Communicator to remember the decision to deny the privilege; Communicator will automatically deny the read-access privilege to any applet signed by Alec B Plumb in the future.

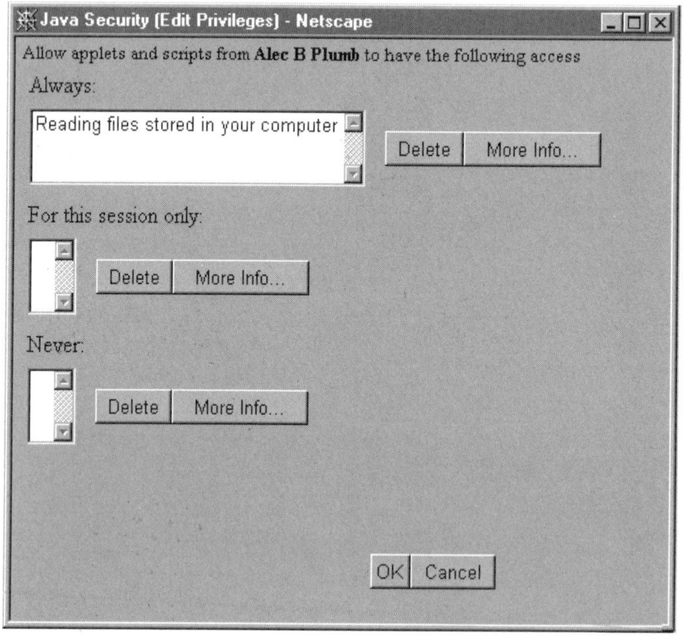

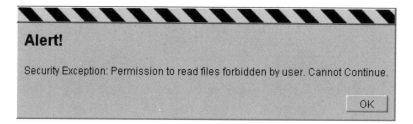

**Figure 4-16**   Alec B Plumb has indefinite read-access privilege.

**Alert!**

Security Exception: Permission to read files forbidden by user. Cannot Continue.

OK

**Figure 4-17**   Signed applet cannot read local files.

A network administrator can use Netscape Mission Control to enable or disable Java or JavaScript, set up the list of publishers, configure the level of access each publisher has, and set up the list of root CAs. The administrator can lock these settings to prevent an end user from changing the corporate security decisions.

Unfortunately, the 4.04 version of Communicator does not provide a way to add a vendor to the list without first running an applet signed by that vendor. Netscape has acknowledged this shortcoming and will support this feature in the near future.

### Java Capabilities API

Developed by Netscape, the **Java Capabilities API** is a set of Java classes that extends the Java security model to enable downloaded signed applets to request permissions and access sensitive computer resources. This API allows a programmer to request a fine-grained access privilege to a resource, enable the privilege, perform the sensitive operation, and disable the privilege. This enable-perform-disable model reduces the scope of code within which an applet can perform unsafe operations, potentially resulting in code that is safer to run and more amenable to security scrutiny reviews.

Listing 4-1 demonstrates a simple Java program that uses the Java Capabilities API to read the user.home system property. Note that reading a system property is a sensitive operation, and an applet confined to the sandbox cannot perform it. The program calls the enablePrivilege method of the PrivilegeManager class with UniversalPropertyRead as argument to request and enable permission to read system properties. If permission is granted, it reads the user.home property; otherwise, it catches the ForbiddenTargetException exception and prints an error message.

**Listing 4-1**  A Simple Java Program that Uses Java Capabilities API

```
// SimplePrivSample.java
package netscape.sample.security;
import netscape.security.PrivilegeManager;
import java.io.*;
public class SimplePrivSample
  implements RunnableSample
{
public void run(PrintStream ps) {
    ps.println("Trying to acquire permission to read system
          properties...");
```

```
    try {
       PrivilegeManager.enablePrivilege("UniversalPropertyRead");
       ps.println("\tSuccess!");
    } catch (netscape.security.ForbiddenTargetException e) {
       ps.println("\tFailed! Permission to read system properties
         denied by user.");
    } catch (Exception e) {
       ps.println("\tFailed! Unknown exception while enabling
         privilege.");
       e.printStackTrace(ps);
    }
    ps.println();
    String property = "user.home";
    ps.println("Trying to get system property (" + property + ")...");
    try {
       String propertyValue = System.getProperty(property);
       ps.println("\tSuccess!");
       ps.println("\t" + property + " = " + propertyValue);
    } catch (netscape.security.AppletSecurityException e) {
       ps.println("\tFailed! Security Violation.");
       e.printStackTrace(ps);
    } catch (Exception e) {
       ps.println("\tFailed! Unknown exception while accessing
                property.");
       e.printStackTrace(ps);
    }
  }
}
```

In the Java Capabilities API model, all access control decisions boil down to who is allowed to do what. The class Principal represents who, typically a signing certificate. Class Target represents access to one or more system resources, and class Privilege represents authorization (or denial of authorization) for a principal to access a target.

The class PrivilegeManager keeps track of which principals have access to which targets at any given time. A signed applet must use this class to request an access privilege to a particular target. PrivilegeManager distinguishes between granting a privilege and enabling a privilege. Granting a privilege indicates that an applet can step out of the sandbox, but the applet must explicitly enable the privilege before it can step out. Note that in Listing 4-1, the PrivilegeManager.enablePrivilege method call grants and enables a privilege at the same time. The rationale for distinguishing between granting and enabling is to further minimize the scope of code that can potentially do unsafe operations. Refer to http://developer.netscape.com/library/documentation/signedobj/capsapi.html for detailed information on the Netscape extensions to the Java security model.

Java Capabilities API does provide a fine-grained API to control access to system resources and allow a programmer to precisely limit areas of code that perform sensitive operations. There is, however, a trade-off. All the existing Java code must be changed to take advantage of these capabilities, and programmers must be trained to effectively leverage this API. The Authenticode 2.0 model, on the other hand, takes a much less drastic approach, as we shall see shortly.

### Signed JavaScript Programs

A JavaScript program can use LiveConnect to call the Java Capabilities API and step out of the sandbox. Object signing supports the signing of JavaScript files, inline scripts, and event handler scripts. You can obtain more information about signed JavaScript codes at [NETS97b].

## Authenticode 2.0 and Microsoft Internet Explorer 4.0

IE 4.0 provides a key feature, called security zones or trust zones, to group Web sites together based on their trust levels and customize the security privileges of each zone. Similar to Object Signing, Authenticode 2.0 [MICR97e] supports intermediate levels of trust for Java code, but it uses a different approach to designate these levels.

### Security Zones

A **security zone** is a group of Web sites in which you have the same level of trust. As a result, if you download active content from two Web sites within the same security zone, you are willing to grant them the same privileges to access resources of your computer. For example, if you run an applet from one site and allow it to write to local files, you are likely to grant an applet from the other site the same write privilege. IE 4.0 provides a menu with more than 50 options and allows you to precisely define your level of trust with the Web site within a security zone. The menu options include

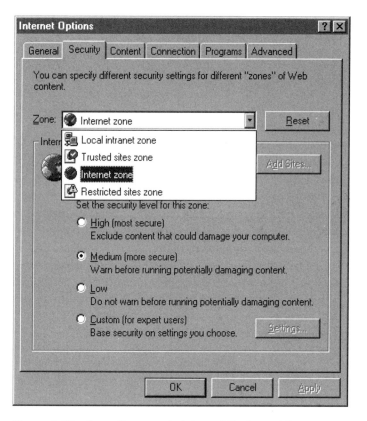

**Figure 4-18**    Security zones in Internet Explorer 4.0.

settings for ActiveX controls and plug-ins, Java applets, Active scripting, JavaScript, and user authentication. IE 4.0 predefines four security zones, as shown in Figure 4-18. Note that you can customize the security settings of each of these zones.

The **Local Intranet Zone** is for Web sites within a local area network, usually protected by a firewall. You can consider these sites to be absolutely trustworthy and grant them unrestricted access privileges to your computer. The **Trusted Sites Zone** includes sites that are on the Internet, but you have a high level of trust in their integrity and are willing to give them access to some of the resources on your computer. The Web sites of your brokerage, your bank, and your friends are good examples of trusted sites. The **Restricted Sites Zone** is the black list. It contains sites that contain damaging active content—you are not willing to grant these sites any privileges. The **Internet Zone** contains everything else on the Internet—you neither trust nor distrust these sites.

## Trust-Based Java Security

Working in conjunction with security zones, the Java security model [MICR97d] in Authenticode 2.0 and IE 4.0 provides a trust-based approach to managing the security threats of downloaded Java applets. Each security zone has a set of assigned trust levels for Java code (see Figure 4-19), which you can customize based on your comfort level, experiences that you have had with the zone, and reputation of sites within the zone. IE 4.0 can then sandbox applets downloaded from the Internet Zone, while giving free reign to applets downloaded from the Trusted Site Zone, if these are your comfort levels.

If an applet requires privileges to sensitive client computer resources that do not exceed its trust level, it runs without your intervention. If an applet requires more privileges, which are not explicitly denied, IE 4.0 will present you with a

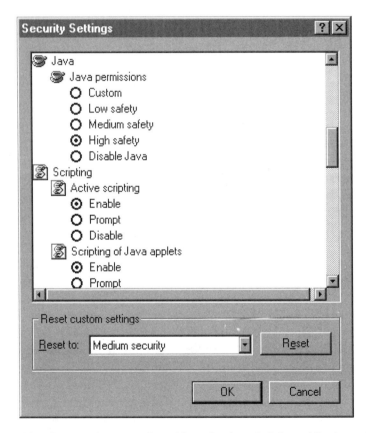

**Figure 4-19**    Customizing security settings for Java in Internet Explorer 4.0.

dialog box listing all the expanded privileges and their associated risks. You will have to make a yes-no decision and determine whether you trust the applet to run with the list of expanded privileges. An applet that does not receive expanded privileges will still run, but all of its attempts to access forbidden privileges will result in security exceptions. A well-designed applet should capture these security violations and take an alternative course of action.

How does IE 4.0 know which access privileges an applet needs to run? **Privilege signing** enables a software publisher to specify the set of all the privileges that a Java class needs and securely incorporate them into a signed .cab file. When downloading an applet, IE 4.0 inspects the signature of its signed .cab file, determines all the privileges requested by the applet, and uses the security zone associated with the applet to decide whether it should allow the applet to run, automatically deny some privileges, or consult you. The Authenticode 2.0 model for privilege signing is very different from Netscape's Object Signing. With Authenticode 2.0, a signature conveys the set of all the privileges used by signed Java classes; Object Signing embeds hard-coded privilege requests in Java source code. As a result, it is less expensive to migrate existing unsigned Java code to signed Java code using the Authenticode 2.0 technology.

**Privilege scoping** enables a trusted class to precisely define and limit the range of code for which a privilege is granted for use. Privilege scoping minimizes the threat of untrusted code spoofing trusted code into inadvertently calling it with privileges that it otherwise cannot obtain. **Package manager** allows you to install class libraries or Java Beans [FEGH97] locally on your machine without being forced to give them free reign over your computer resources. Traditionally, local Java classes have had unlimited access privileges to sensitive resources. Although this level of trust is appropriate for standard Java class libraries, it might not be appropriate for third-party Java Beans or other classes that are not system libraries.

### Timestamping

One of the shortcomings of Authenticode 1.0 and Netscape Object Signing is that a software publisher cannot associate the time that it has signed a piece of code with the signed code. The signature of signed code, therefore, expires after the validity period of the certificate ends, forcing the publisher to resign its code every year (assuming certificates are valid for one year). So much for virtual shrink-wrapped software!

Authenticode 2.0 fixes this problem. Through a timestamping service, a software publisher timestamps its signature and incorporates the timestamp, code, signature, and other relevant information in an Authenticode 2.0 data structure. A browser uses the timestamp to verify that the publisher had signed the code with a key pair that was valid *when* the code was signed. With the timestamping feature of Authenticode 2.0, a properly signed, virtually shrink-wrapped software remains "shrink-wrapped" even years after the publisher's certificate expires.

## Summary

Web surfing involves a bidirectional information exchange. When you visit a Web site, content is downloaded from the site into your browser, and you may leave behind personal information at the site. The presence of active content in the Web poses a number of security threats to you. Once downloaded, active content can potentially have the same access privileges to your computer as software installed from a floppy disk or a CD-ROM. Hostile active content can find and send out sensitive information stored in the computer, damage files, disable the computer, or annoy you. The World Wide Web has shifted the security problem from protecting a server from hostile clients to protecting a client from malicious servers.

The original model of downloading content from the Web has changed the notion of buying shrink-wrapped software from a neighborhood store. The neighborhood store has given way to hundreds of thousands to Web sites that either sell software over the Internet or have active content in their Web pages. Authenticode and object signing technologies leverage digital signatures to enable software vendors to provide virtual shrink-wraps for the software they release via the Web.

Finally, everything comes down to trust-based software management and managing risk. You manage risk by having absolute trust in some sites, no trust in other sites, and some trust in everything else. You let active content from absolutely trusted sites have free reign over your computer, disable active content from untrustworthy sites from being downloaded to your computer at all, and give active content from sites in the gray area restricted access to your computer.

## References

[BANK95]    Bank, J. *Java Security,* December 1995, http://www-swiss.ai.mit.edu/~jbank/javapaper/javapaper.html.

[BLAZ96]    Blaze, M., J. Feigenbaum, and J. Lacy. "Decentralized Trust Management," *Proceedings of IEEE Symposium on Security and Privacy,* May 1996, pp.164–173.

[CHU97]    Chu, Y., J. Fcigenbaum, B. LaMacchia, P. Resnick, and M. Strauss. "REFEREE: Trust Management for Web Applications," *Proceedings of the 6th International World Wide Web Conference,* 1997, pp. 227–238.

[FEGH97]    Feghhi, J. *Web Developer's Guide to Java Beans,* Scottsdale, AZ: Coriolis Group, Inc., 1997.

[NETS97a]    *Netscape Object Signing: Establishing Trust for Downloaded Software,* Netscape Corporation, 1997, http://developer.netscape.com/docs/manuals/signedobj/trust/owp.htm.

[NETS97b]   *JavaScript Security in Communicator 4.x,* Netscape Corporation, 1997, http://developer.netscape.com/docs/manuals/communicator/jssec/contents.htm.

[MICR96a]   *Proposal for Authenticating Code via the Internet,* Revision 1.1, Microsoft Corporation, April 1996, http://www.microsoft.com/security/tech/authcode/authcode.htm.

[MICR96b]   *Microsoft Authenticode Technology: Ensuring Accountability and Authenticity for Software Components on the Internet,* Microsoft Corporation, October 1996.

[MICR96c]   *Signing Code with Microsoft's Authenticode,* Microsoft Corporation, December 16, 1996.

[MICR97d]   *Trust-Based Security for Java White Paper,* Microsoft Corporation, April 1997, http://www.microsoft.com/java/security/jsecwp.htm.

[MICR97e]   *Microsoft Security Management Architecture White Paper,* Microsoft Corporation, May 1997, http://www.microsoft.com/ie/security/?/ie/security/ie4security.htm.

Chapter

# 5

# Secure Messaging and S/MIME

Securing an e-mail message in an open network requires **writer-to-reader security,** in which the message is protected from the moment it leaves a sender's mailing tool until it arrives at a recipient's mailing tool. Writer-to-reader security requires secret-key cryptography for confidentiality, public-key cryptography for authentication and nonrepudiation, and a formal public-key infrastructure for accountability. The material in this chapter builds upon many of the abstract ideas presented in Part I and serves as an excellent demonstration of their practical applications.

There are too many secure messaging protocols. Some, such as Privacy-Enhanced Mail (PEM) and X.400, have a sound theoretical foundation but have not received commercial vendor endorsement due to a lack of interoperability with the Internet mail system. Another, Pretty Good Privacy (PGP), is very effective for a small community of casual e-mail users but has shortcomings when scalability and accountability become requirements. Even worse, these protocols are not interoperable.

It seems, however, that one protocol is compatible with the Internet mail, has been recognized by the commercial vendors, such as Netscape and Microsoft, and is being deployed at a large scale in the marketplace. The large-scale deployment allows e-mail users to exchange secure e-mail without worrying about interoperability issues. A large part of this chapter is devoted to covering this protocol, which is known as S/MIME (Secure Multipurpose Internet Mail Exchange).

We will also provide detailed coverage of Netscape Messenger and Microsoft Outlook Express. Although the presented material does serve as a comprehensive tutorial on these two applications, the real objective of the presentation is to give you an understanding of how a secure e-mail tool *might* work. There are many other S/MIME-compliant mailing tools, the coverage of which is beyond the scope of this chapter.

## S/MIME

In 1995, several software vendors, led by RSA Data Security Inc., collaborated on a specification for secure messaging. Named S/MIME, the specification outlines the application of two security mechanisms, digital signatures and encryption, to enhance unsecure e-mail with authentication, integrity, and confidentiality services. The application of S/MIME, however, goes well beyond securing e-mail and allows many other software products, such as electronic data interchange (EDI) software and online electronic commerce services, to incorporate security.

S/MIME stands for Secure MIME. MIME is a set of specifications that provides a way to interchange text in languages with different character sets. It also enables multimedia e-mail among many different computer systems that use Internet mail standards.[1] S/MIME builds on top of two Public-Key Cryptographic Standards (PKCS) *de facto* standard formats, PKCS #7 and PKCS #10, developed by RSA Data Security, Inc. S/MIME enjoys a very strong commercial vendor acceptance, and many products already released to the marketplace, such as Netscape Messenger and Microsoft Outlook Express, support S/MIME.

## S/MIME Security Services and Mechanisms

S/MIME provides four security services that a traditional **mail user agent** (MUA) can apply to messages it sends or receives to protect message originators or recipients from a variety of threats in an open network. An MUA is a software program that allows a user to prepare messages, submit them, and receive messages. An MUA may be a sending agent, which helps users compose and send messages, or a receiving agent, which assists users in receiving messages. In this document, we may refer to an MUA as simply an agent. Table 5-1 enumerates these services and the mechanisms used to implement them.

**Table 5-1** Security Services Provided by S/MIME

| Security Service | Security Mechanism |
| --- | --- |
| Message origin authentication | Digital signature |
| Message integrity | Digital signature |
| Nonrepudiation of origin | Digital signature |
| Message confidentiality | Encryption |

---

1. The material in this section is based on *S/MIME Version 2 Message Specification* [SMIM97] . The IETF (Internet Engineering Task Force) S/MIME Working Group is currently working on another set of documents, *S/MIME Version 3 Message Syntax* and *S/MIME Version 3 Certificate Syntax*, to make the S/MIME specification an Internet standard. The material presented in this section, therefore, may change as the S/MIME specification evolves. Visit http://www.rsa.com/smime for the latest news on S/MIME and http://www.ietf.org/html.charters/smime-charter.html for the ongoing work at the IETF to standardize S/MIME.

**Message origin authentication**   This service provides a recipient with assurance that the message has been sent by the claimed originator. Note that the *From* field in an unsecure message does not provide any assurance for the identity of the originator because an impostor can set this field to any value.

**Message integrity**   The message integrity service provides assurance that the content of the message has not changed while in transit from an originator to a recipient.

**Nonrepudiation of origin**   This service protects a recipient from an originator later denying that he has sent the message or arguing that the message he has sent was different from the one the recipient claims.

**Message confidentiality**   Message confidentiality protects the contents of a message against unauthorized access by eavesdroppers while en route from an originator to a recipient.

These services are typically applied at the discretion of a human user. For example, when sending an e-mail message, you might decide to encrypt or digitally sign your e-mail. S/MIME services can also be used in automated message transfer agents (MTAs) that do not require any human involvement, such as automatic signing or encryption of fax messages sent over the Internet.[2]

The application of S/MIME security services is not limited to e-mail—any transport protocol that transmits MIME objects can leverage these services. For example, because the Hypertext Transfer Protocol (HTTP) transports MIME objects, it can use S/MIME to secure the communications between a Web browser and a server. S/MIME has also been applied to exchange digitally signed EDI data over the Internet (http://www.commerce.net/news/cnet_edi.html).

## Weak versus Strong Encryption

S/MIME-compliant agents can support a variety of secret-key encryption algorithms because the underling PKCS #7 syntax standard used for encryption is quite general (see Chapter 7).

An S/MIME agent typically supports 40-bit RC2 and triple-DES, although triple-DES may not be available due to export restrictions. The encryption algorithms provided by a particular S/MIME agent depend on factors such as the supporting legal structure, export restrictions, or agreements between private parties. Furthermore, a receiving agent may have encryption capabilities that differ from those of the  sending agent. For example, a receiving agent may be able to decrypt

---

2. Panasonic has announced a fax machine that sends S/MIME messages over the Internet, either to another fax machine or to a PC.

triple-DES, whereas a sending agent may not be able to encrypt under triple-DES. We refer to encryption under 40-bit RC2 (or a comparable algorithm) as **weak encryption** and triple-DES (or a comparable algorithm) as **strong encryption.**

The decision to use weak or strong encryption when sending a message depends on a variety of factors, such as encryption capabilities of a sending agent, decryption capabilities of a receiving agent, user preferences, private agreements, and so on. If the sending agent employs weak encryption to ensure successful decryption by the receiving agent, it may run the risk of an eavesdropper intercepting and decrypting the message. If the sending agent employs strong encryption, however, the receiving agent may not be able to decrypt the message. To address such issues, S/MIME supports a **capabilities attribute,** which allows a receiving agent to announce its decrypting capabilities in order of preference.

When an S/MIME agent sends a message to multiple recipients, some of the recipients may not be able to decrypt a strongly encrypted message. In this case, the agent may decide to use weak encryption for those recipients and strong encryption for the others. An eavesdropper listening to the agent's traffic, however, can determine the content of the message by simply decrypting the message that was encrypted with a weak algorithm. Strong encryption in this case may not provide any added security over weak encryption.

## Public-Private Key Pair Length

S/MIME uses public-key cryptography to create digital signatures and encrypt the secret key used to encrypt a message under a recipient's public key. We will explain the notion of encrypting a secret key under a public key in a subsequent section. An S/MIME agent must support the use of RSA key pairs for signing and encryption; it can, however, support additional encryption and signing algorithms and announce them via the capabilities attribute.

The RSA public key certified in an S/MIME certificate and its corresponding private key must have a key length of between 512 and 1024 bits. It is recommended that the key pair have a length of at least 768 bits because 512-bit keys are considered to be cryptographically unsecure. Some of the S/MIME agents in the United States, however, generate only 512-bit keys to get more advantageous export licenses.

## S/MIME Certificates

An **S/MIME certificate** is essentially the same as a personal or client certificate with the requirement that the e-mail address of the certificate subject (owner) must appear in the subjectAltName X.509 v3 extension field. A sending S/MIME agent should ensure that the e-mail address in the *From* header of an e-mail matches the Internet e-mail address in the signer's certificate; a receiving agent must perform this check again and react appropriately if it fails.

An S/MIME certificate should at a minimum provide assurance that the subject of the certificate has the corresponding e-mail address certified in the certificate. A higher grade S/MIME certificate may provide further assurances, such as certifying the identity of the certificate subject. If you receive e-mail that is digitally signed by a lower grade certificate, all you know is that it has come from the claimed e-mail address. E-mail signed by a higher grade certificate may also attest to the identity of the person who sent it. Note that in both cases, you can develop trust in the integrity of the *content* of the e-mail, that is, the fact the e-mail has not been tampered with while in transit.

You can obtain an S/MIME certificate from a third-party CA, which may issue different grades of S/MIME certificates. VeriSign, for example, issues Class 1 and Class 2 S/MIME certificates. A Class 1 certificate certifies the e-mail address, whereas a Class 2 certificate certifies the identity of the sender as well as his e-mail address. Figure 5-1 shows a VeriSign Class 1 S/MIME certificate. Note that if you have multiple e-mail accounts and you want to send signed e-mail from all of them, you need to have a certificate for each account.

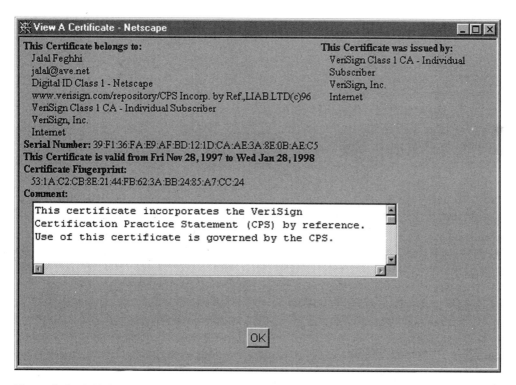

**Figure 5-1** A Netscape VeriSign Class 1 S/MIME certificate.

An S/MIME agent can generate a key pair, get identity information from a user, create a certificate registration request, and submit the request to a CA, who may transform the request into a certificate and return it to the agent. S/MIME leverages PKCS #10 to create a certificate request and a form of PKCS #7 to return a certificate. Alternatively, an S/MIME agent may have no capability for creating key pairs or requesting certificates—it relies on another application, such as a Web browser, to perform the certificate request processing.

## Including a Certificate Chain and a CRL with a Signed Message

When a recipient receives a signed message, it needs to have a valid certificate chain for the message originator to verify the signature. A sending S/MIME agent can optionally include a certificate chain for the signer when it sends a signed message to increase the likelihood that a recipient can verify the signature. Furthermore, a recipient should have access to a recent certification revocation list (CRL) to ensure that the certificate used to sign a message is not revoked. A sending agent can also include a CRL with a signed message and provide it to a recipient in addition to a certificate chain and the actual message.

Including your certificate when you send a signed message, however, has a drawback. A certificate may occupy 1 to 3 kilobytes of space, and a chain of two certificates may require about 4 kilobytes for transfer and storage. If you send a signed message to 1000 people, which may ultimately happen if you post a message to a newsgroup or a large mailing list, and include your certificate chain, you may waste a lot of bandwidth and storage. Including CRL information with a message is even worse because CRLs can become quite large.

One alternative to including certificate and CRL information with a signed message is to provide a recipient with a reference to a location where such information can be found. The recipient can then decide whether to verify the signature and can download the signer's certificates from the designated location. Note that if a recipient has already stored the signer's certificates from a previous correspondent, she can verify the signature without accessing the download location. Virtual business cards (if supported by an e-mail tool) can be used to provide a recipient with certificate location information.

The decision to include certificates with a signed e-mail depends on a variety of factors, such as the capabilities of a recipient for storing certificates, the capabilities of a recipient to access a directory service, and the size of the community of e-mail users. In a small community, we expect that e-mail users have already stored other users' certificates locally on their computers—including certificates when sending e-mails may waste network bandwidth. In larger communities, however, including certificates or reference locations where certificates can be found may be appropriate.

## Interoperability

RSA Data Securities Inc. has defined a matrix of interoperability tests, which checks an S/MIME product against a reference implementation of S/MIME for conformance testing http://www.rsa.com/smime/html/interop_center.html. S/MIME-compliant messaging products should be interoperable, meaning that you can, for example, send an encrypted e-mail message from Microsoft Outlook Express to a recipient who uses Netscape Messenger to receive and process e-mail.

Another interoperability consideration concerns backward compatibility of S/MIME products with traditional user mail agents. Obviously, a non-S/MIME e-mail product cannot process encrypted e-mails because it does not understand the S/MIME format types, nor does it have any decryption capabilities. How about signed e-mail messages? The S/MIME specification defines two alternative methods to sign e-mail, one of which is compatible with non-S/MIME e-mail products. A non-S/MIME e-mail product can display signed e-mail if the sending S/MIME product employs the backward-compatible method to prepare signed e-mail. Note that the S/MIME specification recommends that sending S/MIME agents use the backward-compatible method.

## Creating S/MIME Messages

S/MIME leverages PKCS #7 cryptographic message syntax format to secure a MIME entity by wrapping it into a PKCS #7 object. The PKCS object is itself wrapped as a MIME entity and transported by a transport mechanism that handles MIME data to recipients. A recipient extracts the PKCS object from the transported MIME entity, unwraps the object, and recovers the original MIME entity.

PKCS #7 describes a general syntax for data that may require cryptographic operations, such as digital signatures and encryption. PKCS #7 defines six content types to handle cryptographically enhanced data, three of which are used in S/MIME: data, signed data, and enveloped data. **Data content type** refers to arbitrary data, such as ASCII text files, which may not have any internal data structure. **Signed content type** specifies a data structure to accommodate a digital signature, all the required algorithm identifiers, certificates, CRLs, and other signer-related information. This content type supports authentication of origin, integrity, and nonrepudiation of origin services. **Enveloped-data content type** describes a data structure to include data encrypted under a secret key, the secret key that is encrypted under the RSA public key of each recipient, recipient identifiers, and algorithm identifiers. Enveloped data supports the confidentiality service.[3]

---

3. We use the term **enveloping** to refer to the process of encrypting data with a secret key and encrypting the secret key with a public key. The term **unenveloping** refers to the reverse process of decrypting the encrypted secret key with the corresponding private key, recovering the secret key, and decrypting the data with the secret key.

We now discuss how a MIME entity is prepared before security services are applied to it, the construction of a PKCS #7 object, and wrapping of the object as MIME data. The entity is first converted to a canonical form and then encoded for transfer. Appropriate security services are then applied and a PKCS object is created, which is wrapped into a MIME entity and transported. When an agent receives an S/MIME message, it removes the security services and recovers the original MIME entity. The recovered MIME entity is typically passed to a MIME-capable user agent, such as a traditional e-mail product, for further decoding and presentation to the user.

A MIME entity that is to be enveloped or signed must be converted into a **canonical form** that is unique and unambiguous in the environment where its digital signature is generated and the environment where the signature is verified. The canonicalization of MIME entities whose major type is text is especially important because text often has different representations in different environments. For text MIME entities, the canonicalization involves converting the line endings to the pair of characters <CR> <LF> and choosing a registered character set. If text is not canonicalized prior to transportation over a network, its representation may change in transit or in a receiving environment, causing its digest not to match the accompanying digital signature.

An S/MIME implementation should perform **transfer encoding** to a MIME entity before applying security services to it. The standard Internet Simple Mail Transport Protocol (SMTP) infrastructure can handle only 7-bit text. Although many segments of the transport infrastructure now handle 8-bit or binary data, it cannot be guaranteed that the entire path between an originator and a recipient is 8-bit clean. A MIME entity that is not 7-bit data, such as 8-bit text or binary data, should be transfer encoded into a 7-bit representation prior to any cryptographic enhancements. Quoted-printable and base-64 encodings are two techniques for encoding 8-bit text or binary data into 7-bit text.

### Encrypted Message

As we mentioned in the preceding section, the message is first canonicalized and then transfer encoded. The agent then generates a random secret key, which is used to encrypt the message. The specific secret-key algorithm used to generate the secret key may be RC2, triple-DES, or another algorithm—a user may or may not have control over the secret key algorithm or key length. The agent then encrypts the secret key with the RSA public key of each recipient using RSA encryption; the RSA key pair may have a length anywhere from 512 to 1024.

The agent packages the encrypted message, encrypted secret key, algorithm identifiers, and any other relevant data into an enveloped-data PKCS #7 object. This object is coded with the basic encoding rules (BER) encoding of ASN.1 syntax and then

```
Content-Type: application/pkcs7-mime;
      smime-type="enveloped-data";
      name="smime.p7m"
Content-Transfer-Encoding: base64
Content-Disposition: attachment;
      filename="smime.p7m"

MIAGCSqGSIb3DQEHA6CAMIACAQAxggGeMIHMAgEAMHYwYjERMA8GA1UEBxMISW50ZXJuZXQ
xFzAV
BgNVBAoTD1Z1cmlTaWduLCBJbmMuMTQwMgYDVQQLEytWZXJpU21nbiBDbGFzcyAxIENBIC0
gSW5k
aXZpZHVhbCBTdWJzY3JpYmVyAhAMjHzzqNyZ+4Kxk5Uj7tiwMAOGCSqGSIb3DQEBAQUABEA
ggkl4
49deRn6GazAcpQ2jO1y4zuqRibpLx/KxEZ9/1qO91ZzP9g9IoN8YWzJaOBt+d4ItUjII/tX
cQfvz
```

Figure 5-2   A sample encrypted S/MIME message.

base-64 transfer encoded. The transfer encoding is required because the PKCS #7 object is binary and cannot be transported over the traditional 7-bit SMTP infrastructure. Do not confuse this encoding with the encoding of the canonicalized message. Finally, the agent wraps the encoded PKCS #7 object into a MIME entity using **application/pkcs7-mime** content type. Figure 5-2 shows a sample encrypted message.

### Signed Message

S/MIME supports two alternative methods to sign MIME data. The first approach uses the multipart/signed format and application/pkcs-signature type, whereas the second approach uses the application/pkcs-mime format with the parameter smime-type set to signed-data. The multipart/signed format is the preferred method because it allows a mailing agent that does not recognize S/MIME to handle a signed message and display it to a user. The second format, however, is not backward-compatible and precludes existing UMAs from displaying signed e-mail.

Signing a message using the preferred method entails the following tasks. The message is canonicalized, transfer encoded, and then hashed using the SHA-1 algorithm to create a 20-byte message digest. The message digest is signed by encrypting it with the originator's private key to create a digital signature over the message. The digital signature, algorithm identifiers, certificates of the originator (optional), and any other pertaining data is packaged into a signed PKCS #7 object, which is translated in ASN.1 and transfer encoded. The resulting object is inserted into a MIME entity of application/pkcs-signature type. This MIME entity and the original message are then wrapped into another MIME entity as multipart/signed and transported. Because the message signature is detached from the actual message, a UMA that is not S/MIME compliant can still display the message, although it cannot verify the signature. Figure 5-3 shows a sample signed message.

### Signed and Encrypted Message

To compose a signed and encrypted message, an S/MIME agent can sign the message first and then nest it in an enveloped message, or it can envelope the message and nest the enveloped message in a signed message. This flexibility originates from the PKCS #7 syntax standard, which permits different PKCS content types to be arbitrarily nested inside each other. An agent may support one or both methods when sending a message—the agent may allow a user to specify the method if it supports both options. Note that an agent must be able to receive and process an arbitrary nesting of messages within reasonable resource limitations of the recipient computer.

```
Content-Type: multipart/signed;
    protocol="application/pkcs7-signature";
    micalg=SHA-1;
    boundary="----=_NextPart_000_0053_01BCF822.D6CF0800"

------=_NextPart_000_0053_01BCF822.D6CF0800
Content-Type: text/plain;
    charset="iso-8859-1"
Content-Transfer-Encoding: 7bit

This message is digitally signed.

------=_NextPart_000_0053_01BCF822.D6CF0800
Content-Type: application/pkcs7-signature;
    name="smime.p7s"
Content-Transfer-Encoding: base64
Content-Disposition: attachment;
    filename="smime.p7s"

MIAGCSqGSIb3DQEHAqCAMIACAQExCzAJBgUrDgMCGgUAMIAGCSqGSIb3DQEHAQAAoIIIVDC
CAjww
ggGlAhAyUDPPUNFW81yBrWVcT8glMA0GCSqGSIb3DQEBAgUAMF8xCzAJBgNVBAYTA1VTMRc
wFQYD
VQQKEw5WZXJppU2lnbiwgSW5jLjE3MDUGA1UECxMuQ2xhc3MgMSBQdWJsaWMgUHJpbWFyeSB
DZXJO

------=_NextPart_000_0053_01BCF822.D6CF0800--
```

**Figure 5-3**  A sample signed S/MIME message.

Signing a message first and then enveloping the signed message has the advantage that the enveloping obscures the signature. The only way an eavesdropper can determine the originator of the message is by looking at the *From* field, which is not reliable. The advantage of enveloping the message before signing is that the message signature can be verified without removing the enveloping, which requires the private key material of the recipient. An automatic signature verification system can then verify a signature and take an appropriate action before the message ever reaches the recipient.

# Microsoft Outlook Express

Outlook Express is an e-mail utility program that comes as a part of standard installation of Microsoft Internet Explorer. Outlook Express conforms to the S/MIME version 2 specification.

The North American (U.S. and Canada) version of Outlook Express supports 40-bit and 128-bit RC2, DES (56 bits), and 112-bit triple-DES secret-key encryption algorithms. The export version of Outlook Express, however, currently supports only 40-bit RC2. Outlook Express can decrypt 112-bit triple-DES and 64-bit RC2 encrypted messages, but it cannot send messages using these algorithms. SHA-1 is the message digest algorithm used in Outlook Express.

## Obtaining an S/MIME Certificate

You must have an S/MIME certificate to send digitally signed e-mail. Click on the **Tools|Options...** menu in Outlook Express and then click on the **Security** tab to view the security options shown in Figure 5-4. To apply for a certificate, click on **Get Digital ID...** to visit a Web page that lists the certification authorities from which you can get a certificate for Outlook Express. As this book went to press, this page lists only VeriSign; we therefore use VeriSign S/MIME certificates throughout this section to demonstrate the capabilities of Outlook Express.

Choose a certification authority from the list and fill out the enrollment form. For a VeriSign Class 1 Digital ID, you need to provide only your name, e-mail address, and billing information if you are enrolling for a full-featured certificate. Complete and submit the form. If the enrollment is successful, you will receive e-mail from VeriSign that contains a PIN and instructions on how to pick up and install your certificate (see Figure 5-5).

Requiring a PIN to pick up a Class 1 S/MIME certificate and sending the PIN via an e-mail serves as a confirmation method to ensure that a person applying for an S/MIME certificate provides the correct e-mail address during enrollment. Note that VeriSign does not perform any further identity confirmation checks for Class 1

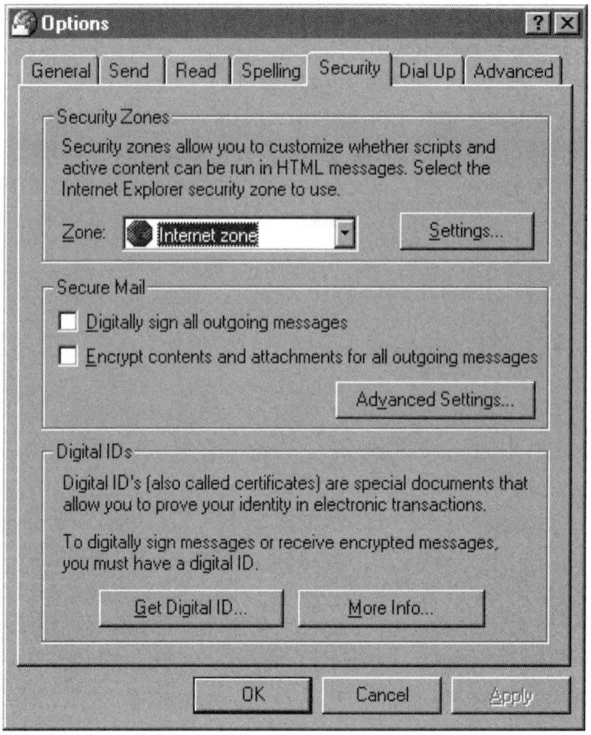

**Figure 5-4**   Security options in Outlook Express.

Digital IDs. A message digitally signed by a Class 1 S/MIME certificate provides assurance to a recipient that the message originated from the claimed e-mail address. It does not, however, provide any assurance about the identity of the person who sent the message. If an organization or a group of e-mail users needs assurance about the identity of the sender of an e-mail message, they can purchase higher-grade certificates, such as VeriSign Class 2 Digital ID, or use VeriSign OnSite and take charge of the authentication process. VeriSign OnSite is described in Chapter 10.

Follow the instructions in the e-mail to install your certificate. As a part of the installation process, you can view your certificate and verify its content, as shown in Figure 5-6.

## Assigning the Certificate to an E-Mail Account

After you have installed your S/MIME certificate, you need to assign it to your e-mail account. Click on the **Tools|Accounts...** menu in Outlook Express and then choose the **Mail** tab to list the e-mail accounts that you have set up on your com-

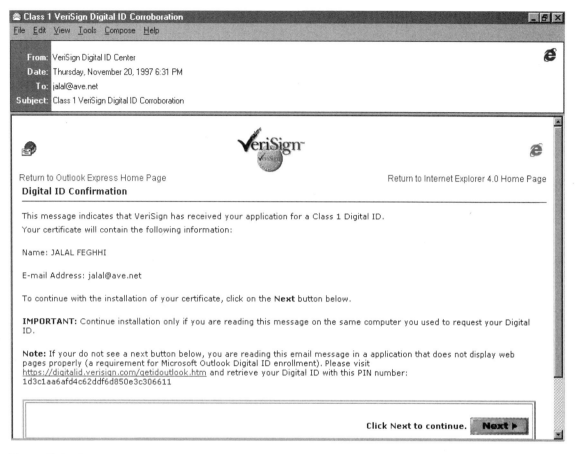

**Figure 5-5** Confirmation e-mail containing the PIN.

puter. Select the appropriate e-mail account, click on **Properties,** and then choose the **Security** tab to view the security properties of your e-mail account. Refer to Figures 5-7 and 5-8 for screen shots.

To assign your S/MIME certificate to the e-mail account, check the **Use a digital ID when sending secure messages from:** box and click on the **Digital ID...** button. As Figure 5-9 illustrates, a dialog box appears that lists all the currently available S/MIME certificates. Choose your S/MIME certificate and click on **OK.**

## Backing Up Your Certificate and Private Key

If you lose your private key, you can no longer sign your messages nor can you decrypt messages that are sent to you encrypted. (Note: We are assuming that you are

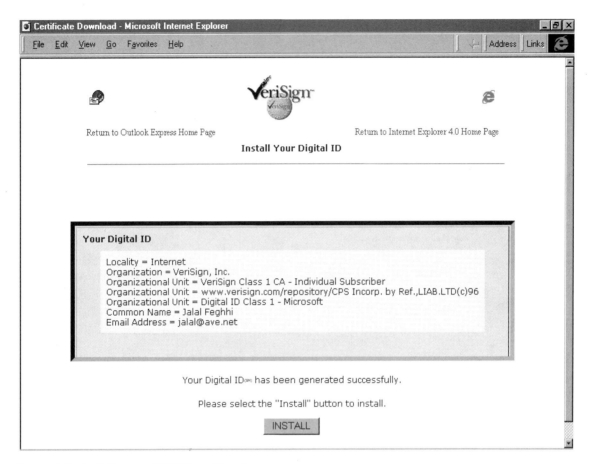

**Figure 5-6**  Installing an S/MIME certificate.

using the same key pair for both digital signature and encryption. Outlook Express version 4.17 supports only one key pair, although future versions may support two key pairs, one for signing and one for encryption. See the Single Key, Dual Key, Multiple Public-Keys per Individual section in Chapter 2.)

You can revoke your old certificate, obtain a new one, and resume sending signed messages. You cannot, however, decrypt messages encrypted with the old private key. All such encrypted messages are lost, unless you can somehow recover your lost private key through a key recovery service or have backed up the private key yourself.

To back up your private key, use the **View | Internet Options...** menu from Internet Explorer, choose **Content | Personal...** to view your personal certificates, select the appropriate certificate, and click on **Export....** In the **Export Personal Certificates** dialog box, type a password and a file name. Internet Explorer will

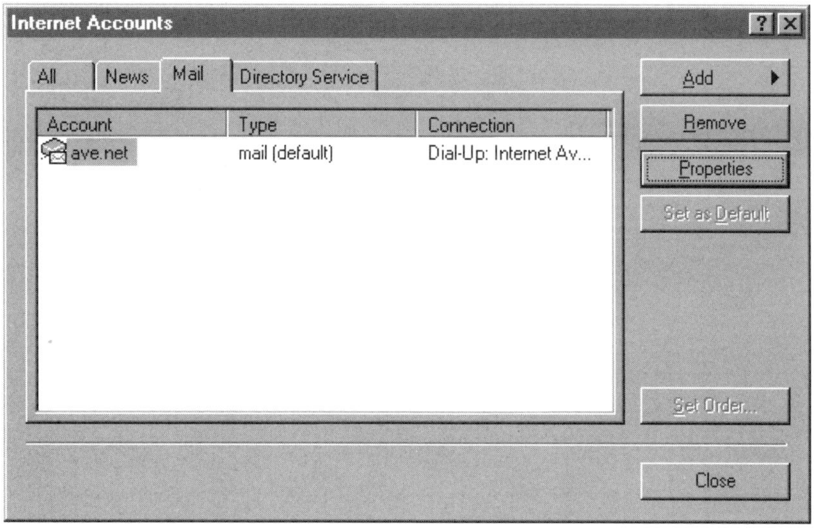

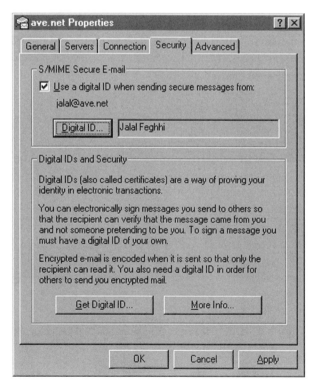

**Figure 5-7**  Available Internet accounts.

**Figure 5-8**  Internet account security properties.

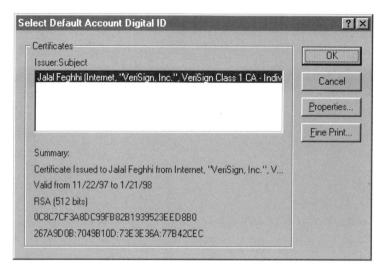

**Figure 5-9**  Available certificates for an Internet account.

save your certificate and private key to the file and encrypt the file with the password. It would be preferable if you saved your private key on a removable media, such as floppy disk, to minimize the chance of an attacker attempting to obtain your encrypted private key and crack it.

## Sending a Digitally Signed Message

You can now send a digitally signed message to anyone on the Internet. Note that you do not need to have a person's S/MIME certificate to send her a signed message —sending a signed message only requires the sender to have a certificate. A good way to experiment with sending signed messages is to send yourself a signed e-mail.

Prepare an e-mail message to yourself and then choose **Tools | Digitally Sign** menu from the menu bar. You can also sign a message by clicking on the **Digitally sign message** icon, which is an envelope with a red ribbon on the tool bar. Note that Outlook Express indicates that it will sign the message by placing a red ribbon in the e-mail subject line, as shown in Figure 5-10.

Figure 5-11 illustrates how Outlook Express informs a recipient that a message has been digitally signed. Pay attention to the security field of the message, which indicates that the message has been digitally signed and verified. It would be constructive to take a closer look at this message before Outlook Express removes the signature.

Figure 5-10  Sending a signed message.

Figure 5-11  Receiving a signed message.

Make sure the signed e-mail window is active. Click on the **File | Properties** menu, choose the **Details** tab, and then click on the **Secure Message Source...** button. Outlook Express displays the source of the message, part of which is shown in Figure 5-12. As you can see, the body of the message, *This message is digitally signed*, is still in plaintext. The message also includes a chunk of binary data, which contains the digital signature of the message and your certificate.

## Importing a Person's Certificate to the Address Book

You must have a person's S/MIME certificate if you want to send her an encrypted e-mail. In this section, we discuss methods for importing a certificate to the address book.

```
Return-Path: jalal@ave.net
Received: from jalal (ppp21.ave.net [206.24.126.171]) by mail.ave.net (8.7.1/8.7.1) with
SMTP id PAA14141 for <jalal@ave.net>; Sun, 23 Nov 1997 15:11:26 -0800 (PST)
From: "Jalal Feghhi" <jalal@ave.net>
To: "Jalal Feghhi" <jalal@ave.net>
Subject: Digitally signed
Date: Sun, 23 Nov 1997 15:16:55 -0800
Message-ID: <01bcf865$e5e4e560$9c7e18ce@jalal>
MIME-Version: 1.0
Content-Type: multipart/signed;
        protocol="application/x-pkcs7-signature";
        micalg=SHA-1;
        boundary="----=_NextPart_000_0053_01BCF822.D6CF0800"
X-Priority: 3
X-MSMail-Priority: Normal
X-Mailer: Microsoft Outlook Express 4.71.1712.3
X-MimeOLE: Produced By Microsoft MimeOLE V4.71.1712.3
X-UIDL: 880326723.000

This is a multi-part message in MIME format.

------=_NextPart_000_0053_01BCF822.D6CF0800
Content-Type: text/plain;
        charset="iso-8859-1"
Content-Transfer-Encoding: 7bit

This message is digitally signed.

------=_NextPart_000_0053_01BCF822.D6CF0800
Content-Type: application/x-pkcs7-signature;
        name="smime.p7s"
Content-Transfer-Encoding: base64
Content-Disposition: attachment;
        filename="smime.p7s"

MIAGCSqGSIb3DQEHAqCAMIACAQExCzAJBgUrDgMCGgUAMIAGCSqGSIb3DQEHAQAAoIIIVDCCAjww
ggGlAhAyUDPPUNFW8lyBrWVcT8glMA0GCSqGSIb3DQEBAgUAMF8xCzAJBgNVBAYTAlVTMRcwFQYD
VQQKEw5WZXJpU2lnbiwgSW5jLjE3MDUGA1UECxMuQ2xhc3MgMSBQdWJsaWMgUHJpbWFyeSBDZXJO
aWZpY2F0aW9uIEF1dGhvcml0eTAeFw0SNjAxMjkwMDAwMDBaFw0yMDAxMDcyMzU5NT1aMF8xCzAJ
BgNVBAYTAlVTMRcwFQYDVQQKEw5WZXJpU2lnbiwgSW5jLjE3MDUGA1UECxMuQ2xhc3MgMSBQdWJs
```

**Figure 5-12**   Details of a signed message.

## Importing a Certificate from a Signed Message

The easiest way to add the certificate of a person to the address book is to ask her to send you a signed message, which typically includes the certificate of the signer as an attachment. Let's add your certificate to the address book using the signed message that you just sent to yourself. Later, you will use this certificate to send an encrypted message to yourself.

Open the signed message that you sent yourself, choose **File | Properties**, and then select the **Security** tab to get the dialog box shown in Figure 5-13. Click on the **Add Digital ID to Address Book** button of the dialog box to display the properties associated with the sender, as shown in Figure 5-14. You can use the **Digital IDs** tab of the properties dialog box to examine the certificate before accepting it. Click on **OK** to accept the new contact and add it to the address book. Click on the **Address Book** icon inside Outlook Express to view the contents of the address book. As Figure 5-15 illustrates, the address book should contain your name and indicate that you have a certificate by displaying a red ribbon on the card next to your name.

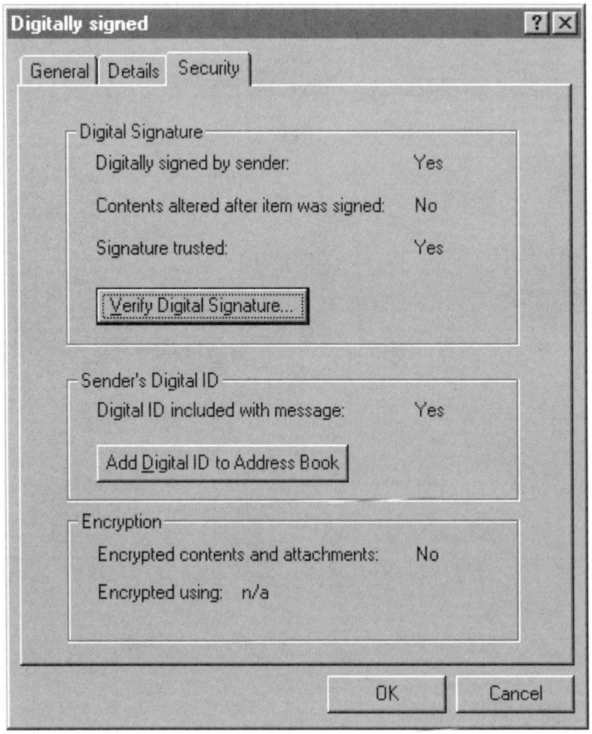

**Figure 5-13** Security properties dialog box of a signed message.

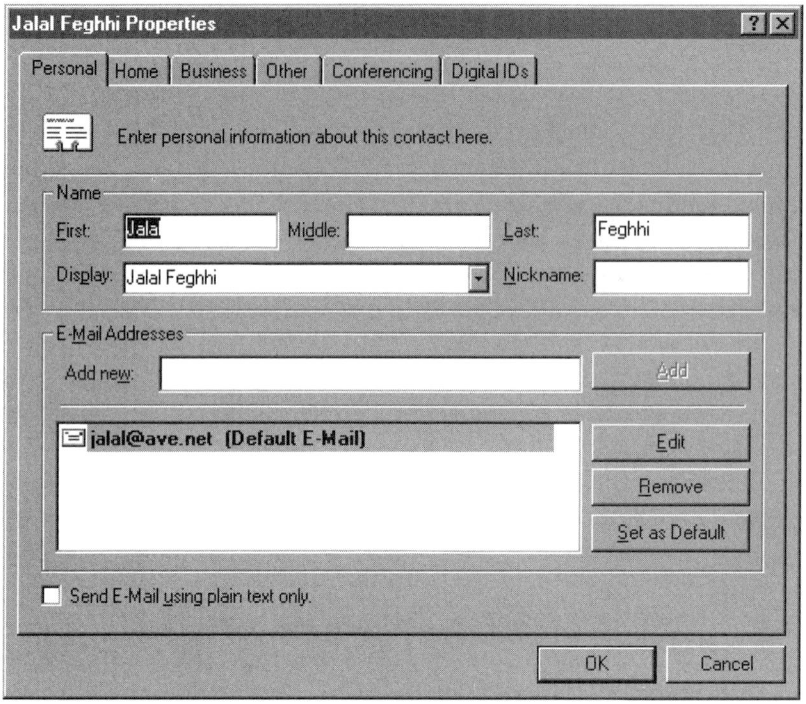

**Figure 5-14**   Adding a contact to the address book.

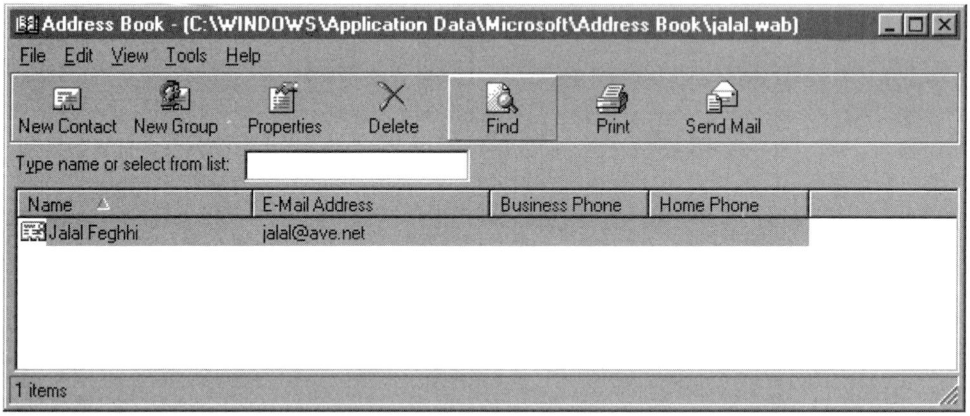

**Figure 5-15**   A red ribbon in the address book indicates a contact has a certificate.

## Importing a Certificate from a Directory Service

Outlook Express supports the Lightweight Directory Access Protocol (LDAP) for accessing directory services to find people and businesses. In particular, you can use a directory service to import a certificate for someone to whom you wish to send encrypted e-mail. Outlook Express comes with built-in access to a number of popular directory services; you can use the **Tools\|Accounts** to add additional directory services.

In the address book, click on the **Find** icon in the tool bar. Choose the directory service, fill out information about the person whose certificate you want to find, and click on the **Find Now** button. As Figure 5-16 shows, the address book displays a list of records that match the search criteria. Choose the appropriate record and click on the **Add to Address Book** button to create a new contact. You can also use the **Properties** button to examine a record.

## Importing a Certificate from a File

You can import a certificate to the address book from a certificate file encoded in binary PKCS #7 format. You can obtain the file from a directory service, a CA, or from

**Figure 5-16** Using a directory service to import a certificate.

a floppy disk that you may have exchanged with someone. In the address book, create a new entry for the contact or double-click an existing one, choose the **Digital IDs** tab, and click on the **Import...** button. Specify the file name and click on **Open** to import the certificate.

### Importing a Certificate from a Certification Authority

If you know which CA has issued your friend's certificate, you may be able to search the CA's repository and import her certificate directly into your address book. We shall illustrate the required steps by importing Peter Williams' certificate from the VeriSign repository.

Go to http://digitalid.verisign.com/query.htm, and search for Peter's certificate by his e-mail address peter@verisign.com. From the list of matched records, choose a Class 1 certificate issued for Microsoft, and click on the certificate to view its details. Choose the desired download format as someone else's digital ID for Microsoft, and download the certificate, as illustrated in Figure 5-17.

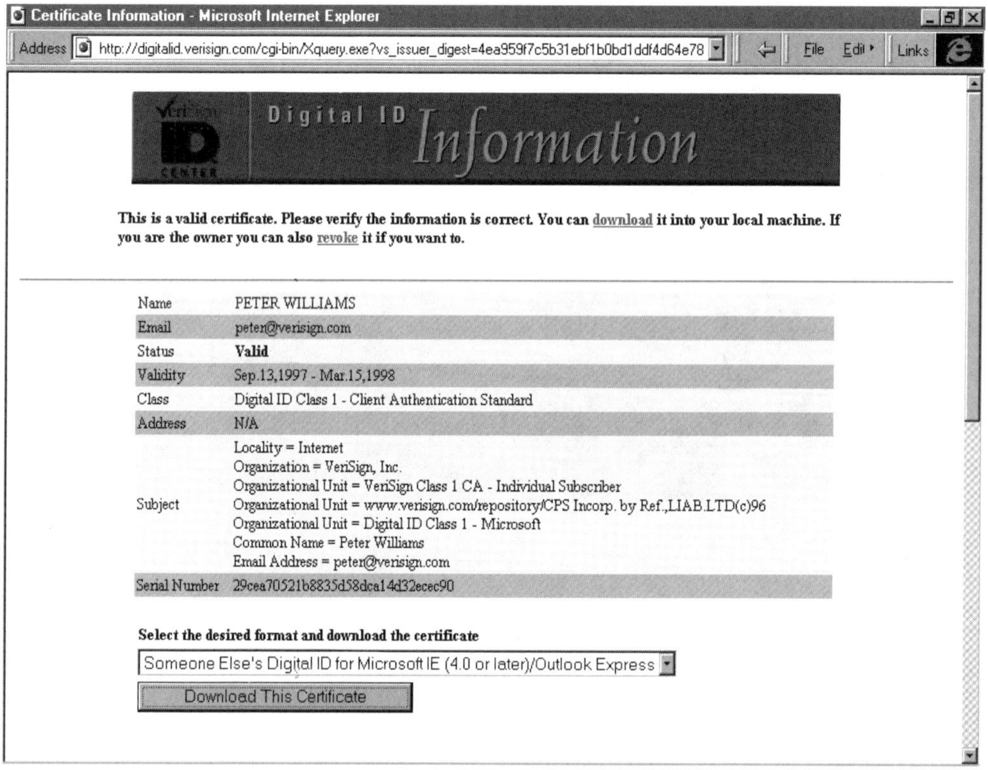

**Figure 5-17**  Downloading a certificate from a certification authority.

In the **File Download** dialog box, choose **Open this file from its current location** radio button and click the **OK** button. Internet Explorer brings up the **Digital ID** dialog box, which allows you to view the certificate and add it to the address book (see Figures 5-18 and 5-19).

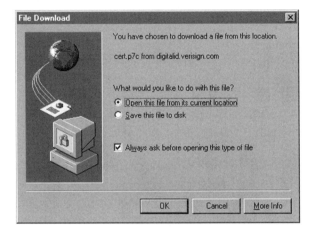

**Figure 5-18** Open the certificate file from its current location.

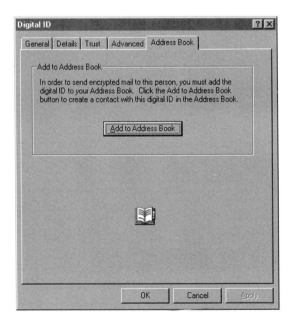

**Figure 5-19** Digital ID dialog box.

## Sending an Encrypted Message

To send an encrypted message to a friend, you need to have her S/MIME certificate in the address book. In the last section, you added your S/MIME certificate to the address book. You can now experiment with encrypted e-mails by sending an encrypted message to yourself.

Prepare an e-mail message to yourself, and then choose **Tools | Encrypt** menu from the menu bar. You can also encrypt an e-mail message by clicking on the **Encrypt message** icon, which is an envelope with a lock on the tool bar. Note that, as shown in Figure 5-20, Outlook Express places a lock in the e-mail subject line to indicate that it will encrypt the message.

Figure 5-21 illustrates how Outlook Express informs a recipient that a message has been encrypted. Pay attention to the security field of the message and the lock symbol, which indicate that the message has been encrypted. Figure 5-22 shows the source of this message before it was decrypted by Outlook Express. You can obtain the source by clicking on the **File | Properties** menu, choosing the **Details** tab, and then clicking on the **Secure Message Source...** button.

Suppose an eavesdropper monitoring your outgoing or incoming e-mail sees the message of Figure 5-22. He can still obtain some information, such as subject, recipient, and date sent. The body of the message, however, is encrypted. Whether he can decipher the message depends on a number of factors, including the length of the encryption key and the potential value to be gained in decrypting the message.

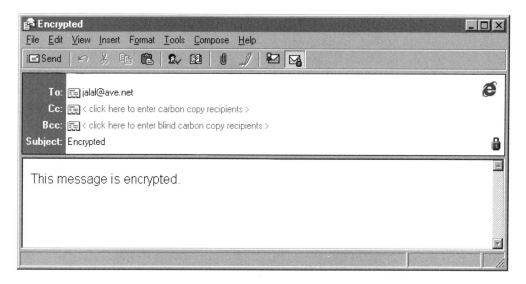

**Figure 5-20**  Sending an encrypted message.

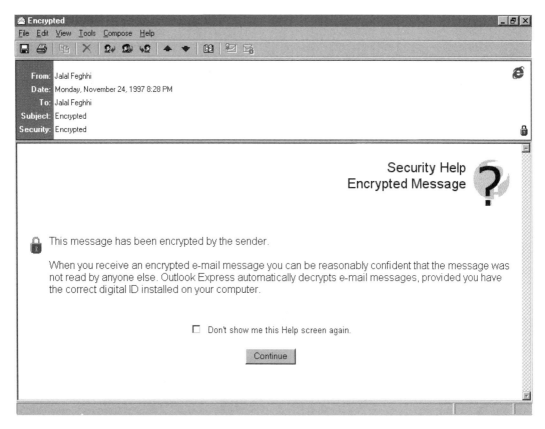

**Figure 5-21**   Receiving an encrypted message.

## Automatically Signing or Encrypting a Message

You can configure Outlook Express to automatically sign or encrypt your messages. From the main window, click on **Tools|Options...,** choose the **Security** tab, and then select the appropriate check boxes in the **Secure mail** area. Note that Outlook Express will warn you if you attempt to send an encrypted message to someone for whom you have not established a certificate.

## Trust Status of a Certificate

Typically, you trust a person's certificate and are willing to add it to your address book because you trust the CA who has issued the certificate. It is possible, however, that a person has an S/MIME certificate from a CA that you do not recognize. In such a case, you do not want to trust all the certificates that are issued by that

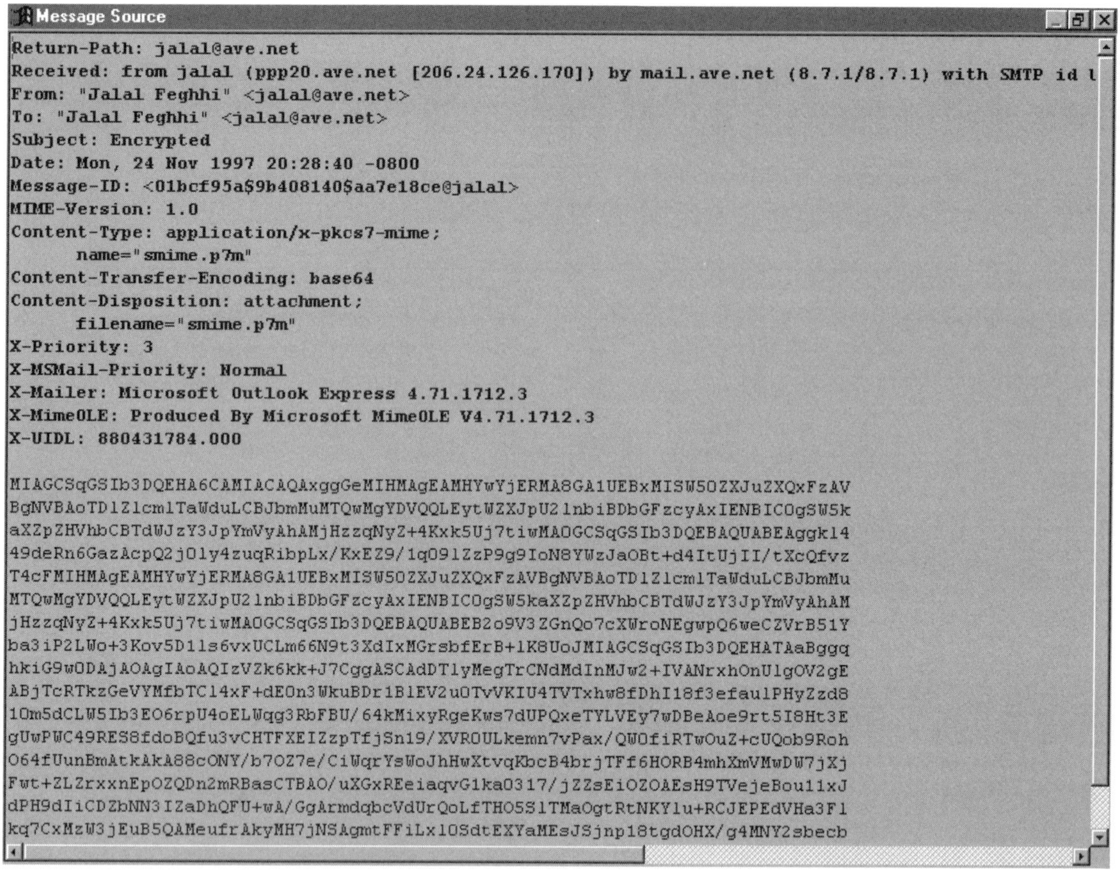

Figure 5-22 An encrypted message.

CA, but you still want to trust this person's certificate. Outlook Express allows you to do this.

To view or edit the trust associated with a certificate, double-click the name of the contact in the address book—for this example you can use your own record, which should have a certificate. Click the **Digital IDs** tab, select the digital ID whose trust level you want to modify, click **Properties**, and then choose the **Trust** tab (see Figure 5-23).

The **Certificate trusted for** area of Figure 5-23 indicates that this certificate can be used for both encryption and authentication, and the **Edit Trust** area describes the origin of the trust in the certificate. The **Inherit Trust from Issuer** option indicates that you trust the certificate because you trust the issuing CA. The **Explicitly Trust this Certificate** means that you want to trust this certificate regardless of whether you trust its issuing CA. **Explicitly Don't Trust this**

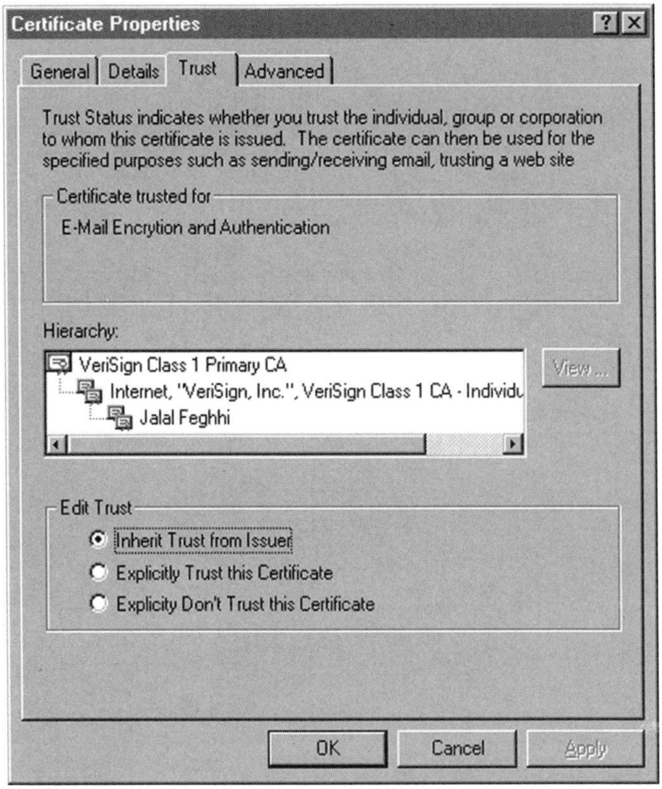

**Figure 5-23**   Trust properties of a certificate.

**Certificate** is useful when you do not trust the certificate. Using this option is preferable to removing the certificate, because you will be warned if an e-mail message contains an untrusted certificate.

# Netscape Messenger

Messenger is Netscape's Web-based, S/MIME-compliant messaging tool, which comes bundled with Netscape Communicator. It supports encryption and digital signing, and provides an interface to popular directory services to export or import digital certificates. Messenger supports domestic and export-level public-key and secret-key encryption. The export-level secret-key encryption is currently 40-bit RC2.

Figures 5-24 and 5-25 illustrate the Messenger main security window (it was necessary to take two screen shots to capture the entire window). This window

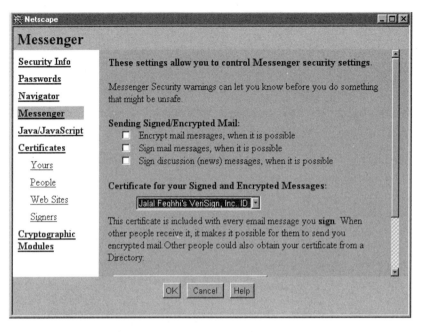

**Figure 5-24**   Messenger main security window.

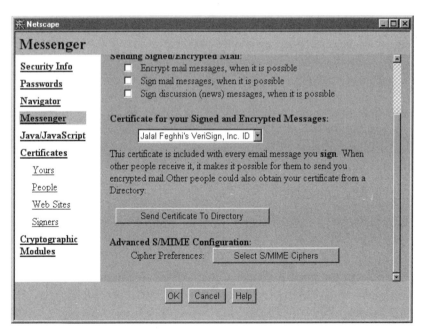

**Figure 5-25**   Messenger main security window (continued).

allows you to instruct Messenger to automatically digitally sign or encrypt your messages, choose an S/MIME certificate if you have more than one, export your certificate to a directory service, and select ciphers to be used. Figure 5-26 shows the interface for exporting a certificate to a directory service, and Figure 5-27 shows the secret-key algorithms available for encryption. Note that the domestic-grade Messenger might support more algorithms than are listed in Figure 5-27.

**Figure 5-26**  Directory service interface for exporting a certificate.

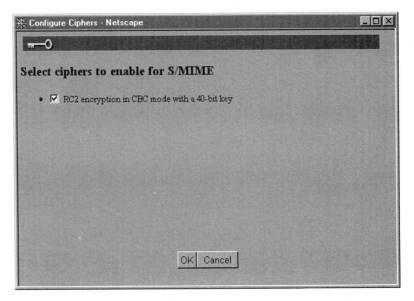

**Figure 5-27**  List of supported secret-key algorithms.

## Sending a Digitally Signed Message

Once you have installed an S/MIME certificate in Communicator (you can obtain S/MIME certificates from http://digitalid.verisign.com/smime.htm, you can start sending digitally signed messages. To sign a message, you can either instruct Messenger to automatically sign all outgoing messages or you can click on **Message Sending Options** when composing a new message and then select the **Signed** check box (see Figure 5-28).

As Figure 5-29 demonstrates, Messenger affixes a special logo to designate a signed message. Clicking on the **Security** icon brings up the **Security Info** window

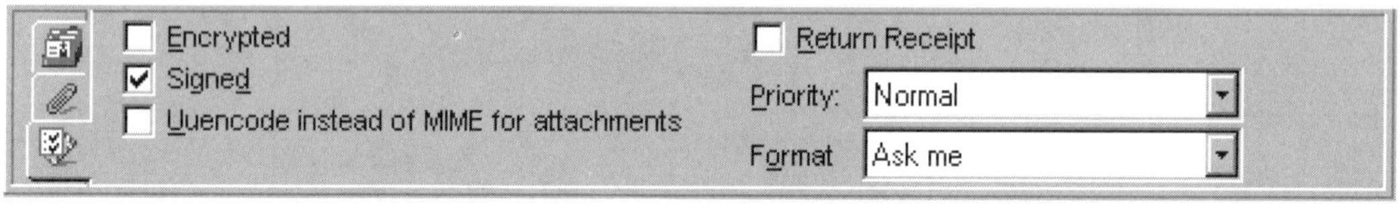

**Figure 5-28**   Options for sending a message.

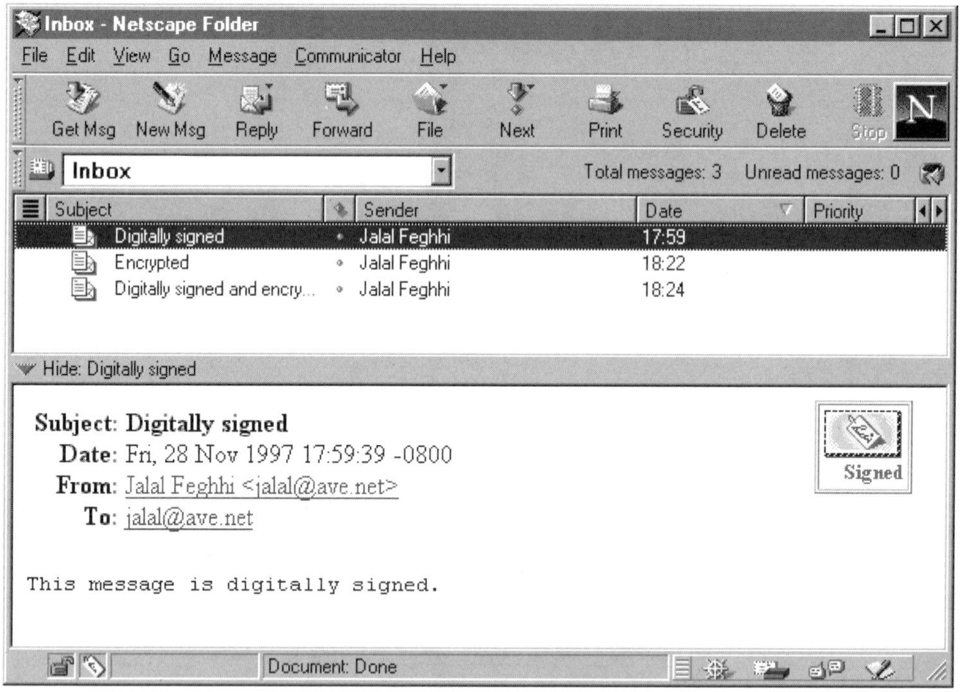

**Figure 5-29**   Messenger's GUI to display a signed message.

shown in Figure 5-30, which displays more information about the signed message, such as the date and time the message was signed. This window also allows you to view the signer's certificate.

## Sending an Encrypted Message

The procedure for sending an encrypted message in Messenger is the same as that for sending a signed message. You must, however, have a certificate for each recipient. If you click on the **Security** icon when preparing an encrypted message, Messenger informs you whether it has appropriate certificates to encrypt the message. The Security window allows you to search a directory service to import a certificate if you do not have a certificate for a recipient (see Figures 5-31, 5-32, and 5-33).

## Sending a Digitally Signed and Encrypted Message

You can apply both digital signature and encryption security mechanisms when you send a message with Messenger. Messenger affixes a special logo, shown in Figure 5-34, to designate a message that has both security mechanisms applied to it.

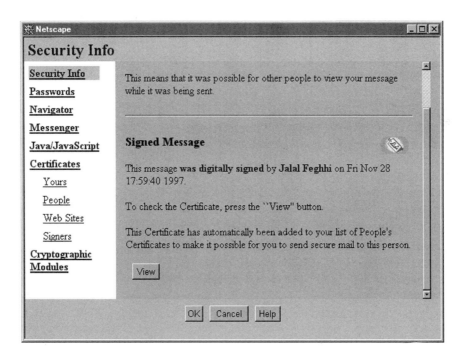

**Figure 5-30**   Security Info window shows the status of a message.

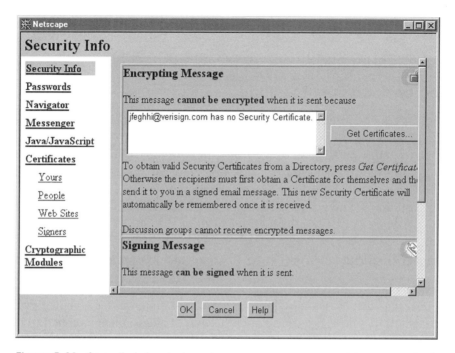

**Figure 5-31**   Security Info window shows a message cannot be encrypted.

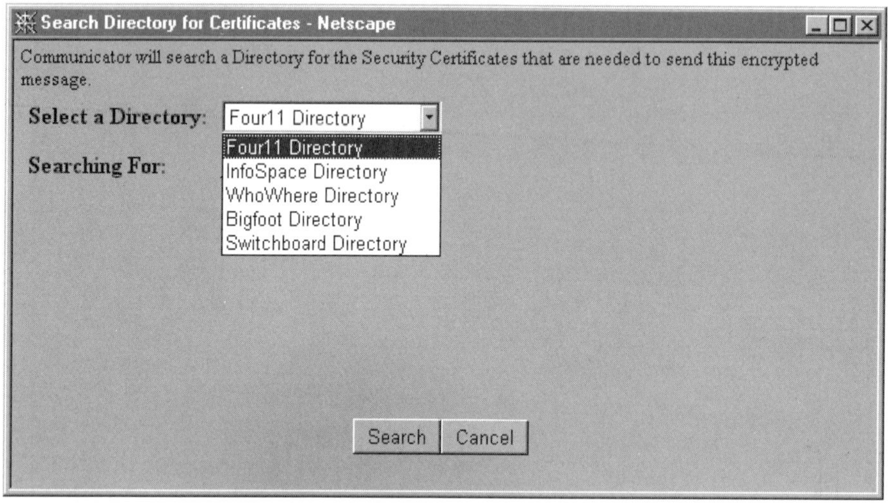

**Figure 5-32**   Searching for a recipient's certificate.

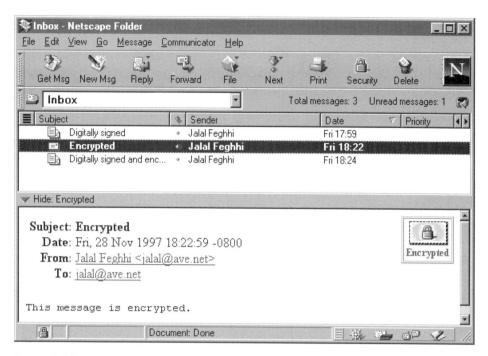

**Figure 5-33**  Messenger's GUI to display an encrypted message.

**Figure 5-34**  Messenger's logo to display a signed and encrypted message.

## PEM, MOSS, PGP, and X.400

There are many other ways to make e-mail secure. In this section we provide an introduction to some of these approaches. See [FORD97] for a more detailed discussion.

### PEM

Started in the late 1980s, **Privacy Enhanced Mail** (PEM) [LINN93] was the first serious project by The Internet Engineering Task Force to provide secure e-mail over the Internet. PEM uses digital signatures and encryption to implement all the security services that S/MIME has. PEM specifies a symmetric-key and a public-key approach to key management, although only the public-key specification was implemented.

PEM defines its own message format to wrap unsecure e-mail with security services. The PEM message format is based on 7-bit text messages and is not compatible with MIME. As a result, it did not receive strong commercial acceptance and its widespread deployment never materialized.

## MOSS

The Internet Engineering Task Force continued its attempts to provide secure messaging for the Internet with **MIME Object Security Services** (MOSS) [CROC95]. Instead of defining its own message formats, MOSS employed MIME and specified two new MIME content types (multipart/signed and multipart/encrypted) to support encrypted or digitally signed messages.

MOSS suffered from a lack of detailed specification, which caused interoperability issues between MOSS implementations. Furthermore, MOSS does not define a rigid public-key infrastructure. Similar to PEM, MOSS did not receive much commercial acceptance and was never deployed in a large-scale environment.

## PGP

**Pretty Good Privacy** (PGP) [ZIMM95] is a specification and a software product, freely available from Massachusetts Institute of Technology. PGP uses digital signatures and encryption to provide all the security services that PEM, MOSS, and S/MIME define. PGP specifies its own message formats, but they can be converted to MIME content types and handled by MIME-enabled messaging agents.

PGP defines its own public-key infrastructure and relies on e-mail users to exchange keys and establish trust in each other. The informal relationships between various PGP key holders create a *web of trust,* which differs from the well-structured, formal relationships designed to provide accountability. PGP is suitable for a small community of users who exchange casual e-mail, but it becomes unmanageable for large groups of users. PGP is inappropriate for environments that require accountability, such as electronic commerce applications.

## X.400

**X.400** is a set of standards developed by the International Telecommunication Union (ITU), International Organization for Standardization (ISO), and International Electrotechnical Commission (IEC). Although X.400 has the most comprehensive set of security services of any standard, X.400 secure messages cannot be transported over the Internet mail infrastructure, but they can be sent over the Internet through mail gateways.

## Summary

S/MIME uses digital signature and encryption security mechanisms to provide message origin authentication, message integrity, nonrepudiation of origin, and message confidentiality security services. S/MIME uses X.509 v3 certificates, formal public-key infrastructure, and the PKCS #7 and PKCS #10 standards. S/MIME supports a variety of secret-key encryption algorithms, although higher grade encryption is subject to export controls.

S/MIME is compatible with MIME and defines a handful of new MIME types to accommodate encrypted or signed messages. An S/MIME implementation applies security services to a message and creates a PKCS #7 object, wraps the PKCS object into a new MIME entity, and transports it over the Internet mail system. A receiving S/MIME implementation unwraps the MIME object, removes the security services, and recovers the original message. S/MIME has a very strong commercial vendor acceptance, and S/MIME implementations, such as Netscape Messenger and Microsoft Outlook Express, have already been deployed in the marketplace.

## References

[CROC95]   Crocker, S., N. Freed, J. Galvin, and S. Murphy. *MIME Object Security Services*, Request for Comments (RFC) 1848, Internet Activities Board, 1995.

[FORD97]   Ford, W., and M. Baum. *Secure Electronic Commerce: Building the Infrastructure for Digital Signatures and Encryption*, Prentice-Hall, Englewood Cliffs, NJ, 1997.

[LINN93]   Linn, J. *Privacy Enhancement for Internet Electronic Mail, Part I: Message Encryption and Authentication Procedures*, Request for Comments (RFC) 1421, Internet Activities Board, 1993.

[SMIM97]   *S/MIME Version 2 Message Specification*, Internet Draft draft-dusse-smime-msg-07.txt, 1997.

[ZIMM95]   Zimmerman, P.R. *The Official PGP User's Guide*, MIT Press, Cambridge, MA, 1995.

Chapter

# 6

# Web Server Security, Certificates, and Access Control

The security of a Web server is of paramount importance. Attackers have traditionally attempted to take advantage of a server's vulnerabilities and penetrate the server. An administrator can use a variety of safeguards to protect a server from rogue clients. The discussion of all such safeguards is beyond the scope of this book, but [GARF97] provides a good discussion of this subject.

This chapter concentrates on the use of certificates to enhance the security of Web servers. A server can require clients to provide their certificates when they attempt to access a resource. The server can then use the certificate to log detailed information about the user, gather information about users, and enforce access control.

The subject of access control and authorization is particularly important because many system penetrations succeed as a result of failure to enforce such control. We, therefore, devote most of this chapter to covering how a server can use certificates to enforce access control. We will also demonstrate how a programmer can use Microsoft Active Server Page (ASP) to obtain a client certificate and easily retrieve its fields without worrying about the ASN.1 format.[1] Finally, we will discuss proxy servers and the use of digital signatures to block untrusted code.

## Microsoft ASP, Certificates, and Access Control

A Web server page can serve as an authorization point and enforce the access-control security policy of an organization. A properly configured Web server can ask a client to submit its certificate when it accesses a page, authenticate the client, and make the client certificate available to the requested page. The page can then use the certificate to determine the client's access privileges, perhaps using an access-control database, and enforce the local access-control policy.

---

1. VeriSign provides a plug-in called Certificate Decoder Ring (CDR) for Netscape servers that accomplishes the same task for Netscape CGI programs.

Microsoft ASP technology provides a user-friendly interface to obtain a client certificate from within an ASP page and retrieve the certificate fields, such as the subject distinguished name, issuer name, and validity start date. A user of the interface need not worry about the details of decoding an ASN.1-encoded certificate. The user simply retrieves a field by specifying its name and the interface implementation deals with the certificate format details. In essence, ASP treats the certificate like a collection object and provides access to its fields while hiding its implementation details.

## ASP and Certificates

Microsoft **Active Server Page** (ASP) is a server-side scripting environment used to create and run dynamic, interactive Web server applications. ASP files, which have .asp extensions, are text files that contain text, HTML tags, and script commands. ASP supports Microsoft Visual Basic Scripting Edition (VBScript) and JScript scripting languages. When a Web browser accesses a page with an .asp extension on a site, the Web server first reads the page, executes all the scripts, and then sends the resulting HTML page to the browser.

ASP supports six built-in objects to access HTTP requests sent by a browser, create a response to a browser, store information about a particular user, access the methods and properties on a server, and support transactions. One of the built-in objects, the Request object, provides access to all the information passed with a request, such as parameters passed by an HTML form, cookies, and client certificates.

The Request object has a ClientCertificate property, which is a collection object that contains the X.509 certificate from a request issued by a Web browser. If a browser uses a URL starting with https:// instead of http:// to connect to a server and the server requests client authentication, the browser sends the user's certificate with the request and ClientCertificate contains the certificate fields. Otherwise, the ClientCertificate object is empty. The syntax to retrieve the client certificate from the HTTP request is as follows:

```
Request.ClientCertificate( Key[SubField] )
```

The argument Key specifies the name of the certificate field to retrieve. Table 6-1 lists the names of the valid ClientCertificate fields. For example, the following piece of code obtains the entire distinguished name of the client certificate subject:

```
Request.ClientCertificate( Subject )
```

To obtain a particular attribute of the Subject or Issuer field, an optional subfield can be supplied to the Key argument. Table 6-2 lists the supported subfields. Subfields not listed in Table 6-2 can be retrieved by their ASN.1 identifier, which is

**Table 6-1**  Fields of a ClientCertificate Object

| Field | Description |
|---|---|
| Subject | A string that contains the subject distinguished name of the certificate, such as C=US, O=ACME, CN=John Smith. The Subject key can be used with a subfield to retrieve the value of each attribute of the distinguished name, as described in Table 6-2. |
| Issuer | A string that contains the distinguished name of the certificate issuer. The Issuer key can be used with a subfield to retrieve the value of each attribute of the distinguished name, as described in Table 6-2. |
| ValidFrom | The date on which the certificate becomes valid. This date follows VBScript format and varies with international settings, such as 12/13/97 11:59:59 PM in the United States. |
| ValidUntil | The date after which the certificate expires. |
| SerialNumber | A string that contains the certificate serial number as an ASCII representation of hexadecimal bytes separated by hyphens, such as 14-77-E2-00-01-00. |
| Certificate | The binary ASN.1 encoded of the entire certificate content. |
| Flags | A set of flags that provide additional client certificate information. The flag ceCertPresent indicates that a client certificate is present, and ceUnrecognizedIssuer signals that the last certificate in the certificate chain is from an unknown issuer. |

**Table 6-2**  Subfield Optional Parameters

| Subfield | Description |
|---|---|
| C | Country of origin |
| O | Company or organization name |
| OU | Organizational unit |
| CN | The common name of the user |
| L | Locality |
| S | State or province |
| T | Title of the person or organization |
| GN | Given name |
| I | A set of initials |

a list of numbers separated by a period. The following code segment, for example, retrieves the common name attribute of the subject distinguished name and the "2.99.99.1" field.

```
Request.ClientCertificate( SubjectCN )
Request.ClientCertificate( 2.99.99.1 )
```

## Access Control

A server-side ASP can leverage a client certificate to implement a variety of features, such as logging information about the client who has accessed the page, customizing the page depending on the information encoded in the certificate, enforcing authorization, and so on. The features implemented by an ASP depends on a particular application and might vary from one site to another. The ASP ClientCertificate collection object, however, makes it straightforward to access the different fields of a certificate and allows a developer to focus on implementing the application-specific logic as opposed to struggling with parsing the ASN.1 encoded certificate.

Listing 6-1 demonstrates a very simple ASP that uses a client's certificate for access control. The page retrieves the organization attribute of the subject distinguished name and denies access to the page if a client is not an employee of the ACME corporation. A more realistic access-control logic might check other fields of the certificate in addition to the organization name, such as the subject's common name or extension fields, and it may access an authorization database to determine the client's privileges.

**Listing 6-1** A Simple ASP for Access Control Using Certificates

```
<HTML>
<BODY>
<% if (Request.ClientCertificate( SubjectO )=="ACME") then %>
You are authorized to access this resource!
<% else %>
Sorry, you don't seem to be an authorized member of our organization.
</BODY>
</HTML>
```

# Mapping Clients to Windows NT Accounts with Certificates and Access Control

Setting NTFS file access permissions for individual files and directories is the most fundamental way to secure the contents of a Web site on a Windows NT File System (NTFS) hard disk partition. With NTFS permissions turned on, a user who wants to access a resource must belong to a Windows NT user group with the correct permissions for accessing and manipulating that resource. NTFS permissions also support various levels of access to a Web site's content, such as read-only and read-write.

You can configure your Web server to require users who attempt to access a restricted resource to have valid Windows NT account user names and passwords.

Each time a user attempts to access a restricted resource, the Web server authenticates her identity and ensures that she has a valid Windows NT account before it grants access. The server can authenticate a user by relying upon the **mapping** of the information contained in the user's certificate to a Windows NT user account. The mapping can be a **one-to-one mapping,** which maps a specific user's client certificate to an NT user account, or a **many-to-one mapping,** which relates multiple certificates to a single account. After the server successfully maps a user to an NT user account, it **impersonates** the user on the server by granting all the access privileges to the resource as if she had directly logged on to the server and accessed the resource. Chapter 15 will revisit this topic and provide step-by-step instructions on mapping procedures and impersonation.

The one-to-one mapping, however, requires the Web server to have access to a text (ASCII) copy of the user's certificate. Initially, the server may not have such a certificate and may require a setup or registration phase in which a user submits her certificate for mapping. Using ASP server-side scripting and the ClientCertificate object, it is straightforward to write a script that obtains a user's certificate, converts it to ASCII format, and saves it in a file, which can be subsequently mapped to an NT user account. Listing 6-2 illustrates such a script.

**Listing 6-2** An ASP Script to Convert a Client Certificate into an ASCII File

```
'Instantiate the ASP FileSystemObject to create a text file
'
Set fs = Server.CreateObject("Scripting.FileSystemObject")
'Create text file with append mode
'
Set os = fs.OpenTextFile("C:\cert.txt", 8, True )
'Extract encoded certificate text from certificate and
'encode text as 64-bit data
'
uue = "ABCDEFGHIJKLMNOPQRSTUVWXYZabcdefghijklmnopqrstuvwxyz0123456789+/"
os.WriteLine( "-----BEGIN CERTIFICATE-----" )
cer = Request.ClientCertificate("Certificate")
lcer = len(cer)
l = 0

for x = 1 to lcer step 3
 a1 = asc(mid(cer,x,1))
```

```
   if x+1 <= lcer then
     a2 = asc(mid(cer,x+1,1))
     if x+2 <=lcer then
       a3 = asc(mid(cer,x+2,1))
     else
       a3 = 0
     end if
   else
     a2 = 0
     a3 = 0
   end if


   os.Write mid(uue, (a1 and 252)/4 +1 ,1)
   os.Write mid(uue, (a1 and 3)*16 + (a2 and 240)/16 +1 ,1)

   if x+1 <= lcer then
     os.Write mid(uue, (a2 and 15)*4 + (a3 and 192)/64 +1 ,1)
       if x+2 <= lcer then
         os.Write mid(uue, (a3 and 63) +1 ,1)
       else
         os.Write "="
       end if
   else
     os.Write "=="
   end if


   l = l +4
   if l = 64 then
     os.WriteLine("")
     l = 0
   end if
next

if l > 0 then
```

```
os.WriteLine( "" )
end if


os.WriteLine( "-----END CERTIFICATE-----" )
```

## Mapping Client Certificates to Netscape Accounts and Access Control

Netscape servers do not support the notion of impersonation, and clients do not leverage native operating system accounts to control access to resources. Instead, Netscape servers internally associate an application-level access-control list (ACL) with an identified resource and support a rather sophisticated set of matching rules to define when access to a resource is allowed or denied. The rules use host names, IP addresses, user names, or groups to specify the enforcement criteria for access control. Netscape servers go through the following steps to determine whether a client is permitted to access a resource:

1. Is the client's IP address automatically allowed?

2. Is the client's host name automatically allowed?

3. Is the client identified (through password or valid certificate) as one of the allowed users from the database?

4. Is the client's IP address allowed if the user is one of the allowed users from the database?

5. Is the client's host name allowed if the user is one of the allowed users from the database?

As this sequence of steps indicates, Netscape supports three methods of authentication, namely host and IP address, user name and password, and client certificate. In **host and IP address authentication,** access to a resource is determined based on the IP address and host name of the client computer. Access control based on host and IP address is seamless because the user who is attempting to access a resource does not need to provide any authentication information. However, IP addresses are subject to spoofing attacks, and a secure deployment of this technique must be used.

A resource can be configured to require **user name and password authentication,** also called **basic authentication,** during which a user must provide his user name and password to gain access to the resource. Netscape servers store the list of users and groups in an LDAP database, which is either a file store on the Web server computer or an LDAP server on a remote computer. When a user submits his credentials (user name and password), Netscape uses the LDAP database to verify the submitted information. Note that this method of authentication is not seamless because a user must enter his user name and password before he can access a resource unless his name and password are already cached.

Netscape also supports the mapping of a client certificate to a user name and password account, and using the mapped account to enforce access control. If a resource requires **client certificate authentication** for access control, the first time a user accesses the resource he must enter his user name and password to establish his identity. Netscape then maps the user's certificate to his user name and password. After the mapping is established, the user can seamlessly access a restricted resource without ever needing to provide his login and password.

The server uses the client certificate to search the user LDAP database for the user's entry. If the entry is found, the server compares the certificate received against the certificate in the directory. (The details of these two steps may vary depending on the server configuration as described in the next section.) If the two certificates match, the server has successfully mapped the certificate to a user account, which is then used in conjunction with the ACL on the resource to allow or deny access.

## Certificate Mapping API

You can customize the process of mapping a client certificate to a user account by defining how the Netscape Web server searches the LDAP directory for a user's entry. Furthermore, you can specify whether the server should verify that the submitted client certificate matches the user's certificate in the directory. To customize the mapping process, you can edit the `<server_root>/userdb/certmap.conf` file. For details on configuring this file, refer to the *Managing Netscape Servers* manual, which is provided with each Netscape server.

You can also configure the mapping process programmatically through a set of API functions, referred to as the **Certificate Mapping API** functions. The main API function calls three other API functions to find a certificate subject's entry in the directory as described in the following. It first calls the **certificate mapping function,** which uses the submitted certificate and the `certmap.conf` file to generate a base distinguished name (DN) and a search filter. The base DN determines the entry from which the search should begin. For example, if the base DN is `<O=ACME; C=US>`, a subtree search looks through all entries in the directory that have `<O=ACME; C=US>` in their distinguished names.

The base DN and search filter is passed to the **certificate search function,** which actually searches the directory for the certificate subject's entry and returns a list of matching entries. Finally, the main API function calls the **certificate ver-**

**ification function** to narrow down the list to a single matching entry and verify that the entry has a certificate associated with it.

These three functions define the process of finding a certificate subject's entry in the directory. You can write your own version of these three functions, compile them into a shared library or a dynamic linked library (DLL), and modify the `certmap.conf` file to load your library and use the customized functions instead of the default API functions.

# Firewalls, Web Proxy Servers, and Digital Certificates

In this section we discuss how firewalls and Web proxy servers can protect an organization's internal network from the Internet. We also explain how proxy servers can leverage certificates and digital signatures to block untrusted downloaded code from reaching an internal network. You can refer to [CHAP95] and [CHES94] for excellent information about firewalls.

## Firewalls

A **firewall** is a collection of components that protects a network from another network. Typically, a firewall is placed between an internal local area network (LAN) and an external public network, such as the Internet. The internal network, which is secured from the external network by the firewall, is said to be sitting **behind the firewall.** A firewall has the following three properties [CHES94]:

- All inbound and outbound traffic between the two networks must pass through the firewall.

- Only authorized traffic, as defined by the local security policy, is permitted to pass.

- The firewall itself is immune to penetration.

Firewalls can be classified as packet filtering, circuit-level gateways, or application-level gateways. A **packet-filtering** firewall allows a packet to pass or drops a packet based on the packet's source address, destination address, or port number. For example, a packet-filtering firewall can protect a local network by blocking all inbound traffic from the Internet except for the traffic coming from a specified host. In a **circuit-level gateway,** a computer from one network connects to a TCP port on the gateway; the gateway then connects to another computer located on the other network. After the connection has been established, the gateway acts as a wire and simply copies the bytes between the two networks. An **application-level gateway** operates by allowing traffic intended only for a predefined set of applications to pass while denying access to all other applications. For example, an application-level gateway can be configured to pass only e-mail, HTTP, and file transfer protocol (FTP) traffic while blocking all other traffic.

## Web Proxy Servers

A **Web proxy server** is an application-level gateway used to protect an organization's internal network from the Internet while allowing the organization's employees to access the authorized resources on the Internet. The distinction between Web proxy servers and firewalls is blurring as Web proxy server vendors integrate other types of proxy servers, such as WinSock and SOCKS, and packet filtering into their products. The Microsoft Proxy Server 2.0 (http://www.microsoft.com/proxy) is a good example of such a proxy.

A Web proxy typically supports the HTTP, FTP, Gopher, and SSL protocols. A browser running on an internal network must first connect to the proxy if it needs to access a Web site on the Internet. The proxy then connects to the Web site on behalf of the browser, sends the request to the site, receives the response from the site, and forwards the response back to the browser. The proxy never reveals the topology or the IP address of the internal network, making it difficult for an attacker to penetrate the network behind the proxy.

A Web proxy can also allow a Web site behind the firewall to publish on the Internet without compromising the security of the internal network. Through a process called **reverse proxying,** the proxy impersonates a Web site to the external world by receiving requests from outside browsers and redirecting them to the Web site behind the proxy server. The proxy may cache the Web site pages and forward requests to the site only when necessary.

## Blocking Untrusted Code Using Digital Signatures

Because all the traffic between an organization's internal network and the Internet must pass through it, a proxy server has a unique vantage point in protecting internal computers from harmful code. The proxy server can detect potentially harmful downloaded code and eliminate it before it ever reaches an end user's computer. In its security policy, an organization can define what constitutes harmful code and configure its proxy server to block such code.

Digitally signed code can serve as an effective measure in determining what constitutes potentially harmful code. Recall from Chapter 4 that a software developer can use a commercial or an individual software publisher certificate to sign his code (Java applets, ActiveX controls, DLLs, etc.) prior to distribution via the Internet. A proxy server can automatically block all the unsigned code or code signed by an individual publisher. Furthermore, a proxy server can check the digital signature of signed code and remove any signed code whose signature does not verify, thus ensuring that code has not been tampered with while in transit. A proxy server can also maintain a list of trusted publishers and automatically remove code that is not signed by a trustworthy software developer or a commercial organization.

InterScan WebProtect from Trend Micro Incorporated is a good example of a product that blocks unsigned or untrusted downloaded code. InterScan WebProtect is actually an Internet Server Application Programming Interface (ISAPI) application that extends the functionality of Microsoft Proxy Server. This product performs a variety of other types of virus scans, such as cleaning FTP and HTTP virus-infected file transfers and detecting and removing known macro viruses on the fly. Refer to http://www. antivirus.com for more information on the InterScan WebProtect. Finjan Software http://www.finjan.com, Check Point Software Technologies http://www.checkpoint.com, and Network Associates http://www.networkassociates.com provide the same kind of filtering technology.

## Summary

Microsoft ASP technology makes it easy to obtain a client certificate on a server-side ASP page and retrieve its fields. The ASP page can use the certificate to implement the local security policy access control. Furthermore, a Microsoft Web server can map a client certificate to an NT user account and impersonate the client on the server computer, thus enforcing the operating system file permissions.

A Netscape Web server can also map a client certificate to a user account and use the mapped account in conjunction with ACLs to limit access to resources. Netscape provides a Certificate Mapping API to customize the process of mapping certificates to accounts.

Firewalls have been used extensively to protect organizations' internal networks from the Internet while permitting employees to access authorized Internet resources. A Web proxy server is a firewall that typically handles the HTTP and FTP connections, although the functionality of Web proxy servers is approaching that of firewalls as they are beginning to incorporate other capabilities, such as packet filtering. Proxy servers can use Authenticode technology as a basis for blocking untrusted (unsigned) code, code signed by individual publishers, or code signed by untrustworthy commercial publishers.

## References

[CHAP95]   Chapman, D., and E. Zwicky. *Building Internet Firewalls,* O'Reilly & Associates, Inc., Sebastopol, CA, 1995.

[CHES94]   Cheswick, W., and S. Bellovin. *Firewalls and Internet Security: Repelling the Wily Hacker,* Addison-Wesley, Reading, MA, 1994.

[GARF97]   Garfinkel, S., and G. Spafford. *Web Security and Commerce,* O'Reilly & Associates, Inc., Sebastopol, CA, 1997.

# Chapter
# 7
# Integrity and Open Standards

Digital certificates play an important role in assuring various aspects of the integrity of Internet secure communication systems. As we saw in Chapters 4–6, digital certificates are now being used in systems that address real-world communication threats faced by Internet browsers from downloaded, executable content, threats to e-mail authenticity and content confidentiality and threats leading to unauthorized access to Web services. To the user, rightly or wrongly, the certificates often represent assurances that the security of the system *as a whole* functions correctly and effectively. Before we discuss practical certificate issuing and management systems, we will consider security from an implementation-independent viewpoint.

To assure a measure of integrity in a certificate-based security system, implementers of certificate issuing systems or certificate-using security mechanisms may ensure that their products and services can conform to well-engineered, thoroughly reviewed, open standards that specify system and component behavior. As we shall see in this chapter, the applications described earlier share underlying standards and mechanisms and rely upon established integrity resulting from careful, open design and review process.

Summers [SUMM97] quotes Courtney and Ware as "urging using integrity 'to mean that an object has integrity if its quality meets expectations which were determined before the fact'." Attaining verifiable quality generally means measurement, process, and lots of engineering documentation. Some security quality philosophies define "real security" as occurring only when consumers read, understand, and analyze the various standards, software programs, and electronic devices for themselves. Others contend, more plausibly perhaps, that consumer confidence is a function of the recognition of the *brand(s)* attached to security products and services. Successful brands are assumed to lean toward ever-improving standards of quality and integrity, and market themselves on such properties to engage consumer confidence and loyalty.

To understand some of the integrity issues as they affect Internet public-key infrastructure (PKI) brands, in this chapter we provide a high-level introduction to the core technical standards for Internet application security mechanisms. We also overview emerging intervendor agreements concerning the use of PKI by standardized applications. In Part IV, we will address integrity in greater detail, as it relates to the processes of issuing, managing, using, and relying on certificates.

In the first section we discuss the role played by formal specification in security engineering. We reintroduce ASN.1, a system of notation for specifying functionality and syntax in an abstract manner. In the second section, we apply our understanding of formal notation to the specifications of several application-independent security mechanisms. The third section introduces certificate profiles that mandate practices for trust management and constraints on certificate content. Profiles are aimed at the formation of networks of CAs supporting particular classes of standardized security applications. Finally, the fourth section begins our analysis of the theoretical notion of trust. We describe how security applications using underlying protocols such as SSL need to manage "trust points" to securely connect users with no prior mutual relationship.

# ASN.1 and Formal Specification

One mark of a mature technology is that with but little change it can be applied to different problems and operate in different environments. The **Public-Key Cryptography Standards** (PKCS) are a suite of well-documented security specifications that form the basis of many commercial Internet security products and solutions. They are frequently referenced, reused, and refined in public standards addressing certificate-based security systems. In these and other ways they fit the definition of maturity.

As noted in Chapter 2, PKCS standardizes important cryptographic algorithm details. The cryptography elements of the series translate raw mathematics into interoperable schemes for application in cryptosystems. Using X.509 notation, they formally declare algorithms such as RSA to specify associated data formats, processing conventions, and identifiers. Other documents in the series specify algorithm-independent security mechanisms, interchange syntaxes, and programming techniques for interfacing computers to hardware cryptoperipherals. As of June 1998, a new project (PKCS #13) had recently begun formalizing an elliptic curve cryptosystem.

## Notation for Specification Languages

The discipline of communications security has a long history of research and development. Considerable effort has been spent in attempting to "know," by formal scientific and mathematical modeling, whether a given information system or communication component is secure. One of the more useful methods to come out of this program is **formal specification.** With this technique, designers express the behavior of the system in rigorous terms. To aid the process, they may first fashion custom languages,[1] introducing defined terms and constructs with which to express or analyze their designs.

An example of language specification to aid the specification of security mechanisms occurred during the standardization of the Secure Electronic Transaction (SET) standard. The initial SET working group, to which some of the authors of this book contributed their expertise, defined a presentation language. With terms formulated in response to business, technical, and security requirements and using PKCS security constructs as the underlying connectives, the notation enabled precise specification of the security mechanism requirements for protection bankcard-based payment protocols. The resulting language of structured security primitives enabled security analysis to be performed as the design took shape. This language eventually evolved into a set of SET-specific conventions facilitating layered specification and clear determination of security-critical processes.

In the security profession, the **Abstract Syntax Notation** (ASN.1) has been widely used to describe security protocols, interfaces, and service definitions. Well-known usage of the notation includes the X.500 Directory and X.400 Messaging systems, which include extensive security models. Although the OSI protocols underlying these systems have largely fallen by the wayside, as a design tool ASN.1 has survived and indeed grown in the standards-based security field because of its support for rigorous specification. Its notational facility for design abstraction works in tandem with the more basic ability to define syntax for message formats.

## Encoding, Programming, and Analyzing ASN.1

ASN.1 is a notation for expressing syntax of objects and messages. The Basic Encoding Rules (BER) enable data values described by abstract ASN.1 specifications to be represented in concrete form as an array of bytes. (A summary of the relationship between abstract syntax specification and encoding rules is given in Appendix A.[2]) Although programmers may choose to work directly with the encoding of ASN.1 types, generally, encoder/decoder routines are used to translate between the coded form and the native types of the programming system.

To the benefit of all users and vendors of a variety of computing platforms, BER- and DER-encoded[3] data is largely platform-independent, making the resulting

---

1. Using one language to specify another is not limited to academic formalism. English and other spoken languages are commonly represented via signing, written characters, phonemes, and as the "symbols" of lipreading. Each medium uniquely adds and subtracts information to and from the underlying message.

2. The summary of ASN.1 and the encoding rules provided in Appendix A are extracted from "The Layman's Guide to a Subset of ASN.1" (ftp://ftp.rsa.com/pkcs), with permission. This well-respected guide teaches developers about the notation system.

3. To ensure a canonical encoding of a value, some security mechanisms require use of a subset of BER, known as the Distinguished Encoding Rules (DER).

stream of bytes ideal for data transport between computers on open networks. In the main, application developers usually work with ready-built programming objects for high-level ASN.1 types, which shield them from the details of ASN.1 and encoding schemes, or they will use ASN.1 compilers.

## PKCS and ASN.1 Specification

The Public-Key Cryptography Standards (PKCS) are written in a highly structured form but with a minimum of notation. As mentioned earlier, the message syntaxes introduced are not specified in C++ or some other implementation language but in ASN.1. The message syntax descriptions are accompanied by annotations stated in highly technical English, which describe the procedures applications are expected to use to handle the specified data objects, and often define the intended semantics. Listing 7-1 shows an example of a partial syntax.

Nondevelopers need really only know that an **ASN.1 Abstract Syntax** is usually a specification of a list of typed elements that are either primitive (such as integers or octet-strings) or constructed (such as sets and sequences of additional elements). A **type hierarchy** is a collection of type declarations, normally organized in modules[4] that manage declaration scoping. Sequences of message elements forming a message to be transferred often take the notational form of a list of identified fields (e.g., version) and their data type (e.g., Version).

**Listing 7-1** An ASN.1 Type Example

```
SignedData ::= SEQUENCE {
        version                 Version,
        digestAlgorithms        DigestAlgorithmIdentifiers,
        contentInfo             ContentInfo,
        certificates            [0] IMPLICIT
                                ExtendedCertificatesAndCertificates
                                OPTIONAL,
        crls                    [1] IMPLICIT CertificateRevocationLists
                                OPTIONAL,
        signerInfos             SignerInfos
}
```

If you imagine the term SEQUENCE in Listing 7-1 to be the commencement of a C++ interface definition (perhaps named ISignedData) and each field to generate

---

4. PKCS is a little unusual in that the original standard did not use ASN.1 module notation.

a putField( ) and setField( ) method, you will have a fairly good understanding of ASN.1 usage.[5]

Similarly, should you see SET OF *<something>*, such as the SET OF Attribute shown in Listing 7-2, you can imagine this construct to be implemented as an unordered array of nonrepeating values, or for those who prefer pure interface notions, an enumeration object listing the interface pointers to each object representing a value.

Being abstract, a type such as SEQUENCE OF INTEGER is not limited to the built-in capabilities of programming platforms; the list of integers is logically infinite, as is the length of integer values. Of course, pragmatic designers will set constraints to limit the generality of such types. Modern ASN.1 specifications often formalize type size and processing constraints to induce greater interoperability between implementations that may otherwise impose different maximum values in practice. The formal specification of the SET protocol is an example where very elaborate ASN.1 type and value constraints are specified. In contrast, PKCS is written in simpler ASN.1.

In summary, ASN.1[6] plays a role similar to the one that external data representation (XDR) conventions play in industry-wide remote procedure call (RPC) technologies or the network data representation (NDR) conventions play in Microsoft's DCOM. The following excerpt from [KALI 93], a part of the RSA Data Security, Public-Key Cryptography Standards document suite developed by RSA Laboratories and partners, concludes our short introduction to ASN.1:

> It is a generally accepted design principle that abstraction is a key to managing software development. With abstraction, a designer can specify a part of a system without concern for how the part is actually implemented or represented. Such a practice leaves the implementation open; it simplifies the specification; and it makes it possible to state "axioms" about the part that can be proved when the part is implemented, and assumed when the part is employed in another, higher-level part. Abstraction is the hallmark of most modern software specifications.

> One of the most complex systems today, and one that also involves a great deal of abstraction, is Open Systems Interconnection (OSI, described in X.200). OSI is an internationally standardized architecture that governs the interconnection of computers from the physical layer up to the user application layer. Objects at higher layers are defined abstractly and intended to be implemented with objects at lower layers. For instance, a service at one layer may require transfer of certain abstract objects between computers; a lower layer may provide transfer services for strings of ones and zeroes, using encoding rules to transform the abstract objects into such strings. OSI is called an *open system* because it supports many different implementations of the services at each layer.

---

5. Microsoft Windows CryptoAPI2 uses precisely this technique when providing programmable ASN.1 object classes (see Chapter 3).

6. More background and tutorials on ASN.1-specified security objects can be found in the FIPS PUB 196, "Entity Authentication Using Public Key Cryptography" (http://csrc.nist.gov/fips/fips196.wp6).

OSI's method of specifying abstract objects is called ASN.1 (Abstract Syntax Notation One, defined in X.208), and one set of rules for representing such objects as strings of ones and zeroes is called the BER (Basic Encoding Rules, defined in X.209). ASN.1 is a flexible notation that allows one to define a variety of data types, from simple types such as integers and bit strings to structured types such as sets and sequences, as well as complex types defined in terms of others. BER describes how to represent or encode values of each ASN.1 type as a string of eight-bit octets. There is generally more than one way to BER-encode a given value. Another set of rules, called the Distinguished Encoding Rules (DER), which is a subset of BER, gives a unique encoding to each ASN.1 value.

# Security Mechanisms

To facilitate deployment of a security management infrastructure for public networks such as the Internet, various standardization bodies have made efforts to specify common message and information handling procedures. Application-independent and environment-independent security mechanism definitions and techniques for digital signatures and digital enveloping have been the satisfying result.

## PKCS Facilities, Mechanisms, and Profiles

There are currently 12 fully defined members of the PKCS family, published by RSA Data Security Inc. (http://www.rsa.com/pkcs). Although some of the series have been deprecated or merged, the standards represent the basis for the actual security technology deployed in multivendor Internet application security systems today.

The PKCS address the RSA (PKCS #1) and Diffie-Hellman (PKCS #3) and most recently Elliptic Curves (PKCS #13) algorithms. The PKCS #5 specifies a constructed algorithm for enciphering a data object using a content-encryption key derived from a password. Other PKCS elements specify syntax to represent RSA private keys in a system-independent manner (and potentially protected while stored by the PKCS #5 mechanism), and PKCS #12 specifies an interchange format designed to transfer certificate, trust, and private-key stores between computers.[7] The PKCS #11 standard specifies an API that developers can use as a standard interface to cryptosystem implementations on a wide range of peripherals such as PC cards or smart cards.

The PKCS #10 key certification request and PKCS #7 cryptographic message syntax standards are widely used in the security industry, embedded in such applications as Netscape Communicator and Microsoft Internet Explorer. PKCS #10 and PKCS #7 are used to assist key management and trust-point initialization of SSL,

---

7. Versions of PKCS #12 are used to transfer keying and other materials from Netscape Communicator to Microsoft Internet Explorer, for example.

S/MIME secure e-mail (see Chapter 5), and code-signing technologies such as Authenticode (see Chapter 4). (S/MIME v2 is simply a careful construction of PKCS #7 and MIME applied to the process of protecting MIME-encoded messages. Similarly, Authenticode is another construction of PKCS #7 that uses detached signatures to protect Windows object formats, Java class files, font files, etc.)

PKCS #7 is a general framework for signing and encrypting information objects. Similarly, PKCS #10 is a general framework subscribers or their agents use to request key certification. During profiling, these general standards are normally tuned to the specific threat-models of the environments and applications they are to serve.

## Key Certification Request—PKCS #10

The PKCS #10 standard specifies the format of a message that represents a subscriber's request for public-key certification and states the required handling procedures for message creation and processing. Normally, the response message from a certificate issuer is an X.509 certificate (possibly with other certificates) packaged in a PKCS #7 envelope. The ASN.1 notation for the CertificationRequest type is shown in Listing 7-2.

**Listing 7-2** PKCS #10

```
CertificationRequest ::= SEQUENCE {
          certificationRequestInfo        CertificationRequestInfo,
          signatureAlgorithm              SignatureAlgorithmIdentifier,
          signature                       Signature
}
CertificationRequestInfo ::= SEQUENCE {
          version                         Version,
          subject                         Name,
          subjectPublicKeyInfo            SubjectPublicKeyInfo,
          attributes                      [0] IMPLICIT Attributes
}
Version ::= INTEGER
Attributes ::= SET OF Attribute -- (NB an attribute is a name=value
pair)
SignatureAlgorithmIdentifier ::= AlgorithmIdentifier
Signature ::= BIT STRING
```

The PKCS documents rely upon a smaller number of ancillary declarations from the ITU-T X.500 and other OSI standards. These include the Name and

Attribute types. X.509 also governs interworking requirements controlling the use of signing and hash algorithms used to produce the content of a Signature value.

The PKCS #10 request message is a very simple object. It is intended to convey to a CA information relevant to a decision to certify a public key. In addition to ensuring the integrity of the message, the signature value may be used to determine that the message originator possessed the private-key, which pairs with the public key for which a certificate is being sought.

To support a multialgorithm world, the **SignatureAlgorithmIdentifier** field indicates which signing algorithm is used. The name of the originator and the public key have distinct fields; other information can be placed in the flexible, general-purpose **Attributes**[8] field, which may be used to extend the syntax at will.

The name of the subscriber may be expressed as an X.500 Name. This basic name form is an ordered sequence of relative distinguished names (RDNs), which are just structured sets of name/value pairs. Any naming schema and architecture can be imposed, and fully schematized and constrained directory-based name management is also supported. When used for naming, particular name-centric attribute types (such as emailAddress) are often used. In general, developers are free to invent new naming types, value formats, and schemas for attribute-based name forms, as required. Often the requested name, or a name derived from this value, will be listed in the certificate issued in response to the certification request.

Vendors such as Microsoft have quite properly profiled PKCS #10 specifying the use of particular attributes as PKCS #10 extensions. These enable subscribers or their agents to signal such data as "intended key purpose." This signal may generate a suitable constraint in the resulting certificate that signals the CA's intent that cryptographic mechanisms should limit use of the key. Similarly, ActiveDirectory-managed Names may limit the form of Names to highly constrained schemas to achieve interworking between this directory, the using directory-using applications, and certificate-using systems.

## Digital Signature Processes—PKCS7.SignedData

The structure of PKCS #7 is considerably more complex than PKCS #10, although its ideas are very simple. The PKCS #7 syntax enables you to generate a number of data streams.

The SignedData formatted stream implements a generalized, certificate-based digital signature process.[9] In its default mode, the stream envelops the payload data that has been signed. Then, the one or more digital signatures are affixed.

---

8. An Attribute is simply a name/value pair, similar to the query argument of a URL, such as latest or expired in http://www.jane.roe.com/cgi-bin/document.cgi?latest=true&expired=nothanx.

9. X.800 defines a digital signature as a relatively low-level cryptographic mechanism. We use the term *digital signature* in this book to mean the extension of that mechanism to enable use and/or reliance upon certificate validation during signature verification.

PKCS #7 specifies the generation of a signed-data content-type as a standard security mechanism for general-purpose digital signature creation:

> The signed-data content type consists of content of any type and encrypted message digests of the content for zero or more signers. The encrypted digest for a signer is a "digital signature" on the content for that signer. Any type of content can be signed by any number of signers in parallel. Furthermore, the syntax has a degenerate case in which there are no signers on the content. The degenerate case provides a means for disseminating certificates and certificate-revocation lists.

Listing 7-3 shows the syntax for the SignedData type.

**Listing 7-3** SignedData

```
SignedData ::= SEQUENCE {
        version             Version,
        digestAlgorithms    DigestAlgorithmIdentifiers,
        contentInfo         ContentInfo, -- the inner payload
        certificates        [0] IMPLICIT
                            ExtendedCertificatesAndCertificates OPTIONAL,
        crls                [1] IMPLICIT CertificateRevocationLists
                            OPTIONAL,
        signerInfos         SignerInfos
}
```

An individual signing block (SignerInfo) represents one affixed digital signature (see Listing 7-4). The generalized authenticatedAttributes field allows additional data to be protected by the signing process alongside the signed payload, as exploited in the CRS protocol (see Chapter 10). (Standardized CRS may use more modern versions of PKCS #7 than described here.) A signing block may identify a certificate that may be used to assist signature verification. Any supporting certificates and CRLs that the originator wishes to convey can be represented in SignedData value's certificates and crls fields. The set of affixed signatures is conveyed in the signerInfos field. SignerInfo is declared in PKCS #7, as shown in Listing 7-4.

**Listing 7-4** SignerInfo

```
SignerInfo ::- SEQUENCE {
        Version                     Version,
        issuerAndSerialNumber       IssuerAndSerialNumber, -- pointer
                                    to certs
```

```
        digestAlgorithm              DigestAlgorithmIdentifier,

        authenticatedAttributes      [0] IMPLICIT Attributes OPTIONAL,

        digestEncryptionAlgorithm    DigestEncryptionAlgorithmIdentifier,

        encryptedDigest              EncryptedDigest, -- the signature

        unauthenticatedAttributes    [1] IMPLICIT Attributes OPTIONAL }
EncryptedDigest ::= OCTET STRING -- an RSA signature of a hash value,
                                    in practice
```

A signed-data stream may be used without encapsulating any payload and without any affixed signature thereon. This is commonly known as a **Certs-Only** message. The leftover fields essentially represent a list of certificates and CRLs. This degenerate form of the syntax is ideal as a bearer of the certificate (chain) issued by a CA to a requesting subscriber, as mentioned in the discussion of PKCS #10.

PKCS #7 also specifies an **external signature** variant. Here, the signed data stream does *not* encapsulate the payload. To verify an external, or detached, signature, one must reassociate the signed-data stream with the data that was signed.

### Authenticode's Integrity Policy

As discussed in Chapter 4, Authenticode code signing tools place an encoded PKCS #7 external signature into the DLL, Java class file, or Cab archive being protected. This profile is perhaps one of the most advanced uses of the underlying capabilities of the PKCS #7 technology, in which it is tuned to a specific set of threats and risks. The following list identifies some of the aspects of the technical interworking and policy requirements laid down by the Authenticode specifications:

**PKCS #10/PKCS #7**   The tailored PKCS #10 certificate request process and PKCS #7 response message to key software publishers who will sign content.

**X.509**   The contents of the certificates used when verifying Authenticode signatures.

**Issuing policy**   The policy for identity confirmation under which authorized CAs issue the certificates to publishers of signed content.

**PKCS #7**   The form of the external signature(s) and supporting certificate chains embedded into the signed content (normally).

**Content attributes**   The extensions required for the signature block to indicate the type of content being protected and other properties.

**Integrity concept**   The control objectives of the integrity policy to be enforced during software code downloading, loading, and invocation during which signatures are verified.

The signature object placed in the protected object is usually complete, in the sense that it may contain the full set of certificates and an RSA signature. By verifying authenticity and by enforcing constraints signaled in the signature block, Windows-registered trust providers can enforce required certificate and code authorship validation policies.

Authenticode uses profiled certificates known as **software publisher credentials** (SPCs). It also imposes certificate issuing and revocation procedures upon CAs, who are required to obtain a legally binding **software publisher's pledge** from subscribers. CAs may also provide a related certificate status service and may be required to ensure that Dun & Bradstreet suitably rates an applicant for some grades of SPC. These signals, together with SignedData attributes, enable public and corporate trust administrators to manage the data integrity and authenticity policy for component and software download services for Windows and the Microsoft Internet Explorer platform.

In a recent extension, Authenticode2 uses PKCS #7's facility to bear an additional signed timestamp to the external signature. (See Chapter 4 for more general discussion.) The amendment also enables signed Java class cabinet packages to specify which permissions the object about to be loaded or executed must first obtain from the local authorization manager. The Java Virtual Machine's system class loader and security management classes can enforce the permission model when loading and calling code. Licensing and other concepts can also be derived from Authenticode.

## Digital Enveloping Processes—PKCS7.EnvelopedData

As mentioned earlier, the PKCS #7 standard enables a number of data streams to be generated. The EnvelopedData stream enables users to apply confidentiality services to payload data. The classical PKCS #7 digital enveloping process encrypts and envelops the payload and performs end-to-end exchange of a single content-encryption key to a set of intended recipients.

At first pass, one tends to think of confidentiality in terms of the raw secrecy of the protected payload. However, a confidentiality service more correctly responds to a policy idea. **Privileged access** to the information is **delegated** to those in whom confidence concerning the handling of the plaintext information is expressed by the originator, by virtue of their membership in the set of intended recipients. Confidentiality (in a trusted distributed information processing system) is really the originator's control over the future handling of data by the recipients upon its release from ciphertext form. Encryption is just a means of enforcing a policy-based authorization regime, better suited to distributed than to monolithic information processing systems.

To build such a confidentiality service, an integrity-protected public key distribution mechanism is required. In traditional PKCS #7, EnvelopedData uses the

RSA public-key algorithm to exchange an originator-generated content-ciphering key using the (authenticated) public keys of the intended recipients. The confidentiality service then relies upon the integrity of the certificate-based key distribution mechanism to protect against release of the content ciphering keys to other than authorized recipients.

The syntax for EnvelopedData is shown in Listing 7-5. The (enciphered) payload is present in encryptedContentInfo and the set of recipient tokens is present in RecipientInfos. The intended recipient obtains the content-encryption key for the enciphered content by uncovering the key from the relevant token using the local private keying material. PKCS #7 specifies the generation of an enveloped-data content-type as a standard security mechanism for general-purpose digital envelope creation:

> The enveloped-data content type consists of encrypted content of any type and encrypted content-encryption keys for one or more recipients. The combination of encrypted content and encrypted content-encryption key for a recipient is a "digital envelope" for that recipient. Any type of content can be enveloped for any number of recipients in parallel.

**Listing 7-5** EnvelopedData

```
EnvelopedData ::= SEQUENCE {
          Version                 Version,
          RecipientInfos          RecipientInfos,
          encryptedContentInfo    EncryptedContentInfo
}
```

An individual RecipientInfo is shown in Listing 7-6. Conventionally, issuerAndSerialNumber identifies the certificate used by the originator to authenticate the recipient's public key and to determine the recipient's policy for handling the sensitive payload whose release is ultimately controlled by that certificate. The secret content-ciphering key is present in encrypted form in the encryptedKey value (being deciphered using the recipient's private key), and the key exchange mechanism is identified using the KeyEncryptionAlgorithmIdentifier.

**Listing 7-6** RecipientInfo

```
RecipientInfo ::= SEQUENCE {
          version                 Version,
          issuerAndSerialNumber   IssuerAndSerialNumber, -- of the
                                  recipient certificate
```

```
        keyEncryptionAlgorithm    KeyEncryptionAlgorithmIdentifier,

        encryptedKey              EncryptedKey

}
```

## Nested Security Mechanisms in S/MIME

EnvelopedData is specified for use in securing personal e-mail by the S/MIME specification, along with similar specifications for SignedData. The inner payload of a PKCS #7 stream in the S/MIME profile is always a MIME-encoded object.

The combination of EnvelopedData and SignedData is an effective information object protection standard that is suitable for exchanging messages that require both authentication and confidentiality. An outer digital envelope may convey an inner digitally signed message only to a nominated set of recipients, without revealing to the world the identity of the originator. Of course, the originator may wish to include himself or herself as a recipient in order to be able to decrypt the enveloped message. Alternatively, third parties may countersign messages (encrypted or not) as they pass through value-added networks.

S/MIME and its version 2 conventions for layering PKCS security mechanisms are described more fully in Chapter 5.

## SET Specialization of PKCS #7

The Secure Electronic Transactions (SET) standard is a joint effort of the software industry and several credit card companies (VISA, MasterCard, JCB, and AMEX) to define a secure messaging standard for payment-service transactions passing over open networks. It is anticipated that the underlying security mechanisms and public key infrastructure can be used to protect other classes of financial service transactions, including home banking and bill presentment. Logically, a SET certificate can be used in a PKCS #7–based S/MIME protocol exchange just as well as it can be used in a PKCS #7–based SET protocol exchange. By exploiting the integrity afforded to the system as a whole by its reliance on a certificate-based security infrastructure, SET is positioned as a general-purpose transaction-grade infrastructure for secure electronic commerce.

The security requirements of SET-mediated payment systems are beyond the scope of this book, as are the detailed message flows (http://www.setco.org). However, as the SET technical design relied upon the requirements analysis underlying PKCS #7 and X.509, it is instructive to note how SET layers additional integrity semantics upon the basic security mechanisms. Furthermore, it is valuable to examine the analysis and design method used to produce this timely standard.

To address the needs of secure messaging and transactional security, a set of security primitives was specified. The underlying PKCS #7 security mechanisms have been revised and extended and duly profiled to support new cryptographic modes of operation. An X.509-based key management system was specified along with a conformance and accreditation program to enforce a certificate-based control system. Advanced use of ASN.1 specifies precise processing and interworking requirements and enables easier automated conformance testing of vendor implementations.

Appropriately protected messages are communicated between the parties in secure flows. The primitive security operators refine and extend the PKCS #7 digital signature and digital envelope mechanisms. Additional countermeasures address threats due to the transactional environment, replay and receipt vulnerabilities inherent in connectionless message-switching networks, and the need to provide selective field confidentiality with varying strengths of encipherment. With only minor changes, SET was able to profile PKCS #7 mechanisms to satisfy these sophisticated requirements for a transaction-grade messaging infrastructure. Whereas S/MIME addresses the secure point-point e-mail problem, the transaction-ready SET protocol addresses the secure multiparty messaging problem.

Readers are referred to [SET Book 3] for definitions of the SET signing and encryption primitives and the architecture of the message-switching system in which they serve to protect and enforce the information flows required for transactional security. Additional description of SET certificates is presented later in this chapter.

## Certificate Profiles

As described in Chapter 3, X.509 is a general-purpose standard that defines a framework for authentication infrastructures supporting communication systems. As intended by the ISO international agreement process, various groups have specified profiles representing concrete agreements concerning particular integrity requirements. A **certificate profile** is a specification of certificate field content in terms of the required syntax and semantics. It may also include specification of the procedures for creating and processing certificate values.

A certificate profile may include conditions for determining whether aspects of implementation are conforming to requirements. Advanced profiles tuned to specific operational infrastructure deployments may also delineate the organization, roles, and procedures of the CAs issuing certificates, revoking registrations, and handling compromise. In many cases, other elements of the certification process address factors such as evaluation criteria for trusted engineering and accreditation of authorities by auditors.

The purposes and assumptions of a functional profiling activity are often diverse. Requirements for certificate profiles can range from the need to enforce mandatory security policies across the four military services to the need to maintain legally protected client/attorney or doctor/patient confidences. The risks to data communications security in a given community often drive the design of a certificate profile. Risk management is perhaps the dominant design criterion. Careful statement of the assumed operating conditions of the users' equipment and the training and capabilities of the users and administrators to respond to normal and adverse situations must be addressed.

We will review two X.509 certificate-profiling initiatives,[10] and highlight how they uniquely address aspects of the key distribution problem. (Appendix B describes the various certificate extensions supported in Microsoft Windows products, most of which correspond to public intervendor standardization efforts):

**PKIX-1**   The IETF's PKIX working group has specified a draft certificate profile aimed at satisfying an application-independent certificate-based key distribution mechanism. This profile is intended to be used by Internet standard applications.

**SET**   The SET standard specifies the contents of cardholder, merchant, and payment gateway certificates, along with the content of certificates issued to SET CAs. SET deploys a fixed hierarchy of issuing authorities and carefully regulates the intended purposes for which particular certificates should be used. The SET profile invents engineering mechanisms for managing certificate distribution and revocation in huge communities.

## PKIX-1

The Internet Engineering Task Force's Public Key Infrastructure, using X.509 (PKIX) working group has largely agreed upon a certificate profile whose design aims to fashion a robust infrastructure for classical Internet applications. PKIX-1 is one of a number of draft documents that describes the working group's current round of agreements.

### Profile Content

PKIX-1 addresses the following topics in its seven main sections:

**Section 1**   A profile of the format and semantics of certificates and certificate revocation lists for the Internet PKI. The processing of certification paths in the Internet environment is stated.

**Section 2**   The requirements that inspired the creation of the profile and the assumptions that affect its scope.

---

10. See also http://www.armadillo.huntsville.al.us/Fortezza_docs/sdn706r30.doc and the related /Fortezza_docs/appreq11.doc file for a certificate profile of a command and control system.

**Section 3**   The architectural model and the relationship to previous IETF and ISO standards.

**Section 4**   The tailored X.509 version 3 certificate.

**Section 5**   The tailored X.509 version 2 certificate revocation list (CRL).

**Section 6**   The specification of a PKIX path validation procedures and requirements.

**Section 7**   Description of procedures for identification and encoding of public key materials and digital signatures.

## *Integrity Design*

The original assumptions driving the IETF's vision of an Internet PKI are outlined in Section 2 of an early version of the PKIX-1 specification (see http://www.ietf.org/internet-drafts/draft-ietf-pkix-ipki-part1-07.txt or succesor versions). Whereas other profiles can often assume fixed infrastructure (e.g., a military command and control system deployment) or a commercial closed environment of contracted parties (e.g., SET), PKIX must include in its scope the needs of the residential Internet community worldwide. The equipment in use across the Internet comes in all shapes and sizes, degrees of conformance to standard, functional capabilities, and quality. Maximum interoperability is the engineering goal that traditionally drives the design of Internet standards. The operational culture asserts that power and authority should be maximally decentralized and user experimentation encouraged. At the same time, the users increasingly expect the underlying network to satisfy their expectations for quality electronic commerce, banking, and entertainment.

To help address the needs of such an environment, the PKIX-1 designers thoughtfully documented the characteristics and assumptions used when formulating the profile. These assumptions help classify the high-level integrity goals of the key distribution mechanism underlying the PKIX Internet PKI:

> **2.1 Communication and Topology:** The expected user's environment is characterized as: *"The users of certificates will operate in a wide range of environments with respect to their communication topology, especially users of secure electronic mail.* ***This profile supports users without high bandwidth,*** **real-time IP connectivity, or high connection availability.** *In addition, the profile allows for the presence of firewall or other filtered communication."* (Emphasis added.)

> **2.3 User Expectations:** The designers express the design assumptions concerning the sophistication of the users, who might be described as the general-public: *"Users*

*of the Internet PKI are people and processes who use client software and are the subjects named in certificates. These uses include readers and writers of electronic mail, the clients for WWW browsers, WWW servers, and the key manager for IPSEC within a router.* **This profile recognizes the limitations of the platforms these users employ and the sophistication/attentiveness of the users themselves.** *This manifests itself in minimal user configuration responsibility (e.g., root keys, rules), explicit platform usage constraints within the certificate, certification path constraints which shield the user from many malicious actions, and applications which sensibly automate validation functions."* (Emphasis added.)

**2.4 Administrator Expectations:** The PKIX-1 designers make risk judgments concerning the needs to bound the impact of infrastructure compromise due to the training of the parties who operate CAs: *"As with users, the Internet PKI profile is structured to support the individuals who generally operate Certification Authorities (CAs).* **Providing administrators with unbounded choices increases the chances that a subtle CA administrator mistake will result in broad compromise.** *Also, unbounded choices greatly complicates the software that must process and validate the certificates created by the CA."* (Emphasis added.)

PKIX-1 specifies many innovative and forward-looking mechanisms designed to enable the Internet PKI to support electronic commerce and lead the formation of a global public PKI. Its greatest asset and its greatest liability simultaneously lie in its attempt to specify a general public infrastructure that meets a diverse range of expectations of quality. It makes many assumptions upon conforming implementation of certificate-path processing by end-systems and a general willingness of end users to cede control over their use of public-key cryptography to third-party certificate issuers. More importantly, the standard (or at this time, the standard-to-be) allows itself to be substituted or augmented by organizations with an identified need for more specialized assurances, suggesting that mass-market certificate-using end-system implementers (such as those producing Internet browsers) will need to plan for a world of multiple-certificate profiles.

## SET

In late 1996, VISA and MasterCard began to work together to lead the banking and software industry in the definition of a Secure Electronic Transaction (SET) standard. The purpose of the protocol specification was to interface Internet users to the credit-card payment networks via SET-enabled merchants. The certificate profile of SET is described in [SET Book 2], sections 4 and 5.

SET was the first attempt to specify an open network payment service using an X.509 v3–based PKI. From the outset, the designers sought to use public-key certification to ensure the system operated with sufficient integrity to meet the audit standards required of financial services offered to the general public.

## *Profile Content*

SET version 1 addresses the following topics related to its certificate profile:

**4.1 X.509 certificate definition**    The certificate definition describes the fields used in the SET X.509 certificate. SET's profile is perhaps the most prescriptive public profile to date. It specifies a naming schema and naming architecture for the X.500 Names used to describe certificate subjects and issuers, and SET-specific Cardholder IDs.

**4.2 X.509 extensions**    The SET specification of X.509 profiles the standard X.509 extensions in terms of their mandatory syntax, presence, or processing requirement when interpreted in the context of SET message processing and certificate issuing. The certificate policy extension is particularly vital as it identifies governing policy in terms of a formal, hierarchical certification domain exhibiting strict delegation of authority.

**4.3 SET private extensions**    The private extensions to X.509-format SET certificates include capability indications (e.g., tunneling of encrypted messages is supported) and requirement signals (e.g., cardholder certificates are required). Custom extensions to the format, which coordinate the activities of end-systems sending and receiving SET messages, are defined. Private extensions also are used to classify and name subjects in the payment industry.

**4.4 Certificate profiles**    The formal section of certificate type profiles lists each X.509 extension and identifies how/when they are used for each of the different types of certificates used in SET, for each type of key (signing or encryption).

**5 Certificate revocation list and BrandCRLIdentifier**    SET goes beyond the CRL mechanisms established in the X.509 Authentication Framework by specifying use of a BrandCRLIdentifier together with a profile of X.509 CRL v2–format extensions. The BrandCRLIdentifier (BCI) was created for SET. It lists the current CRLs within a given brand (e.g., VISA). In many ways, this construct distributes knowledge on which CRL the latest revocation information is located.[11]

## *Integrity Design*

The designers of the SET certification profile used the certificate policy extension as a fundamental tool for controlling transactional integrity in a multiparty system and to organize the various categories of player in the bankcard-based payment industry. The expectations of both the banking community and consumers are high,

---

11. One can see a future use for this structure in distributing location information enabling effective, partitioned, and replicated CRL handling for very large subscriber and relying-party communities.

as are those of regulators and ombudsmen. The nature of the credit industry is to perform risk arbitrage on a massive scale; governments worry about money supply targets; consumers expect statutory rights and limitations of financial exposure due to fraud; controlling financial liability and stability is of paramount concern.

To address the liabilities, SET documents the roles played by each authority governed by SET policy. The roles and requirements for exercising integrity control during cardholder certificate issuing are highlighted in the following list with short quotations from the VISA/MasterCard SET standard [SET Book 3]:

**Root certificate authority**   SET operates a strict hierarchical domain of authority governed by policy. Risk management at the top of such systems is crucial, leading SET to manage the threats by requiring that "the Root CA (RCA) is *kept off-line under extremely tight physical controls.*" (Emphasis added.)[12] As public-key cryptography enables keying material to be public without inherent risk of compromise for long periods, new brand CA certificates and new root certificates will be issued only occasionally and probably in a ceremonial fashion.

**Brand CA**   As an example of a shared industry initiative, it is important that each competitive payment network (MasterCard, AMEX, etc.) is wholly independent operationally, leading SET to enable autonomy yet prescribe required structure in each subdomain. "The Brand CA (BCA) allows for some degree of *autonomy in each Brand's certificate management* [and is] operated under tight physical controls and will be used to *issue Geopolitical and/or Cardholder, Merchant, or Payment Gateway CA certificates ...*" (Emphasis added.)

**Cardholder CA**   The cardholder CA (CCA) responds to subscriber requests for certificates linked to their cardholder account. As part of performing authentication management (see Chapter 8), "the CCA *maintains relationships with card issuers* to allow for the verification of Cardholder accounts." As part of its role in performing key management (see Chapter 8), a CCA does not generate CRL for cardholders, although SET does require CCAs to accept responsibility for the critical distribution of CRLs issued by the root, brand, geopolitical, and payment gateway CAs.

SET is a complex specification. It relies upon many of the lessons learned from large-scale systems standardization in exploiting formal specifications. In many ways, it continues the security model and approach laid down in the X.400 (1988) messaging standard. It does not make the mistake of introducing wholly new messaging layer technologies, however. SET is to be provided to consumers via Internet mass-market

---

12. Formal policy models can differ in their treatment of root keys. For example, the VeriSign Root is a registration authority, not a certification authority.

products (such as Windows, Java, and Internet browsers) using the World Wide Web and e-mail for transport. SET mixes operating policy and key distribution to great effect, using formal authority delegation to structure the traditional roles of the vertical banking/payment industry. SET is especially tuned to solve very concrete multiparty, regulated liability issues, and overlaps considerably with PKIX-1 in its use of certificate policy mechanisms and system accreditation to assure the public of service quality and security.

## Trust Points

Commencing with a quotation from [SHAN48], Edgardo Gerck leads an Internet discussion http://www.mcg.org.br/trustdef.txt with the assertion, used with permission, that:

> *In Information Theory, information has nothing to do with knowledge or meaning. In the context of Information Theory, information is simply that which is transferred from a source to a destination, using a communication channel. If, before transmission, the information is available at the destination then the transfer is zero. Information received by a party is that what the party does not expect—as measured by the uncertainty of the party as to what the message will be.*

> Shannon's contribution here goes far beyond the definition (and derived mathematical consequences) that "information is what you do not expect." His zeroth-contribution (so to say, in my counting) was to actually recognize that unless he would arrive at a real-world model of information as used in the electronic world, no logically useful information model could be set forth!

> Now, in the Internet world, we have come to a stand off: either we develop a real-world model of trust or we cannot continue to deal with limited and fault-ridden trust models, as the Internet expands from a parochial to a planetary network for e-commerce, EDI, communication, etc.

> And, what would be this "real-world model of trust" for the Internet world? Here, akin to Information Theory, trust has nothing to do with friendship, acquaintances, employee-employer relationships, loyalty, clearance, betrayal and other hard to define concepts.

> In the concept of Generalized Certification Theory (see http://www.mcg.org.br/cie.htm), trust is simply "that which is essential to a communication channel but which cannot be transferred from a source to a destination using that channel."

Dr. Gerck's underlying observation that the integrity of certificate-based security systems (such as the X.509 Authentication Framework) hinges upon the very notion of trust is very valuable.[13] Although trust is defined by the X.509 standard in terms of integrity—a CA is expected to reliably perform its user authentication and certificate registration duties—this does little to establish any *conceptual* properties of trust itself as a basis for building secure *systems*.

As anticipated by the ISO process, local environments are expected to profile and tailor the X.509 Authentication Framework. In this way, they can address the integrity requirements of national, application, community, or personal needs. ISO data communications standards are generally constructed assuming that islands of user interoperability will form, and the economic or social benefits of networking will inevitably cause systems to link together over time. X.509 does not impose a particular economic or social model of integrity, however. Such telecommunications standards generally limit their scope to stating technical matters. Models of integrity and trust in a particular space are best left to the communities of interest, governments, and industry forums, which are most familiar with these groups' specific needs.

Given the *laissez-faire* trust doctrine pervading X.509, how is trust being managed in practice in the first generation of X.509-based, Internet-consumer security products? What trust standards are being established? What do they address? To answer these sorts of questions, we examine what is perhaps the most highly accessible form of public-key cryptography: the application of Netscape's Secure Socket Layer (SSL) to protect the World Wide Web's HTTP. (The profiled combination of SSL and HTTP is known as **HTTPS**.) In HTTPS, SSL works to resolve secure URLs such as https://www.netscape.com, as discussed in detail in Chapters 14 and 15. We focus our analysis of SSL in terms of the **trust policies** that need to be formulated and the **trust decisions** that must be made. Then, we can address the central issue of all certificate-based security systems: **trust points.**

## Netscape Secure Socket Layer

The SSL protocol[14] establishes secure connections between two TCP protocol machines. In the form of HTTPS, it is often closely associated with electronic commerce Web sites that enable users to post such personal details as credit card numbers over encrypted sessions when buying mail-order goods and services. Accessing resources at HTTPS URLs normally causes SSL security to be invoked in both client and at the server.

---

13. Gerck is a member of the Meta-Certificate Group (MCG). MCG is an international nonprofit open group with Web site at http://www.mcg.org.br.

14. See http://search.netscape.com/newsref/ssl/3-SPEC.html for an SSL specification and http://search.netscape.com/newsref/std/tunneling_ssl.html for SSL tunneling information.

An Internet browser initiates one or more SSL sessions, negotiating an agreed-upon set of security services via standardized connection and session handshake procedures. Services might include data integrity and user-data confidentiality. Upon completion, the agreed-upon security services are provided for both user and housekeeping SSL-protocol data alike.

Application data streams generated by HTTP, NNTP, POP3, and SMTP sessions are nominally protected by an SSL protocol layer implemented by a socket provider, having passed through a transport layer interface such as WinSock. Generally, mass-market implementations establish a conventional unprotected socket connection and then apply the negotiated security services to the data streams before transferring the output to the communications system via the socket. As the SSL protocol does not require any particular handling of certificates exchanged during the handshake, implementations generally address trust policy and trust decisions for themselves.

### The SSL handshake

The **SSL handshake** is an exchange of cryptographically protected messages that establishes a security context for subsequent information flows. The design ensures the integrity of the establishment procedure and agrees on all shared keys. The precise flow and sequence of messages depends upon the cipher-suites being negotiated by the parties according to their own capabilities and requirements.

By relying upon certificates to distribute the public-keys of the parties, the HTTPS application can offer the user assurances of peer-entity authentication, data integrity, and (optionally) data confidentiality. User and server certificates are exchanged and validated, as required, during each handshake procedure; the authenticated public keys normally act to ensure a secure handshake procedure.

To control the integrity of the key distribution mechanism, common cipher-suites enable chains of certificates to be exchanged, terminating at a special public key known as a **root key,** or at a self-signed public key acting as a root key. Root keys can be as globally known or locally known as a certificate-user's risk-management strategy demands. In certificate-based key distribution systems, a root key is the basic embodiment of a trust point.

The interaction of trust processes with the SSL handshake's optional reliance on certificates is particularly visible during SSL client authentication. **SSL Client Authentication** is a server-invoked handshake procedure that enables that server to identify and authenticate an originator of SSL session data. The security mechanism used to provide client authentication depends upon the cipher-suites chosen by the two parties. For RSA-based users, client authentication proofs rely upon digital signatures computed over session variables. For Diffie-Hellman–based communities using certificates, the proofs are tied to the process of agreeing upon the SSL master secret to be used by both parties.

How does the client know which certificate to send? How does the server know which certificate to ask for or to accept? These tactical questions concern trust policy, trust decisions, and trust points administered by end-systems. What happens when a certificate expires during a long session? Can anyone issue a certificate containing my public key? Must one use the same certificate with a particular server every time? These strategic questions concern trust management and trust models normally administered by the security management systems of the communicating parties.

## Trust-Point Discovery

Earlier we introduced the fundamental notion of a trust point. A **trust point** is a public key pertaining to a CA trusted to reliably authenticate subjects prior to issuing the digital certificates used during entity authentication. That CA is often a trusted third party. A **trust decision** is made at the moment a user chooses to rely upon the integrity policy associated with a trust point. **Trust-point discovery** is the process of evaluating CA integrity disclosures in light of the trust policies used by the communicating parties to reach agreement upon a *common* trust point. A **trust policy** is a set of local security policy rules that control how users delegate their trust during trust-point discovery.

In the SSL world of mass-market browsers, trust points are often represented as records in a local database of public keys. Membership in the list means that an automated browser will, in practice, rely on the integrity associated with a given trust point, and thereby help secure the key distribution mechanism and the security context. The browser manufacturers embed some trust points. Users may also add trust points manually at will and may be prompted to do so upon receiving SSL handshake messages. The combination of administrator configuration, user interface dialogues to assign trust, and user vigilance constitutes today's process for making trust decisions.

As a part of the client authentication message exchange, the SSL server may indicate the trust points that it is willing to accept as suitable for its purposes. This list currently takes the form of the names of CAs issuing user certificates or managing trust networks (see Chapter 12). The client uses the references to either rapidly obtain a certificate from one of the associated CAs or, more conventionally, selects a certificate that has already been issued.

The trust-point discovery process available in today's products tends to be rather limited. Almost invariably, the list of server-supplied names is simply a preconfigured list at the server; no intelligence is used to select which trust points should be indicated on a particular session handshake. Similarly, selection by the client of a matching certificate tends to be delegated to interactive users for the first time, and this decision is often automatically assumed for subsequent handshakes with the same server.

## Summary

Interoperable security systems rely upon implementers to produce conforming implementations of well-analyzed technical standards to ensure the integrity of the security system. Formal security mechanisms may be used to document technical security specifications, such as the Public-Key Cryptography Standards (PKCS). PKCS uses ASN.1 as its notational basis.

Standard security mechanisms include public-key certification requests, digital signatures, and digital envelopes. PKCS documents specify the underlying facilities, mechanisms, and algorithm profiles, addressing specifically RSA (PKCS #1), Diffie-Hellman (PKCS #3), and most recently Elliptic Curves (PKCS #13).

The PKCS #10 key certification request and PKCS #7 cryptographic message syntax standards are used widely in the security industry and are embedded in such applications as Netscape Communicator and Microsoft Internet Explorer.

The PKCS #10 Certificate Request usually generates an X.509 certificate in response, packaged, possibly along with other certificates, in a return PKCS #7 envelope for transport. The SignedData syntax may also be used as a digital signature service. The degenerate "certs-only" SignedData syntax provides a means for disseminating certificates and certificate revocation lists.

The EnvelopedData syntax may be used as a digital enveloping process. It enables users to apply confidentiality services to data. EnvelopedData uses public-key cryptography to exchange or agree upon the secret enciphering keys, and it relies upon certificate-based key distribution to protect the exchange and agreement mechanisms.

An X.509-based key management system may be specified in a PKCS #7 profile to enforce a public-key–based control system via conformance and accreditation processes. SET certificates are examples of profiled X.509 certificates, which are designed to be used alongside SET primitive security operators that have refined and extended the basic PKCS #7 digital signature and digital envelope mechanisms.

A certificate profile is a specification of certificate field content in terms of the required syntax and semantics. It may also include specification of the procedures for creating and processing certificate values. The risks to data communications security in a given community often drive the design of a certificate profile. PKIX-1 and SET are two examples of profiles that address the needs of their interworking communities.

PKIX-1 addresses a world in which the equipment in use comes in all shapes and sizes, degrees of conformance to standards, functional capabilities, and quality. Maximum interoperability is the engineering goal. The SET profile mixes operating policy and key distribution, using formal authority delegation to structure the traditional roles of the vertical banking/payment industry. SET is careful to address liability questions, and it overlaps considerably with PKIX-1 in its use of certificate policy.

The Netscape Secure Socket Layer (SLL) provides data integrity and user-data confidentiality services. User certificates are exchanged and verified during the SSL handshake procedure to perform certificate-based key distribution. A root key is the basic embodiment of a trust, and it represents integrity policy. In today's systems SSL delegates trust handling to the careful execution of integrity-inducing policies of the CAs issuing the certificates. In the trust-point discovery process, a trust point is a public key that pertains to a CA. A trust policy is a set of local security policy rules that control how users delegate trust during trust-point discovery.

# References

[KALI93] Kaliski, Burton S. *A Layman's Guide to a Subset of ASN.1, BER and DER*, Technical note, revised November 1, 1993.

[SET Book 3] SET, *Secure Electronic Transaction Specification Book 3: Formal Protocol Definition*, Version 1.0, May 31, 1997.

[SHAN48] Shannon, C. *A Mathematical Theory of Communications*, Bell Systems Technical Journal, 1948; 27.

[SUMM97] Summers, R. *Secure Computing—Threats and Safeguards*, McGraw-Hill, New York, 1997, http://ourworld.compuserve.com/homepages/rsummers/tableofc.htm.

# Part III
# Security Management Practice

Part III is motivated by a desire to empower the decision-maker attempting to make sense of the public-key infrastructure deployment choices offered by the emerging security industry.

Certificate-based security systems have been on the technology shelf for many years alongside multimedia e-mail and Internet telephony. The integrity benefits of digital certificates are just beginning to be explored by corporations seeking to invest in process automation and critical networking infrastructure. Decision-makers are excited by the prospect of finally being able to enter the world of electronic commerce using mostly automated security management. Users are also excited at the extension of privacy guarantees; California Republic residents have additional means to assert their Constitutional right to expect privacy, for example.

In this part we concentrate on institutional use of PKI systems. As with many markets at the beginning of their mainstream appreciation, specialist and generalist vendors alike are gearing up to compete for market share.

How is a middle manager charged with deploying secure e-mail throughout the company to make sense of the options? What are the options? How can you see beyond the marketing and obtain a clear view of the requirements that a product, service, or some product/service hybrid satisfies?

The three chapters of this part address the practicalities of security management using digital certificates, as seen through the eyes of some of the businesses seeking to supply technology, know-how, expertise, and solutions in an increasingly mainstream security market. In profiling these companies' offerings, we have the goal of enabling readers to learn a little about the nature of the underlying requirements. The precise nature of particular products should be determined by contacting the vendors directly.

In Chapter 8 we consider the big picture of certificate-based security management systems. We profile several certification authority product and key management solutions from famous-name and lesser-known suppliers. From a wide range of possible candidates, we have picked a set of products that embodies distinct visions of the management process. As a result, buyers should be well positioned to formulate for themselves criteria that will enable them to determine required features.

In Chapter 9, we present a profile of commercial services that perform public-key infrastructure management on behalf of customers. Without comparing the market players, we attempt to decipher the messages that providers are currently using to define the buyer's problem space.

In Chapter 10, we consider the functional model underlying distributed security management based on digital certificates. Different roles and responsibilities naturally occur when issuing and managing certificates. Some companies will prefer to perform some or all of these roles in-house. Others may outsource high-assurance data processing, while keeping decision-making and policy formulation under tight local control. Chapter 10 highlights the VeriSign OnSite initiative and various underlying technologies used in distributing security management to explore the promise of local registration authorities and joint risk management.

Readers are also encouraged to refer to the projects presented in Parts V and VI to obtain practical experience on using and issuing digital certificates.

# Chapter
# 8

# Security Management Solutions

Security architects design management policies and practices to administer enterprise-wide control systems. As we will discuss in detail in Part IV, control systems are used in security management to enable *policy-based* administration.

A security management system design methodology can aid the enterprise system architect in deploying certificate-based security systems. Security solutions meet enterprise-specific needs by carefully integrating certificate technology with traditional business transaction processing systems. Generally, the architects, designers, and their buyers will use off-the-shelf security management products to implement their systems, or they will use the services of specialized providers. Regardless of technology or service provider, the security system will require solution-level design. By focusing on security policy specification as a design methodology, one can use its focus on organizational management and system design principles to exploit certificate-based security systems for their true worth.

A security management system's protection philosophy characterizes the culture of control required by the enterprise to protect and share its information and system assets. By functionally modeling the overall information system along with its operational environment, system architects can schematize specific goals and problem constraints, identify control objectives, and finally design a solution that implements the security policy and enforces the required regime of organizational control.

Certificate servers and similar off-line workstation-based products are an emerging class of security management product. They help organizations tap the potential of certificate-based key distribution to manage and enforce workgroup security in intranet and extranet scenarios. By implementing information system security management processes using configurable or programmable certificate servers, designers can directly instrument their own control regimes. Alternatively, by using certificate and security management toolkits, developers can implement specialized certificate issuing and management systems that feature requirements absent from standard products or services.

## Design Methodology for Intranet CA Solutions

Certificate servers will probably soon become widely deployed in corporate intranets. The current and coming generation of certificate server product is either tightly coupled with the network operating system login process or operates from a central data center as an enterprise server on the corporate LAN. It is to be expected that solution and key management service companies will step into the design space to assist enterprises specify, deploy, and configure their systems. Some hybrid solutions will opt to use local registration authority (LRA) methods and protocols, outsourcing some specialized or expensive parts of the local CA management process to service providers as appropriate.

A solution-centric security management system design methodology has as its outcome a specification of the complete security system covering enterprise needs in the environment under control. The design process should describe four aspects of the target system:

**Concept**    A clearly articulated concept-of-operations statement should be drawn up stating how the certificate-based security system meets the security policy. It should also state which methods will be used operationally to control and coordinate the various security management procedures (see Chapter 13).

**Mission**    A mission-specific security policy should be formulated that identifies the control objectives to be established by the organization and sets expectations of the protection to be afforded to each category of asset. Control objectives are statements of intent for an organization's security management practices. They should be developed responding to generic vulnerabilities, such as minimizing the impact of CA compromise or ensuring accountability of trusted personnel.

**Model**    The distributed information system requiring protection should be modeled in terms of its discrete information processing and communication components.

**Distribution**    A functional and physical distribution strategy should be formulated after performing a thorough risk analysis. The risk analysis[1] should identify and quantify threats to the distribution of information system components across communication links in the target environment.

Identifying operational threats and the organization's control objectives in a highly systematic manner should deliver flexible, yet effective, policy-based security management solutions.

---

1. See an overview of risk management at http://isd.redstone.army.mil/ar38019/ar38019ch5.html.

# Policy-Based Design

The scope of security policy is very wide. Interested readers might consult the wide-ranging Government Accounting Office critique at http://www.us.net/softwar/gao2.html of U.S. government agency security to learn how policy should saturate the very fabric of user organizations.

For the purpose of illustration, we now attempt to provide an example, in very summarized form, that addresses the suggested methodology of design. For each aspect described in the preceding section, we characterize an actual system as best we can—given the paucity of citable source material. We feature the Electronic Key Management System (EKMS) used by portions of the U.S. military for a wide range of cryptographic keying needs.[2] This example is used purely as an academic model, however. Our objective is merely to enable readers to scope a large-scale security management solution; we are not suggesting that enterprise needs will be driven by the many and varied factors that motivated and constrained EKMS.

## Concept and Mission

Under the tutelage of the National Security Agency, the U.S. Department of Defense is using the services provided by the **Electronic Key Management System** (EKMS). EKMS[3] is a total communications security (COMSEC) management system that encompasses all aspects of a key management architecture. This covers key management services, COMSEC material distribution, and logistics support. The system has been established to supply electronic key services to COMSEC devices in a secure and timely manner, and it has grown to service additional device and program requirements over time.

EKMS provides COMSEC managers with an automated system capable of ordering, generation, production, distribution, storage, security, accounting, and access control over keys. Planned features of EKMS include automated auditing capabilities to monitor and record security-relevant events, account registration, and extensive system and operator privilege management that will provide flexible access control to sensitive keys, data, and functions within the system.

EKMS hinges upon the activities of the **Central Facility** (CF), which provides a broad range of capabilities to the military services and other government agencies. The CF is capable of generating keying material, performing seed conversion

---

2. See http://www.us.net/softwar/firefly.html. This section is a summary of a SOFTWAR Web page, used by permission of the SOFTWAR site's maintainer, Charles R. Smith. Further context is provided in [BORG92].

3. The name "EKMS" is somewhat historical and often referenced in the literature. EKMS, as used in this book, is unrelated to any commercial product with the same acronym.

and rekey, maintaining compromise-recovery capability, processing orders for both physical and electronic keys, and electronically generating and distributing keying material.

## Model and Distribution

The CF is the foundation of EKMS. Traditional paper-based keys, **Secure Telephone Unit** (STU-III) keys, **Secure Data Network System** (SDNS) keys, and other electronic keys are managed by a single CF.

The CF interoperates with other EKMS elements through a variety of media, communication devices, and networks through direct distance dialing using STU-III (data mode) secure telephones, and/or secured dedicated links. The full implementation features a TCP/IP-based message service as the primary method of communication with the CF. This message service permits EKMS elements to store EKMS messages that include electronic keys for later retrieval by another EKMS element.

The **Local Management Device** (LMD) is central to EKMS. It is composed of a service- or agency-supplied commercial off-the-shelf (COTS) personal computer (PC). The LMD platform hosts **Local COMSEC Management Software** (LCMS), which will provide the interface between the LMD, the **Key Processor** (KP), and other EKMS elements.

When the LMD and KP are used in tandem, the account manager may order and account for all forms of COMSEC material, store key in encrypted form, perform key generation and automatic key distribution, perform COMSEC material accounting functions, and communicate directly with other EKMS elements.

The KP is a trusted component of EKMS. It performs cryptographic functions, including encryption and decryption functions for the account, as well as key generation and electronic signature operations. The KP is capable of secure field generation of traditional key.

Locally generated key can be employed in cryptonet communications, transmission security applications, point-to-point circuits, and virtually anywhere else paper-based keys have been used traditionally. Electronic keys can be downloaded for further transfer, or "fill," into the **End Cryptographic Unit** (ECU).

### Security Policy and System Design

Many security researchers have analyzed the general idea of security policy. They largely agree it is a multifaced response to a range of security problems. It is centered on "the set of laws, rules, and practices that regulate how an organization manages, protects, and distributes sensitive information" [TCSEC].[4]

---

4. See http://www.disa.mil/MLS/glosrefs.html#glossary and Chapter 13 for a discussion of TCSEC.

[CHIZ92] discusses the use of security policy in (or *as*) the system development process. The key, he argues, is to avoid two obvious traps when procuring security systems: the acquisition of the latest class of product to be announced just because it is all the rage and the tendency to use super-secure products to protect low-value assets to ensure that the job gets done right. Instead, you should focus selection of solution components upon the analysis of actual needs and requirements.

There are various types of security policies (see Chapter 13 for additional discussion). When used appropriately, they provide "a tool to properly assign both responsibility and accountability for security in the organization as a whole, and the organization's information technology systems specifically" [CHIZ92]. We present quotations from [CHIZ92] on the detailed process of using security policy as a basic tool for security solution design. Advanced readers may wish to refer to the original paper for additional discussion of the variations of policy proposed.

> Any system development starts with a mission, or more specifically a perceived need. In the realm of security, this need corresponds to the *security policy objectives,* which are themselves an expression of the security needed for the mission. The mission sponsors then proceed to identify the mission requirements in terms of everything required to perform the mission and the approach to accomplishing the mission. This corresponds to the *organizational security policy,* which lays out all of the responsibilities for security in accomplishing the mission.

> Next, the mission sponsors identify a role for information technology in the mission and develop a plan for its use in the context of the mission. This phase of system development corresponds to the . . . *Information Technology System Security Policy.*

> Finally, actual technology is procured to accomplish the automated aspects of the mission. This technology may be general-purpose, commercially available technology or technology that is designed and built specifically for the mission. In either case, there should be a corresponding *Information Technology Protection Policy* that describes what shared resources the technology manages and how it provides the means to protect those resources from being shared unintentionally. The final step in the system development process is to integrate the technology into the mission.

# Products

Having described the process of designing a security solution applying digital certificate management, we turn our attention to some of the products for building certificate issuing systems and operational security solutions. To assist the organization of the various summaries and commentaries, we break our survey into three sections:

**Certificate toolkits and platforms**   Programming libraries or shared object DLLs that reside on popular computers, handling X.509 certificates, certificate revocation lists, their storage, access, and general management.

**Certificate servers**   Network responders that implement management protocols enabling remote users to request certificate issuance and management and perform remote key management.

**Certificate authority workstations**   Dedicated workstation computers performing generally off-line, high-assurance certificate issuing and management and cryptographic device management.

## Certificate Toolkits and Implementation Platforms

### *SECUDE*

**SECUDE** is a research output of the German national research laboratory GMD (http://www.darmstadt.gmd.de/secude/technical/htm). It is primarily a source-language development kit that provides cryptography, OSI security mechanisms, PKCS support, commercial API access methods such as GSS-API, tools for operating a CA, storage technology for handling software user keys, directory support for certificate and CRL distribution, and smart card support.

SECUDE's CA Management supports certificate issuing, maintaining revocation lists, and administering users, featuring various key-generation and certification models. In one model, users can generate their own keys, which are then certified by the CA. In another, the certification authority both generates and certifies keys for users. The CA Management facilities can be hosted as a Web site to perform on-line certification. User data is accessed from a database, using a manufacturer-independent interface.

The SECUDE standard package is shipped with an application that provides security commands in a UNIX-style shell interactive environment, supporting both basic and advanced users alike. The SECUDE security shell is part of each supported platform, and it allows the scripting of custom issuing and management scenarios.

SECUDE supports the European ICE-TEL certificate profile for X.509 v3 extensions, including: Basic Constraints, Subject Alternative Name, Issuer Alternative Name, KeyUsage, Certificate Policies, CRL Distribution Points, Authority Key Identifier, and Subject Key Identifier. The open architecture enables the software to also support IETF certificate profiles aimed at the Internet market, and enterprise- and vendor-specific extensions as required.

SECUDE is ported to many operating systems and has recently begun to be commercialized via integration with SAP/3.

## Microsoft CryptoAPI

**CryptoAPI** from Microsoft provides many of the same facilities as SECUDE. It goes beyond supporting toolkit solutions, however, by integrating certificate support functionality directly into the Windows operating system. Windows has adopted X.509 certificate technology to help protect its own integrity and secure distributed operating system services.

Using Win32 conventions, the core functions are exported to all developers, enabling them to build certificate-issuing and -using applications. Furthermore, the architecture enables Microsoft and third parties to extend Windows to meet evolving needs for certificate technology extensions in the area of formats, fields, and management protocols. (See Part VI for indirect use of CryptoAPI certificate support facilities when extending the Microsoft Certificate Server. Also, see the section on Java support for X.509 and other certificate formats in Chapter 3.)

## Entrust Technologies' Entrust/Toolkit

For developers making Entrust-aware applications for Entrust-PKI customers, the **Entrust/Toolkit** from Entrust Technologies provides a suite of security functions in a variety of packages tuned to security environments, much like SECUDE and CryptoAPI (http://www.entrust.com/toolkit/). These functions handle files, real-time data exchange, and IP-network key and security session negotiation procedures using the added-value features of Entrust key and certificate management. The toolkits provide standards-based APIs to the advanced functionality of the Entrust additions to standard key management protocols and local key handling. Entrust/Toolkit is aimed at developers who do not have specialized security expertise.

Entrust/Toolkit provides a cryptographic kernel validated according to the FIPS 140-1 standard and supports industry-standards algorithms.

## Intel CDSA

The **Common Data Security Architecture** (CDSA) is a specification of APIs and an extensible framework from Intel. It is not so much a commercial toolkit for developers as an initiative to define a comprehensive approach to security service and security management for computer-based security applications (http://developer.intel.com/ial/security/cdsa/FAQ.htm).

CDSA is logically a cross between the product concepts of SECUDE, Entrust/Toolkit, and CryptoAPI. It is designed to make computer platforms more secure for applications. There are several layers in the CDSA model. For our purposes we are interested in the **Common Security Services Manager** (CSSM), which provides management of the security infrastructure in a manner consistent across multiple platforms.

Protection of the platform from compromise of CSSM policies uses self-checking technology and allows checking process add-ins. The **Embedded Integrity Services Library** (EISL) and the **Integrity Services Library** (ISL) are used to verify and create integrity credentials in this regard.

Application-centric digital certificate features include the **Certificate Services Manager** (CSM), which is responsible for handling digital certificates and certificate revocation lists as abstract data types in much the same way as SECUDE. The **Trust Policy Manager** (TPM) controls which actions can be performed by a certificate subject, and features the ability for organizations to field multiple trust policy modules. It is similar to CryptoAPI-related Windows Trust Providers (http://premium.microsoft.com/msdn/library/sdkdoc/wintrust6037.htm).

## Certificate Servers

In the following summaries, we attempt to identify the distinctive features of the server platforms, rather than list all their features and benefits. In most cases, basic standards, conformance requirements, interfaces, and system components capabilities are common across the vendors, including the Microsoft Certificate Server, which we do not describe here. (We use this product in Part VI to explore the practical art of certificate issuing in detail.)

### *Baltimore Technologies' UniCERT*

Baltimore Technologies' **UniCERT** is a general-purpose certificate server transaction processing system (http://www.baltimore.ie). The design highlights the use of the PKCS series of de facto industry standards and targets the issuance and management of certificates by SSL- and S/MIME-enabled Internet applications. UniCERT is founded upon support for the emerging architecture and protocols of the IETF PKIX draft specifications for management protocols. The product offers a suite of self-standing server products that communicates with users and local registration authorities using PKIX-based PKI products (see Chapter 10).

UniCERT is a platform for public key certification. In terms of client/server architectures, registration agents (RAs) interact with the certificate management ports provided by a certificate authority (CA) server. The CA process services certificate application and revocation requests from UniCERT RAs, which, in turn, interface to the local or remote user equipment.

Two classes of end-user interact with the RA: direct registration agents (parties that interface with RA processes directly) and remote user agents (remote parties that apply for certificates). The issuing engine features a highly configurable policy engine suitable for controlling multiple issuing authorities, and you may deploy smart card tokens to control access to the UniCERT servers by administrators.

UniCERT runs on both Windows NT and UNIX. The product can issue certificates using the certificate profiles expected by Netscape Navigator–compatible Web browsers that support HTTPS, S/MIME, and SET. It also enables the deployment of escrow/recovery solutions for user keys.

### Entrust Technologies' WebCA

WebCA is Entrust Technologies' entry level certificate server (http://www.entrust.com/webca). Long known for setting the open standards for certificate and key management software in UNIX distributed network security systems, Entrust Technologies has now also adopted the simple PKCS-based Internet key management technology and security standards in order to interwork with security clients using Internet protocols. WebCA is a Windows NT product that piggybacks on a Web server. The issuing authority interface is constructed as a server-centric, forms-based Web application.

Two classes of users interact with the CA via the Web server: administrators and certificate applicants. Configurable templates enable specification of the contents of certificate fields, and the product is tuned toward the generation of SSL, S/MIME, and Netscape Object Signing certificates. The Entrust process for issuing digital certificates has two stages when the trusted user base is known. Administrators can load the names into a bulk-load file, generate one-time passwords, and distribute them to users through a secure, out-of-band method; the approved individuals then retrieve their certificates using their passwords to authenticate themselves. End users can retrieve their certificates in a single session.

Operational security of the issuing system is largely a function of the security provided by the Web server platform and/or the host operating system. As Netscape and Microsoft platforms (principally) extend their capabilities to include native smart card and cryptoacceleration support and strong cryptography, these features will be available to WebCA administrators. Based on Entrust technology, there are integrity-checked audit records of all system activity, and a 1024-bit software RSA CA signing key and cryptocapability. User information is encrypted in the Entrust/WebCA database, which may make it difficult to locally extend the product except when using Entrust/Toolkit technology.

WebCA scales to 5000 users when used with **Entrust/Directory,** but the certificate management can be interfaced to X.500 directory systems when more certificates are required.

### IBM Registry

**IBM Registry** is a security platform that enables IBM customers to deploy public key infrastructure business solutions (http://www.internet.ibm.com/commercepoint/registry/index.html). It is a part of the CommercePoint family of products and services designed for Internet commerce players. IBM supports Internet merchants and payment processors using the SET protocol (see Chapter 7).

As one might expect, the IBM initiative in public key infrastructure management is not limited to selling mere technology or a platform product. Big Blue has sought to define an infrastructure solution space (http://www.software.ibm.com/commerce/registry/need-uses.html).

The IBM Registry product concept concentrates on end-to-end security design that protects both communications and the storage of registration data. Using the idea of a bank vault, the **IBM vault** software provides certificate registrants with an access-controlled region of personal data storage space on a remote server. Access to the data and security operations such as signing and encryption can be gated by the use of digital certificates.

Customers will be able to use the finished product alongside a schema-customizable X.500 directory, which can serve as a general-purpose directory and a general enterprise-wide management control point for user security attributes, including roles and privileges.

The product is being designed both for enterprise use and for use by service bureaus. The transaction-processing environment is based on Web protocols and standards. The nature of Web standards allows for full distribution and separation of registration and certification processing, flexible customization of the authentication management procedures, and the required corporate styling of Web page content and layout.

### Netscape Certificate Server

The **Netscape Certificate Server** is intended to serve as the security management hub for enterprise-wide intranet computing systems (http://merchant.netscape.com/netstore/servers/certificate.html). Certificate Server is a member of the Messaging and Collaboration group of Netscape SuiteSpot servers. It is designed to complement other elements of this enterprise infrastructure solution, working particularly closely with the Directory and Messaging servers.

As a system, the Netscape Certificate Server provides a forms-based Web interface to public operations invoked by client applications and privileged operations used by certificate issuing agents. These agents process requests and publish certificates and status indications to a directory service.

The certificate server processes and configuration are managed through the **Netscape Administration Server,** which integrates the certificate service into a common management framework and toolset. Other elements of the security solution include Proxy Server, Directory Server, and the Enterprise family of Web application servers, some or all of which may be required to fully use the Certificate Server. Used together and when hosted upon a well-configured secure operating system, these servers enable customers to deploy a secure operational facility.

Certificate Server enables the Netscape security model and may optionally issue certificates containing Netscape-defined certificate extensions. These extensions are generally supported by both Netscape and Microsoft browser products. By default, software-based cryptographic signing processes are used.

Certificate Server can manage a hierarchy of issuing authorities. Netscape client products can exploit the control extensions placed in authority certificates to learn the type of certificate issued. Similarly, keys can be signaled as restricted for use in only particular elements of the Communicator suite, such as S/MIME in Netscape Messenger. Similarly, extensions can indicate that a given certificate represents a CA and perhaps that a given CA is the last in a chain.

Some general-purpose Netscape extensions include:

**netscape-cert-type**    Limitation on the use of a certificate.

**netscape-revocation-url**    URL used to check certificate status.

**netscape-cert-renewal-url**    URL that points to a certificate renewal form.

**netscape-ca-policy-url**    URL for a Web page describing issuing policies.

**netscape-ssl-server-name**    An SSL server host-name expression.

**netscape-comment**    A comment to the user when the certificate is viewed.

## VeriSign OEM

VeriSign OEM is the retargeting of the software that runs VeriSign's CA center into a cross-platform, shrink-wrapped product. The major architectural components of the product are the (SQL) Query Manager, Transaction Manager, Signing Server, and Middleware Framework:

**Query Manager**    Serves as the database interface layer and supports the presentation of query results with a wide range of options.

**Transaction Manager**    Ensures the integrity of certificates while managing their lifecycle.

**Signing Server**    Manages software- and hardware-signing units.

**Middleware Framework**    Provides a communications middleware between Web servers, Query Manager, Transaction Manager, and the Signing Server.

VeriSign OEM supports local registration authorities and serves as a turnkey system to issue client, Web server, IPSEC, and SET certificates. To ensure the integrity of the system, the product distinguishes between CA operator, LRA operator, and subscriber roles, and it uses certificates to control access to privileged operations.

The major functional components of the product are the following:

**Signer hierarchy management** This component creates signers and creates arbitrary complex hierarchies between them.

**Signer name space management** The OEM product allows a customer to segment the name space of a signer into independently managed jurisdictions (currently, only organization and organizational unit attributes can be used to segment the name space). Each jurisdiction can define its local control rules, policies, and customized certificates. The Web-based GUI enables customers to easily configure certificate extensions and attributes.

**Certificate lifecycle management** VeriSign OEM provides a complete Web-based interface to query a database based on a wide range of options and perform lifecycle management operations, such as approving certificate enrollments or revoking a certificate.

**Subscriber services management** This component contains a complete set of Web pages to enable end users to enroll for different types of certificates and request lifecycle management operations.

**Directory system management** The OEM product is tightly coupled with LDAP-compliant directory servers and can populate them with certificate and CRL information.

**Workflow management** For environments with high transaction volumes, the workflow support allows incoming certificate lifecycle management requests to be assigned to different operations and tracked.

### Additional Reading

Many other vendors offer integrated certificate servers or related management system components. The following URLs list some additional vendor offerings:

**Xcert (LDAP)** http://www.xcert.com/

**GNS (Microsoft Access)** http://champlain.gns.ca/text/products/pkimanage.html

**Techop (SECAM)** http://www.techop.demon.co.uk/key.htm

**Entegrity/COST** http://www.entegrity.com

## Certificate Management Workstations

### CertCo

CertCo's **Root CertAuthority** specifically addresses the issuance of certificates to Certification Authorities (http://www.certco.com/products/rootcal.htm). Based on the RFC 1422–specified concept of hierarchical domains of certifiers in which root CAs delegate authority down a certification chain, CertCo offers a product dedicated to managing the perceived risks faced by such a critical component of a hierarchical security system.

To minimize the risk of an operator commissioning a fraudulent certification, Root CertAuthority private key management controls and offers multilevel control over the certificate-issuing approval process. Established practices of separation of duty and multilevel control over critical control functions may be enforced using cryptographic secret-sharing techniques controlling the arming of the certification system and/or access to the signing key.

Root CertAuthority operates on a Windows NT Server system, relying for additional operational and lifecycle assurances on procedural safeguards by the operator and strict control over the PCMCIA and other cryptographic devices used to sign or arm the certification system. The design of the product allows for distribution of components over networks. However, we classify this product in the workstation category when it is used to control signing keys of certification authorities, as we imagine that such a function will be performed only off-line and in a shielded manner.

## NSA CAW

Since 1985, BBN[5] has worked with National Security Agency engineers to develop secure architectures for data messaging and networking. The NSA-developed **Certificate Authority Workstation** (CAW) product, now sold commercially by GTE, is an integral component of the Department of Defense's Defense Message System infrastructure (http://www.disa.mil/D2/dms/dms2.html).

The functions of NSA CAW include:

**Key management**  The CAW manages Key Encryption Algorithm (KEA) and Digital Signature Algorithm (DSA) key pairs, and the data storage keys for CA and approved users. KEA and DSA parameters are loaded onto Fortezza cryptocards, which are used by end users and CAs alike.

**Hierarchy management**  The CAW generates configuration data and builds certificates that establish a hierarchy of certificate authorities, enforcing names and authorization constraints.

**Card and certificate management**  The CAW builds and signs certificates, including the user's public keys. The certificate is loaded onto a CAW-programmed

---

5. See http://www.bbn.com/products/security/caw.htm. Additional BBN PKI products are described at http://www.bbn.com/products/security/skcms.htm. BBN is now a unit of GTE Internetworking.

and managed token, such as a Fortezza PCMCIA cryptocard. It then initializes and loads certificate and related data onto the cards. The system manages privileges, maintains backup data, and, at the end of a certificate's life cycle, issues CRLs.

**Directory system management**    Operating in an X.500 directory environment, the CAW posts certificates, CRLs, and compromised key lists (CKLs) to the directory so users can access the information they need to perform secure messaging operations.

**Audit support**    Audit records supply security-critical information to administrators and auditors.

## Summary

Design management policies and practices enable organizations to create management control systems. A security management system's requirements are determined by the required culture of control over asset protection.

A security management system design methodology aids deployment of certificate-based security systems. Information system security management processes may be implemented using programmable certificate servers. Certificate and security management toolkits enable local or specialized certificate issuing systems. Intranet Security management systems will probably be the first environment to see large-scale deployment of certificate servers.

In the category of toolkits that provide components for building certificate issuing and management systems, a sample of vendor products includes SECUDE, Microsoft's CryptoAPI, Entrust Technologies' Entrust/Toolkit, and the Intel-sponsored CDSA.

In the category of certificate servers, a sample of vendor products includes Baltimore Technologies' UniCERT, Entrust Technologies' WebCA, IBM Registry, the Netscape Certificate Server, and VeriSign OEM.

In the final category of traditional certificate authority workstations, a sample of vendor products includes CertCo's RootAuthority and the NSA's Certificate Authority Workstation, commercialized by GTE/BBN.

## References

[BORG92]    Borgoyne, E., and R. Puga. "An SDNS Platform for Trusted Poducts," *Proceedings, Volume II, 15th National Computer Security Conference, 1992.*

[CHIZ92]    Chizmadia, D. "Some More Thoughts on the Buzzword 'Security Policy'", *Proceedings, Volume II, 15th National Computer Security Conference, 1992.*

[TCSEC]    Trusted Computer System Evaluation Criteria, DoD Standard S200-28-STD, December 1985.

# 9

# Certification Services

In this chapter, we analyze the emerging public key certification service industry. Although centralized order-processing service centers have existed for paper and electronic keys in the military for many years, only recently have commercial services become marketable. However, seemingly firm concepts and philosophies for managing cryptographic technology must change. These systems must now accommodate profit and loss, competition, and the need of markets to measure, openly, the quality of businesses that operate as true, trusted third parties.

A protection philosophy provides a context for analyzing the protection mechanisms that a trustworthy system provides.[1] In traditional secure system design, trust is a technical matter largely concerned with engineering and operational assurances. In the commercial world, trust is the name of the game itself, particularly in the service industries of banking, trading, and insurance.

To help buyers of certification service understand what these assurances mean, we begin by describing a process view of CAs. We define the work that must be performed to deliver key management functionality and credible assurance to real users. We suggest that a way to distinguish among the offerings of the market leaders in certificate-based commercial trust management is to establish how they bundle such elements together.

Our analysis of the Internet service-delivery infrastructure that automates traditional third-party trust arbitrage is the main topic of the chapter. Technical security architectures such as the X.800 model overviewed in Chapter 1 describe security in terms of interactions of signals within an information systems' communication subsystem. We extend this idea, conceiving of a commercial security architecture modeling reliance on the assurances of CAs as the means to instrument consumer and business-to-business trust practices across the Internet.

---

1. A *protection philosophy* is an informal description of the overall design of the system that delineates each of the protection mechanisms employed. It is a combination of formal and informal techniques used to show that the mechanisms are adequate to enforce the security policy. See http://www.disa.mil/MLS/glosrefs.html.

Based on this view of the emerging Internet trust market, we highlight a number of service providers now offering trusted third-party certification and secure IP-networking services.

## Elements of Service

It is widely believed that a large number of ordinary businesses are now planning to field their first generation of CA services, much as they planned corporate-LAN e-mail services a decade ago.

As Microsoft, Lotus, Netscape, and Novell (along with players yet unknown) evolve their secure network operating system platform features, parties may come to depend upon these systems and middleware offerings for enterprise-wide security management. Others may choose application-solution or technology products such as those discussed in Chapter 8. To solve some or all of their requirements, corporate security officers may also opt to outsource part of the security management process using local registration authority (LRA) systems as discussed in Chapter 10.

Regardless of the form used to field a certification service, buyers and planners require a vendor-independent, form-independent analytical model with which to compare, contrast, and understand what the provider market is offering. In the next section, we present the elements of just such a model attempting to identify the underlying elements of a CA, stripped of all commercial angles, technical detail, and marketing concepts.

It is common to regard the act of subscribing to a certification service as one in which one files a registration requesting the privileges to thereafter request, renew, replace, and revoke that registration. We term this the **5Rs model.** As each privilege is used, a certificate is issued or status information updated. However, this description is the view from the door, so to speak; it is the user looking in on a finished concept. We need to look behind the scenes at the internal processes of the CA.

In our CA Work Product model, we identify nine items that are indirectly delivered when using a CA's external management interface. We term each item an **element of service.** The elements of service fall into three control categories:

**Internal controls**    Compromise of an internal control may impact a particular group of subjects and relying parties by undermining authentication quality. Careful physical and personnel screening practices must augment internal controls.

**Security controls**    Compromise of a security control may impact the secure communications of particular parties by undermining their confidence in the assurances of a particular certificate-based security system. Compromise of cryptographic materials controls associated with signing devices could compromise historical transactions and could require very costly compromise recovery process invocation to limit damage and rebuild transactional integrity.

**Administrative controls**    Compromise of an administrative control may impact an entire community's readiness to rely upon a third-party certificate-based security system or, worse, any third-party involvement in certificate-based security systems.

We identify work products as being performed by a CA operator rather than the CA. We use the term **CA** in this context as the embodiment of management authority to perform the various certification steps using a fielded system, and we use the term **CA operator** to stand for the MIS department, LAN manager, or contracted service company performing CA duties.

## Internal Controls

Four of the elements of service address internal controls:

- Authentication management
- Certificate issuance
- Certificate management
- Name management

The amount of trust in a CA operator's internal controls[2] is measured by the recommendations of an independent auditor's report. The auditor examines the controls placed in operation and tests their operating effectiveness using standards such as the Statement on Auditing Standards (SAS) No. 70 [SAS 92].

### Authentication Management

**Authentication management** is the ongoing process of creating and maintaining an accurate register of subject authentication information. A CA operator will always use its own records system to control the status of authentication information

---

2. In our model, the work products in the category of internal controls are intended only as an academic description for actual internal controls. Operating companies would be likely to supplement controls related to certification transactions by many others addresssing specific operational vulnerabilities.

for the members of its user community. The operator's staff may use records accessed from the systems of others to confirm the identity of subjects or rely upon another party to represent that a given user's identity has been confirmed (see the LRA Model section in Chapter 10).

An affirmative confirmation usually causes an auditable filing action to create or update records in the system. The registered records may be made available for inspection and review. An open registry may enable subjects and the public to contest the recording actions on many grounds with a view to seeking potential revocation or modification.

## Certificate Issuing

The action of issuing a digital certificate can have many meanings according to the context, laws, or policies under which it is performed. A CA operator issues a certificate upon digitally signing any piece of information using a signing key the CA has designated as restricted for the purpose of certificate issuing. False issuing is a threat to any certificate-based security system, and it is difficult to address with only technical safeguards. **Certificate issuing** is usually contingent upon authentication management and by definition occurs only upon use of a signature key to sign a certificate message.

The act of issuing does not necessarily make a certificate valid or convey the authority to use the private key associated with the public key listed. Issuance acts usually distinguish between subject and authority certificates.

## Certificate Management

As we will discuss in considerable detail in Chapter 12, it is vital to ascertain the validity of a certificate when relying upon a certificate. An issued certificate's validity may be controlled by conditions laid down in a subscriber agreement and, once posted, be represented to the world by status information in one or more certificate repositories. **Certificate management** is a registration process, similar to authentication management, where certificate values are controlled by filing, records management, and dispute resolution processes.

Public-service CAs usually build legal protocols into subscriber and relying-party agreements enabling the registry of certificates to be accessed via publicly available repositories and possibly directories. Certificate management processes may serve as a means for giving formal notice about certificate status. Revocation is an element of certificate management, as is recovery from authority compromise.

## Name Management

The X.509 Authentication Framework assumes that **naming authorities** will issue and manage names. A CA will perform authentication management referring to both those names and supporting identity confirmation material. A CA must have a cogent story to tell concerning its use and reliance on names. **Name management** governs naming architectures and schemas, primitive and compound name registration, and record management processes.

Should a public-service CA choose to act as a naming authority operator for its subscribers, it is possible to regard the resulting certificate as a protected name registration, much like a registered trademark. Use of names by CAs, public or private, should conform to community naming standards and use character sets that are meaningful to those user communities. Using exclusively Greco-Latin characters in China is unlikely to produce a useful system, for example.

Although a real party accountable to a real-world security policy should always be bound to a subject name in an issued certificate, the accountability binding need not be publicly known from the published name. Primitive name acceptability can be based on universal or local criteria, and primitive names can be as real or imaginary as the user community desires.

## Security Controls

Three elements of service address security controls:

- Key management
- Key distribution
- Certificate distribution

The amount of trust in a CA's security controls depends on accreditation of the Certification Practice Statement (CPS) (see Chapter 11) governing the CA's and user community's operations and the auditor's report on the effectiveness of the internal controls to ensure that the material obligations upon the CA, as laid down in the CPS, are being met. The quantities measured for key distribution address liability, whereas for certificate distribution they address the quality of service provided by the CA to users requiring timely access to up-to-date certificate registries on a $24 \times 7$, 365 days/year basis.

### Key Management

The effectiveness of a cryptographic security mechanism usually depends upon the effectiveness with which the keys are managed. **Key management** is the process that ensures that, throughout their life cycle, keys are handled according to the threats faced by the keyed security service, in a given operational environment, and understanding as time progresses risks of cryptographic compromise inevitably increase. The work product is represented by the management controls used by a CA to notify a community that certificates need replacing, that a compromise or revocation event has occurred, a naming record has been suspended, a device is being retired, and so on.

Activities in cryptographic keying materials management include generation, destruction, assignment, and renewal (see Chapter 13). Public keys in certificate-based security systems undergo key management through the related activities of request, replacement, renewal, and revocation of digital certificates. CAs usually provide a manual or on-line means by which users can request key management services for their certified keys.

Chapter 10 presents an overview of two protocols designed for semiautomated key management. PKCS standards can also be used, and indeed are used every day as a very simple and effective semiautomated key management protocol for public keys as demonstrated by a wide range of SSL- and S/MIME-enabled security products. CAs deploy data centers and network servers capable of performing transaction processing in the manner required by these protocols and thereby enable certificate users to interface with their remote services.

## Key Distribution

We use the term **key distribution** throughout this book in a limited way. Key distribution is a security mechanism that, for the *asymmetric* form of key distribution, enables a subject's *public* key to be accepted into a receiving user's public key database in a way that allows the receiving party to determine its authenticity and to determine that it is bound to the named subject.

Certificates are one technique for performing key distribution. A common consequence of public key distribution is that additional symmetric keys may then be easily and securely shared between authenticated parties. They need to rely, principally, upon only the underlying certified keys to be assured that a secret is transferred confidentially to others when suitable trustworthy certificate-enabled security mechanisms are used. Another consequence of public key distribution is that the resulting keys may be used to verify digital signatures.

A CA may specify the purposes for which the public key is intended to be used. Certificates intended to distribute public keys to S/MIME applications may be distinct from those used to key IPSEC routers, or they may enable use of a given key for any purpose. Key distribution can be segmented into regimes serving the needs of digital signature consumers, as opposed to encryption service users, which require parties to effectively have multiple key pairs and certificates, even for a single application such as privacy-enhanced e-mail.

## Certificate Distribution

Having published a large number of certificates in a repository, a CA must enable a community of users and relying parties to obtain and then use them when using security services. **Certificate distribution** is a mechanism that enables relying parties to access the records in a certificate registry, repository, or directory in a timely and accurate fashion.

As user communities become larger and more dispersed, there are engineering scaling problems to be solved while providing effective and timely access to a centralized registry. Once access to a registry database is distributed via a directory mechanism, additional engineering and security problems are introduced. Directory protocols require both the entries storing certificates and the directory access points to be distributed across a wide-area network. However, major directory initiatives from companies such as Novell, Cisco, and Microsoft are underway.

Careful naming design by a CA or precise construction of indexes in on-line directories allow users to search for and list the entries of users and their certificates. A CA might also enable users to print a URL on their virtual business cards to a Web resource fronting the CA's repository acting as a simple directory available to all. A CA's service must provide the telecommunications capability to satisfy the engineering demands placed on a directory-based information retrieval service by large communities and have strategies in place to cope with peak demand.

## Administrative Controls

Two elements of service address administrative controls:

- Policy management
- Domain management

Administrative controls are currently measured in terms of rather subjective trust valuations of CAs such as high, medium, or low. Over time, objective measures may be determined based on number of interconnections to other trusted domains, the stature of subscribers and partners, the financial stability of the providers, the number of years of publication of audit reports, the conformance of policy to established criteria, and such metrics as the number of complaints or delays in dealing with compromise alerts and incidents.

### Policy Management

We discuss certificate policy in Chapter 11. A CA may enter into contractual relationships with subscribers, relying parties, and other members of a management domain of related CAs. A certification practice statement will codify the governing rules for the community. A CA operator may offer one or more policies, and users must be prepared to correctly determine the policy under which any given certificate was originally issued.

A CA should document its policy and practices and justify how and why it represents the assurance associated with the certificate issuing and management processes it controls. A CA's operational effectiveness should be independently audited on schedules laid down in policy commitments.

Should a CA pass obligations to subscribers concerning trustworthy systems or pledges of performance, it should be prepared to enforce subscriber agreements.

A CA should have the wherewithal to agree or enforce policy recognition with other CAs, should it join or operate a trust network requiring policy conformance.

### Domain Management

A certification service provided by a CA operator may be organized so that distinct issuing authorities, organized as a **domain** of CAs, issue different types and classes of certificates. (See Chapter 13 for a discussion of certification domains.) A CA that offers different assurances to relying parties should be able to clearly articulate the restrictions and differentiating properties in terms of purpose limitations and liabilities of the parties.

A CA operator may allow other operators to manage CAs within the domain and may engage in interdomain certification, allowing networks of domains to form larger and larger communities of users who can mutually authenticate. A CA service may enable automatic procedures for exchanging the certificates used to perform interdomain certification.

## A Commercial Internet Security Architecture

As a communications phenomenon, the Internet is entering middle age. The culture of pioneers, universities, high-technology companies, and curious users musing on the meaning of cyberspace is giving way to the culture of infrastructure, which supports both liberal, open communications and traditional business. Economics and media politics will inevitably push the Internet into its final form as a regulated, intelligent broadcast network as is being pioneered by @Home and other cable, satellite, and copper-broadband businesses.

A commercial security architecture, which integrates digital certificates, will need to address two aspects of the PKI role:

**Virtual services**    The single PKI is the instrument that enables commercial marketing of products and services in the on-line medium and the means to conduct day-to-day government. Digital certificates are issued like marketing coupons on the one hand and as institutional logos on the other. In less overtly commercial service uses, the infinitely flexible certificate replaces the cinema club membership card, the ration card, the reservation receipt, the savings stamp, the customer loyalty card, the Internet parking ticket, the income tax filing receipt, the fishing license. . . . The **financial services** view of the service business is a variation on this theme. The single PKI enables banks, insurance companies, and sales networks of professionals to underpin commerce by assuming their traditional intermediary role as trusted third parties during commercial transactions. By using legislation and regulation to favor accredited banks and insurers as trust providers in the Internet space as they are favored in traditional infrastructures, financial service providers can maintain their preeminent position in control of the flow of money. In this view, PKI is used to manage trust in terms of the delegation of authority to handle financial transactions.

**Telecommunications**    Aimed at particular business communities, PKI management systems enable subscribers to access a variety of value-added encryption services offered by the telecommunications and ISP companies. Telecommunications companies provide global, regional, and private PKIs to distinct sectors of corporate markets that need to span wider and wider business and financial culture divides when trading. The **software systems** view of the telecommunications business is a variation on this theme, with more limited scope. A PKI is merely a distributed computer system's security subsystem that enables corporate security officials to control a set of managed, networked resources processing corporate information. The software, solution integration, and computer services industries sell security solutions much as they sell other solutions to institutional needs for managed computing.

## Virtual Services

Business has an opportunity to adapt digital certificates as a vehicle for conducting traditional forms of commerce, banking, trading, and so on in the on-line medium. The security services enabled by public key cryptography can, of course, protect transactions across the hostile open communications networks. However, additionally and perhaps uniquely, the organization of the public key infrastructure may realistically emulate the very economic structure and organization of the various sectors of commerce and industry.

The trust relationships that factor into business become the basis for structuring digital certificate issuing and management. To promote reasonable levels of trust and produce a conducive, self-regulating environment for all to use, government authority will probably be used to create a (hopefully nonexclusive) professional-grade service industry of public service CAs and commercial outsourcing providers to help businesses operate their own CAs.

## Telecommunications

The role of the telecommunications company in the face of the Internet revolution is perhaps one of seeing opportunity for extension of traditional telecommunications management, service, and sales. Telecommunications companies generally strive to avoid commoditization of their services; laying cables and transferring bits for a fee is the last thing a profitable company in a mature competitive market wishes to do. Adding value by selling management services with such properties as enhanced reliability, connectivity, and security is a traditional means of selling more valuable *managed* networks to residential subscribers and corporate users.

The telecommunications industry would like users to conceive of their PCs as intelligent network terminals. Of course, Novell, Apple, and Microsoft (and most users) tend to view the world in terms of the PC; the telephone and cable companies are simply access points to the world beyond the home or office. These two views must eventually converge. Does the consumer perceive the world in terms of the PC desktop or the Internet service provider? Who will influence if, when, and how other commercial brands get consumer attention?

The computer and telecommunications industries have traditionally vied for control over the consumer's access point to networked information. IBM and AT&T, as progenitors of the industries they lead, failed to obtain monopolies in *both* computing and global networks. When it comes to trust, however, the schism of views is critically important. Will one inherently trust the network, allowing the network provider to obtain and verify one's incoming certificates, say? Or will validation occur at the PC by the user? Is the end user a mere consumer of trust managed and gauged by others or a key player in the trust market? As we will see in Chapter 12, these questions open many issues relevant to secure electronic commerce and the roles played by on-line consumers and on-line providers.

## Certification Services Providers

In this section, we describe four certification service providers. We do not necessarily assert that all these companies embrace the analysis contained in the foregoing section. Companies featured here represent only a sample of actual service providers.

### Digital Signature Trust Company

The Digital Signature Trust Company (DST) is a subsidiary of Zions National Bank and works with other elements of the bank to implement a standards-based PKI (http://www.digsigtrust.com/). It offers CA services and a service bureau that hosts the CAs of businesses and government agencies. The company is significantly involved in the Utah state government's program to implement a regulated, statewide public-key infrastructure supporting the needs of Utah companies.

DST was the first licensed CA in the state of Utah and operates its CA services in accordance with legislative and regulatory requirements. A feature of all Utah-regulated CAs is their required focus on repository services. DST plans to levy per-transaction fees on those who publish, list certificates, or otherwise obtain access to PKI-related information in its repository. In relying upon information obtained from licensed repositories, companies gain specific protections of Utah state law when conducting electronic commerce transactions that rely on public-key infrastructure techniques. Similarly, companies offering public-key infrastructure services obtain certain limitations on liability.

### GTE CyberTrust

GTE CyberTrust is the brand name of a suite of CA products and services from GTE Government Systems Corporation. As a telecommunications company and as a defense contractor, GTE has long been involved in the manufacture and use of high-speed encryption devices for secure U.S. government voice and data communications. GTE leverages experience in having provided networked electronic key management services to U.S. government national security agencies.

In recent years, GTE has begun to leverage its engineering and design expertise in secure system and component design to provide commercial CA products and services. Having addressed and satisfied the trusted engineering and review procedures required by defense contracts, GTE is able to provide a disciplined response to large corporate customers with specialized networking or security requirements. GTE security design consultants played a critical and respected role in the specification of the SET standard, for example, and have assisted MasterCard with its SET certification service pilot program.

In the enterprise market, the CyberTrust Customer-Branded Service is an outsourcing arrangement whereby customers obtain the ability to issue SET and/or SSL digital certificates (see http://www.cybertrust.com/services/CAServiceOffer.html). Using the GTE data centers, the customization service enables enterprises to create and project their own brands and security management concepts to the public. Based on customer-provided authorization criteria, GTE will perform the functions of a [local] Registration Authority.

### TradeWave

TradeWave Corporation uses Entrust Technologies software to provide key management services to virtual private networks (VPNs; see http://www.tradewave.com). A VPN is usually a closely knit group of trading partners whose intercompany communication channels are protected by a shared and mutually trusted security system.

Frequently, trading partner agreements may be established across the private network facilitating a communal environment for electronic data interchange (EDI).

The company offers custom CA solutions and security network products that are tightly integrated with on-line key management servers. The operational security protocols together with certificate-based key management protect the transactions between the trading partners linked over the Internet by the VPN.

TradeWave relies heavily upon the centralized-control management philosophies of the Entrust Technologies suite of security components in its TradeVPI and TradeAuthority programs (see http://www.tradewave.com/products/cabuyer.html and http://www.entrust.com). The dominant feature of the TradeWave service model is its support for local registration authorities (LRAs). Security administrators interact with the TradeAuthority service bureau using a remote administration tool with which they manage user registrations and the associated lifecycle of keys. (Chapter 10 presents the LRA concept in more detail.)

The protection philosophy can perhaps be best described as one in which a user's access to workstation or network-delivered security services is centrally managed by security administrators exploiting the ability of the solution to impose fine-grain access control. The administrator of the domain is always in charge of and responsible for the security service usage when controls are imposed using a centralized key management concept.

## VeriSign, Inc.

VeriSign is well known as the CA that allows Netscape and Microsoft Web servers to fully exploit built-in SSL security features enabling them to authenticate themselves to users across the Internet. Many thousands of companies have sent business records to VeriSign's DigitalId Center. Authentication management staff then work with customers by e-mail and telephone to confirm their net-identities before issuing certificates. In partnership with software manufacturers and Internet service providers, VeriSign has essentially defined the business of issuing secure server certificates.

Individuals worldwide have obtained VeriSign personal certificates that enable them to perform SSL-based login to secure servers. Close integration of VeriSign public services (and those of its competitors—see http://www.microsoft.com/ie/ie40/oe/certpage.htm and http://search.netscape.com/assist/security/partners/overview.html) with Netscape Communicator and Microsoft Outlook enables them to also sign e-mail messages and create privacy-enhanced (i.e., encrypted) messages using the S/MIME secure mail protocol.

VeriSign established its reputation as a public CA enabling others to communicate and engage in commercial transactions (see https://digitalid.verisign.com). It operates facilities in the United States and Japan and provides local service in other countries through partnerships with major companies such as British Telecommunications.

VeriSign also operates corporate certification services on behalf of enterprises via its VeriSign OnSite program and runs SET issuing services for credit card companies and a number of banks.

OnSite is VeriSign's local registration authority outsourcing service in the enterprise market. It is targeted at Fortune 10,000 organizations and government agencies deploying intranet, extranet, and electronic-commerce solutions that require digital certificates for access control or secure messaging. VeriSign OnSite includes software that can be installed at the customer site or hosted at VeriSign as well as back-end certificate processing services run by VeriSign to help enterprise customers quickly set up their own certification authority services. As featured in Chapter 10, when used in conjunction with the CRS protocol, OnSite enables enterprise customers to integrate the process of certificate registration, authentication, and certificate issuance into an automated, high-volume transaction system.

In summary, VeriSign's strengths lie in its disclosure of its certification practices, the auditing of its service delivery infrastructure, and its policy of first-to-market innovations and options for delivering certificate-related services. In February 1998, VeriSign became a public company, embracing the additional scrutiny and public accountability that such status brings to trusted third parties.

### Additional Reading

Certification authorities lists are provided at the following URLs from which readers can research additional concepts for designing a certification and key management service.

**QMW law:** http://www.qmw.ac.uk/~tl6345/ca.htm

**ICE-TEL:** http://auchentoshan.cs.ucl.ac.uk:8877/trustfactory/trustfactory.htm

## Summary

The emerging public key certification service industry deliverables can be described in terms of elements of service. Elements of service fall into three control categories. Internal controls address compromise of the quality of authentication. Security controls address compromise of communications security. Administrative controls address compromise of confidence and trust in transaction-processing environments.

Internal controls assure a CA's processes in authentication management, certificate issuing, certificate management, and name management. Security controls assure a CA's processes in key management, key distribution, and certificate and CRL distribution. Administrative controls assure a CA's processes in policy and domain management.

The trust infrastructure for delivering commercial and banking services together with telecommunications infrastructure gives rise to a commercial security architecture. The aim of such an infrastructure is to enable security services enabled by public-key cryptography to protect transactions across the hostile open communications networks.

The Digital Signature Trust Company offers CA services and a service bureau that hosts the CAs of businesses and government agencies. State laws regulation may enable certain companies to obtain certain limitations on liability.

VeriSign is a public CA and solution provider to enterprises via its VeriSign OnSite program. VeriSign relies on its Certification Practice Statement and auditors' reports to represent its trustworthiness.

GTE CyberTrust is a suite of CA products and services from the GTE Government Systems Corporation. GTE leverages experience in providing networked electronic key management services to U.S. government agencies.

TradeWave Corporation provides key management service to virtual private networks (VPNs). TradeWave offers custom CA solutions and security network products that are tightly integrated with on-line Entrust key management servers.

## References

[GARF97] Garfinkel, S., and G. Spafford. *Web Security and Commerce,* O'Reilly and Associates, Sebastopol, CA, 1997.

[SAS92] AICPA, "Reports on the Processing Transactions by Services Organizations," Statement on Auditing Standards, No. 70, April 1992.

Chapter

# 10

# LRAs and Enterprise Solutions

Local registration authorities (LRAs) are an emerging class of certificate-based security management solutions. They help corporations secure their intranets, extranets, and electronic commerce solutions by tapping into the potential of digital certificates. LRAs allow an organization to keep tight control over the authentication process for issuance of digital certificates while outsourcing the more difficult key management processes to third-party CAs. Due to its economics and ease of use, many organizations will probably opt for this model of joint responsibility to deploy certificate-based solutions. This is similar to the business practice of outsourcing payroll processes while keeping internal control over who gets a salary increase.

In this chapter we present a model that captures the relationships of a CA with its subscribers and shows the roles, functions, and responsibilities of a CA. By taking a close look at this model, we will develop the LRA model for deploying public-key infrastructure (PKI) technologies within an organization. We will then discuss two protocols for managing the lifecycle of certificates. These protocols enable different components of a PKI (CA, LRA, and end users) to exchange on-line messages to request or deliver PKI services. At the end of this chapter, we will examine VeriSign's OnSite commercial LRA service.

## The CA Model

In Chapter 3 we discussed certification authorities (CAs) and explained that a user applies to a CA for a certificate through a certificate registration form. The CA, after confirming the identity of the applicant, generates a certificate and distributes it to the user. The CA may use a variety of in-band or out-of-band processes to verify the identity of an applicant, including accessing a third-party consumer authentication database, asking the user to appear in person to present an identification card, phone calls, and so on. Figure 10-1 presents an abstract model to capture the underlying operation of a CA.

As Figure 10-1 illustrates, a CA performs authentication, certificate distribution, and key management. **Authentication** is the process of verifying that you are who

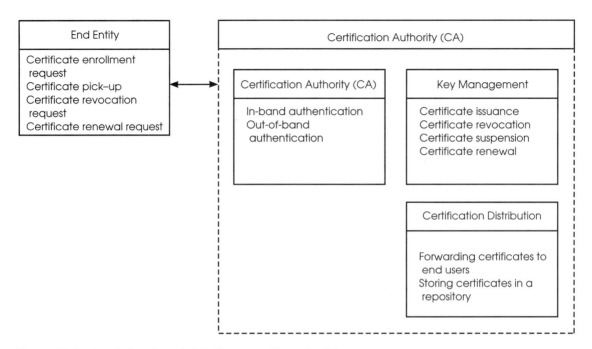

**Figure 10-1** An abstract model for the operation of a CA.

you claim you are. **Certificate distribution** is the task of forwarding a certificate to a subscriber after the CA has verified the user's identity and issued a certificate. Note that a CA typically stores the issued certificate in its repository and provides external access to the repository, thus allowing the certificate to be distributed to any party.

**Key management** includes certificate issuance, revocation, suspension, and renewal. Key management is an integral part of operating a CA and is a major factor in determining how trustworthy the CA is perceived to be. For example, if a CA's facility is not physically secure, an intruder may be able to break in and issue a rogue certificate. Similarly, a dishonest CA employee may issue a rogue certificate in exchange for money. Key management is the most important value-added feature of a third-party CA, and its reliable operation requires substantial capital expenditure, security expertise, and know-how.

The salient point of Figure 10-1 is that the CA performs key management as well as authentication. Although as providers of trust it is natural for a CA to perform both key management and authentication, in certain situations, tight coupling of these two tasks poses some limitations.

If a CA is managing a large, geographically dispersed population, requiring users to physically appear at a central CA location for authentication might be difficult to accomplish. It would be more practical if local offices, such as post offices, conveniently located in different geographic areas, could register users, confirm their identities, and contact the CA for certificate issuance. The CA would then provide key management services for local branches, who register and authenticate users. Furthermore, decoupling key management from authentication enables corporations and organizations that want to deploy public-key technologies to outsource key management while imposing a tight control over the registration and authentication processes. In the next section, we will discuss this scenario in detail and introduce an alternative to the CA model.

# The LRA Model

In some situations practicality, not convenience, requires the decoupling of key management from authentication. We will explain this situation with an example, and then we will present the LRA model. At the end of this section, we will compare the LRA model with the CA model.

## Outsourcing Key Management Services

High Tech, Inc. has deployed public-key technology and digital certificates throughout all of its offices in Europe. The company's security policy states that all e-mail correspondence between offices must be encrypted for privacy using S/MIME. The company has incorporated the task of requesting a certificate into its hiring process and requires all new employees to obtain a certificate upon hiring.

Amy Smith, who has just joined High Tech, Inc., accesses an internal Web page, enters her personal information in the form, and submits it to apply for a S/MIME certificate, as prescribed by the hiring process. The personal information includes her name, Social Security number, and a unique personal identification number (PIN) that was given to her when she was hired. An administrator working for High Tech, Inc. receives the submitted application and authenticates it using the internal human resources database. The authentication involves ensuring that the information submitted in the form matches the information in the database and that the PIN Amy provided is the same one assigned to her. Furthermore, the administrator may ask Amy to personally appear at his office and present her identification card.[1]

After the administrator authenticates Amy's application, he sends a certificate enrollment request to a third-party CA that provides key management services to High Tech, Inc. The CA ensures that the certificate request has originated from an authorized administrator working for High Tech, Inc., issues a certificate for Amy, and returns the certificate to the administrator or directly to Amy. Note that the CA

---

1. The process that an administrator follows to authenticate the certificate request may vary from an organization to another. We are not attempting to model this process here.

makes no attempt to verify the identity of Amy Smith—as far as the CA is concerned, the certificate request is preauthenticated.

For this scenario to work, High Tech, Inc. needs to have control over the authentication process. Otherwise, the company would be forced to give the CA access to its human resources database, and providing such access clearly does not work because the database contains confidential and proprietary information and introduces a security risk. Furthermore, if High Tech, Inc. does not have control over the authentication process, it would be forced to follow the CA's authentication process instead of its own internal process.

Delegating the authentication process to High Tech, Inc. has many more advantages than simply preapproving certificate requests. When Amy leaves the company, the administrator can ask the CA to revoke her certificate because she is no longer affiliated with High Tech, Inc. Similarly, when Amy's certificate expires, the administrator can ask the CA to renew her certificate on Amy's behalf. Similar to the certificate registration scenario, the CA considers all such requests to be preauthenticated, provided they come from authorized personnel from High Tech, Inc.

## Introduction to the LRA Model

Figure 10-2 presents a model to capture relationships between end users, an LRA, and a CA. The LRA performs a variety of tasks, such as assigning distinguished names to subscribers, receiving certificate applications, confirming identity information, checking identification cards, revocation reporting, accepting renewal requests, distributing hardware tokens, or collecting obsolete tokens. The LRA can also generate key pairs for subscribers, archive key pairs, and recover lost key pairs.

It is critical to understand that an LRA does not perform any key management functions. An LRA authorizes requests, such as certificate issuance or revocation, on behalf of a CA; it must contact the CA for the actual issuance or revocation of a certificate. The ultimate decision to actually carry out a requested service, however, rests with the CA. The CA has the discretion to reject a certificate request from an LRA if the request conflicts with its practices. Furthermore, the CA has the discretion to modify the content of a certificate request, for example, by changing its subject name or adding extension fields. The LRA or the user, however, can decline such altered certificates.

Note that the LRA model addresses the shortcomings encountered when a CA attempts to authenticate geographically dispersed people. People who need high-assurance digital certificates requiring personal presence can go to a local post office, for example, and apply for a certificate. The post office would provide application forms, check personal information against an identification card, and submit the applications to a central CA. The process of applying for a certificate would be similar to applying for a passport. When you apply for a passport, however, you cannot designate the agency that should issue the passport. When you

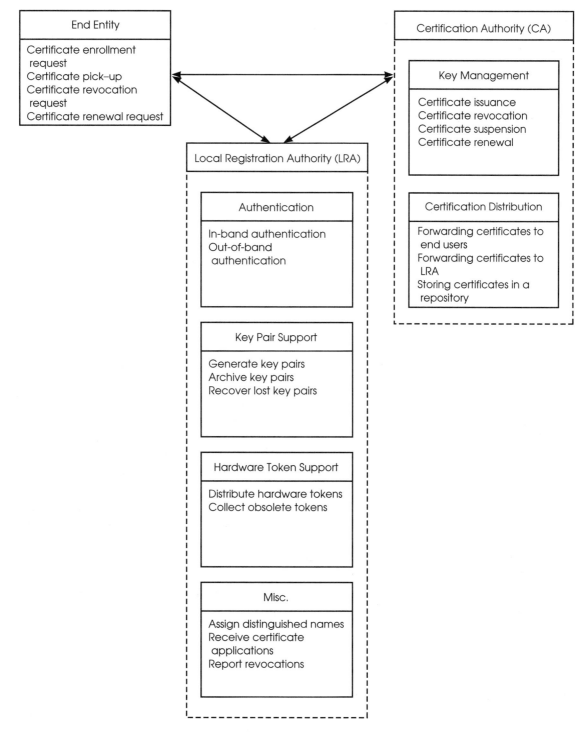

**Figure 10-2** An abstract model for the operation of an LRA.

apply for a digital certificate, the post office may supply you with a list of CA service providers to choose from.

The LRA model also addresses the needs of corporations and organizations who need tight control over registration and authentication. Corporations who need to deploy public-key solutions can act as the LRA for their employees and then outsource key management services to a CA.

# Models of Deployment for LRA

The model of Figure 10-2 prescribes that an LRA should have control over the authentication process. To deploy an LRA in a organization, however, we need a better understanding of how subscribers requesting certificates, the LRA performing local authentication, and the CA providing key management services interact with each other. We discuss three such models in this section. To simplify the presentation of these models, we concentrate on certificate enrollment requests as a typical key management service. Later in this chapter, we will revisit two of these models and present two commercial LRA implementations.

## CA Queues Requests for LRA

Let's explain how the three parties involved in an LRA service interact to implement an LRA service using our previous example, High Tech, Inc. Amy Smith accesses a Web page hosted by the CA to enroll for a digital certificate, enters her personal information and her assigned PIN, and submits her application. The request for the certificate is sent directly to the CA, which provides key management services for High Tech, Inc. After the CA receives her application, it sends Amy an e-mail to inform her that her certificate request has been received and is being processed.

The High Tech, Inc. **LRA administrator** (LRAA) accesses a designated, access-controlled LRAA page hosted by the CA to view the enrollment requests. He views Amy's enrollment request, checks her personal information and her PIN with the human resources database, and approves the request. Once approved, the CA generates a certificate for Amy and sends her an e-mail, which informs her that her certificate request has been approved and provides instructions for certificate pickup.

The CA must control access to the LRAA page and ensure that only the authorized personnel of High Tech, Inc. can view enrollment requests and process (approve or reject) them. The CA can use the password-login model to authenticate LRAAs, or it can require them to present a special certificate to gain access to LRAA pages.

Amy Smith may never be aware that a third-party CA has been involved in the overall process of requesting and obtaining her certificate. Even though she has accessed a page hosted by the CA to enroll for a certificate, the CA can customize the enrollment page for High Tech, Inc. Furthermore, High Tech, Inc. can hide the external URL to the CA page from Amy by providing an internal URL, which actually maps to the CA URL.

## LRA Queues Requests

In this model, High Tech, Inc. hosts the enrollment and LRAA pages and queues the enrollment requests internally at its own location instead of the CA. The High Tech, Inc. LRAA accesses the internal queue of pending requests and processes them according to the company's authentication policies.

After the LRAA approves a request, he needs to submit the preapproved request to the third-party CA. He can call the CA, mail the required forms, or send the request electronically, perhaps using an agreed-upon protocol. The significant restriction on the method of communications is that the CA must be able to ensure that the request originates from the LRAA. Recall that in the previous model, the CA satisfies this requirement by tightly controlling access to the LRAA pages. In the next section, we will describe a possible method based on digital signatures.

## Automated Processing

In this section, we present a model to automatically process certification requests instead of queuing them for manual processing by the LRAA. The model uses an agreed-upon protocol to communicate programmatically between the LRA and CA and digital signatures to establish the authenticity of the communications.

When Amy Smith submits her request for a certificate, the Web server CGI program accesses the human resources database to authenticate the request. If authenticated, it creates a certificate request message, digitally signs it, and sends the signed message to the CA. The CA receives the message, verifies its authenticity, interprets its content, and then issues a certificate for Amy. The CA creates a message containing the certificate, signs it, and sends it to the High Tech, Inc. Web server CGI program, which verifies the CA signature and delivers it to Amy.

Note that in this model, it is essential to have an agreed-upon protocol between the CA and LRA. Furthermore, the protocol must enable the CA and LRA to ascertain the origin of exchanged messages. In the next section, we will describe two such protocols.

# PKI Management Protocols

As public-key technology integrates with common products such as e-mail tools, browsers, routers, and firewalls, there is an ever-increasing need for a standard interface to public-key services and certification products to enable secure communications. Through this standard interface, a certificate-using product can programmatically enroll for a certificate, query and retrieve a certificate, request a revocation, or update its key. An S/MIME e-mail tool, for example, could prompt you for personal information, send a certificate request to a CA, receive your certificate, and install it on your machine. A common interface facilitates the development of public-key products and allows them to interoperate with any provider of public-key services after they are deployed in target environments.

A common interface also plays a significant role in implementing local registration authorities. Because an LRA is essentially a reseller of third-party CA key management services, it is necessary to establish an interface to such services to support a high-volume transaction channel between an LRA and a CA. Furthermore, because LRA service requests are considered preauthenticated, the CA must be able to programmatically ascertain that such requests originated from the LRA.

A common interface is also useful to facilitate communications between two CAs. In Chapter 3, we suggested that a large-scale, Internet-wide deployment of public-key systems must support the existence of multiple CAs and the relationships between them. We also presented two models to capture such relationships. An interface to enable CA-to-CA communications will be useful to support such relationships and create cross-certifications between different CAs.

Currently, the public-key infrastructure certification products, LRAs, and CAs provide interfaces to their services that range from proprietary to published as IETF Internet Drafts. **Certificate Request Syntax** (CRS) (ftp://ftp.ietf.org/internet-drafts/draft-ietf-smime-crs-00.txt) and **Internet X.509 Public Key Infrastructure Certificate Management Protocols** (PKIX-CMP) (ftp://ftp.ietf.org/internet-drafts/draft-ietf-pkix-ipki3cmp-06.txt) are two interfaces that have been published as IETF Internet Drafts. In the following sections, we will discuss CRS and PKIX-CMP. We will provide a rather comprehensive overview of CRS because the authors have been involved in the design of the CRS protocol and have insight into its creation. We will also provide an introductory overview of PKIX-CMP; you can refer to the provided reference for detailed information.[2]

Although it might be too early to conjecture which protocol will find widespread adoption by commercial vendors and will be deployed in PKI-based products, the CRS protocol may be better positioned for two reasons. First, a number of commercial vendors participated in its design, and it is more likely that they will adopt and promote this protocol. Second, CRS is based on de facto Public-Key Cryptographic

---

2. As this book went to press, there was an ongoing effort to harmonize the CRS protocol with the PKIX-CMP protocol. Regardless of the outcome of these efforts, we feel that the material presented here is valuable and helps the reader understand the *role* of a management protocol in implementing a public-key infrastructure and the *fundamental* requirements of such a protocol. Refer to http://www.ietf.org/html.charters/ pkix-charter.html for the latest developments.

Standards (PKCS), whereas PKIX-CMP defines its own data structures, making it more difficult and time consuming for commercial vendors to understand the protocol and implement it in their products.

## CRS

Published in November 1997, CRS is a protocol coauthored by Cisco, Netscape, Microsoft, Sun, and VeriSign for exchanging on-line messages between an end user and a CA. The CRS protocol is based on PKCS #10 and Cryptographic Message Syntax (CMS), which extends the PKCS #7 standard. Although the CRS protocol has a generic design and is extensible, its current specification is slanted toward supporting on-line communications between an LRA and a CA. This protocol needs to be extended to address the exchange of on-line messages between all components of a PKI, particularly CA-to-CA and initial registration of end users for certificates.

The CRS protocol supports a transaction-based pair of request and response messages between a client and a server. A **transaction** typically consists of one request message followed by one response message. For example, an LRA can send a preauthenticated certificate registration request to a CA, which immediately returns the issued certificate in the response, completing the transaction.

Through the use of **transaction IDs,** however, a transaction can span many pairs of request-reply messages, potentially over a connectionless transport protocol such as HTTP. A client may generate a transaction ID and retain it until the server responds with a message that completes the transaction. Note that the server always includes the transaction ID that it received from the client in its response messages. Transaction IDs are useful when a server cannot immediately fulfill a request or the connection between a client and a server breaks down and the client needs to resynchronize its state with the server. For example, when an end user sends a CA a registration request that requires out-of-band authentication, the CA sends the end user a response to indicate that it cannot immediately fulfill the request. The end user can go into a polling state and use the transaction ID to retrieve its certificate at a future time.

A request or response message consists of a message body and one or more service indicators. The **message body** contains the request that a client makes or the response that a server returns, whereas **service indicators** provide contextual information about the message body. For example, the body of a request might contain a PKCS #10 certificate request, while the service indicators convey additional information about the PKCS #10 request such as the CRS protocol version and the transaction ID. In this section, we refer to the message body as **payload.**

The CRS protocol secures the integrity and nonrepudiation of the exchanged messages through digital signatures. The originator of a message computes the digest of the message, signs it with its signing private key, and affixes the digital signature to the message; the receiver of a signed message uses the originator's public key to verify the authenticity of the message. The Digital Signature algorithm (DSA) and RSA can be used to sign messages. Signing of exchanged messages allows a CA, who communicates with an LRA over an unsecure channel, to automatically process incoming preauthenticated requests from the LRA. Similarly, an LRA or end user can use the CA's public key to verify the authenticity of incoming messages from the CA.

The CRS protocol can also secure the confidentiality of exchanged messages. The sender of a message envelopes the message body by encrypting it with a symmetric cipher and then encrypting the encryption secret key with the recipient's public key. Both Diffie-Hellman and RSA key transport can be used to protect the secret key. Note that CRS protects only the payload of a message—the service indicators are not encrypted. The receiver uses its private key to decrypt the secret key and then uses the decrypted secret key to decrypt the payload.

CRS can secure exchanged messages against replay attacks. The originator of a message optionally includes a **nonce** (a random number) in the message and retains the value of the nonce. If included, the recipient of the message must include the received nonce in its reply message. Upon receiving the reply, the originator compares the received nonce against its retained nonce and considers the reply for further processing if they match. When the recipient includes the originator's nonce, it also includes its own nonce, which is useful if a transaction spans more than one pair of request-reply messages.

### Transactions

The CRS protocol currently defines three transactions, as listed in Table 10-1. An end user uses these transactions to request PKI services from an LRA or a CA; similarly, an LRA uses them to request PKI services from a CA. To become an all-encompassing PKI interface, CRS must address the following three areas. First, it must define new transactions to support other LRA-to-CA requests, such as key update and certificate update. Second, it should specify how an end user that does not have a certificate can authenticate itself to an LRA or a CA and register for a certificate. Third, the CRS protocol should address the requirements of CA-to-CA communications, such as requests for cross-certificates and cross-certificate renewals. CRS has an extensible design, and we expect more transactions to be defined to support these.

A client enrolls for a certificate by sending a PKCSReq to a server, and the server responds by returning the requested certificate and its associated nonroot CA certificates in a CertRep message. The ability to sign messages in this transaction is quite useful, and it enables an LRA to send preauthenticated certificate requests to a CA. In a variant of this transaction, a client enrolls for two certificates with DualReq, requesting a certificate whose public key is certified for encryption only and another certificate whose public key is certified for signing only. The server returns both certificates with the DualRep response.

**Table 10-1** Transactions Defined by the CRS Protocol

| Transaction | Messages | Description |
|---|---|---|
| Certification of a public key | PKCSReq, CertRep DualReq, DualRep | A client enrolls for a certificate. A client enrolls for a dual certificate. |
| Certificate and CRL retrieval | GetCert, GetCRL, CertRep | A client retrieves a certificate or a CRL. |
| Certificate revocation | RevReq, RevRep | A client requests certificate revocation. |

A client uses the certificate retrieval transaction to download an already issued certificate from a server. This transaction is useful for state recovery within resource-constrained PKI clients, such as low-end IP routers, which do not retain their certificates in nonvolatile memory. If a CA or LRA maintains an LDAP database of certificates, a client also has the option of using the LDAP protocol for certificate retrieval. Similarly, a client can use CRS to download the latest CRL from CA. Note that signing messages in this transaction is of lesser value compared to certificate enrollment because certificates and CRLs are already integrity-protected by the issuing CA via a signature block.

An end user initiates a certificate revocation transaction with an LRA, or with a CA directly, through RevReq to revoke its certificate. If the end user is requesting the revocation because it has lost its private key, it cannot sign the request. If its private key is compromised, the end user can sign its request, but the signature cannot be trusted. Therefore, signing a certificate revocation by an end user is not very meaningful. The end user can use a challenge password to authenticate itself in this case. An LRA, however, is in a much better position to receive a revocation request from an end user, authenticate the request by out-of-band or in-band procedures, and forward a revocation request signed by its private key to the CA.

## Messages

The CRS protocol currently supports eight messages. A message contains a message body (payload) and a set of service indicators. The payload of a message can be optionally encrypted; the payload (encrypted or not) and the service indicators should be integrity-protected by providing a signature block. Note that the service indicators cannot be encrypted and are passed as cleartext. Table 10-2 enumerates the messages currently supported by CRS.

The PKCSReq message consists of a PKCS #10 certificate signing request; it may also contain a challenge password attribute and a set of X.509 extensions. The challenge password can later be used to authenticate an end user when it requests a PKI service, such as a certificate revocation. In response to a PKCSReq request from an end user or an LRA, a CA returns the requested certificate and all of its associated

**Table 10-2** Messages Defined by the CRS Protocol

| Message | Description |
|---------|-------------|
| PKCSReq | A PKCS #10 request for a certificate. |
| CertRep | Response to a PKCSReq, GetCert, and GetCRL. |
| GetCert | Request to query and retrieve an end user's or CA's certificate. |
| GetCRL | Request for the CA's CRL(s). |
| DualReq | Request for separate signature and encryption certificates. |
| DualRep | Response to a DualReq request, containing a signature certificate, an encryption signature, and all of their associated nonroot certificates. |
| RevReq | Request to revoke a certificate. |
| RevRep | Response to a certificate revocation request. |

nonroot certificates in a CertRep message. An end user can request two certificates, one designated for signing and the other for encryption, in a single DualReq message. When a CA receives a DualReq request, it returns both certificates in a single DualRep response.

GetCert and GetCRL are used to retrieve certificates and CRLs from a CA's repository, respectively. The CA responds with a CertRep, returning an appropriate certificate or CRL. The RevReq handles the case where an end-entity has lost its private key and authenticates itself by a challenge password. In this case, the request need not be signed if it contains the challenge password.

### Service Indicators

Service indicators provide contextual header information for a message body. For example, a client or a server uses the messageType service indicator to determine the type of the message (PKCSReq, CertRep, etc.) that it has received. Service indicators are passed as cleartext. The sender of a message, however, hashes the service indicators together with the message body and then signs the digest, thus protecting them for integrity. Service indicators are also called **authenticated attributes** because any changes made to them during transmission can be detected. If sending service indicators as cleartext poses a security threat, a confidentiality service at the transport layer, such as HTTPS, can be used. Table 10-3 lists the service indicators and provides a brief explanation. The messageType, pkiStatus, and failInfo are mandatory and must be present in all messages.

## PKIX-CMP

PKIX-CMP attempts to define a comprehensive set of on-line protocol messages that define all the relevant aspects of certificate creation and management among an end user, LRA, and CA. These messages support interactions between a CA and a client system (an end user or an LRA) with which a key pair is associated, or be-

**Table 10-3** Service Indicators Defined by the CRS Protocol

| Service Indicator | Description |
|---|---|
| version | The version of the CRS protocol. If absent, a value of 0 is assumed. |
| messageType | This field identifies the type of the message body, such as PKCSReq, CertRep, and so on. |
| pkiStatus | This field conveys the success or failure of a request. |
| failInfo | The failInfo field conveys the reason for a failed request. |
| transactionId | This field identifies a transaction. It is useful when a transaction spans more than one pair of request-reply messages. |
| sendorNonce | The sendorNonce field, together with recipientNonce, provides application-level security against reply attacks. |
| recipientNonce | The recipientNonce field, together with sendorNonce, provides application-level security against reply attacks. |

tween two CAs that cross-certify each other. In the next section, we will provide an overview of the management operations supported by PKIX-CMP.

## PKI Management Operations

PKIX-CMP defines seven categories of management operations to support a wide range of interactions between different components of a PKI. These categories and their associated operations are

**CA establishment**   This group supports the establishment of a new CA and includes operations such as creation of initial CRLs and export of CA public key.

**End-entity initialization**   These operations include importing a root CA public key and requesting information about the options supported by a PKI management entity.

**Certification**   This group supports various operations that result in the creation of new certificates such as initial registration, key pair update, certificate update, CA key pair update, cross-certification, and cross-certificate update. **Initial registration** is the process whereby an end user who does not have a certificate from a CA first contacts the CA or LRA to obtain one. The CA may return the certificate directly to the end user, it may post the certificate in its repository, or it may do both. **Key pair update** supports the regular update of a key pair and the generation of a certificate certifying the new key pair, whereas **certificate update** is the recertification of an existing key pair with a new certificate. **CA key pair update** handles the update of CA key pairs. **Cross-certification** enables a CA to request a cross-certificate from another CA; **cross-certificate update** is the renewal of an existing cross-certificate.

**Certificate and CRL publication operations**    PKI management operations that result in the publication of certificates and CRLs.

**Recovery operations**    An end-entity's key materials used for decryption may optionally be backed up by a CA, an LRA, or a key-backup system. These operations allow the entity to recover its backed up key materials due to failures, such as a forgotten password or a lost key chain file.

**Revocation operations**    These PKI operations result in the creation of new CRL entries when an authorized person informs a CA of an abnormal situation that requires certificate revocation.

**Personal security environment (PSE) operations**    PSE refers to local trusted storage that is required to securely store an end-entity's private key or public key of a root CA. Although PKIX-CMP does not delineate the PSE operations, it defines a data structure that can form the basis of such operations.

## VeriSign OnSite

In this section, we discuss VeriSign OnSite as an example of how a commercial vendor implemented an LRA service. OnSite implements the CA Queues Requests for LRA model discussed earlier.

OnSite (http://www.verisign.com/onsite/index.html) is an LRA service that provides all of the necessary certificate lifecycle services, applications support, and management tools required to deploy public-key technology within an organization. OnSite consists of customized end user enrollment Web pages, administrative control and management Web pages, and a certificate directory distribution service. End users interact with customized, Web-based enrollment forms to request and receive their certificates. The enrollment forms and lifecycle Web pages can be hosted at the organization's site or by VeriSign.

VeriSign promotes OnSite as an LRA service that allows a company to deploy PKI solutions quickly, easily, and inexpensively, as an alternative to do-it-yourself certification products. See Appendix C for VeriSign's analysis of cases when a company acts as LRA and outsources its key management to a CA versus when it installs a certification product and becomes its own CA.

### Certificate Enrollment and Distribution

As Figure 10-3 illustrates, several steps are involved between enrolling for a certificate and picking it up. This section discusses these steps and presents the OnSite service from the perspective of a subscriber.

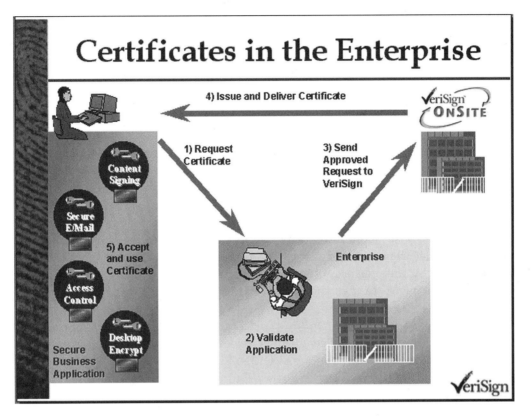

**Figure 10-3** OnSite model for certificate enrollment and distribution.

1. An applicant for a certificate submits a Web-based certificate enrollment form. The form is securely transferred to OnSite, and OnSite keeps the request in pending queue for consideration.

2. The OnSite LRAA uses his smart card to gain secure access to the OnSite administrative Web site. The smart card contains the LRAA certificate, which is required for access. The LRAA reviews the contents of each certificate application in the pending queue and validates the identity of the applicant and her affiliation with the organization.

3. If the LRAA validates the identity of the applicant and the information in the enrollment form, he approves the certificate application and instructs OnSite to issue a certificate to the applicant. In the Authentication Models section, we will describe two methods for authenticating certificate enrollments. The LRAA rejects the applicant's application if he cannot confirm her identity.

4. A VeriSign's CA or a CA specifically set up for the organization creates and signs the certificate. The choice of the CA depends on whether the certificates are considered public or private, as described in the Public versus Private Certification section. OnSite sends the applicant e-mail notifying her of the approval. The e-mail includes a PIN and the URL where she can pick up her certificate.

5. Using the PIN, the applicant picks up the certificate at the specified URL and becomes a subscriber if she accepts the certificate. VeriSign publishes public certificates in its repository; private certificates are published by the organization in its own directory.

## Certificate Management

OnSite provides a set of administrative pages that an LRAA uses to interactively manage the lifecycle of certificates, configure subscriber enrollment pages, import root key of a CA, and perform other administrative tasks. OnSite tightly controls access to these pages through the use of certificates (see the Controlling Access to LRAA Web Site section).

In this section we explain OnSite's certificate management operations. These operations result in creation of certificates, rejection of certificate requests, revocation of certificates, and downloading of CRLs. Figure 10-4 illustrates the OnSite's certificate management Web page.

**Process Requests**  This operation presents a list of all certificate applications that are in the pending queue and have not yet been approved or rejected.

**Figure 10-4**  OnSite's certificate management operations.

LRAA reviews the enrollment information for each request, determines whether it meets the authentication rules, and approves or rejects it.

**View Requests**   This operation enables LRAA to search the database of requests for particular applicants over a particular time period. LRAA can further narrow the search by specifying an applicant's name, e-mail address, or state of a request (approved or rejected).

**View Certificates**   LRAA uses View Certificates to search the database of certificates for particular subscribers over a particular time period. LRAA can search by the applicant's name or e-mail address or by certificate serial number.

**Revoke Certificates**   This operation enables LRAA to search for valid certificates and revoke them.

**Download CRL**   This operation allows LRAA to download the latest version of the list of serial numbers of revoked certificates. OnSite regularly updates the CRL, typically nightly.

**Reports**   LRAA uses the Reports function to request various reports on the status and activity of the OnSite service.

**Update Directory**   OnSite maintains a complete history of all certificates that LRAA has approved and prepares certificate directory data files that interoperate with an organization's directory server. LRAA uses Update Directory to generate this directory information into a directory file for import into the organization's directory server.

## Authentication Models

OnSite prescribes two models for enabling an LRAA to authenticate certificate enrollment requests. In this section, we discuss each model at length.

### PIN Model

In the **PIN model,** the LRAA generates a PIN for each subscriber in its domain and sends it to the subscriber in a secure manner (e.g., via First Class postal mail or protected internal organization mail). As an optional extension to this model, the subscriber could be instructed to visit the LRAA to present her ID badge and receive the PIN directly from the LRAA. The subscriber is instructed to enter the PIN in one of the predefined (or comment) fields. The LRAA then approves the certificate request based on a match of subscriber name and the PIN contained in the subscriber application with the list (subscriber name/PIN) locally retained by the LRAA.

### Shared Secret Model

In the **shared secret model,** the LRAA instructs the subscriber to enter during en-rollment one or more unique pieces of information, such as last payroll check num-ber, amount of federal taxes paid, or Social Security number, that are known only by the subscriber and a trusted representative of the organization such as the LRAA. This data is entered in one or more of predefined (or comment) fields as spec-ified by the LRAA. The LRAA then approves the certificate request based on the match of the subscriber name and the shared secret(s).

## Controlling Access to LRAA Web Site

An administrator who wants to act as LRAA for OnSite on behalf of an organization must apply to VeriSign and enroll for a LRAA certificate. VeriSign authenticates the certificate request to ensure that the applicant represents an authorized member of the organization and then sends the administrator a smart card and a smart card reader. Through a Web page, the administrator generates a key pair on the smart card, sends the public key to VeriSign, and receives an LRAA certificate.

When accessing an LRAA page, the Web server engages in a client authentica-tion protocol with the browser and requires the LRAA to present his certificate. OnSite uses the presented certificate to authenticate the LRAA and determine the organization that he represents, which is encoded as an extension field in the cer-tificate. See the Client-Centric Processing section in Chapter 3 for a discussion of using certificates to encode application-specific information.

## Public versus Private Certification

An organization that uses the OnSite service can decide whether its certificates should be public or private.

### Public Certificates

Public certificates are digitally signed by appropriate issuing authority classes within VeriSign's PKI hierarchy, the roots of which are embedded in most popular browsers, servers, and e-mail tools. Because they chain to preinstalled trust points, public certifi-cates typically do not have interoperability problems when used outside of the organi-zation. For example, you can send a digitally signed e-mail using a public certificate to a friend outside of your organization; your friend's e-mail tool will probably recognize the authority who signed your certificate and will not issue any warnings.

### Private Certificates

Private certificates are issued by issuing authorities that are set up specifically for an organization. The root keys of these issuing authorities are not preinstalled in certificate-using systems; they must be imported in a trustworthy manner into all such systems within the organization (OnSite provides a function to import the root key of a CA into an application). To provide interoperability across organizations, other organizations must also be willing to recognize these private authorities and import their root keys.

## Local Hosting

When OnSite first starts up, the certificate enrollment forms and certificate lifecycle services (verifying the validity of a certificate, retrieving a certificate, requesting revocation, etc.) used by subscribers are hosted on a VeriSign Web server. Alternatively, an organization can choose to host these pages on its local intranet server. Called **local hosting,** this option allows an organization to fully customize these pages to suit its needs. When an organization locally hosts these pages, subscribers access the certificate enrollment and lifecycle pages through an internal Web server instead of through the VeriSign server. All the enrollment and lifecycle requests, however, are sent directly to VeriSign.

## VeriSign OnSite Automated Authentication

The CA Queues Requests for LRA model may not meet the needs of every organization. Consider a large company that wants to deploy S/MIME within its organization for its tens of thousands of employees. Although it would be practical for each employee to individually submit certificate enrollment applications, it would be time-consuming and error-prone for an LRAA to manually process all the queued applications. Furthermore, the authentication information that an employee submits to a CA may be sensitive company or personal information. For example, a company may want to implement an authentication policy in which a subscriber provides her Social Security number or the amount of federal tax withheld in the enrollment form. The company, however, does not want to submit such sensitive information about its employees to an external CA.

In this section, we discuss VeriSign OnSite Automated Authentication, an LRA service that implements the Automated Processing model (see the Automated Processing section). OnSite Automated Authentication enables an LRA to exchange on-line signed messages with VeriSign using the CRS protocol. When VeriSign receives a request from an LRA, it checks the request signature to verify that it originated from a known LRA, automatically processes the request, creates an appropriate response, signs it, and sends the response to the LRA. Because VeriSign does not queue the incoming key management requests from LRA subscribers, the LRAA no longer has to manually view and process each request. Furthermore, subscribers do not need to submit any sensitive authentication information directly to VeriSign.

Instead, LRA performs the authentication process internally and sends signed, preauthenticated requests to VeriSign.

A company that acts as LRA on behalf of its employees can automate the internal authentication process. When an employee uses a Web browser to submit a certificate enrollment request, the company's Web server can access an internal authentication database, such as its human resources database, to confirm the identity of the employee. The identity confirmation rules can include checking the submitted personal information against the employee's record in the database, checking the submitted PIN against the one assigned to the employee, and so on. If an enrollment request passes the confirmation rules, the company uses CRS to send a signed certificate request to VeriSign and immediately receives the employee's certificate. If the request fails, the company can notify the applicant about the failure or forward a signed request to VeriSign asking that the request be queued for manual authentication.

## Certificate Enrollment and Distribution

Figure 10-5 illustrates the process of applying for a certificate and retrieving it through OnSite Automated Authentication:

1. An applicant accesses a Web page to enter her enrollment information and authentication data (shared secret or PIN). The applicant submits this data, along with the public key generated by the browser, to the organization's Web server.

2. A CGI program extracts the data and calls a verification function that queries the organization's authentication database and determines the authentication status (approve, reject, or pending) of the certificate enrollment request. The verification function is written by the organization. The enrollment data and the status of authentication are signed by the organization's signing private key.

3. The Web server uses the CRS protocol to automatically send the signed enrollment request to VeriSign. If the verification was successful, VeriSign issues the certificate immediately. If it fails, the request can be queued for manual processing by an OnSite LRAA. VeriSign sends the certificate and serial number to the organization's Web server.

4. The Web server calls a register operation to update the database or LDAP directory server with the certificate and its serial number. This makes the certificate available for downloading by others.

5. The Web server forwards the certificate and its serial number to the applicant's Web browser.

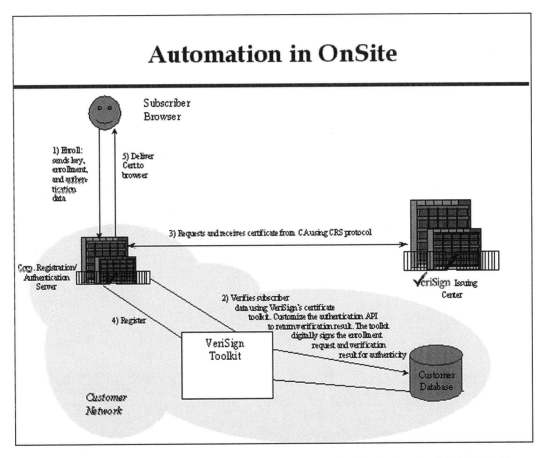

**Figure 10-5**  Certificate enrollment and retrieval through OnSite Automated Administration.

## Summary

Although as providers of trust it is natural for a CA to perform both key management and authentication, there are certain situations where tight coupling of these two tasks poses some limitations. Decoupling of key management from authentication enables organizations to act as the LRA and outsource key management, while maintaining tight control over the registration and authentication processes.

LRA performs a variety of tasks, such as assigning distinguished names to subscribers, receiving certificate applications, confirming identity information, checking identification cards, reporting revocations, accepting renewal requests, distributing hardware tokens, and collecting obsolete tokens. LRA can also generate key pairs for subscribers, archive key pairs, and recover lost key pairs. There are different ways to implement LRA, some of which require management protocols.

# Part IV

# The Trust Dilemma

Part IV is motivated by a desire to empower the decision-maker attempting to make sense of the public-key infrastructure potential and ramifications. Keen observers may notice that this motivation is very similar to that guiding Part III on security management practices. In this part of the book, we look at digital certificates through the eyes of certificate users and those who accredit systems.

Security has traditionally been viewed either as an unwarranted burden forced upon liberal users under pressure from auditors or as some top secret technology deployed to maintain national security. Useful deployment has tended to happen either as a total institutional response or not at all. The openness of the Internet and its technology has changed such perspectives; however, that openness and the mass use of cryptography is both a threat and an opportunity.

The essence of integrity is trust, as we saw in Part II. We will now explore several perspectives on trust itself. If we regard integrity as the regulator of openness, then trust is the spark of electricity with the potential to drive the engines of secure electronic commerce. However, trust is like electricity—it is a dangerous element that must be handled carefully; it can easily shock and burn. Users need to learn to manage both anxiety and overconfidence concerning Internet threats and address risk by managing trust decisions using experience and judgment.

How is the average consumer and computer systems administrator to embrace the responsibilities of trust management? What are the factors? How can one see through the fog of technology and obtain a clear view of the issues to be addressed when making security decisions or deploying security systems? The three chapters of this part address the practicalities of commercial trust management. In describing the issues and opportunities, we have the goal of enabling readers to learn a little about the ephemeral nature of trust itself.

In Chapter 11, we present the topic of certificate policies. Policy enables the administration and management of distributed communications and transactional security. With a view to enabling secure electronic commerce, we consider some of the underlying trust factors. We argue that the embodiment of such policy elements into actual practice provides sufficient rationale for a reasonable person to view the resulting infrastructure as ready for mainstream consumer transactions.

In Chapter 12, we consider the role digital certificates play in enabling a trusted infrastructure. If we are to rely upon security for our daily transactions, what basis do we have to rely on the theories of cryptographers to obtain assurances that we are all indeed protected? Digital certificates represent a sea-change in perspective concerning how we look at the Internet when powerful cryptography is unleashed. To address commerce and consumers, certificates should enable the Internet to mature and embrace brands.

Chapter 13 rounds off the presentation of trust issues by bringing us down to earth on the topic of operational security. We will all increasingly need to face down the specter of the security audit. From a wide range of issues, we pick a set of security procedures that particularly affect the quality of a certificate issuing and management process. Hopefully, users will begin to formulate for themselves criteria that will enable them to measure and validate the claims of trusted third parties, while understanding their own critical role in ensuring the effectiveness of the security system.

# 11

# Certificate Policy and Certification Practice

Transactions are the lifeblood of commerce. To translate into practice the architecture of authentication discussed in Chapter 3, the technology and standards discussed in Chapter 7, and the management systems highlighted in Chapters 8–10, we need a common technical idea that blends these factors together to form a transaction-ready security infrastructure. That idea is certificate policy.

Communication systems have long used policy signals and carefully formulated processing rules to secure the interworking of information systems. However, the potential of certificate policy is greater than merely mitigating the technical security risks faced by two systems. Rather, it can express and control the shared *intent* of the communicating parties. No longer are parties merely key holders, network adapters, or abstract, anonymous users of network security services; they are buyers choosing products, merchants making offers for sale, banks receiving payments, judges considering evidence, and many other possibilities.

We commence our discussion of certificate policy by considering policy generally in communications and management systems. In the main body of the chapter, we then discuss several elements of technical policy that those charged with administering the collective public-key infrastructure must address.

## Transactions and Certificate Policy

In the first three parts of the book, we presented the mathematics, models, frameworks, applications, and technology demonstrating the potential of public-key cryptography and supporting infrastructure to help secure the integrity and confidentiality of communications. Users of mass-market products can now encrypt credit card numbers, guard against viruses, and send signed messages. However, commercial adoption of the same facilities requires something more than mere protection of communication channels. The nature of global business simply requires more than secure communications; it requires trusted transactions.

## Policy and Administration

In a given operating environment, policy is a way to govern the interchange of messages. For the purposes of this book, we define **policy** as the governing principles that control the interchange of messages. Used purposefully, **policy rules** implement the administrative goals of the environments used by parties to engage in information exchange. Secure communications combined with the sound administration of policy can provide the necessary technical assurances that will enable parties to rely upon the integral exchange of electronic information.

When two parties are known to each other, the protocol under which messages flow tends to become standardized in order to promote efficiency and reliability. An authoritative administrative framework and carefully defined set of policy rules codify the intended meanings of the communication acts represented by the exchange of messages. A common administrative framework can establish intended meanings clearly to all before the protocol of messages is concluded.

For our purposes, a **transaction** is a particular set of communication acts intended by the parties to be interpreted against an agreed-upon administrative policy. In commercial transactions, administrative policy governing commercial-grade transactions often invokes legal standards and processes (whose nature we will not even attempt to address).

We define a **trusted transaction** as a transaction conducted under a security policy administered by a recognized security management domain [VARAD]. The use of transactions in technical security models is well established. For example, when discussing role-based security policies, Ferraiolo and Kuhn [NIST] use Clark and Wilson security transforms to mathematically model mandatory access control in terms of transactions assigned to different roles in an authorization scheme.

When using a certificate-based security system, elements of security policy are embodied in the form of a **certificate policy.** It is common to all involved parties and may be expressed formally in terms of transactional integrity and operational reliability requirements. We discuss some of these requirements in Chapters 12 and 13.

## Certificate Policy

Certificate policy is a specialized form of administrative policy tuned to transactions performed during certificate management on the one hand and use or reliance on certificates on the other. Indirectly, certificate policy[1] can also govern the trans-

---

1. Some PKI architectures use the term **CA policy** to distinguish this general notion from **X.509 certificate policy.**

actions conducted using a communications system protected by a certificate-based security system.

In policy-bound management regimes, third-party CAs issue and manage the digital certificates. Acceptance of the policy rules and the governing role of a given certifier enables certificate subjects and certificate users alike to express their consent to be controlled by the rule set of the third party. By subscribing to the certification service of such a CA or when using its services to establish certificate status, the governed parties can signal their common intentions to regard the communications as trusted transactions.

The role of a third-party CA is very similar to third-party practice in the commercial EDI value-added network (VAN) world, in which senders and receivers of messages transported or switched by the VAN obtain mutual integrity assurances through use of the common provider. In many ways, trusted-third-party CAs play the role of *virtual* VANs. Trust networks play the role of the VANs that switch and route messages between subscribers bound to other VANs.

### X.509 Certificate Policy

X.509 certificate policy is but one element of security policy administered by a CA. As we shall see later in this chapter, a host of other certification practices impinge upon the activities of CAs acting as trusted third parties. In some cases, these practices are governed by specific law, in order to have the communication system provide the legal assurances required by the transacting parties. The technical X.509 recommendation, however, does not address these areas.

Through X.509, ISO and ITU-T characterize and specify a general authentication framework for use by communication systems and network applications. Having established a framework, these standards organizations expect others to define security protocol specifications and applications identifying policies that constrain certificate contents. By controlling the critical certificate extensions, such policies and associated enforcement technology can support provision of the security services required by particular applications. (We saw a clear example of a certificate policy schema in Chapter 7, for the SET protocol.)

Facilitating schematization of the extensions to the X.509 certificate message format is a primary motivation for X.509 certificate policy. Conformance and use of content schemas are an important part of implementing trusted transactions. The rule system that enforces the required integrity policy can be managed at the CA and/or at the end-systems during certificate use. Mappings of extension content schemas can also facilitate interdomain integrity policy recognition and management. (We investigate certification domains in Chapter 12.)

The X.509 recommendation specifies many standard extensions that enable remote management of user keys. As we saw in Chapter 7, other organizations have specified additional extension syntaxes and security procedures. X.509 certificate policy can signal the use of particular management procedures for CA key pair up-dating, separation of purpose of certified keys, subject key pair updating, private key usage periods, limitations on the intended use of certificates in different environ-ments, interdomain recognition of key management practices, and use of particular algorithms by specific security mechanisms. (See the X.509 recommendation for full details or our summary of important extensions in Chapter 3.)

X.509 assumes that CAs recognizing particular policy elements will issue policy statements and signal their recognition by including certificate policy identifiers and qualifiers (if any) in the certificates they issue. These may be simple or com-plex. X.509 certificate policy statements have spawned into an entire theory (and indeed competing legal theories) of certificate practice statements, as we discuss later (see http://www.ietf.org/internet-drafts/draft-chokhani-cps-00.txt).

## Administration Frameworks

A commercial transaction normally exhibits the property that two or more parties have consented to be governed by a contract for the sale and delivery of goods or ser-vices. As distance or culture separates the parties and as relationships become more tenuous, international trade conventions often codify best business practices in the form of standards to bridge the trust gap. These guidelines often serve as models for national and local practices. In the field of certificate policy and practice, the International Chamber of Commerce has drafted a statement concerning interna-tional digitally ensured commerce [GUIDEC].

Certificate policies play a critical part in administering trusted transactions. However, the administrative function may go beyond merely protecting the security system per se, as in military uses of cryptography or as contemplated by X.509. Certificate-based key distribution inherently structures and organizes the commu-nication relationships between people.

By profiling certificate content and by tuning certification and usage practices to embody the trust requirements of a particular transactional environment, the process of managing and distributing keys becomes a means to govern (and help protect) transactions by policy. Once administrative policy is devolved from tech-nology, the rules of the day can be set into standards as often as the people affected by them require and desire. When the policy rules are enforced using cryptographic security mechanisms and schema-based certificates, the very flexible certificate ex-tension mechanism becomes a tool to both express and implement those standards.

## Elements of Policy and Best Practices

Defining policy is clearly a critical step in fielding public-key cryptography as an au-thentication infrastructure. If digital certificates are the means of projecting legal assurances that communication security risks are being controlled, then within the scope of policy lies every conceivable security issue. Every common practice, usage, convention, and risk factor must be addressed if the use of a security procedure is to be deemed reasonable under the circumstances. If just one exploitable loophole exists, the integrity of the transaction may be undermined.

It seems a daunting and even impossible task to completely specify a certificate policy. The omission of an adequate qualification over just one issue may render a policy ineffective. By considering the design of certificate policy from a dispute-resolution perspective, we attempt to gain some insight on a process for establishing general administrative and certificate policy.

To control where liability falls, commercial law has evolved to establish practices and security procedures. We now analyze certificate policy assuming that parties will fall into legal dispute. The reader can catch a glimpse of the big issues faced by the policy architect in dealing with future dispute handling. A general, commerce-oriented discussion of certification practice is presented in [GUIDEC]. An example of tailoring an administrative regime certification to a noncommercial environment is being specified by the National Institutes of Health (see http://www.alw.nih.gov/~rmalick/pki/docs/certpolicy/certificate_policyv1.html).

## Records

Creation and maintenance of records lie at the heart of a commercial transaction-processing system. Many record-handling procedures are established with dispute handling in mind. Being prepared for possible disputes requires more than mere records retention, however. You must be prepared to defend the design and operational controls of the systems used to ensure the trustworthiness of the records (see http://www.si.umich.edu/e-recs/Sesam/). Only then can such systems be used by people to rely on records as potential evidence during resolution of legal disputes.

Commercial certificate-based security systems tend to use trusted third parties to manage certificates and administer a common security policy governing the transacting parties. Certificate policy designers need to address the likelihood that being a trusted third party will require constant preparation for trial, in which the CA can be a witness or defendant.

### *Practices*

It falls to a so-called certification practice statement (CPS) to disclose how management control systems guarantee the operations of a CA's security management infrastructure. In large part, the quality of the CPS substantiates the assurances of the CA's security claims concerning its authentication processes.

[GUIDEC] defines a **Certification Practice Statement** as "a statement of the practices which a certifier employs in issuing certificates generally, or employed in issuing a particular certificate." Perhaps the most famous CPS to date is that published by VeriSign, at http://www.verisign.com/repository/cps.

The legal enforceability of a CA's policy may depend upon the effectiveness and completeness of its certification practices and their disclosure. The records demonstrating a CA's compliance with recognized integrity standards are central to its ability to claim that its repository and records system are trustworthy.

## Subscription

Acting as a third-party certifier involves a possibility that the first and second parties governed by the CA's policy will fall into legal dispute. If a transaction is repudiated by one of the parties, the policy and practices of the CA may be challenged as the repudiating party seeks to disclaim responsibility. That party is likely to attempt to show the CA has shown total disregard for transactional security issues; therefore its policy and assurances are worthless. The enforcing party is likely to seek to rely upon the CA's original assurances to show that the policy represents good practice and was reasonably followed. Regardless of who wins, the CA's policies and operational conduct are likely to be closely scrutinized!

Where certificate-based security systems help protect transactions, a user may claim that an apparent loss of security was due to some failure of the trusted third party. The failure could be in the design, the management, or the operation of the system; the failure may come to light only years after the transaction took place. The operators of the CA may be held accountable.

For example, if a user relies upon the assumption that an e-mail message protected under a shared encryption key is assured to be confidential by the wonders of digital certificates, and the content is then published openly due to key compromise, the user may try to hold the CA accountable. If an alleged fraud is committed, it may be easier to sue the CA than the perpetrator. Establishing contracted subscriber relationships and formal processes for claims for faulty certificate reliability are two important commercial practices. Corporate lawyers use contracts and notices to manage liability of CAs much as they would with any service provider.

In a litigious society, the third party needs to protect itself from unlimited liability so that it can function. Binding the parties using a CA's certification services by contract is the lawyer's answer to managing liability. However, the act of subscribing to a formally organized service offers more than a way to protect self-interested CA operators. The protocol for subscription and its embedded legal agreements provides the opportunity for both the first and the second parties to become bound to a common policy.

### *Practices*

A **subscriber agreement** is a precise protocol concluding with a legal agreement between a party requesting key certification and a certifier. The sequence of steps required to subscribe may be disclosed in a CPS. Additional warranties may be offered to applicants during subscription in the form of protection plans. Such plans formalize the claims process and rules for disbursing payment for covered losses (e.g., see VeriSign's NetSure protection plan at http://www.verisign.com/repository/netsure/). In general, they help describe the assurances of the CA in terms of the financial protections offered, sometimes for a fee.

The protocol for agreement results in obligations being passed from the CA to subscriber and vice versa (e.g., see http://www.verisign.com/repository/SUBAGR.html). Whereas an "applicant" shall send a request for key certification, the CA shall "approve" the issuance of a certificate. Whereas a certificate must be applied for, upon acceptance the subscriber may incur duties and responsibilities to, for example, suitably protect private keys. Furthermore, the subscriber may make legal representations to the CA and others upon acceptance.

Subscription to a CA's certificate issuing and managing service is an important element in obtaining the trusted third-party benefits, but because not all communication acts are transactions, all Internet key certifications do not require formal subscription protocols.

## Relying Party Relationships

If the CA is known as the third party, and the subscriber is known as the first party, what term do we use for the second party? The second party is conventionally known as a **relying party.** The relying party expects CA services to be reliable and may assume that when relying on the certificate in the legal sense. The relying party, in our context, is the recipient of a communication event protected by a certificate-based security service. Of course, a CA can be the recipient of such an event, thereby playing the roles of both third party and relying party.

Transactional security requires both parties to a transaction to be bound to a common policy. As the infrastructure of CAs expands, and organizational and residential users sign up for certificates with their choice of trusted CA, it is ever more unlikely that both parties will subscribe to the same CA's service. It cannot be assumed that all CAs will have interworking agreements recognizing each others' practices, just as not all EDI VANs offer arbitrary switching. Consequently, each CA lays out in its policy what reliance means in all the pertinent circumstances it can reasonably claim to control. Procedures for binding parties to the reliance element of certificate policy are usually a side effect of subscription. However, relying parties may not necessarily be subscribers of any CA service; they may simply be recipients of a digitally signed file while visiting a news publisher's Web site.

Relying on certificates is not something that occurs only upon direct receipt of a digital signature, nor does it occur merely in relation to the identification of parties. An S/MIME e-mail originator may rely upon the fact that an intended recipient of a to-be-encrypted e-mail has agreed never to forward messages released under confidence. During message preparation, the originator may inspect the recipient's certificate and note the governing policy. By evaluating the credibility of the CA's CPS and checking the revocation status of the certificate, the originator may then decide to release the data. In this case, reliance has already occurred prior to the actual release of the message. The originator is relying upon the certification act communicated by the digital certificate as a (partial) expression that the recipient is bound to a policy.

It will often be the case that the relying party will interact with a CA or other authority to determine if the certificate is currently operational. At this point the CA may require that party to abide by a **relying party agreement** (see http://www.verisign.com/repository/rpa.html). Given the nature of all cryptographic systems to suffer compromise, one may assume that a judge will require any reasonable party to have checked revocation status. Of course, one may *use* a certificate at one's own risk without *relying* on any representations; however, legal recourse may be limited.

A CA may ensure that the path to obtaining such status information requires the accessing party to agree to be bound to the governing policy. In this way, the loop binding all parties to a common governing policy for a trusted transaction is closed.

## Operational Status

The effectiveness of a legal instrument is always in a state of doubt; nothing is certain—assuming it was valid in the first place. Similarly, what is clearly defined today may be poorly defined tomorrow. The operational status of a certificate is fundamental to the enforceability of policy during dispute handling, particularly once a certificate has expired.

To be useful during disputes, the rules of the policy should be in effect at the time of the hearing (governing the required conduct of the arbitration process) and optionally at the time the events in question occurred (should the parties wish to mandate a security policy). Certificates expire, and they can be revoked at any moment. When processing a transaction, the relying party should establish an evidence trail showing that the act of reliance was validly performed. Each certificate in question should be demonstrably valid, operational, and in effect.

As we discussed earlier, deciding to rely on a certificate requires one to determine its revocation status. Determining that the certificate is operational requires an additional determination. The security service using the certificate must itself have been validly invoked. Designating a certificate as operational implies that the relying party determined that the service was invoked during the operational period of the certificate.

An example may help. Suppose the digital signature on a U.K. contract signed using RSA in January 1975 and validated using a reliable certificate with a one-year expiration period would have been potentially effective until January 1976. Providing we have records that validation occurred in February 1975, we can establish the contract's original validity in the future. We can claim that the operational status of the controlling certificate back in 1975 authenticates the historical document today.

Operational status of the certificate is very relevant to a subscriber both before and after certificate expiration. It is arguably unreasonable to rely upon a digital signature if the verification key is available only using an expired certificate. However, it may be reasonable to use (but not rely upon) one's own expired (and therefore nonoperational) certificate in some circumstances. For example, one may be attempting to decrypt an archived S/MIME encrypted message.

## Practices

A commercial CA will probably provide revocation status information to parties who are willing to be bound to its certificate policy. [GUIDEC] suggests that the notion of a valid certificate is tightly bound to the need to give notice. It defines a valid certificate as "a certificate which its certifier has issued or disclosed to another person in circumstances where that person's reliance on the certificate is foreseeable, unless the certifier timely gives notice that the certificate is unreliable, or unless the certificate is a public key certificate which has been revoked or is, at the time in question, suspended."

By tying the notion of validity to that of giving notice, which [GUIDEC] implies to be a function of a CA when publishing revocation information, we have made a good start.

As a practice, a CA should disclose when a certificate becomes valid. This is usually the moment the certificate is first published in a recognized repository. Mere issuance and signing of the certificate content by the CA does not necessarily make the certificate valid. In some issuing regimes, the applicant may be required to accept the certificate along with all the policy obligations and become a policy-bound subscriber before the CA will publish the certificate.

To address the period between issuing and publication, CA vendors are using the notion of operational period and operational certificate.[2] An issued, signed, operational certificate is not valid until it has been accepted by the subscriber who requested key certification. One cannot reasonably rely upon an invalid certificate, one can argue. But how does one know if a certificate is valid, if acceptance status information is not present in the certificate?

---

2. The VeriSign CPS defines operational certificate as *"Operational Certificate: 'A certificate which is within its operational period at the present date and time or at a different specified date and time, depending on the context'."* See https://www.verisign.com/repository/cps.

The trick performed by the CA's subscription protocol is straightforward. Whereas the certificate was published to the applicant for the purposes of accepting it, there was an obligation in the subscriber agreement that it would not be used prior to that decision. Upon receipt of notification of the decision to accept the certificate, the CA publishes the certificate in its formal repository as an act of giving notice. At that moment, revocation status information should also become available.

Of course, to determine that the certificate is valid, potential relying parties must consult the repository to determine publication status and revocation status. Access to the notice repository may be controlled by a relying party agreement.

Having validated a certificate, additional policy-based conditions usually control the standards for reliance. We do not believe that a certificate is either reliable or unreliable, as [GUIDEC] suggests. Reliability is a subjective matter to be determined by the certificate user, and it requires the management of trust models and the execution of trust policies, as we will discuss in Chapter 12.

### Additional On-Line Reading

The following list of URLs refers to papers and initiatives on policy from additional or complementary perspectives:

**NIH**   http://www.alw.nih.gov/~rmalick/pki/docs/nihpolicy-whitepaper

**Utah**   http://csrc.nist.gov/pki/twg/utah/index.htm

**Utah critique**   http://www.softwareindustry.org/issues/docs-org/digsig.pdf

**IETF**   http://www.ietf.org/internet-drafts/draft-chokhani-cps-00.txt

**ABA "guidelines" tutorial**   http://dev.abanet.org/scitech/ec/isc/dsg-tutorial.html

## Summary

Certificate policy lies at the heart of transaction systems secured using certificate-based security systems. Legal-grade certificate policy binding may use transactions during certificate management and usage or reliance on certificates. The design of public policies and their administration of large communities will tend to invoke legal standards and processes.

Commercial-grade certificate policies may facilitate electronic writings, certificate-based authentication, and digital signatures. Trusted third parties underpinning public trust will need to qualify their systems for keeping transactional records, their processes for controlling subscription to management services, and their systems for giving notice of certificate status.

Parties in an open community can be bound to a common set of rules either by the process of subscription or the process of reliance. Relying parties may become bound to the policy when accessing certificate status information.

Authority-specific policy rules may specify particular procedures for certificate chain validation. Validating a certificate is a part of the process of relying on a certificate and the assurances supplied by the issuer. Validation of certificates may govern the effectiveness of transactions they control. A CA will disclose when a certificate becomes valid, if validity is not a property of certificate signing.

For a certificate to be published in a repository, and thereby be designated as valid, prior acceptance of the certificate by a subscriber may be required. Upon accepting associated policy obligations, subscribers become policy-bound with respect to their subsequent use of the certificate and related keys.

# References

[CPS] Certification Practices Statement, VeriSign, 1996. http://www.verisign.com/repository/cps.

[GUIDEC] *General Usage for International Digitally Ensured Commerce*, International Chamber of Commerce Electronic Commerce Project, http://www.iccwbo.org/guidec2.htm.

[NIST] Ferraiolo, D., and R. Kuhn. "Role-Based Access Controls," Proceedings Volume II, 15th National Computer Security Conference, 1992.

[VARAD] Varadharajan, V. "A Security Reference Model for a Distributed Object System and Its Application," Proceedings, 15th National Computer Security Conference, 1992.

# Chapter
# 12

# Secure Electronic Commerce

In the field of digital certificate issuing, we use the term **trust network** as another name for a management domain of certification authorities. Monolithic trust-network management processes tend to encounter scaling problems as the size of the CA community desiring interoperability and uniformity for their users grows. Distributing operational responsibility and delegating management authority within the community is a common way to address the underlying engineering and social issues.

Large-scale certificate-based key distribution features scaleability properties that are naturally addressed by established techniques for distributing operational control. As we saw in Part III, a certificate issuing and management system can be functionally distributed into several processes: cryptographic signing, certificate management and distribution, local registration and user authentication, and so on. In addition, as we discussed in Chapter 11, a certificate profile may mandate policy rules over certificate issuing and use. It is instructive to investigate how these design features may be used in combination to control the integrity of a large-scale key distribution system.

To understand some of the integrity factors facing certificate-based security systems, we will analyze their assurances of protection in a key distribution system based upon the process of certificate reliance (see Chapter 11). Our aim is to address how this relates to consumer-friendly commerce on the Internet. By way of introduction we rationalize the security benefits of digital certificate-based security systems by systematizing the notions of integrity, trust, policy, and protection. In the second section, we apply our understanding of certification chains, certificate policies, and management systems to introduce models for organizing CAs into management domains, forming trust networks. The final section addresses the enforcement of technical-PKI security policy and models the essence of trust as we see it, drawing together several threads of discussion to establish what we believe the term **secure** means when used in the phrase **secure electronic commerce.**

## Trusted Key Distribution

Information security and secure system design are two disciplines that are likely to play a significant role protecting the evolving secure electronic commerce infrastructure on the Internet. In this section, we look at what it means for a public key infrastructure to operate as part of a secure system. We will see that certificate-based security hinges on the notion of trust associated with an X.509 certificate-based key distribution mechanism. As trust is the bedrock of traditional commerce systems, it seems vital to understand the means by which trust relationships can be protected by the information systems that enable electronic commerce.

To understand the relationship between public key infrastructures and secure electronic commerce, we analyze the protection problems faced by security mechanisms relying upon public-key cryptography and certificates. Summers [SUMM97] defines a **protection problem** as "a description of some class of restricted behaviors." The basic protection guarantee to be met by a large, certificate-based asymmetric key distribution system is integrity. Perhaps we should apply the protection problem definition and ask what behavior must be restricted to induce integrity in a certificate-based security system.

## Information System Protection

A philosophy of protection for all certificate-based key distribution might be expressed in terms of a cryptographer's axiom:

> If the keys are trustworthy because their distribution system has integrity and the security mechanisms rely upon the keys to be effective, then trust in the keys transfers to trust in the mechanisms.

And from trusted security mechanisms one can provide security services. With trusted security services one can build secure information systems satisfying a security policy such as mandatory integrity.

To answer the question we have posed, we begin by deconstructing two environmental models that introduced correctness and reliability:

**Computer communications**    In Chapter 1, we described the OSI layer model of computer communication. We also described the X.800 security architecture that allows communication systems to address security requirements in terms of a distributed security management model. This framework for placing security services in protocol stacks addresses secure communications in terms of protecting data flow. In the X.800 world, security services restrict data flow by ensuring that the defined layer protocols are followed *correctly* and that the (secure) layer services are delivered to their users without undetected interference.

**Policy rules**    In Chapter 11, we introduced a model of certificate policies and certification practices, which engendered goal-oriented administration of a transactional system. By formulating policy as rules and ensuring that the rules govern meaningful flow of real-world information, a policy-administering organization may protect and control its information processing systems. The protection problem faced by the architect is to ensure the *reliability* of the information by restricting such designation, legally where possible, to only those parties who are using the information in the manner intended by the policy.

In these two models, correctness and reliability are assured by the strength and design of security mechanisms used. When the effectiveness of a security mechanism is founded upon a cryptosystem, protection ultimately relies upon the strength of cryptographic algorithms and the procedures that govern the handling of the keys and other cryptographic materials. We know from our cryptographer's axiom that a security mechanism built using strong cryptography is only as trustworthy as the keys. Reasoning backwards, we arrive at an information system protection hypothesis:

> By protecting the integrity of keys throughout their lifecycle, particularly while distributing public keys over communication channels, we obtain a distributed information system that functions correctly and reliably.

The properties of correctness and reliability in the face of communication threats may be reasonably characterized as precisely the expectations to be met by a protected distributed information system. It is precisely the combination of models for information transfer and the rule systems of certificate policies that makes the design of well-modeled, rule-based security policies that ensure integrity possible. Assuming such practical matters as correct software and controlled operations, our protection theory seems largely complete.

## Certification System Protection

The protection theory propounded in the last section aimed to rationalize the abstract security of practical information systems using protocols such as SSL and S/MIME to guard real-world communications security. However, the logic of the protection hypothesis retains an unknown variable that has particular significance to our book's story. Public keys must be distributed integrally over a communication channel if they are to serve as an infrastructure for the rest of the protection pyramid. That is, the protection theory does not describe the key distribution[1] mechanism it uses in its model. However, it depends upon it. How do we rationalize the integrity of this channel upon which the security of distributed information system processing depends?

Clearly, the supporting argument cannot be based on trusting the information system—that itself relies upon key distribution to guarantee the integrity of its security mechanisms. Therefore, the basis must come from outside the protection theory developed so far.

The short answer, if you have not already guessed, is to rely upon the verifiable assurances of the CAs issuing the digital certificates. A protection philosophy for the effective use of digital certificates might be expressed in terms of the CA's axiom:

> If the CA is reliable because the certificate issuing system is assured, and the assurance rating relies upon effective accreditation of the system, then trust in accreditation transfers to trust in the CA.

And from assured CAs we can obtain an assured certificate-based key distribution mechanism that combines with security services to protect the distributed information system processing. However, we must rely upon real CA operators to perform their duties reliably and faithfully. They must be prepared and required to report fully and honestly all facts and other knowledge to auditors, who should represent the interests of the relying parties.

In terms of our model, a digital certificate is nothing more than a key whose binding to a name is itself protected by a security mechanism—a digital signature. To verify the integrity of the certificate, a signature-validating public key must be obtained using a trustworthy key distribution mechanism. This dependency makes the process of establishing the assurances of certificate-based key distribution mechanisms recursive.

Reusing our technique for analyzing protection problems, we now ask of certificate-based key distribution what behavior must be restricted to obtain integrity in certificate-issuing and management processes.

To answer this question, we deconstruct two further environmental factors, introducing accountability and operational status into the model:

**Accountability**    In Chapter 4, we described a scheme for integrity enforcement based upon processes for ensuring legal accountability. We described a system for arranging binding commitments from software code publishers. This framework for using legal pledges (during certificate-issuing processes) to address the technical threats of malicious code in the future (when used by rely-

---

1. Recall the discussion of key distribution in Chapter 9.

ing parties) establishes the **accountability** of the various parties against binding standards of expected behavior. For our purposes, the important property is that parties become bound to an integrity policy,[2] and are accountable to it.

**Operational status**    In Chapter 11, we introduced operational status as a vehicle for deciding the enforceability of a binding commitment during a dispute over accountability in the future. By crafting commitments for particular communities of subscribers and relying parties, third-party CAs help guard against repudiation of communication acts. The protection problem faced by the ultimate consumer of security services is to ensure the **operational status** of the commitments when the important communication event occurs and, subsequently, during any dispute over its nature. The effectiveness of binding agreements in the future depends upon the operational status of the original commitments.

In these two models, and particularly as policy becomes increasingly bound by law, accountability and operational status are ensured by nontechnical[3] accreditation, audit, and arbitration processes. Inspection, investigation, and criteria for evaluation are the tools used by accounting companies; repository records and operational management policies are the subject of audits; and formalized pleadings are the stuff of arbitration. We know from the CA's axiom that a CA assured by accreditation is only as reliable as the accounting firm performing the accreditation. Reasoning backwards, we arrive at a certification system protection hypothesis:

> By assuring the process of issuing and managing digital certificates, particularly by assuring the distribution of trust points, we obtain a trusted public-key certification system that engenders accountability of communicating parties and the operational status of transactions.

Convolving the hypothesis of our certification system with that for our information systems and assuming such practical matters as correct software and controlled CA operations, our protection theory seems largely complete.

## Trust Models

The protection theory propounded in the last section aimed to rationalize the abstract security of practical certification systems such as those described in Part III.

---

2. To be more exact, the Authenticode security policy mentioned features discretionary integrity with strong accountability.

3. The use of *nontechnical* here does not mean the scientific means of accreditation is limited; rather, it denotes that noncryptographic means are used.

However, the logic of the protection hypothesis retains an unknown variable that is even more significant to our book's story than the last time we used this phrase. Trust points must be distributed using assured means, but the protection theory does not describe how to assure the trust points it uses in its model. How do we rationalize the assurance of trust points upon which our certification systems and information systems depend?

Fortunately, in response to the need for analysis we can now introduce a new factor—the trust model—rather than endlessly deconstruct the environment in which one makes security decisions. A **trust model** is the class of decision processes used by relying parties to accept and use the assurances of one or more trust points.

### *Trust Chain Validation*

We learned in Chapter 3 that digital certificates can form chains, each link offering the assurance of the issuing authority of the integrity of another certificate or a user's public key. Having determined the chain, the relying party usually reaches for a validation key that can be authenticated by noncertificate means—a trust point, in the language of Chapter 7. The validation key is just the public key a relying party must reach for to begin chain validation, as defined in Chapter 3.

It is appealing to believe that all certificates will chain to either one or a small number of trust points, also known as root keys. In general, a **root key** is a trust point controlled by one or more authorities operating under a publicly known and respected security policy. The validation key used to commence certificate chain validation is often a root key, but it doesn't have to be. This trust point can also be the public key of the relying party's enterprise CA or the relying party's own public key in PKIs that operate without third-party CAs. Assessing these trust point issues is precisely the subject matter of each certificate user's trust policy.

A **certificate chain** is a list of certificates. The public key listed in any certificate in the chain issued to a CA can be used to validate at least one other certificate in the chain. A **trust chain** is a certificate chain for which there is at least one certificate that a relying party can validate using a trust point previously accepted into the controlling trust policy. A certification path is just a trust chain that has been reduced to exclude redundant certificates, as defined by the user's trust policy.

Commonly, a trust chain is a preordered list of authority certificates and a subject's certificate, where the authority certificates represent a cascade of CAs, each controlling the integrity of the next. A root key embedded in an SSL-enabled browser may enable an HTTPS user to accept and validate the inbound certificate chain from the Web server as a certification path. The validation process may even be wholly automatic, with the result being displayed as a padlock icon or a blue line.

Without belittling the simplicity and effectiveness of the embedded root key design, we can reiterate what we learned from our more advanced tour of *potential* SSL trust mechanisms in Chapter 7. Interactive discovery of common trust points can serve as a general-purpose mechanism for negotiation and agreement. Intelligent, parameterized discovery processes can perhaps be expected to one day replace those based on embedded root key infrastructures.

### Certification Path Discovery and Trust Policy

Just as embedded root key designs can limit trust point determination processes, so can notions of fixed, preordered certificate chains limit the scope for intelligent certification path discovery algorithms. Flexible mechanisms for choosing paths through a certification graph enable negotiation factors other than controlling legal terms to be addressed by searching processes. Multiparty, constraint-satisfying graph-reduction innovations can be expected to emerge in future generations of SSL- and IPSEC-based communications security products. This is perhaps especially true of IPSEC,[4] where the multicast-ready nature of the underlying Internet protocol it secures could support negotiation of trust parameters that affect many parties simultaneously.

In the space between intelligent, multicast, dynamic path negotiation and simple acceptance of fixed, embedded trust points lies an opportunity to exploit interdomain certificates. It is useful to link the notion of local trust points, interdomain certificates, and certification paths to illustrate a simple but powerful trust policy tailored to individuals.

If a relying party's trust policy designates as its only trust point that user's CA's public key, trust delegation can be controlled as required by the user's trust policy. The user can select and vet distant authorities for some determined purpose and according to personal criteria, much as you subscribe to channels from a satellite-broadcasting network. By authorizing a CA to issue one or more restricted personal interdomain certificates to the trust points heading acceptable remote domains, the relying party can implement the policy rules to enforce a personal trust policy. The interdomain certificate will not only establish the required interdomain relationships, by virtue of the key certification, but may contain the control extensions specializing that delegation to meet the user's requirements.

Of course, some users might share an interdomain certificate prepared by the CA on behalf of an entire class of relying parties when their requirements are identical, or a LAN administrator may impose an organizational reliance policy by restricting the availability of interdomain certificates.

A trust policy becomes operational when an incoming certificate chain is received from a Web server, for example, and local certification path validation begins. In our discovery method, the relying party's personal set of all interdomain certificates is

---

4. IPSEC (the standardization of mechanisms assuring the integrity and confidentiality of Internet protocol packets) is likely to be shipped worldwide with Microsoft NT 5 and CISCO routers in 1999.

logically added to the inbound chain. Reduction of the chain of many certificates to a valid trust path then occurs. A common reduction would result in the simple addition of a single interdomain certificate to the front of the inbound chain.

Validation of an X.509 certification path during trust policy enforcement requires conforming implementations to address critical extensions found in the certificates. A relying party's path validation algorithm can choose to regard the extensions as mandatory automated policy rules, particularly whenever one of its own interdomain certificates is processed. Furthermore, local enforcement rules can be formulated and set when an interdomain certificate is requested to dominate and control all other policy-rule processing performed as one traverses the remaining certificates during chain validation. Such a certificate would probably be at the head of the chain, so its extensions can logically drive a relying party's requirements for path validation, automating local trust policy in practice. Furthermore, the set of available interdomain certificates can drive the initial process of certification path discovery.

## Distributing Trust Management

Whether the enabling technology is an SSL handshake supported by X.509-format certificates or a less well-known certification scheme, such as Meta-Certificates (see Chapter 8 and http://www.mcg.org.br/), the mixing of third-party assurances with dynamic trust negotiation enables distributed trust management on a large and flexible scale.

To answer the question posed at the outset of this discussion, centralization of trust management and security policy enforcement is the behavior that must be restricted to induce integrity in any certificate-based security system. Only then is the relying party protected. In terms of electronic commerce, only when consumers are empowered to decide for themselves can they be held responsible for the trust decisions that underpin every electronic commerce transaction. (Similar arguments can be made for military command and control systems.)

To understand a consumer-centric notion of trust, we need to characterize how trusted third-party CAs can work with branded names of merchants on the one hand and consumer-centered trust policies on the other to provide consumer-navigable trust networks.

## Trust Networks

Internet users are increasingly familiar with Internet Web site naming domains. It is quite intuitive when navigating to http://www.microsoft.com/security to expect to be presented with information in the knowledge domain of Microsoft Internet security technologies. However, names are not always intuitive. For example, it is not obvious from the name that the Defense Information Service Agency publishes downloadable information security courseware from its INFOSEC training facility at http://www.disa.mil/ciss/itf/cwdown.html.[5]

Users are becoming increasingly familiar with the idea that the domain name component of a URL (e.g., www.disa.mil) can be associated with a particular type of object. To the average user, http://www.msn.net is an access port to an on-line network service. It is quite distinct from a home page at http://www.microsoft.com. Whether a user's recognition of brand names as network or corporation objects is affected more by investments made in advertising the MSN and Microsoft names or by the associations of .net or .com is the subject of much debate.

Consumers do seem to expect that for some object or service located by a name, a particular organization will be responsible and accountable for managing information and services at that site. Consumers expect to be able to infer the nature of a site from its name, which may also suggest availability of particular information resources and services by brand association.

As branding conveys indirect notions of trust to users, we explore the relationships between naming and digital certificates, and the organization of trust networks as a means of projecting Internet brands to consumers. Of course, some CAs are themselves a kind of Internet brand—very high-profile brands responsible for reliably authenticating the identities (and brands) of others.

## Certification Domain Management

Authentication of the names of subjects is an integral part of digital certificate issuing. As a part of the process of authentication, name management is intimately related to certificate management. The management practices of certification domains are conceptually very closely related to the management practices of naming domains, which are regions of administrative control over sets of name spaces.

We define a **certification domain**[6] as a region of administrative control over sets of certified resources, managed by one or more identified organizations. For our purposes, the resources managed by the certification authorities conforming the domain are the authority and subject public keys. The managing organization is the CA, or the set of CAs in that domain upholding a common administrative policy.

CAs normally perform authentication management and confirmation of identity before they issue certificates to subjects. Normally, they list the subject's representative

---

5. http://www.disa.mil/ciss/dodfm2.html links to an order form where security briefing and computer-based training materials may be ordered, currently at no cost.

6. X.509 does not standardize the concept of a certification domain. Security domains in general, however, are an established standardized security management system construct.

names or other particular information in the certificates to aid identification by relying parties. Although they are formally independent, naming domain management and certification domain management are often intertwined.

When addressing the key distribution problems facing a wide-area infrastructure, certification authorities naturally form certification domains to certify the public keys of (named) subjects in the large community. The domain structures often mirror the domain structures used to organize the subject names. For example, a network of CAs forming a national certification domain may mirror a naming scheme in which subjects are identified using country and state/province of residence attributes, as managed by naming authorities at country and state/province levels.

One or more CAs in a certification domain may perform the functions of domain manager. A **certification domain manager** operates certificate issuing and management services that may control and represent other issuing authorities within the administrative region.

## Representing Authority and Integrity

As we discussed in Chapter 11, the practices of authorities performing public-key certification are increasingly expected to be disclosed in the form of formal policy statements. The particular authority acting as certification domain manager may authoritatively represent all members of the domain to the world as being governed according to a particular CPS, and thereby provide a measure of uniformity and integrity.

A commercial-grade CPS characterizes and limits assurances relevant to the intended use of the various classes and types of digital certificates which the issuing authorities comprising a domain issue and manage. Given that integrity is the measure of key distribution, the trust decisions of relying parties for the entire domain are likely to be based partially on the disclosures made in the CPS.

As public-key infrastructure becomes more widespread and integrated into (or arguably *becomes*) the electronic commerce infrastructure, distinct domains will inevitably adopt interconnection practices. Through interworking, they will form suites of uniform public services, or larger and larger private networks. As the authoritative representative, the certification domain manager is a natural player to lead or undertake interdomain management duties and issue interdomain certificates.

A **trust network** is a public certification domain.[7] It discloses a complete and coherent CPS, reasonably accounts for its own material observance to the practices

---

7. One can view a virtual private network (VPN), as discussed in Chapter 9, as a private certification domain.

disclosed therein to public accountants, and accurately certifies public keys pertaining to the public. It offers its integrity policy and root keys as trust points to a network of related CAs, and establishes a point of public presence with which to perform interdomain certification.

There are as many ways to organize trust networks as there are ways to organize names. We can look to the institutions and structures of societies themselves to determine some of the models for organizing a network of trust networks.

## Network Organization

Organizing a collection of trust networks into a national and international infrastructure requires a set of considerations similar to those faced by any large business organizing field offices. Will there be one office per town, one salesperson per unit of population, or one thousand dollars of investment per unit of dollar transactions? Each principle suggests different models of structure and organization, each with natural advantages and disadvantages.

Across the diverse and transnational Internet, the principles driving trust network interworking will probably adapt social conventions and practices across industrial, cultural, commercial, and political lines. The nature of trust is such that it and enabling technologies such as PKI will almost certainly mimic the environments into which they enter.[8]

By way of example, we identify five potential models for structured networks of trust networks:

**Residential locale**   In the residential model, subjects are organized by political divisions and administrative regions of states, or economic areas. Tied to such structures may exist rights to vote, obligations to pay sales and income tax, and, importantly, a certain regional pride. One can envisage political entities such as government agencies at national and local levels certifying the public keys of their residents. Residents may be local businesses (whose registrations could be delegated to the local chamber of commerce) or homeowners, apartment dwellers, or registered individual voters.

The administration of a government-centered PKI is likely to be guided by public policy, the culture of the political representation in the locality, and the execution of government privileges as upheld by public audit standards and/or the local political process. Under bilateral or multilateral agreements, governments will agree to share registrations.

---

8. If the society is anti-individual, PKI will be anti-individual. If the society is probusiness, PKI will be probusiness. If the society is ruled by an autocrat, the PKI will be autocratic.

**Organizational affiliation**    In the organizational model, the axis of management and control transfers to private associations and to natural, vertical industry groupings. Whether privately for their own account or for the purposes of trade, an organization may certify public keys by listing individuals and trading partners who are in some way affiliated with its affairs, as an employee, contractor, customer, partner, member, creditor, or franchisee—the forms of affiliation are endless.

The internal administration of the organization's security systems are likely to be guided by management control policies, the culture of the workplace, and sound management practice as dictated by an industry association.

**Official and governmental**    Distinct from residential notions, officialdom may decide to exercise control over a party's activity when using cryptographic mechanisms for official purposes. Submitting a digitally signed annual income declaration may require one to solemnly swear to its truthfulness to be legally recognized. A U.S. government agency's notice to an individual of liability for military service may be deemed to have been duly served only if verified using a certificate issued by the General Services Administration, for example.

Official control is likely to seek to extend its control over strong cryptography and/or the keys, and/or the public key management infrastructure. National governments may require users of such paraphernalia to register its use or obtain it from official sources, much as telephone equipment was once regulated. The scope of official regulation is wide, and the motives political.

**Postal**    Some of the strongest investigative power present outside of prosecuting and judicial authorities is placed in the hands of national postal services. Historically, the postal service has been used to conduct official business with people and commerce between peoples and to engender a free flow of information between people separated by distance. National postal services are often backed by centuries of laws and regulations governing transactions communicated by mail. These properties culminate in statutes controlling mail fraud, and tough postal regulations embrace sweeping rules for newspaper registration, mail-order buying, and advertising by mail and the protection of addressing information.

The network of branch post offices and the existing systemization of residences by street addresses and ZIP codes would seem to be an ideal basis for a public key infrastructure when used to support personal, private Internet communication.

**Peer association**    Unaffiliated individuals associate in a variety of patterns. Peer networking via the Internet has made peer association a more common occurrence than that engendered by more traditional letter and journalistic forms of communication. Chat rooms, mailing lists, newsgroups, multiparty computer games, and virtual reality avatars are all examples of informal Internet social affiliations. The social groups formed under such circumstances tend to be dynamic and large. They operate largely without authority structures. Nothing inherent in the notion of a certification domain requires the CAs of which it is conformed to be *third* parties. PKI technology enables each individual to be a CA, should he or she so desire. The identity projected to peers in such structures can be highly anonymous but nonetheless highly rigorous. Relying parties can know only that a communicating party is the same party as last time. Much like older currency and payment systems that allowed individuals to issue notes and endorse the credit of others based on a system of peer recognition of status and value, certification structures may follow the lines of peer-to-peer valuation of trustworthiness.

Although requiring self-management and being somewhat difficult to administer, peer structures are remarkably adept at focusing organization on the most subtle of criteria. Control over the management of your own keys can be an important part of asserting a reasonable expectation of privacy.

### Network Models

As public certification domains are trust *networks,* we can also apply networking terms to describe the relationships within and between domains. We define **intranet trust** as the set of relationships within a network of issuing authorities conforming to a single domain. The relationships between trust networks or between a trust network and other parties are designated as a form of **extranet trust.**

Commercial third-party CAs and CA operators who perform outsourced trust network management for others may use classical hub-and-spoke relationship models, as seen in the trusted, value-added network EDI business. Well-known brands may use the management services of telecommunications or other specialized companies who provide trust network or VPN outsourcing network services. This model is very similar to how large retail brands use EDI value-added network providers today to provide trusted transport and delivery of business messages.

## A Consumer's Trust-Policy

Before consumers will trust certificate-based key distribution as the infrastructure for electronic commerce, they need to have confidence that the underlying public key infrastructure engenders secure communications and transactions. But we have yet to see a systematization of a process that would assure us that key distribution is indeed a complete or effective method capable of meeting these expectations.

To grow the certificate management infrastructure at the rate required to keep pace with the expected growth rate of Internet users over the next 10 years, we must now reduce the many issues we have seen attached to digital certificates down to a sound bite. One cannot expect the average merchant or shopper to read a book as theoretical as this merely to gain confidence in certificates.

We believe that the outcome of this process must be simple and is inherently competitive and commercial. We summarize our own prediction as:

> Digital certificates will represent familiar brand names on the Internet.

To aid the reduction process, we conclude our analysis of consumer-centric trust management by summarizing the brand-protection elements, and presenting the generic process of reliance as the point at which all the factors come together for consumer decision. It is this process that must embrace and use branding to adapt the technology of PKI to consumer needs.

## Elements of Brand Protection

In this book, we have introduced four components that are useful for constructing a theory of reliance on brands and their reputations:

**Protection philosophy**    Earlier in this chapter, we rationalized a protection philosophy that establishes that one can secure the public keys, assure the quality of the issuing authorities, and authenticate the communicating parties. Using a securely keyed security system and reasonably trusted software, the consumer can access a secure communications and transaction-ready infrastructure.

**Effective representations**    We described in Chapter 11, the protocols entailing effective representation and assurance. These provide a means to transfer obligations between CAs, subscribers, and relying parties. When delivering products and services over an infrastructure guarded by certificate-based security systems, the opportunity exists to automate and handle product liability, warranties, and all the other ancillary features of real commerce.

**Trust points**    In Chapter 7, we described how trust-point determination has the potential to automate commercial-grade negotiation processes and facilitate dynamic learning of trust networks by consumer terminals.

**Policy-based risk management**    We saw also in Chapter 11 how contractually enforceable policy can be bound to certificates and how all parties to a transaction can be bound to a governing set of rules. Consumer-protection laws and other regulations can reduce the risk of loss to socially acceptable levels.

But how can we know that, when combined, these trust components will act together to satisfy the expectations of consumers? Will they inspire enough confidence that people will shop with the same familiarity at Internet stores as they do at the local grocery store? Will merchants accept Internet-style payment with the same charm they accept credit cards today?

### Consumer-Centered Trust

There are two missing pieces in the trust puzzle when addressing users such as the average consumer engaged in shopping or the average shopkeeper engaged in shipping and accepting credit-card payment:

> **Operational security**   Operational security of the public-key and communications security infrastructure on real computer systems in real deployment situations is one piece. Chapter 13 is dedicated to a discussion of this topic in the context of security policy.
>
> **Security policy enforcement**   This concerns a user-friendly way to enforce each individual's trust policy.

We recognize that there is, of course, nothing even remotely user-friendly about the terminology or meaning of *enforcing trust policy* as we understand this idea in this very technical book. We must endeavor to reduce user involvement to the traditional activity of consumers: *deciding* which brand to trust today. As security system designers, we must leave it to media people to find the icons, metaphors, and appropriate advertising to deliver the branding messages effectively.

## Trust-Policy Enforcement

The idea of a trust policy provides a framework within which individual assurances of trust can be composed to satisfy the security goals of consumers. Establishing credible enforcement of a personal trust policy is the key to obtaining consumer confidence in the effectiveness of a *secure* electronic commerce infrastructure.

Trust-policy rules for ensuring integrity can be discretionary (as with the Authenticode code signing scheme) or mandatory (as when using cashless smart cards and phone cards). The consumer's trust-policy enforcement software will need to make largely automatic, real-time determinations restricting user-system behavior to maintain the required levels of integrity, leaning toward mandatory rules. At the same time, these same individuals must be properly involved, leaning toward discretionary rules. Software designers have a difficult set of choices to make when addressing the needs, interests, and short attention spans of the average consumer when managing their own trust decisions. An example of the difference between mandatory and discretionary integrity regimes during trust-policy enforcement can be seen in the process used by merchants when accepting credit card payment instructions.

Merchants have a choice of strategies for managing the risk of not receiving the money, despite having delivered their product or service to the customer. They can validate the cardholder-account's operational status by going on-line to obtain a receipt and authorization code from the acquiring bank. In doing so, they gain a large measure of relief from certain types of fraud. On the other hand, they can avoid the cost and take the risk of nonpayment themselves. In a mandatory regime, merchants have no choice but to validate all consumer transactions with the bank, or else have their processing privileges revoked. In a discretionary regime, they can self-insure when they desire. Some parties, banks and governments particularly, argue that mandatory integrity should be imposed to ensure society as a whole is best protected.

Automated trust-policy enforcement has two high-level processes in either a mandatory or a discretionary design:

**Trust points**   Security decisions to accept a security service must ensure that usage of a trust point is limited to the conditions laid down in the relying parties' trust model and any prescriptions of the trust network regarding limitations on purpose or use thereon.

**Meeting relying-party obligations**   The relying parties must meet their obligations to validate certification paths according to the technical controls embedded in the certificates and requirements of any relying-party agreements. Users must also properly protect their private key(s) and accept appropriate responsibility for any loss of control.

In the consumer space, choosing between mandatory versus discretionary trust policy enforcement is almost a matter of personal freedom and privacy values. If consumers wish to authenticate a signed e-mail without obtaining the latest CRL or going on-line or to use the message content after the sender's certificate has expired, they have a natural right to do so. Such a user must be willing to take the risk of being spoofed or misled, however, in return for not signaling to the world when a reliance decision is made, and such a user may forfeit the right to claim strong liability protections. Only with a real opportunity to override external policy can users be free. Only then is it credible that the consumer really trusted that brand.

## Summary

In the field of digital certificates, a trust network is another name for a management domain of certification authorities. Certification chains, certificate policies, and management systems are combined to form models that organize large structures of CAs, forming trust networks.

Trusted key distribution requires information system protection and certification system protection. Trustworthy keys are derived from the integrity of their distribution mechanism. Trusted security mechanisms provide security services. Security services enable information systems to satisfy security policies.

The protection of the certificate-based key distribution mechanism is recursive. Trust requires that the process of issuing and managing digital certificates and the distribution of trust points be assured. Trust engenders accountability and operational status.

Trust models control the use of trust points when processing trust chains. A trust point can also be the CA's public key of the relying party's CA or the relying party's own public key in PKIs that operate without certification authorities. Appropriate controls form the subject matter of each certificate user's trust policy.

A trust chain is a certificate chain for which there exists at least one certificate that a relying party can validate using a locally valid trust point. A certification path is a trust chain reduced to exclude redundant certificates.

Intelligent trust policy facilitates certificate path discovery. Interdomain certificates enable the relying party to enforce flexible wide-area trust policies.

Issuing authorities naturally form domains to certify the public keys of (named) subjects. A trust network is a certification domain. A common form of network organization is extranet trust. Network models address the relationships between trust networks in addition to the relationships between a trust network and other parties.

A consumer's trust policy must be easy to understand and use. Representing familiar brands on the Internet is one mechanism. To adapt branding to the Internet, there must be user-centric trust. Users must have the power to enforce their own security policies. Relying parties must make semiautomatic, real-time decisions to maintain security. Decisions to accept a security service that requires the use of trust points is guided by the relying party's trust model and may be controlled by the reliance requirements of the trust networks.

# Reference

[SUMM97] Summers, R. *Secure Computing: Threats and Safeguards,* McGraw-Hill, New York, 1997, http://ourworld.compuserve.com/homepages/rsummers/tableofc.htm.

# 13

# Computer Security Management

In this chapter, we address a situation that is becoming more common in large corporations: middle managers are being charged with deploying PKI key management technology in a trustworthy manner. No doubt some will choose to operate their CAs in existing in-house data centers. Others will outsource processing, while retaining critical aspects of management control in-house.[1]

What constitutes adequate care and attention when selecting secure system products? What security controls ensure proper management of a data center? What is involved in engaging a system security auditor? What forms of documentation are required to substantiate due care and attention? What is a proper management response to the issues of computer security for a key management center and a corporate environment addressing public-key cryptography in general?

We begin our response to these questions with a discussion of security policy. Policy infuses organizational and community controls into the operation of key certification services and embodies the trust values required by the users of a CA's service.

The buyer of outsourcing certification services and the buyer of key management products are alike in needing to control quality. Both must control the fielding of CA-based key management capabilities to ensure it satisfies corporate security goals. We will explore quality in terms of system certification, accreditation, trusted facilities, and operational and lifecycle assurances.

## Security Policy and Trust

We learned in Chapters 11 and 12 how certificate policies can facilitate the administration of entire trust networks. Trust networks best embody the trust values of a subscriber community when their own form and management styles closely model the form and management styles of the community they serve. Inevitably, some cultures

---

1. This is much like the business practice of outsourcing payroll processes to printers and envelope-stuffers while maintaining internal control over who gets a salary raise.

will be liberal and others conservative. Certificate policies and allied certification practice statements (see Chapter 11) serve as the foundation for a user community's trust decisions, and are an important, consumer-friendly facet of the more general idea of collective security policy.

In Chapter 8, we briefly focused on security policy from the perspective of a security solution designer's methodology. Architects can use policy to generate security management solutions that integrate certificate-based security systems in business systems and thereby express the required culture of management control. In this chapter, we view the flip side of the coin, considering the viewpoint of the user community, which requires measures of technical assurance of the correctness and effectiveness of PKI before assigning its trust.

It is our contention that a community's propensity to trust a shared security system will increase when security policy rules match the security controls desired by the community in form and style. The principles that lead a skeptic to trust the effectiveness of trusted third-party management controls are described in detail in [SUMM97]: individual accountability, authorization, least privilege, separation of duty, auditing, redundancy, and risk reduction. These are all examples of properties exhibited by the operational culture of a **trusted facility**—the data center out of which one operates a trusted computer-based certificate issuing service.

## Types of Policy

Although sometimes criticized for its focus on military access controls, the groundbreaking Trusted Computer Systems Evaluation Criteria (TCSEC) is perhaps one of the most integrated perspectives on computer security policy:

> In summary, protection requirements must be defined in terms of the perceived threats, risks, and goals of an organization. This is often stated in terms of a security policy. It has been pointed out in the literature that it is external laws, rules, regulations, etc., that establish what access to information is to be permitted, independent of the use of a computer. In particular, a given system can only be said to be secure with respect to its enforcement of some specific policy. [TCSEC]

Applied to organizations, three types of security policies are generally agreed upon as covering the important viewpoints of a secure system:

**Corporate security policy**   The set of laws, rules, practices, and so on, scoped to the needs of an individual *user* organization.[2]

---

2. User organizations can sometimes be distinguished from infrastructure organizations such as trusted third parties and trust-network operators. Alternatively, user organizations can operate their own trust networks.

**Systems security policy** A contrasting systems-oriented perspective of security controls described in terms of the means by which engineering and operational behavior is regulated to achieve required control objectives.

**Technical security policy** A product design perspective aimed at demonstrating that use of computing resources and the processes for automatically handling information are properly regulated in accordance with the sensitivity of the data to loss of control.

Detailed policy documents used to satisfy the auditors who advise the public are valuable intellectual property. Readers can obtain a sample of the kind of material to be addressed in a complete policy by taking a look at Chapter 8 of the forward-looking *National Industrial Security Program Operating Manual* (NISPOM) [NISPOM]. (See http://www.fas.org/sgp/library/nispom/chap08.htm.) Other vital aspects of procedural security generally useful to any commercial or industrial security-conscious facility are addressed throughout the NISPOM.

## Technical Security Policy for PKIs

In Chapter 12, we briefly discussed mandatory integrity policy and related it to the notion of reliance on certificates. During *automated* security policy enforcement, the technology essentially makes the reliance decision for the user. The user's software will normally apply appropriate technical safeguards to counter the relevant threats. To believe in the reliability, a trusting user community requires operational and lifecycle assurances.

**Operational and lifecycle assurances** address the effectiveness of the design, engineering, manufacturing, and deployed integrity of the devices and supporting infrastructure used to perform automated reliance on certificates and security mechanisms. Additionally, they address the trusted facilities and the means to recover from disasters without suffering compromise.

The lifecycle assurances of a device or system are a critical aspect of technical norms for trust, particularly in environments where mandatory policies are the norm. An Internet consumer community may, however, simply trust a (branded) device to do its job correctly when helping them rely on certificates. Such a process would be similar to the way people trust ATMs to correctly manage bankcard PINs today. We term such devices and systems **trusted devices** and **trusted systems.** They are trusted to enforce the technicalities of security policy.

# Accreditation and Trusted Systems

To examine vendor claims concerning trusted systems and products, the computer and software industry has adopted a set of evaluation criteria. Originated by the

Department of Defense during the Cold War to help protect automated storage and processing of classified military and intelligence information, the **Orange Book** lists the features and requirements of trustworthy, automated information processing systems.

The Orange Book is more formally known as the **Trusted Computer System Evaluation Criteria** (TCSEC).[3] The TCSEC introduces a rating system to qualify products and systems as they satisfy ever more stringent requirements. Versions of the TCSEC embracing database and network models interpret the criteria. The network interpretation is known as the **Red Book,** in which interpreted[4] criteria model a tightly coupled networked information system. **Common criteria** work (http://csrc.nist.gov/nistpubs/cc/), which represents modern, international efforts in the area of information assurance, addresses the needs of commercial security systems and component products.

## Certification Marks

The idea of the security evaluation process is that operators of trusted products look for a certification mark. The **certification mark** assures such users that, at a minimum, various criteria have been satisfied, having been properly inspected and evaluated. Put another way, you probably will not have to do your own (extremely expensive) evaluation if you can quote to an auditor the rating issued by the U.S. government.[5]

The SET initiative discussed in Chapter 8 has a similar certification mark scheme to defense- and intelligence-related security systems. It is applied to SET-conforming products and payment brand-authorized operational processes.[6] Certification of products and systems is becoming increasingly related to the business of commercial (public key) certification authorities, particularly when a CA's certification practices address a certificate subject's expected operating conduct in addition to authentication and key management.

For example, the CA service operated by the American Institute of Certified Public Accountants (AICPA) (in collaboration with VeriSign) governs some Web site operations. The evaluation criteria are more general than those associated with the SET marks. A larger U.S. merchant accepting SET transactions is likely to show both Webtrust and SET logos. One may apply for and obtain an AICPA Webtrust

---

3. See http://www.disa.mil/MLS. Also see [CSB] for explanation and commentary. Another excellent overview is at http://developer.novell.com/research/appnotes/1997/november/02/03.htm.

4. See http://bilbo.isu.edu/security/isl/comsecsm.html for background on TCSEC interpretations.

5. See http://www.armadillo.huntsville.al.us/Fortezza_docs/missi1.html#impdocs for NSA certification programs linking cryptographic device and key management requirements for specific applications.

6. See http://www.setco.org/aboutmark.html.

SSL site certificate and then use the associated logo[7] to assure the public that the on-line *selling* process is properly controlled for consumer quality. The merchant may also apply for and use the SET logo to point buyers to a safe *payment* mechanism, having deployed a (certified) SET-complying payment system.

## Trusted Systems Accreditation

Of course, no general criteria set can control risks found in a specific environment or affecting a particular resource. Consequently, a site security officer (or the shopkeeper) must accredit the deployment of even certified products.

**Accreditation,** in the restricted sense of trusted product and system certification, is the process of:

1. Determining the risks present in the local information-processing environment.

2. Determining that the nature and ratings of certified products are sufficient to adequately control the risks once operational and deployed.

For its own information systems management purposes, the U.S. Army (http://isd.redstone.army.mil/ar38019/ar38019ch3.html#3-5) defines accreditation of automated information-processing systems (AIS) and networks more formally:

> Accreditation is the formal declaration that an AIS or network is approved to operate as follows:
> (1) In a particular security mode of operation and security classification level.
> (2) With a prescribed set of minimum environmental, technical, and non-technical security countermeasures.
> (3) Against a threat assessed by the supporting [intelligence] staff office.
> (4) In a properly secured area in a clearly-defined operational environment.
> (5) Under stated short- and long-term goals.
> (6) With stated interconnections to other AIS or networks.
> (7) At an acceptable level of risk for which the accrediting authority has formally assumed responsibility.

Accreditation can be seen from various management angles. Like security policy, it is a multifaceted response. It responds to the need to measure, maintain, and control assurance in various real-world operational circumstances:

**Responsibility assignment** Accreditation is the official management authorization to operate an AIS or network. An accreditation statement assigns security responsibility.

---

7. See http://www.cpawebtrust.org/consumer/index.html and page 629 of [SUMM97].

**Perimeter**   Accreditation addresses the system's perimeter, its boundary, and its relationship to other AIS and networks in a particular infrastructure. The perimeter surrounds the specified set of equipment and peripherals under control.

**Fixed and deployable assets**   Accreditation must address each operational environment of the AIS for both fixed and deployable configurations. The accreditation must clearly establish procedures for transition between the two environments.

**Integration**   AIS that provide remote access to a larger, clearly defined system do not require individual accreditation, but they must follow the security requirements of the larger system.

## A Sample FC2/E3 Rating

As an example of product evaulation and certification, we now consider the path followed by Microsoft on behalf of developers and users who apply its NT Server Internet transaction platform for security-critical processes, which are likely to be the subject of critical and very serious audit. (NT developers include the Netscape Certificate Server, Entrust WebCA, CertCo RootAuthority, and the VeriSign OEM product suite.) The OS vendor has dutifully followed formal trusted product evaluation and follow-up recertification procedures throughout the design and implementation of Windows NT 3.5.1 and its successor versions. It received a trust rating from two well-respected institutions: the National Security Agency and the Information Technology Security Evaluation Criteria (ITSEC) Board of the European Community.[8] The Windows NT Server 3.5.1 (including network configurations) certification statement is available from U.K. ITSEC (http://www.itsec.gov.uk/cgi-bin/cplview.pl?docno=36). A related statement indicates that the more recently introduced Windows NT Server 4.0 is under evaluation (http://www.itsec.gov.uk/cgi-bin/cplview.pl?docno=122).

The FC2 rating is becoming the baseline for commercial-grade operating systems. For security-critical activities such as certificate issuing and management, FC2-rated networked systems perhaps represent the absolute minimum level of trust required in a computing platform. However, buyers who obtain FC2-rated systems must install, configure, and operate the product in a manner that preserves the FC2 conditions to reap the benefits.

The risks to authentication and key management due to the vulnerabilities of an FC2 system are severe; a commercial CA would probably employ special risk-

---

8. See introductory materials at http://www.itsec.gov.uk/docs/introgds.htm and http://crsc.nist.gov/secpubs/itsec.txt.

mitigation tactics when using an FC2-based key management system. These would almost certainly include the use of special-purpose peripherals designed for certificate and CRL issuing and deployment of significantly heightened operational and physical security procedures.

## Trusted Facilities

To convince auditors that a site is indeed a trusted facility, a review of its documentation and practices should establish that operational behavior indeed conforms to a security policy. As the need for greater trust is encountered, the documentation requirements address more details concerning the underlying platforms, products, and administrative, and operational procedures.

In the field of information assurance, the process of formalized documentation exists mainly to help substantiate a vendor's assurance claims. The process is necessarily pursued throughout the lifecycle of the secure computing system.

**Implementation**   Documentation should prove the ability of security mechanisms to enforce the security policy.

**Operations**   Operational manuals for users and administrators should explain how to apply security mechanisms.

**Maintenance**   Documentation should enable security officials to determine what effect a change may have on security *before* the change is performed.

Of particular importance to CA operators is the advice concerning operational manuals. In a CA's operational manual a careful administrator should define a hierarchy of roles for those who maintain the system.

The procedure design should emphasize separation of duties to control internal threats. Special consideration should be given to separating the privileges assigned to engineering developers from those assigned to operators and authentication management users. Facilities must exist to assign temporary privileges to auditors, inspectors, evaluators, and others as needed.

The Orange Book lays down requirements for a **security features user's guide** and the **trusted facility manual** (TFM). These are discussed in detail in [CSB]. The TFM in particular describes the procedures to be used by security officials when selecting security options.

## Cryptographic Materials Protection

As we saw in Chapter 12, when a security system is built upon a cryptosystem and the asymmetric key distribution underpinning the security mechanisms uses digital certificates, the entire edifice of protection hinges upon the security of the wider key management system. On the one hand, placing security control points in the hands of infrastructure providers helps isolate and localize the areas where heightened operational security must be ensured. On the other hand, users tend to be more impacted by failures when relying upon critical infrastructure designs.

The scaling and distribution properties of CAs, certification domains, and autonomous, off-line enforcement of certificate-based security policy by end-user systems embraces replication and redundant engineering practices. These techniques can be used to address infrastructure failure modes. Assuming reasonably trustworthy software is in place at all points (particularly in the key management centers associated with CAs), the assurance of the system as a whole comes down to one requirement: Protect the user's private keys.

To emphasize the importance of this protection requirement, for the purpose of public key infrastructure, we define a trusted facility in terms of a private key protection policy. A **trusted facility** is a data center that completely protects each of the private keys used by a CA operator during authentication, certificate issuing, and key management.

### Certificate Servers and Key Management Systems versus Signing Devices

In Parts V and VI of this book, we present a number of projects that involve various aspects of certificate issuing and management. In these examples, the general-purpose computer serves as the cryptographic device, and it executes the mathematics of signing.[9] The secure operating system security mechanisms are used to protect the critical signing keys against key compromise and misuse. Once the signing service is armed, the trusted computing base security enforcement functions protect the management system from unauthorized (distributed) access to the certificate issuing and management functions.

We use the term **cryptographic materials** to mean cryptodevices or equivalent software modules, arming tokens, passwords, random data streams, electromagnetic signals, and any cryptographic key in ciphertext or plaintext (obviously). Other materials include related operational objects such as envelopes, packaging, containers, seals, serial numbers, and so on that are used to protect keys and cryptodevices. (In paranoid environments, all ciphertext generated by a given class of cryptodevice is considered to be cryptographic material.) Cryptodevices may be

---

9. The underlying CryptoAPI architecture module does not restrict the certificate server to software signing. Furthermore, the system design facilitates back-end remote operation of the certificate server from the Web server (or other entry modules), which provides network transaction entry points.

evaluated against such criteria as the FIPS 140-1 and be issued a certificate of evaluation to certify individual component trustworthiness.[10]

Control of cryptographic material lies at the heart of traditional communication security, as described in the Electronic Key Management System (see Chapter 8). Related management procedures are also a critical aspect of a well-managed commercial security system for the same reason. The ISO 11568 series of standards for the banking industry address best commercial practice to date. Concerning symmetric key security systems, work on public key practices and standards is advancing quickly both in the banking community and in government agencies (e.g., the Department of Defense's Defense Messaging System).

### Cryptographic Materials Management

Materials management procedures can be categorized two ways: those directly addressing keys and those addressing the devices that access and apply keys:

**Keying material control**   Material handling requirements include key generation, loading, usage, storage, backup, destruction, archiving, and termination. Public keys[11] are naturally shared with parties other than their owners during third-party involvement in their generation, escrow of private keys (if any), disclosure to intended recipients, and archival. Keying materials management procedures often require the use of dual-control and split knowledge techniques to control residual internal threats represented by trusted personnel. A dual-control technique ensures that a cryptographic key is under the control of two or more users when it is not under the exclusive control of the trusted device. Split knowledge ensures that knowledge of any component of the key does not convey any knowledge of the resultant key.

**Cryptographic device controls**   Materials controls on cryptodevices assure the security of cryptographic keys throughout their lifecycle while not in the exclusive custody and charge of a trusted person. Perhaps the most important control of all is one that ensures that the plaintext keys are available to trusted cryptodevices that are themselves subject to stringent lifecycle and custodial handling procedures.

Details on diligent custodial procedures for handling cryptographic materials can be obtained from the NASA Handbook 1600.6, NASA Communications Security

---

10. See http://www.signet.org.au/Spyrus/prod_guide/pc_cards/fips140.htm for an example.

11. Secret keys are subject to largely the same requirements as public keys when used to implement a non-certificate-based key distribution mechanism such as ANSI X9.17, Kerberos, or those used in Racal Datacryptor networks.

(COMSEC) Manual (http://nodis.hq.nasa.gov/Library/DirectivesNASA_WIDE/
Procedures/Organization and Administration/N_HB_1600_6.html).

### Creation of Authority

To formally endow an installation of a certificate-issuing system with authority, executive management should hold a formal ceremony. The act of creation of authority to issue certificates could be witnessed by third parties to attest to the solemnity and content of the process. For high-integrity operation of infrastructure authorities and for intercompany and interdomain certification, accrediting officers may wish to videotape proceedings and lodge sealed copies of the tapes with escrow agencies. Authority creation generally encompasses long-term signing key generation and initialization of cryptographic devices.

Creation of authority is a very serious (pseudo-) legal act that is somewhat analogous to registration of a change in a company's articles of incorporation to address new products and markets. Corporate counsel should be actively involved to ensure that all due precautions have been taken to entitle the CA to exercise the authority it claims and to maintain a credible document trail. The chief security officers of the organizations responsible for the CA and/or the operation of the CA should accredit the installation after establishing that the operational procedures are adequate to maintain the original level of security.

When initializing crypto peripherals and generating signing and key management keys for CAs, a hierarchy of logical control levels should be employed. A PIN (or stronger user authentication) scheme should be used to securely transfer initialization and custodial responsibility from the manufacturing domain to a site security officer and then to an authorized user. Such state transitions should ideally alter the permanent state of the device's persistent memory, with PINs being represented outside the device only in a secret-shared form.

Separation of duties enforced via physical and logical access restrictions should be employed to reduce the risk of compromise of a given PIN. Key-generation ceremonies require dedicated rooms and equipment, TEMPEST countermeasures (when appropriate), trusted personnel specially trained in security procedures, dedicated equipment and facilities for witnesses, and the audio-visual recording of all actions in the controlled space.

## Operations Security

In certificate-based security systems, it is vitally important to ensure that cryptographic materials are under control at both the CA operator's data center and the general subscriber's workstation. However, the CA operator has a wide range of system security threats to be concerned about for the data center as a whole.

It is beyond the scope of this chapter to detail the requirements for commercial CA data centers. In summary, therefore, we present a few of the more vital topics directly relevant to a CA operator's ability to operate a trusted facility housing one or more certificate servers.

## Data Centers

The management practices governing the operations of a data center that hosts certificate servers should be tuned to the fact that the security of potentially millions of transactions each day hinge upon the center's security. Although public key and digital certificate designs can limit the impact of compromise, certain operational compromise can lead to total loss of user confidence.

For certificate-based security system designs that use a prearmed network device to sign and issue certificates, highly accountable, manual processes are required to control trusted device reinitialization and rearming. Due attention should be paid at all times to ensuring the integrity and availability of the CA repository. In some cases, confidential and private information must be safeguarded.

Logging information should be generated and stored in a tamperproof manner. For each event in the lifecycle of a user or authority key, the logs of a CA should be able to recreate the conditions that lead to the change in state of a user key. Similar logs should exist for each authority signing or key management key. The purpose of logging is to enable the CA to justify decisions to auditors and anyone relying on the information as evidence and, of course, to track down problems and glitches.

Perhaps the most trusted elements in a key management center using general-purpose commercial operating systems are the people who must be relied upon to act in good faith. A good management orientation for prospective security employees could be based in part on material purportedly used to orient new NSA employees who are charged with protecting and upholding public trust in the national security arena (see http://www.personal.umd.umich.edu/~nhughes/htmldocs/nsa.html).

### Trustworthy Installation

System installation and initialization are very significant events in the life of a certificate server. Earlier, we discussed the accountability issues related to the creation of authority during cryptographic device initialization and key generation. However, it is important to note that an unreliable, unattributable installation of the operating platform compromises the initialization systems and the operational servers alike. In such a situation, any number of parties can claim that the system is inherently unreliable. As we discussed in Chapter 11, when attempting to repudiate a security service relying upon CA-issued certificates, claimants will use any excuse to suggest the security service that binds them was unreliable.

Only trusted and trained personnel should have access to the computer on which security-critical software is to be loaded. The equipment should be procured from reputable dealers and be used directly from (intact) packing crates. Seals, alarms, and courier procedures may be deemed necessary for some components, such as specialized cryptographic signing devices. Should a component be returned for repair, this process must be performed in reverse. Administrators should be diligent: operating systems, middleware, and application software should always be licensed, holograms and serial numbers established as authentic, and proper version and change control established for upgrades, fixes, and custom modifications.

### Fault Tolerance

Fault tolerance of CA operator equipment and telecommunications and preparedness of the facility to withstand various forms of natural disaster are topics likely to be addressed only by commercial CAs. However, as before, for sites that must prepare for the worst, careful design and documentation that demonstrates preparedness are crucial. Accrediting officers need to plan to recover from technological or natural disasters, and the legal aftermath due to any disruption in service. The planning of a trusted facility necessarily includes preparation for the eventuality of failure and disaster.

### Shared Systems and Data Separation

If a site is operating as a CA service bureau, outsourcing clients may require particular equipment to be used to process and store key management transactions. Inevitably, much of the facility infrastructure will be shared, but there may be a need to strictly separate part of the transaction flow. In shared, distributed computing facilities, such policies may be enacted through careful physical administration of LAN segments and by exercising tight control over external network access ports and packet routing paths using firewalls and IP subnetting.

## Physical Security

Many consumers will validly measure reliability and security of a CA service operator in terms of the amount of "bricks and mortar" surrounding its trusted facility. The presence of armed guards and steel safes will no doubt provide further reassurance. [MART73] gives background on criteria for the construction of vaults and closed areas.

A documented physical-site policy can enable an audit of the management controls used to protect a site against physical threats. The following excerpt presents an example of a physical plant management control regime (published by permission of U.S. Naval Computer and Telecommunications Command). A sound physical security regime will eliminate a number of external threats and will usually inculcate personnel security awareness.

## 1. PERSONNEL ACCESS, IDENTIFICATION AND MOVEMENT

[corporate badge issuing regimes, and personnel requirements for visible identification...]

## 2. BUILDING SECURITY

a. Each [local authority] has primary responsibility for the internal security of the spaces/offices assigned. It is the responsibility of each directorate [local authority] to enforce internal security regulations in their assigned spaces. All security violations and practices dangerous to security will be reported to the Security Officer.

b. The headquarters building will be secured at the end of the normal workday or anytime not occupied by assigned personnel. All unnecessary utilities will be secured and all external doors, windows, and other openings which could provide access will be secured and locked.

c. Individuals required to work in the building after normal working hours will be responsible for the integrity and security of their working area. The command duty officer (CDO) will be notified when an unoccupied space is to be opened.

d. Where there is evidence of possible forced entry into the building or spaces the CDO will be notified immediately. The CDO is responsible for notifying [authority] and the headquarters security officer.

## 3. SECURITY CHECKS

a. The command Duty Petty Officer (DPO) will conduct a thorough security check of all spaces at the end of normal working hours. The DPO will check for unsecured spaces; unsecured security containers and classified material; burn bag storage; computers secured, media stored; and general safety.

b. Security violations/discrepancies found during the DPO security check will be reported to the CDO who will initiate a Security Discrepancy Notice. The command Security Manager will be notified the following work day of the violations.

## 5. PHYSICAL SECURITY SURVEY

a. The headquarters Security Officer will conduct a detailed physical security survey at least annually. A physical security survey differs from an inspection in that a survey covers an in-house formal assessment of the headquarters physical security program. The survey will allow the Commander to review what security measures are in effect, what areas need improvement, and provide a basis for determining priorities for funding/work accomplishment.

b. Results of the physical security survey will be retained until completion of the cognizant inspector general command inspection or a minimum of 3 years, whichever is greater.

6. PHYSICAL SECURITY REVIEW BOARD (PSRB). The headquarters Security Officer will be the command's representative on the [authority] Physical Security Review Board which meets annually to discuss security concerns and matters of the host command and how they will affect the tenants.

7. PHYSICAL SECURITY REVIEW COMMITTEE (PSRC)

a. Responsibility. The Commander will designate a PSRC to advise and assist in applying the standards of and implementing the physical security and loss prevention program of this headquarters. The committee will:

(1) Assist in determining requirements for and evaluating security afforded to areas of this activity.

(2) Advise on establishment of restricted areas throughout the headquarters.

(3) Review draft physical security and loss prevention plans or recommended changes prior to submission to the Commander.

(4) Review reports of significant losses or breaches of security and recommend improvements to the Physical Security and Loss Prevention Program.

b. Membership. The PSRC will, as a minimum, include the following membership:

(1) Security Officer (chairperson)

(2) Security Manager

(3) Operations Security Officer

(4) AIS Security Officer

(5) Designated security coordinator from each directorate.

c. Meetings and Minutes. Committee members or their representative will meet as required, but at least quarterly. Minutes of the meeting will be made a matter of record and such records will be retained until completion of the cognizant Inspector General command inspection, or 3 years, whichever is greater.

8. KEY AND LOCK CONTROL. A strict key and lock control program will be managed and supervised by the security officer. Included within this program are all keys, locks, padlocks and locking devices used to protect or secure restricted areas, activity perimeters, security facilities, critical areas, classified material, sensitive material and supplies. This program will not include keys, locks and padlocks used for convenience, privacy, unclassified, administrative or personal use. Guidelines for key control officer, key custodians and requirements for rotation and maintenance can be found in . . . .

Excerpt source: U.S. Naval Computer and Telecommunications Command, used with permission.

## Summary

Computer security management is the process of using security policy to govern the secure system such as that supporting a public key certification service.

Certificate policies are a type of security policy. They administer the quality of a certificate-based key distribution mechanism, rather than computer system security or personnel issues addressed by classical security policy. System security policy is a systems-oriented perspective on the process of regulating behavior to achieve the results desired by the organization. Technical security policy ensures that security services are effective with respect to the policy rules.

To bridge the gap between policy and operations, trusted systems should be accredited. An accreditation statement affixes security responsibility. Beyond the trusted products and systems to be deployed, trusted facilities must also be managed in such a way that its culture and practices support the security policy. An organization that aims to operate a secure system should document its practical instructions in the form of a security features user's guide and a trusted facility manual. This documentation explains the roles of the security administrator, system administrator, and system operator in establishing, operating, and maintaining a secure environment.

Cryptographic materials require special protection measures. Although certificate servers and key management systems are subject to stringent security policy management controls, the signing devices are subject to independent lifecycle management regimes that protect the critical signing keys from key compromise and misuse. Once the signing service is armed, the secure systems trusted computing base security enforcement functions can be relied upon to protect the keyed community against unauthorized access to the certificate- and CRL-issuing capability.

Operations security should be addressed with due regard for established practices for maintaining professional data centers with high availability and robustness. Special attention should be paid to the threats to operation of CA-based key management services. Physical network topology together with packet routing and routing table distribution and management practices may be exploited to enforce data path separation where asset knowledge or failure contamination is unacceptable.

## References

[SUMM97]   Summers, R. *Secure Computing—Threats and Safeguards,* McGraw-Hill, New York, 1997, http://ourworld.compuserve.com/homepages/rsummers/tableofc.htm.

[MART73]   Martin, J., *Security, Accuracy, and Privacy in Computer Systems,* Prentice-Hall, Englewood Cliffs, NJ, 1973.

[CSB]   Russell, D., and G.T. Gangemi, Sr. *Computer Security Basics,* O'Reilly & Associates, Sebastopol, Calif.

[NISPOM]   National Industry Security Program Operating Manual, Department of Defense S2200-22-M, January 1995.

[TCSEC]   Trusted Computer System Evaluation Criteria, Department of Defense Standard S200-28-STD, December 1995.

# Part V
# Web Security and Certificates

Part V explains how to use digital certificate technology to set up secure Web communications. SSL security is where the certificate revolution finally began in earnest on the Internet.

In the heady days of the Netscape revolution, Internet shopping malls run by companies such as MCI and AT&T sought to offer on-line secure merchants environments in which to engage in digital commerce and receive payment from the public. Creation of the SSL protocol was the result, and digital certificates were used to authenticate the malls to consumers everywhere and help set up basic privacy and security. To ensure that other malls could also compete, RSA Data Security set up a unit to issue certificates. Starting from a dozen malls receiving certificates, the secure server community has grown to encompass tens of thousands of companies, and growth shows no sign of slowing. An international CA industry has evolved from those pioneers of Internet electronic commerce.

In Chapter 14, we show, step-by-step, how to set up a secure Web server to use SSL-protected communications between a client and a server and how to configure a Web server to authenticate Web clients who present certificates. In Chapter 14, we deal with the practical aspects of enrolling a server with a CA. We explain how to create a request and work with a trusted third-party CA (VeriSign), an LRA (VeriSign OnSite), and a corporate certificate issuer (Microsoft Certificate Server) to obtain the necessary certificate. We see how to install the Web server certificate using the security management tool and consider some of the options for configuring SSL.

In Chapter 15, we introduce the user to processes for establishing and using SSL client authentication. As with secure Web servers, we see how to work with VeriSign CA, VeriSign OnSite LRA, or Microsoft Certificate Server to obtain personal certificates. We then set up a Web server to demand and require personal certificates and integrate them with access control mechanisms to protect server resources.

Chapter

# 14

# Secure Web Communications— Server Authentication

Server authentication is an important security service that allows a Web client to identify the Web site it is communicating with. Web servers and browsers provide this service by supporting the Secure Socket Layer (SSL) protocol. To use SSL, a special type of digital certificate, called a **server certificate,** needs to be obtained and installed on the Web server. In this chapter, we will cover three common approaches to obtaining such a certificate and will show how to use a server certificate to configure SSL on a Web site.

## Server Authentication

Web communication is a two-way street, where information is transferred between a Web client (browser) and a Web server in both directions. Valuable information can be sent between a browser and a server. In such cases, the user running the browser may need to make sure that

- The information is sent to the right Web site.
- The information is transferred in encrypted form.

Web servers and browsers can provide such an assurance by supporting a server authentication service such as SSL. Whenever you communicate with a Web site using a URL that starts with HTTPS, you are using SSL. The browser then executes a server authentication protocol in which it makes sure that it is communicating securely with the Web site you specified in the URL. Note that you cannot just replace HTTP with HTTPS in any URL to make the Web communication secure. To use HTTPS, the resource should already reside on a Web site that is secured with SSL.

## Setting Up SSL on a Web Site

To use SSL, you need to obtain and install a server certificate on your Web site first. A server certificate contains identification information that enables the Web clients to authenticate the identity of a Web site—typically the fully qualified DNS name, such as www.netscape.com. The first step in getting a server certificate is to create a server certificate request. The second step is to obtain the server certificate using your server certificate request file. There are three ways to obtain such a certificate. In the first approach, you process the certificate request locally using your own certificate server. In the second approach, which is more common, you send the certificate request file to a CA, where the request is processed and a server certificate is issued and sent to you. The third approach involves the use of local registration authorities (LRAs). Finally, you install the certificate on your Web site and configure it to use SSL.

In the following sections, we show how to set up SSL on an IIS Web site. We will use Key Manager, a program shipped with IIS, to generate a public/private key pair and create a server certificate request file. We then present three scenarios for obtaining the server certificate. In the first scenario, we use the Microsoft Certificate Server to process the certificate request file and issue the server certificate. In the second scenario, we walk through the steps to apply for a server certificate using the services of VeriSign, and then we discuss the use of VeriSign OnSite LRA service to obtain a server certificate. But first, let's start with an overview of IIS, which we will be using for our Web site.

### Microsoft Internet Information Server

**Internet Information Server** (IIS) is Microsoft's suite of Internet server applications. On NT Server platforms, IIS includes the following server applications:

- HTTP Server
- FTP Server
- Transaction Server
- Index Server
- Site Analyst

IIS complies with HTTP 1.1 standard (RFC 2068) and the SSL 3.0 protocol. In addition to Common Gateway Interface (CGI), it also supports Active Server Pages (ASP)—Microsoft's server-side scripting environment—and the Internet Server API (ISAPI) to enable extending the functionality of the Web site.

IIS uses **Microsoft Management Console** (MMC) as its administration interface. MMC is Microsoft's new integration platform for application administration that is used by all server applications, such as those included in IIS, Mail Server, and News Server. Figure 14-1 shows how IIS components integrate with MMC.

Figure 14-2 displays the properties of an IIS Web site. We will be using the **Directory Security** tab of this dialog box later in this chapter. To find more information about IIS or to download the latest version of IIS, you can visit Microsoft's IIS home page at http://www.microsoft.com/iis.

## Key Manager

**Key Manager** is a standalone program that is integrated into IIS to facilitate the following key management tasks:

- Generating cryptographic keys

- Creating server certificate requests

- Installing server certificates

- Exporting and importing of cryptographic keys

You will use Key Manager to create a server certificate request for your IIS Web sites.

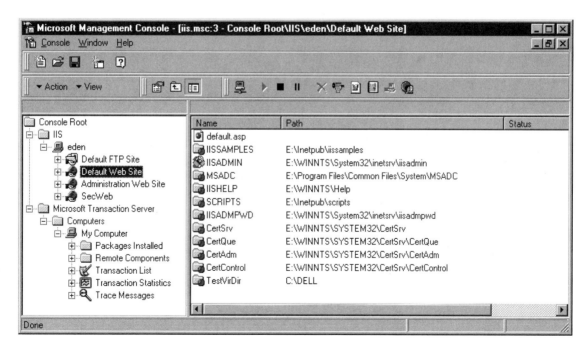

**Figure 14-1** Microsoft Management Console.

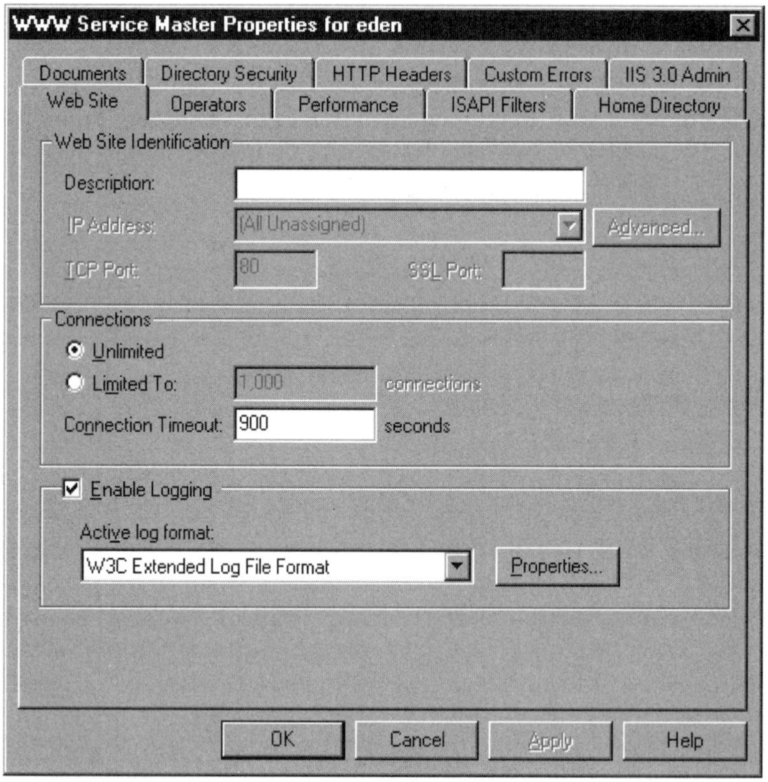

**Figure 14-2** Properties of an IIS Web site.

## Creating a Server Certificate Request

To create a server certificate request for an IIS Web site, follow these steps:

1. Run MMC by selecting **Internet Service Manager** from the Microsoft Internet Information Server program menu.

2. Launch Key Manager by clicking on the **Key Manager** icon on the MMC tool bar. If the **Key Manager** icon is not displayed, select **Internet Information Server** on the left pane of MMC.

3. Select **Create New Key** from the Key menu of the Key Manager window (Figure 14-3).

4. Select **Put the request in a file that you will send to an authority** and assign a name to your certificate request file (Figure 14-4). Click **Next.**

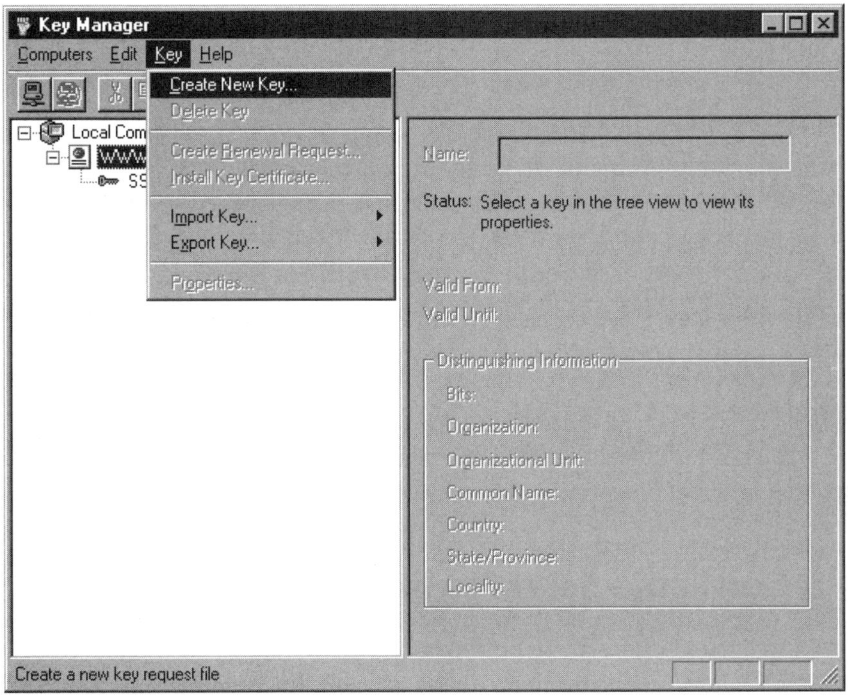

**Figure 14-3** Create a new key pair in Key Manager.

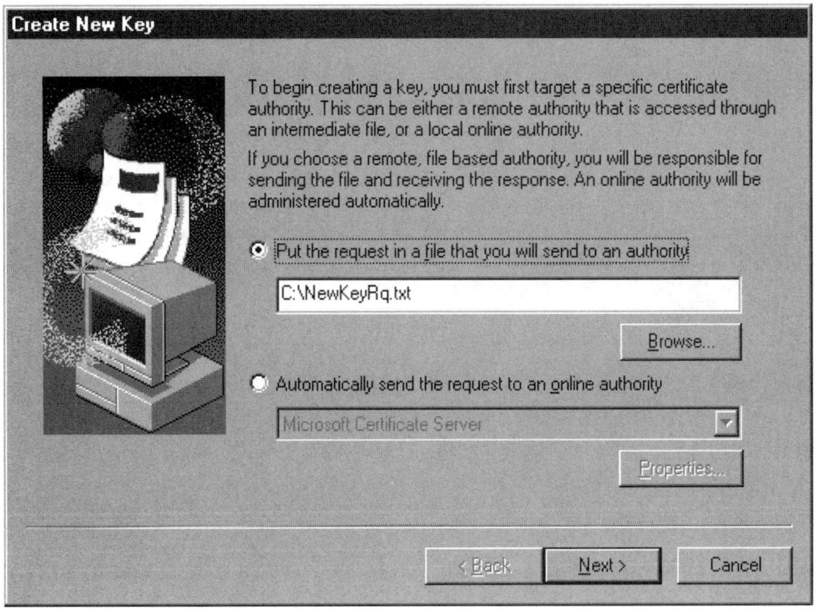

**Figure 14-4** Assign a name to the certificate request file.

5. Assign a name and a password to your key pair (Figure 14-5) and click **Next.** The key name will appear in the Key Manager window after the key is generated. The password is used to encrypt the private key, and it will be needed later when you install the certificate.

6. Provide information about your organization (Figure 14-6). For the **Common Name** field, use the complete name of your Web server as you expect it to be used in an URL (e.g., www.netscape.com). Click **Next** and follow the instructions in the remaining dialog boxes to finish the process.

7. Save the new key by clicking on **Commit Changes Now** in the Computers menu in the Key Manager window.

You have just generated a public-private key pair and a server certificate request file that contains information about your organization, Web site, and your public key. The next step is to get a server certificate using this certificate server request.

## Using a Certificate Server to Issue a Server Certificate

As mentioned earlier, one way to obtain a certificate is to process a certificate request yourself using your own certificate server. In this section, we walk you

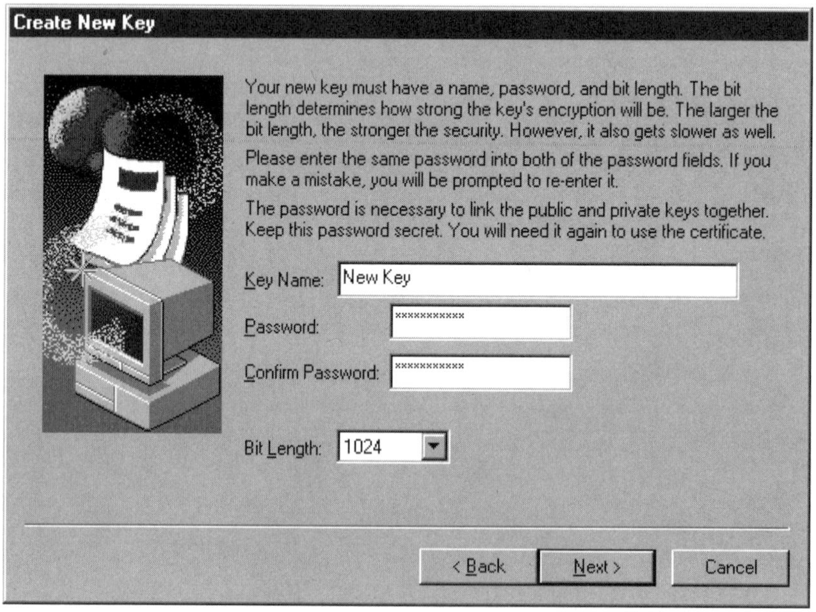

**Figure 14-5**  Choose a name and a password.

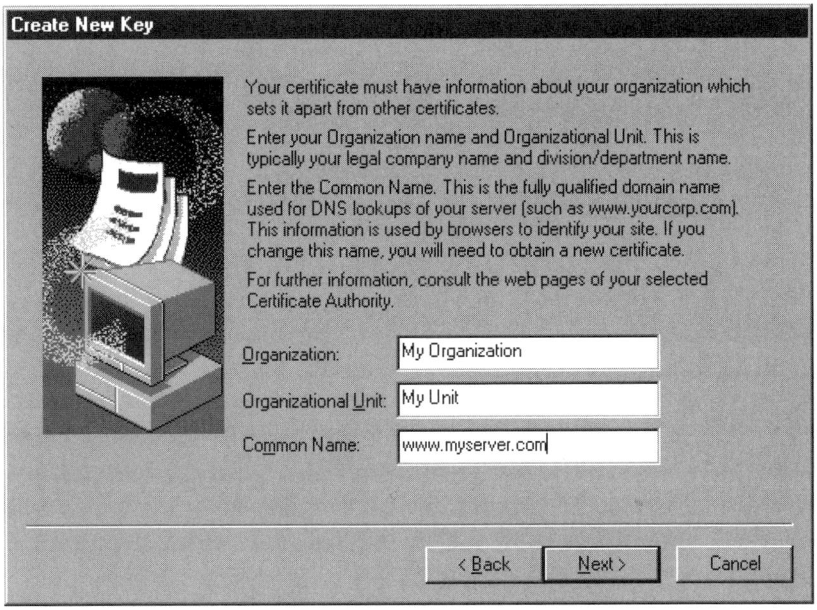

**Figure 14-6**  Provide information on your organization and Web site.

through the process using the Microsoft Certificate Server, available on NT Server platforms. You will revisit the Microsoft Certificate Server (called the Certificate Server from now on) in Part VI.

To issue a certificate using the Certificate Server, follow these steps:

1. Launch the certreq program by selecting **Process Certificate Request File** from the Microsoft Certificate Server program menu. (You can also use the command-line version of the certreq program. Type **certreq /help** in a command prompt window for more information on how to use this program.)

2. Specify the path to your certificate request file and a name for the certificate output file in the dialog boxes that appear. The certreq program sends your certificate request to the Certificate Server for processing. If the request is accepted, a certificate will be created and saved to the specified output file. Note that you need to be in the administrative group to be able to use the Certificate Server utility programs.

## Getting a Server Certificate from a CA

In the preceding section, you used your own certificate server to issue a server certificate. Although this approach may work fine, for example, for an intranet, sometimes you need to get a server certificate from a CA to exploit public trust in a well-known CA. With local certificate servers you cannot easily interoperate with people outside of your intranet. Even within your intranet, the public keys of certificate servers must be securely imported as trusted roots in all certificate-using applications. As an example of the second approach, follow these steps to apply for a server certificate using VeriSign's on-line certificate enrollment service:

1. Create a server certificate request as explained in the Creating a Server Certificate Request section.

2. Point your Web browser to http://digitalid.verisign.com (Figure 14-7) and click on the **Enroll** icon.

3. Select **Web Servers** under **Organizations** on VeriSign's enrollment page.

4. Select **I want a Digital ID for Testing purposes only**. VeriSign's Test Server Certificates are free, valid for a limited time, and good for testing purposes only. We use them here just to show the steps involved in obtaining a server certificate from a CA.

5. Select **Microsoft** from the list of available server software vendors. Note that after you click the **Select** button on this page, you switch to a secure Web communication channel. This is because you are about to provide personal information. Read the information about the steps you are about to take carefully (Figure 14-8).

6. Select the **Begin** button to start the process.

7. Cut and paste your certificate request in the specified area and provide all the information requested. Read the VeriSign Test CA Certification Practice Statement (CPS) before proceeding (you can find more information on CPS policies in Chapter 11).

8. Select **Accept** to proceed and submit the request. If your request is accepted, an e-mail will be sent to you containing the server certificate issued by VeriSign.

9. Cut the certificate part starting at the BEGIN CERTIFICATE line up to and including the END CERTIFICATE line from the e-mail and save it to a new text file. You will use this file later when you install the certificate, as explained in the Installing a Server Certificate section later.

Because you are using a free testing version of VeriSign's server certificate, the certificate that has signed your server certificate (VeriSign's Test CA certificate) is not preinstalled in your browser. (If you had obtained a non-test certificate from VeriSign, you would not have to preinstall the root.) This is also true if you use your own certificate server to issue a server certificate, because the root certificate of your certificate server is not preinstalled in any browsers either. As mentioned in Step 7 in

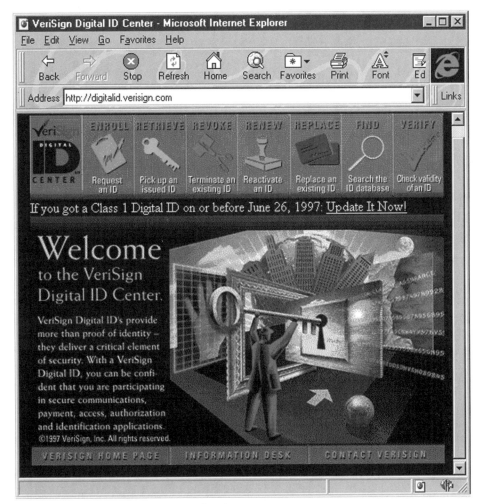

**Figure 14-7**  VeriSign's Digital ID Center.

Figure 14-8 and again in the final page when you finish your enrollment with VeriSign successfully, you need to install this Test CA certificate. Your browser will then be able to validate the server certificate installed on your Web server during an SSL communication. Installation of root certificates in a browser is covered in a later section.

## Getting a Server Certificate from an LRA

A third way to obtain a server certificate is through an LRA service such as VeriSign's OnSite (http://www.verisign.com/onsite/index.html). OnSite allows you to

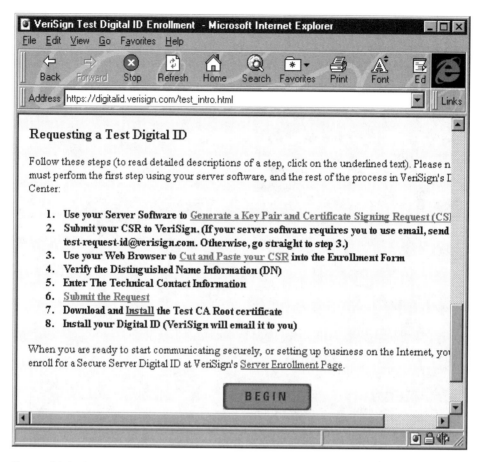

**Figure 14-8** Steps to apply for a Test Server Certificate.

maintain tight control over the authentication of server enrollments while out-sourcing key management to VeriSign CA. Furthermore, OnSite enables you to issue certificates under the VeriSign public PKI hierarchy and eliminate the inter-operability issues encountered when a certificate server issues server certificates. See Chapter 10 for a detailed discussion of LRA and OnSite and Chapter 15 for the steps required to set up the OnSite service.

## Installing a Server Certificate

After you obtain a server certificate, you need to install it on your Web site. Follow these steps to install a server certificate on an IIS Web site:

1. In the Key Manager window, select the key corresponding to the certificate. The key has a red flag because it is not installed yet.

2. Select **Install Key Certificate** from the Key menu (Figure 14-9).

3. Open the file containing your server certificate in the Open dialog box.

4. Key Manager prompts you for your password. Enter the password you chose during the key generation.

5. Select **Add** in the Server Bindings dialog box to choose the IP address and port number this certificate should bind to. The IP address and port number you use here should match the IP address and port number your secure Web site is bound to when you set up your secure Web site (see the Enabling SSL on a Web Site section for more information). This step is necessary because in IIS you can have multiple Web sites with each site binding (listening) to a different port number or IP address. IIS uses this binding to find the server certificate that

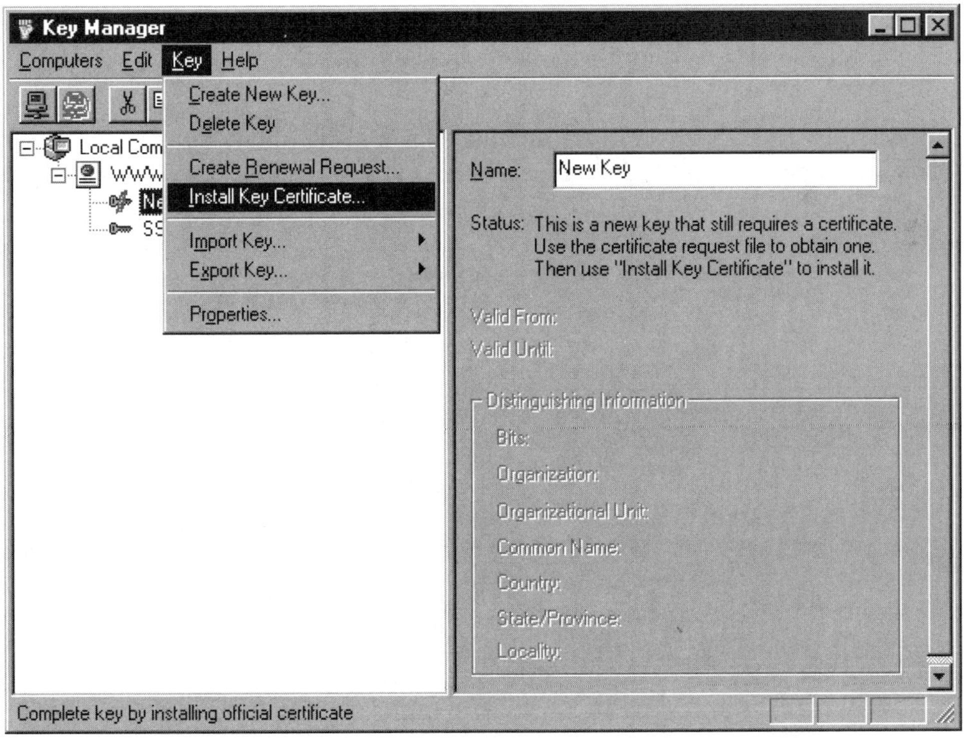

**Figure 14-9**  Install the server certificate.

corresponds to each Web site. The default setting shown in Figure 14-10 works fine if this is the first certificate you install.

6. Click on **Commit Changes Now** from the Computers menu in the Key Manager window.

The red flag on the key in the Key Manager window should disappear once you successfully install the certificate. You are now ready to enable SSL on your Web site.

## Enabling SSL on a Web Site

Now that you have installed a server certificate on your IIS Web site, you can configure it to use SSL. IIS allows you to require a secure channel at three different levels. You can require SSL for all the resources on a Web site, for all resources in a directory, or you can require SSL only for a specific file. To show how this works, we will create a new Web site and require SSL at the Web site level. To do this, follow these steps:

1. Right-click on your computer icon in MMC and select **Create New** from the menu and **Web Site** from the submenu (Figure 14-11). Enter a description for the new Web site.

2. Specify the IP address and port number this Web site binds to. Because the default Web site is already listening on port 80, you need to use a different port

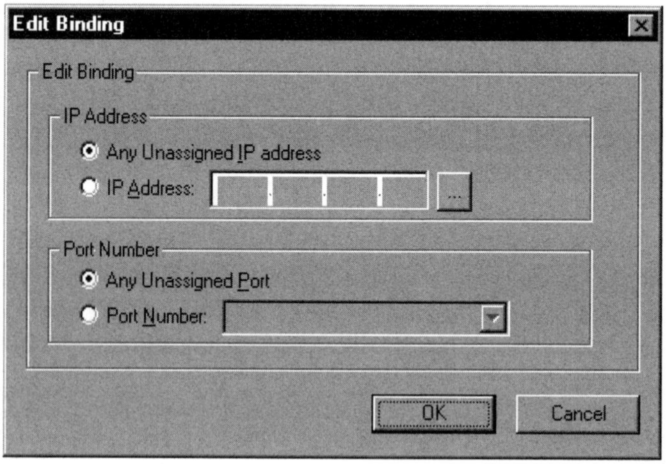

**Figure 14-10**  Setting certificate bindings.

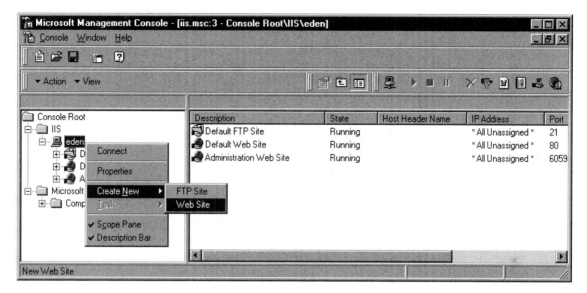

**Figure 14-11**   Create a new IIS Web site.

number so that there will be no conflict (Figure 14-12). The SSL port number should be set to 443, which is the default value specified by the SSL protocol.

Follow the remaining steps to assign a root directory to your new Web site and choose your Web site access permissions. You can start with read-only permission and change the permissions later at different levels. When you are finished, you will see the new Web site on the MMC's left pane.

To set up SSL on this new Web site:

1. Select the **Directory Security** tab from your Web site's properties dialog box.

2. Click the **Edit** button under the **Secure Communications** tab.

3. Select **Require Secure Channel when accessing this resource** (Figure 14-13) to allow only a secure communication to access the resources on this Web site. This means HTTPS must be specified in URLs that point to any resources residing on this Web site.

Your new Web site is now set up to use SSL.

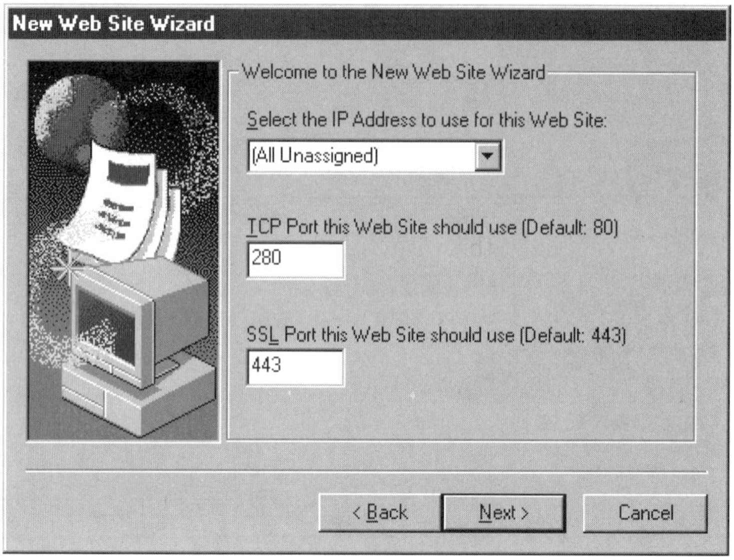

**Figure 14-12**  Set the IP address and port numbers.

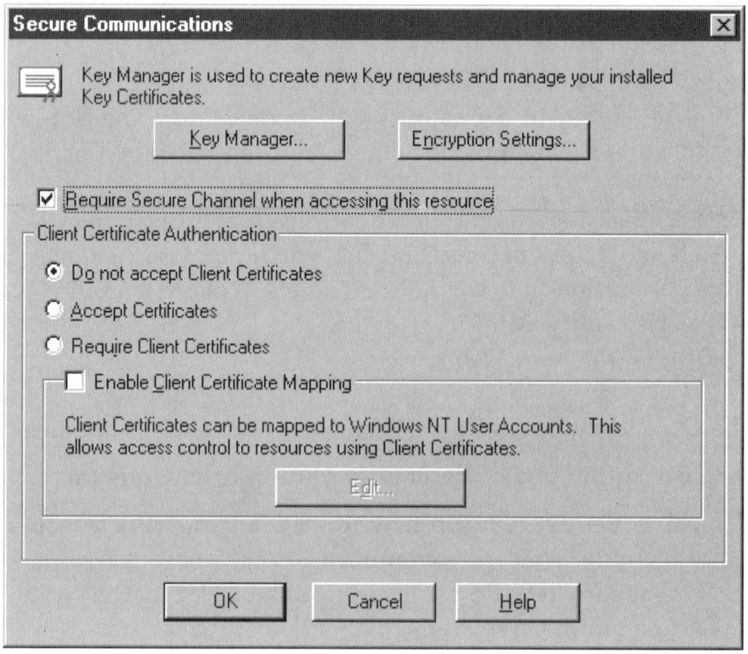

**Figure 14-13**  Require Secure Channel.

# Establishing an SSL Connection

A browser establishes an SSL connection with a Web site after it successfully authenticates the Web site and makes sure it is communicating with the site the user has specified in the URL. To authenticate a Web site, a browser needs the root certificate of the CA that has issued the Web site's server certificate. Because it is not safe to download a root certificate via unsecure channels, root certificates need to be preinstalled in the browser or otherwise installed by the user separately. The root certificates of major public CAs are preinstalled and, in most cases, you don't need to worry about their installation. In certain situations, however, such as when you use your own certificate server, you need to take extra steps to download and install the root certificate in your browser. This was also the case earlier when we obtained a test server certificate from VeriSign, because VeriSign signs its test certificates with a Test CA whose root certificate is not preinstalled. In the next section, we see how to install the root certificates of the Certificate Server and VeriSign's Test CA in a browser.

## Installing Root Certificates in a Browser

One way to install a root certificate is to download the file containing the certificate over the Web. Using the file MIME type, a browser recognizes that it is downloading a root certificate and can install it if you open the file. Root certificates should be distributed using a secure channel because they represent the origin of the trust. That is why root certificates of public CAs are preinstalled in browsers or, in cases where you need to download them over the Web, they reside on Web sites that are secured with SSL.

To install the root certificate of your Certificate Server in your browser, follow these steps:

1. In your browser, load the Certificate Server Administration Tools page located at http://servername/CertSrv.
2. Select **Certificate Enrollment.**
3. Select **Install Certificate Authority Certificates** (Figure 14-14).
4. Select the root certificate of the Certificate Server you want to install.
5. Select **Open this file from the Internet** in the download dialog box.
6. Select the appropriate items from the **Available Usages** and click on **OK** to install the certificate (Figure 14-15).

When you open a root certificate, you are presented with a dialog box similar to the one shown in Figure 14-15. Because a root certificate can be used for different

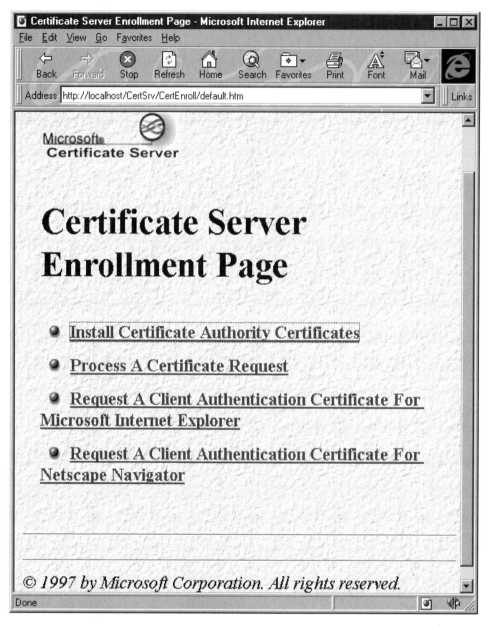

**Figure 14-14**  Install certificate authority certificates.

authentication purposes, you need to specify the authentication purposes you want the certificate to be used for. A root certificate can be used for client authentication (discussed in Chapter 15), server authentication, secure e-mail, and software publishing (downloading code over the network). In the preceding example, we selected the server authentication usage.

You can install VeriSign's Test CA certificate by navigating to https://digitalid.verisign.com/cgi-bin/getcacert (or by clicking the **INSTALL** button on the last page of the enrollment process) and then selecting **Open this file from its current location** in the download dialog box. As explained earlier, after you open the file, enable the certificate, select server authentication for the usage, and press **OK** to install the certificate.

Your browser now has the necessary root certificate and is ready to make an SSL connection with your secure Web site.

## Establishing the Connection

To establish an SSL connection with a Web site, all you need to do is to use HTTPS instead of HTTP in the URL. When HTTPS is used, a browser initiates an SSL handshake with the Web site and makes sure it is communicating with the Web site specified in the URL. All the communication with the Web site is also encrypted. For example, to communicate with the secure Web site you created earlier, create an HTML file named index.htm in the root directory of the Web site and point your browser to https://myserver/index.htm. Because you required an SSL channel when

**Figure 14-15** Installing a new root (site) certificate.

you set up your secure Web site, you will get an error message indicating that SSL is needed if you use HTTP instead of HTTPS in this URL.

## Strong Data Encryption

When you use SSL to communicate with a Web server, a symmetric key will be chosen for data encryption during the SSL handshake protocol. This symmetric key is used to encrypt all the information sent between the browser and the server. The cryptographic strength of your communication depends directly on the length of this symmetric key. The Web browser and server products currently available allow two data encryption key lengths: 40 bit and 128 bit. To require 128-bit encryption in an IIS Web site, for example, you select **Encryption Settings** in the Secure Communications dialog box (see Figure 14-13).

Although the U.S. export restrictions on data encryption strength in Web browser and server technologies are constantly changing, new changes demonstrate an interesting and important paradigm shift in the configuration of cryptographic environments that use public-key cryptography to control the strength of data encryption. Let's look at both the conventional and the new approach.

### Conventional Approach

The conventional way to restrict the strength of data encryption is to have two completely separate classes of cryptographic environment: a low-strength (normally 40 bit) and a high-strength (64 bit and above) class. While low-strength cryptography can be exported worldwide, there are strict restrictions on distribution of high-strength cryptographic components. Strong cryptography is now generally available to all U.S.-based companies. U.S. companies that need to use strong encryption in their non-U.S. offices, however, may go through special procurement and key escrow procedures to use high-strength cryptographic components abroad.

### Using Public-Key Cryptography to Control Encryption Strength

A recent U.S. export policy move allows a mixed cryptographic environment in which both high- and low-strength cryptography are supported in browser technology. In the new approach, the strength of data encryption is determined at connect time by the information available in the server certificate. For a server certificate to turn on the strong data encryption in a browser, it should contain special X.509 extensions and be issued only by certain authorized CAs.

Based on the new U.S. export policy, browsers having a mixed cryptographic configuration will use strong data encryption only when they communicate with a Web site that has a server certificate issued by an authorized CA that contains these security extensions. If these extensions do not exist, the communication is conducted using low-strength data encryption. Currently, only VeriSign is authorized to issue such special server certificates to U.S. and some foreign financial institutions.

You can find more information about these certificates (called Global Server Digital ID by VeriSign and Server Gated Cryptography by Microsoft) at http://www.verisign.com/globalserver/MSglobalfaq.html (Microsoft server), http://www.verisign.com/globalserver/NSglobalfaq.html (Netscape server), or Microsoft's main security page at http://www.microsoft.com/security/.

## Summary

Web sites can use the SSL protocol to provide secure Web communication based on server authentication. To enable SSL on a Web server, you need to obtain and install a server certificate on the server first. You can issue a server certificate using your own certificate server, obtain one from a well-known CA to benefit from public trust in such an organization, or use an LRA service.

A recent change in U.S. export policy allows flexible support for strong data encryption in the new generation of browsers, where strong data encryption is used only when a server certificate containing special X.509 extensions is detected. Currently, all U.S. and most foreign financial institutions can obtain such certificates, and only VeriSign can issue them.

Chapter

# 15

# Secure Web Communications— Client Authentication

Client authentication is another security service that you may need for secure Web communications. Just as a Web client might want to identify the Web server it is communicating with, a Web server might also need to know the identity of the client. Some security policies require client authentication before allowing any communications or any access to Web resources to take place. An on-line banking system, for example, must authenticate a customer before allowing any transactions on the customer's account. In this chapter, we will examine various client authentication methods with a focus on SSL client authentication. See Chapter 6 for restricting access to server resources.

## Client Authentication

**Client authentication** is a process by which a server determines the identity of the client attempting to communicate with it. Client authentication has always been an important aspect of client/server computing because servers, which have access to valuable information, need to reject any communication requests from unauthorized clients. In secure Web communications, as we will see in this chapter, there are different client authentication methods. These authentication methods vary in their security strength. Also, not all Web browsers support all client authentication methods. You should consider these two issues before you add client authentication to your secure Web server.

## Client Authentication Methods

There are different methods for authenticating Web clients and restricting access to resources residing on a Web server. In this section, we examine four different authentication methods: anonymous, basic, NT challenge-response, and SSL client authentication. As in Chapter 14, we will use IIS to show how each method is implemented.

## Anonymous Authentication

In **anonymous authentication**, all clients are simply considered authenticated. Choose this authentication method when you want to make your Web resources available to everybody. In IIS, an anonymous user account, named IUSER_*computername* by default, is used when accessing a resource anonymously. When anonymous access is selected, IIS uses this account to log on clients who attempt to access the resource. Clients are permitted to access the resource if the anonymous account has permission to access the resource. So, in IIS, to use anonymous access you need to enable anonymous access and give the anonymous account permission to access the resource.

In IIS, you can use anonymous access for all resources on a Web site, for all files in a specific directory, or for a single file. For resources on NTFS partitions, access permissions can be set from the **Security** tab in the file or directory properties dialog box. You can find more information on anonymous access and how to set it in the IIS documentation.

## Basic Authentication

The **basic authentication** method is the standard method for collecting user name and password information. When basic authentication is enabled, users attempting to access a resource should enter their user names and passwords in a dialog box rendered by the Web browser. The browser uses this information to establish a connection to the Web server. In IIS, the name is assumed to be the name of a valid NT user account. After IIS verifies the password, it uses this account to log on the user. IIS permits users to access a resource if the specified account has permission to access the resource.

Although basic authentication is a widely used industry standard, it is not recommended because of security reasons. Web browsers using basic authentication transmit user names and passwords in unencrypted form, which are susceptible to eavesdropping. If you need to use this method, however, consider enabling SSL on your Web site. If SSL is enabled, all communication between the client and server, including password information, will be encrypted.

## NT Challenge-Response Authentication

The **NT challenge-response authentication** method authenticates users without requiring the transmission of actual passwords across the network. In an NT challenge-response authentication process, the browser uses cryptography to prove its knowledge of the current user's login and password to the Web server. If the authentication fails, the browser prompts the user for his Windows NT account information and will use the new information using the same Windows NT challenge-response method to establish the connection. In this method, the actual password is never transmitted over the network.

Windows NT challenge-response authentication is most effective in an intranet environment, where both Web clients and servers are in the same NT domain and users have browsers that support this method. Currently, only Microsoft Internet Explorer supports this authentication method.

## SSL Client Authentication

**SSL client authentication** is based on public-key cryptography, in which the user's client certificate is used to verify his identity. In this method, supported in SSL 3.0 and higher, the Web browser and server transfer a series of messages using the private and public key of the user. During this process, the server essentially authenticates the client by verifying that he is the true holder of the presented client certificate. In public key cryptography, the true holder of a certificate is basically the person who has the private key associated with the public key contained in the certificate.

Certificate-based authentication is very secure because it is based on long cryptographic keys. There is also no need for as many login accounts on the Web server because multiple client certificates can be mapped to one user account. Certificate-based authentication is also very powerful because it is possible to regulate Web access based on specific properties of the client certificates. For example, if a Web site needs to provide information only to employees of a specific company, it can simply use the client certificate authentication method to allow access to users who hold client certificates issued to the employees of that company. (See Chapter 6.)

Using IIS, you can configure a Web site to automatically map one or more client certificates to an appropriate Windows NT account. The Web site then uses this account to log on the user and to check for access permissions. It is possible to use any information available in a client certificate, such as the user name or organization name, to configure the Web site's mapping of the client certificate to a Windows NT account.

SSL client authentication is available in SSL-enabled Web sites. During client authentication, a Web site may ask the browser for the certificate of the user who is trying to access the resource. If there are no client certificates or the user refuses to send a certificate, the connection will not be established. For client authentication to work, a user needs to have a client certificate. Let's see what a client certificate is and how you can get one.

# Client Certificates

Client certificates contain information such as user's name, user's public key, the certificate validation period, information on the issuer of the certificate, and so on. Like other certificates, client certificates can be customized through their X.509 extensions. Client certificates customized for banks, for example, can contain information about the bank account of the customer holding the certificate.

There are currently three different ways to obtain a client certificate. You can use your own certificate server to issue one. You can get a client certificate from a third-party commercial CA, or you can get one from an LRA. In the following sections, we will show how to obtain a client certificate using each of these methods.

## Issuing Client Certificates Using a Certificate Server

One way to get a client certificate is to issue it yourself using an internal certificate server. As in the case of server certificates we talked about in Chapter 14, to get a certificate, you should first create a certificate request file and then send it to your certificate server for further processing. In this section, we will show you how to get a client certificate using Microsoft Certificate Server and IIS.

To obtain a client certificate from the Certificate Server, use the following steps:

1. In your browser, load the Certificate Server administration page located at http://servername/CertSrv.

2. Select **Certificate Enrollment Tools** to go to the Certificate Server enrollment page.

3. Select **Request a Client Authentication.**

4. Fill out the certificate enrollment form and press **Submit Request.** If you are using Internet Explorer, a Credentials Enrollment wizard may appear. The Credentials Enrollment wizard is an ActiveX control downloaded by the enrollment page. It generates a key pair for you (Figure 15-1) and creates a certificate request containing your personal information and your public key. The Web browser sends this request to the server. Later versions of IE use a newer version of this control, which by default does not have any graphical user interface. If you don't see this wizard, you are running the new version.

5. If Certificate Server accepts your request and issues a certificate, the Certificate Download Web page will be loaded. Click on **Download** to download and install your new client certificate.

You now have a client certificate issued by the Certificate Server. Note that, because this certificate is signed by an internal certificate server, a Web server can verify your client certificate only if it has the root certificate of your certificate server.

## Getting a Client Certificate from a CA

Another way to obtain a client certificate is to get one from a CA. Obtaining a client certificate from a recognized third-party CA has the benefit that the CA's root key is preinstalled in most Web servers. You, therefore, do not need to install your internal certificate server root key into your Web servers. The process for obtaining a

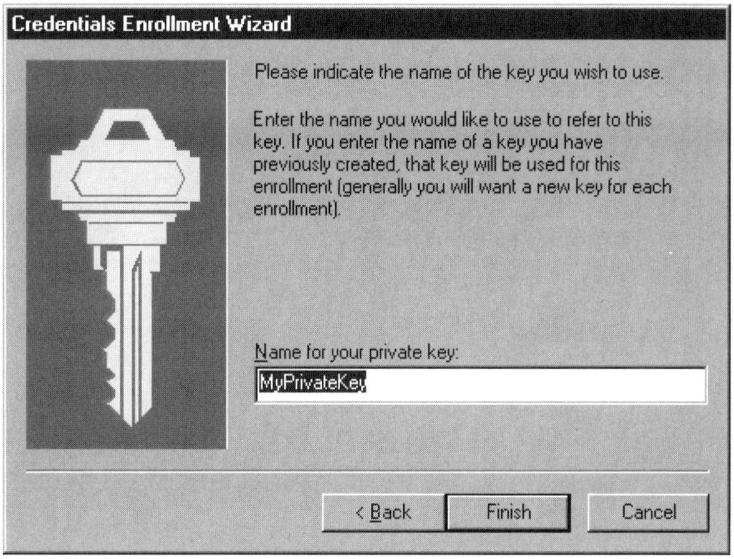

**Figure 15-1**  Credentials Enrollment Wizard.

client certificate from a CA is always defined by the CA. For example, to obtain a client certificate using VeriSign's on-line enrollment service, follow these steps:

1. Point your Web browser at http://digitalid.verisign.com (Figure 14-7 in Chapter 14) and select the **Enroll** icon.

2. Under Web Browsers, select the appropriate link for your Web browser type. In our case, we follow the Microsoft link.

3. Select the class of your certificate (Figure 15-2). You can select a Class 1 or a Class 2 client certificate. These classes are VeriSign-specific and their difference is basically in their level of assurance. Class 2 certificates have a higher assurance level and cost more. To show the steps, we select the Class 1 logo at the top left and apply for a free Class 1 certificate, which is valid for six months.

4. Fill out the enrollment form and select the trial version of Class 1.

5. Read the CPS at the bottom of the page. To continue, you need to accept it.

6. Select **Submit.** The Credential Enrollment Wizard may launch to generate your key pair and a certificate request. If a wizard pops up, follow the instructions to create a certificate request file and send it to VeriSign. If your request is accepted, VeriSign will e-mail you a reference number and directions on how to download and install your certificate. Follow the directions in the e-mail to retrieve and install your certificate.

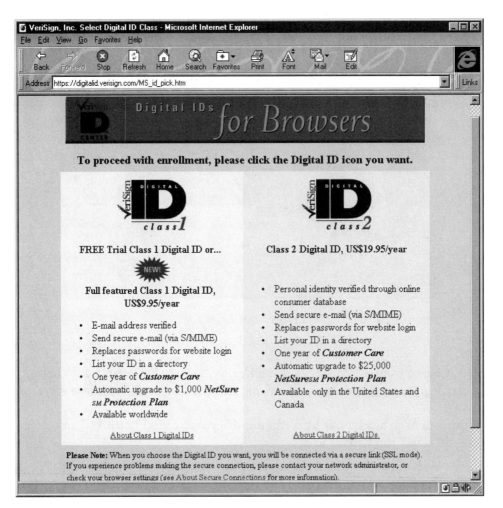

**Figure 15-2**   VeriSign's client certificate enrollment page.

After you install your client certificate, you can communicate with Web sites that require SSL client authentication. You can also use your client certificate to sign or encrypt e-mail messages. Refer to Chapter 5 for more information on how to use your client certificate to sign e-mail messages.

## Getting a Client Certificate from a Local Registration Authority

A third alternative to obtain a client certificate is through an LRA outsourcing service. By using an outsourcing service, an organization can maintain tight control over the authentication of client enrollments while outsourcing key management to a third-party certification authority.

In this section, we use the VeriSign OnSite test drive (http://www.verisign.com/onsite/index.html) to demonstrate how you can quickly set up your own certification authority and start issuing client certificates to people within your organization. OnSite can issue client certificates under the VeriSign public PKI hierarchy and thereby eliminate interoperability issues encountered when a certificate server issues client certificates. See Chapter 10 for a detailed discussion of LRA and OnSite.

Access the OnSite test drive home page at http://www.verisign.com/onsite/testdrive.html. This page, shown in Figure 15-3, explains the steps required to deploy the evaluation edition of OnSite. Follow the instructions and fill out the forms as required. Figure 15-4 shows the main form that you need to fill out. The fields **Company/Department/Agency** and **Dept/Div/Proj** are particularly significant, and together they establish an affiliation. After you provide all the necessary information and accept the OnSite test drive agreement, your browser will generate a key pair and VeriSign will issue you a special administrator client certificate. This

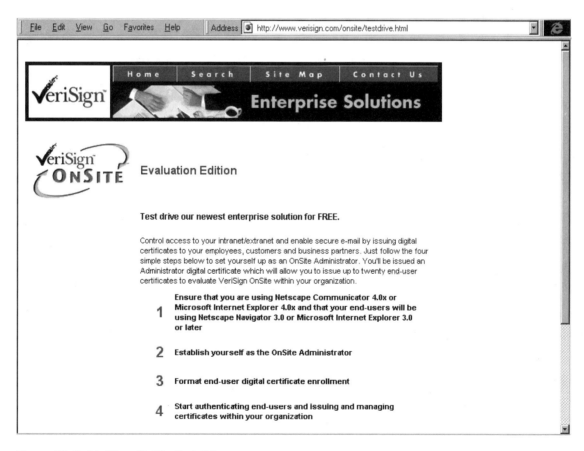

**Figure 15-3**  VeriSign OnSite Test Drive.

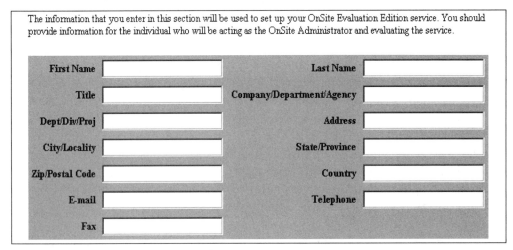

The information that you enter in this section will be used to set up your OnSite Evaluation Edition service. You should provide information for the individual who will be acting as the OnSite Administrator and evaluating the service.

| First Name | | Last Name | |
| Title | | Company/Department/Agency | |
| Dept/Div/Proj | | Address | |
| City/Locality | | State/Province | |
| Zip/Postal Code | | Country | |
| E-mail | | Telephone | |
| Fax | | | |

**Figure 15-4** The main form to apply for OnSite evaluation copy.

certificate contains information that uniquely identifies your affiliation and is used by OnSite during client authentication to distinguish administrators belonging to different affiliations from each other.

After you have obtained your OnSite administrator certificate, use the Enrollment wizard (shown in Figure 15-5) to configure subscriber pages and identify the fields that should appear in client certificates. Click on the **Continue** button and enter your e-mail address, as shown in Figure 15-6. Figures 15-7 and 15-8 illustrate how to configure the subscriber enrollment pages to capture information from subscribers. Finally, you need to decide which fields should appear in the client certificates, as shown in Figure 15-9.

After you customize the subscriber certificates, OnSite will generate customized enrollment pages for your affiliation and inform you of the URL (see Figure 15-10). You can now access this URL to request a client certificate for yourself or supply it to people within your affiliation so they can start enrolling for client certificates.

With an LRA service, you are in charge of authenticating subscribers and approving or rejecting their certificate enrollments. To perform such administrative tasks, you need to provide your administrative client certificate and access the OnSite Control Center, which is shown in Figure 15-11. Refer to the discussion in Chapter 10 or OnSite documentation for details about the OnSite Control Center.

## Enabling SSL Client Authentication

Before you can enable the client authentication method, you need to configure your Web site to use SSL. IIS allows you to require client authentication at three differ-

**Figure 15-5**  OnSite Enrollment Wizard.

ent levels: for the whole Web site, for all files in a directory, or for a specific file. In this section, we enable the client authentication method at the Web site level for the IIS Web site we created in Chapter 14. (Refer to this chapter to learn how to configure SSL on an IIS Web site.)

To enable client authentication in IIS, follow these steps:

1. Run MMC and select your Web site.
2. Select **Properties** from the pop-up menu.
3. Select **Edit** under **Secure Communications** on the **Directory Security** tab.
4. Select **Require Client Certificates** in the Secure Communications dialog box (Figure 15-12).

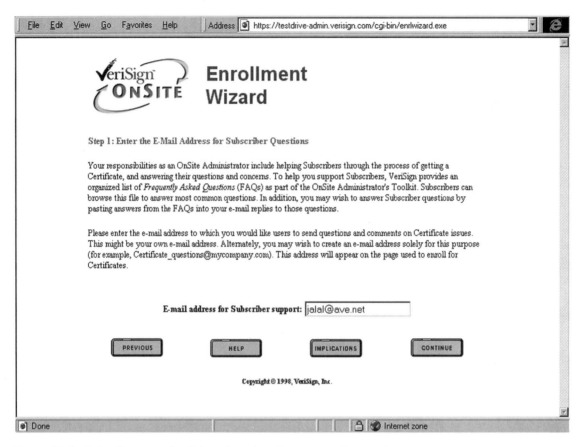

**Figure 15-6**   Selecting e-mail address for subscriber support.

Once you require client certificates at the Web-site level, any browser that attempts to access a resource is asked to send a client certificate during the SSL communication. Moreover, access is allowed only if the client certificate is validated. Note that if you get your client certificate from an internal certificate server, you need to first install the root certificate of your certificate server in IIS. Otherwise, IIS cannot validate your client certificate.

If you now try to download a file from this Web site, a dialog box will pop up in the Web browser informing you that the server is asking for a client certificate. This dialog box has a list of your client certificates. You need to choose which certificate should be sent to the server if you have more than one.

Enabling the client authentication method is the first step in certificate-based authentication. The Web site really needs to do something with the client certificates. IIS can be configured to map a valid certificate to a user account for access

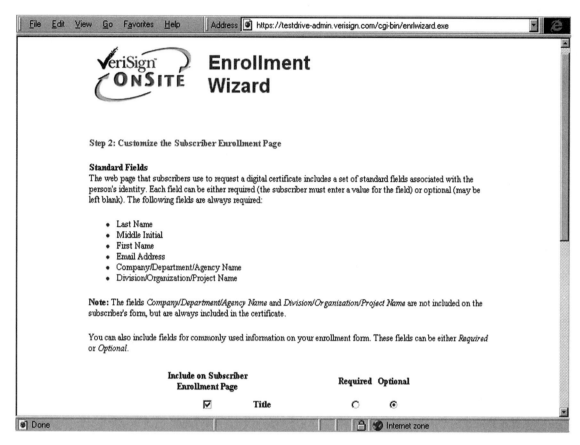

**Figure 15-7**  Customizing the subscriber enrollment page.

control. Client certificates can also be used in server-side programs that need more information about the clients who are requesting resources.

## Mapping Client Certificates to User Accounts

When we enabled the client authentication method in the preceding section, we basically configured IIS to ask for a Web user's client certificate and make sure it is valid. After making sure the certificate is valid, IIS will log on the user using the NT account enforced by other (anonymous, basic, or NT challenge-response) authentication methods. IIS also provides a mechanism for mapping client certificates to NT accounts directly based on the information contained in the certificates. This mapping is part of the authentication process before access to the resource is allowed. If

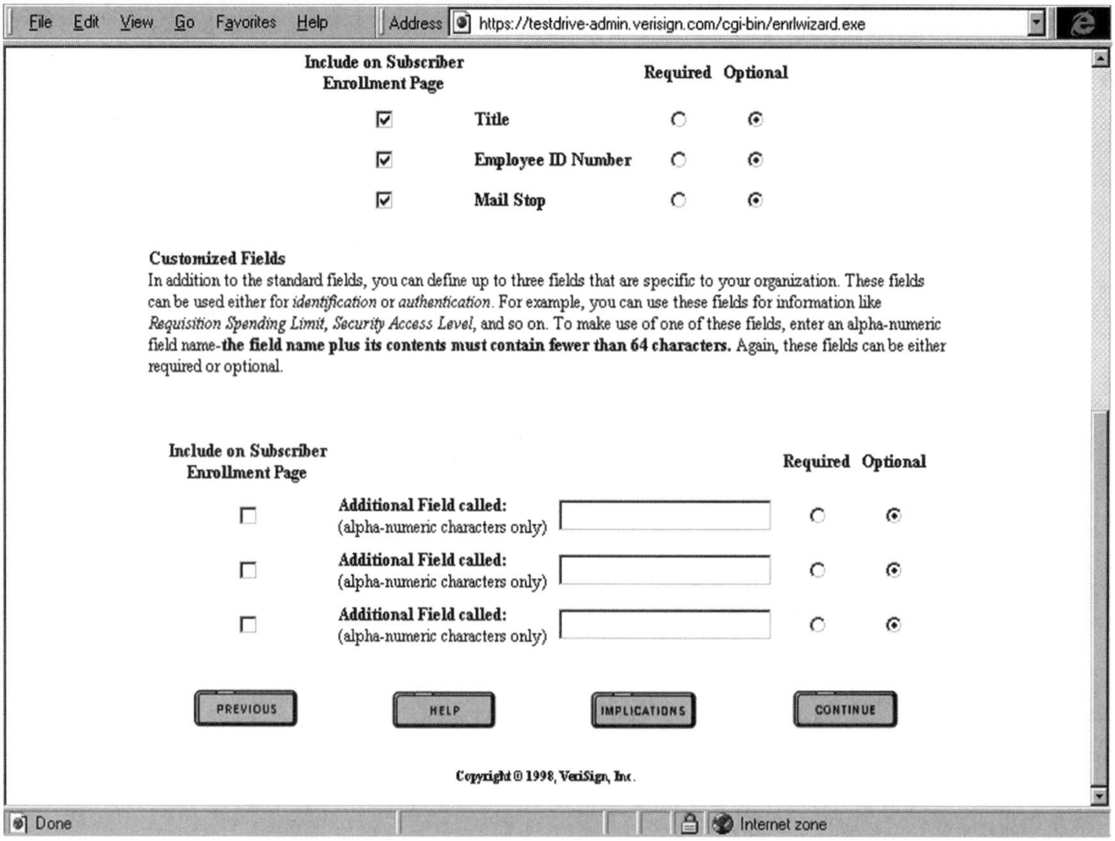

| | File | Edit | View | Go | Favorites | Help | | Address | https://testdrive-admin.verisign.com/cgi-bin/enrlwizard.exe | | |

| Include on Subscriber Enrollment Page | | Required | Optional |
|---|---|---|---|
| ☑ | Title | ○ | ◉ |
| ☑ | Employee ID Number | ○ | ◉ |
| ☑ | Mail Stop | ○ | ◉ |

**Customized Fields**

In addition to the standard fields, you can define up to three fields that are specific to your organization. These fields can be used either for *identification* or *authentication*. For example, you can use these fields for information like *Requisition Spending Limit*, *Security Access Level*, and so on. To make use of one of these fields, enter an alpha-numeric field name—**the field name plus its contents must contain fewer than 64 characters**. Again, these fields can be either required or optional.

| Include on Subscriber Enrollment Page | | | Required | Optional |
|---|---|---|---|---|
| ☐ | Additional Field called: (alpha-numeric characters only) | | ○ | ◉ |
| ☐ | Additional Field called: (alpha-numeric characters only) | | ○ | ◉ |
| ☐ | Additional Field called: (alpha-numeric characters only) | | ○ | ◉ |

[ PREVIOUS ]　　[ HELP ]　　[ IMPLICATIONS ]　　[ CONTINUE ]

Copyright © 1998, VeriSign, Inc.

Done　　　　　　　　　　Internet zone

**Figure 15-8** Customizing the subscriber enrollment page (continued).

the authentication succeeds, IIS uses the mapped NT account to log on the client and access the resource.

To enable mapping of client certificates to NT accounts, follow these steps:

1. In MMC, right-click on a Web site (or directory or file), and then select **Properties.**

2. Select the **Directory Security** tab (or the **File Security** tab for files). Click on **Edit** under Secure Communications.

3. In the **Secure Communications** dialog box (Figure 15-12), select **Enable Client Certificate Mapping** and click on **Edit** to define mapping rules.

4. Choose the **Basic** tab and click **Add.**

5. In the Open dialog box, open the certificate file you want to map to an NT account.

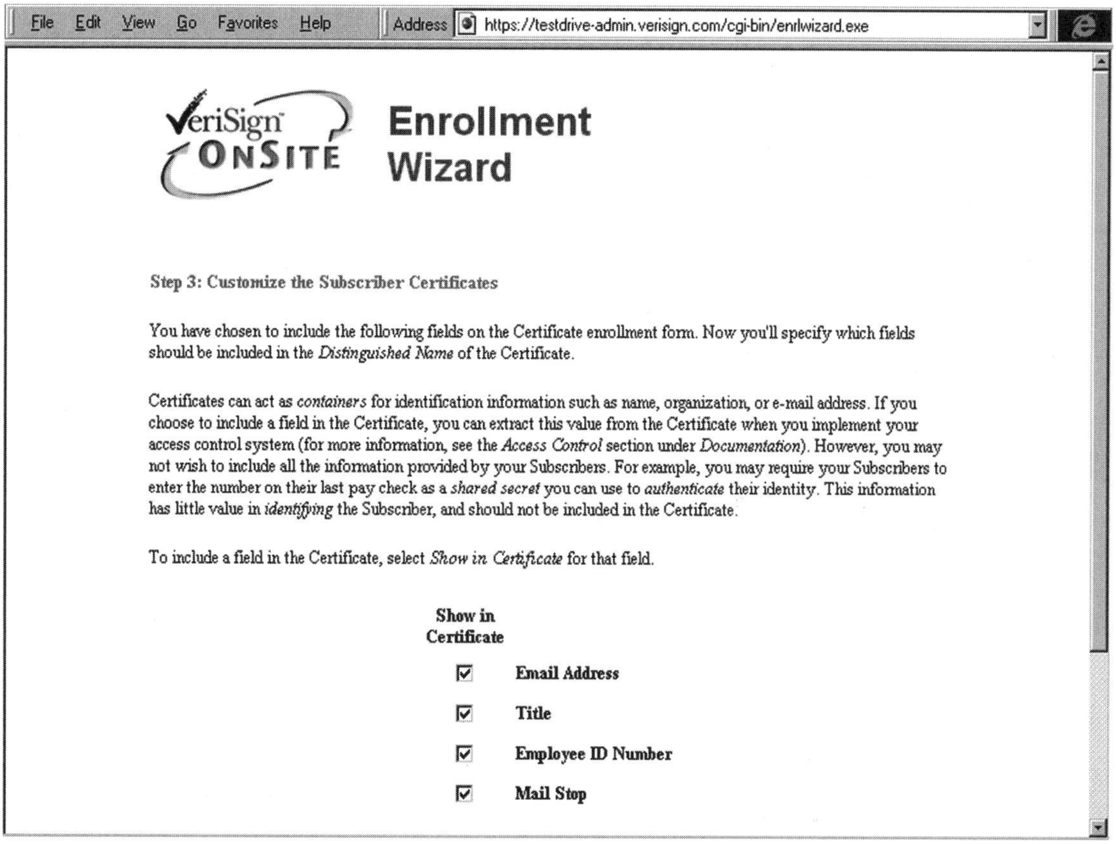

**Figure 15-9** Customizing the subscriber certificates.

6. In the **Map to Account** dialog box (Figure 15-13), assign a name to the mapping and enter a Windows NT account name and password. Click **OK.**

7. In the **Confirm Password** dialog box, reenter the password and click **OK.**

You have now mapped one certificate. Because we have already required client certificates, any user attempting to access our Web site should have a valid client certificate. Also, only users that have the mapped client certificates can access the resources on this Web site. It is possible to map multiple certificates to the same account by repeating the procedure for each certificate.

One potential problem with the above approach is that you need to have certificates of all the clients of your Web site. One way to work around this is to write ASP scripts to save certificates of your clients first. (See Chapter 6.) Another option

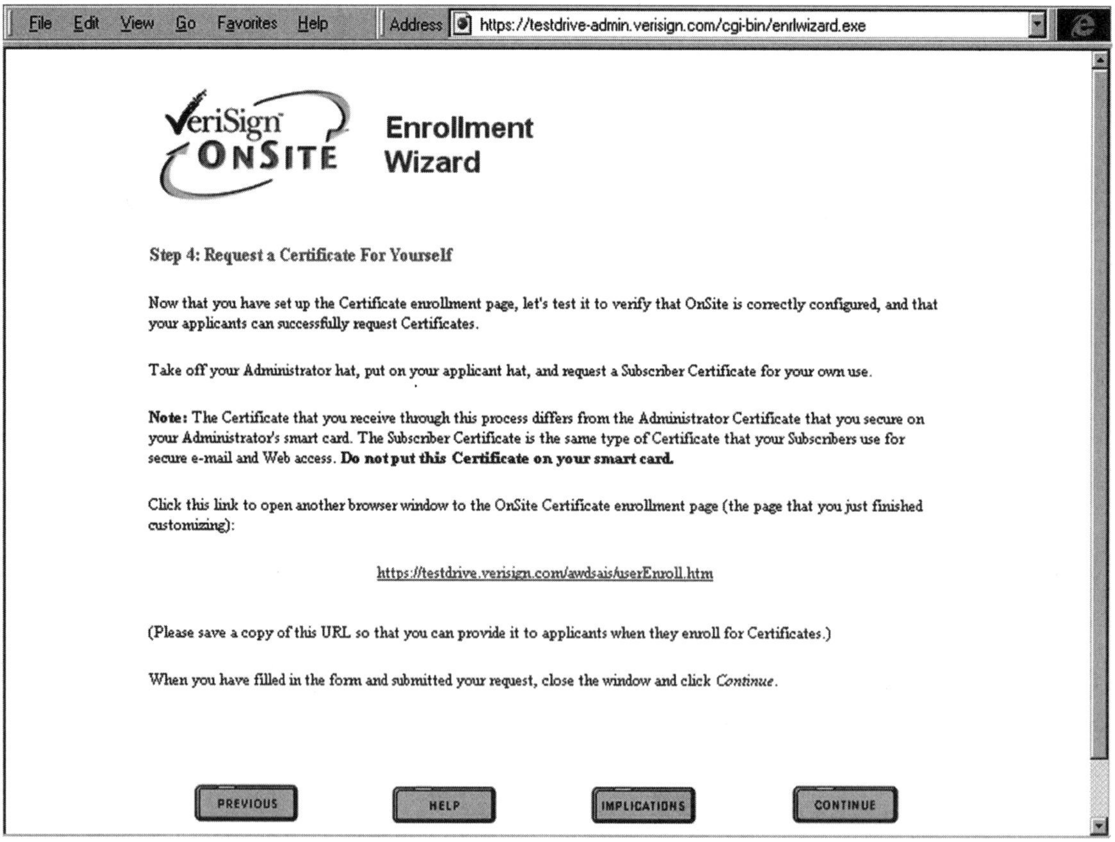

**Figure 15-10**  The URL to enroll for client certificates.

is to use the **Advanced** tab in the Account Mapping dialog box to enable and set wildcard client certificate matching.

To use wildcard client certificate matching:

1. Follow steps 1–5 of the preceding section.

2. Select the **Advanced** tab and select the **Enable Wildcard Certificate Matching** check box.

3. Click on **Add.**

4. In the **Description** box (Figure 15-14), assign a name to the mapping rule.

5. Under **Issuers,** select **Match on all Certificate Issuers which I trust** to check client certificates against all certificate authorities available on your Web

**Figure 15-11**   OnSite Control Center.

site, or select **Match on selected certificate issuers** and then click **Select** to choose specific certificate authorities. Click on **Next.**

6. Click on **New** in the **Rules** dialog box.

7. In the **Edit Rule Element** dialog box (Figure 15-15), use the Certificate Field and Sub Field item lists to select the fields and subfields of the client certificates you want the Web site to look for. In the **Criteria** text box, enter the matching criteria. For example, if you want to allow communication only within the United States, use subfile **C** (country) of field **Subject** and set **Criteria** to **US.** Click **OK.**

8. Repeat Step 7 to add as many matching criteria as needed.

9. In the **Rules** dialog box, click **Next.**

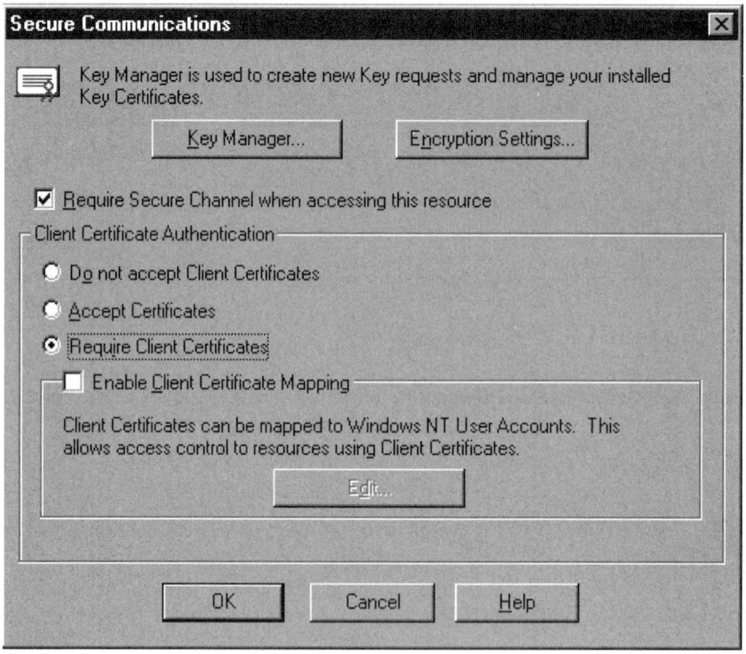

**Figure 15-12** Require Client Certificates.

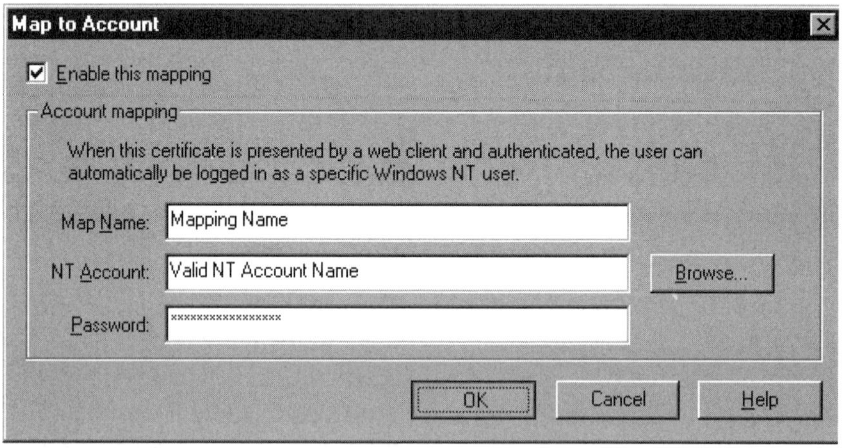

**Figure 15-13** Enter Windows NT account name and password.

**Figure 15-14**  Select which certificate authorities to accept.

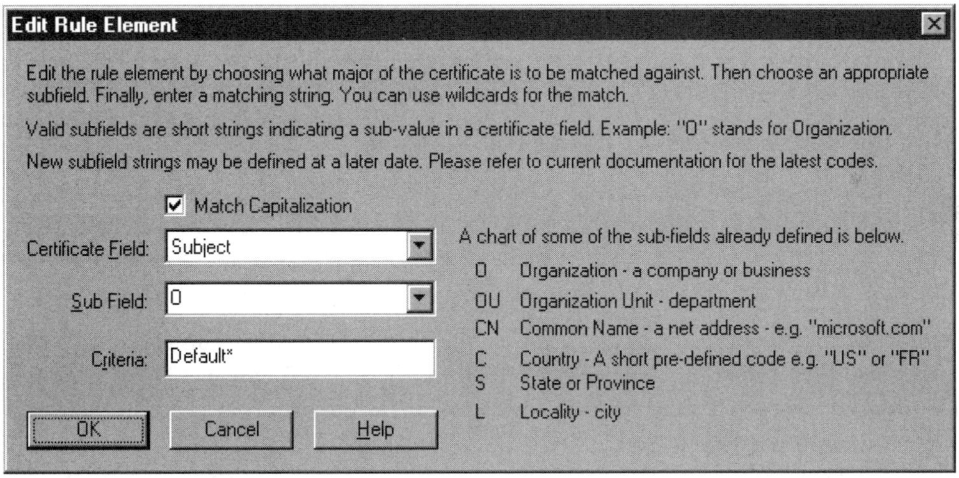

**Figure 15-15**  Define a matching rule.

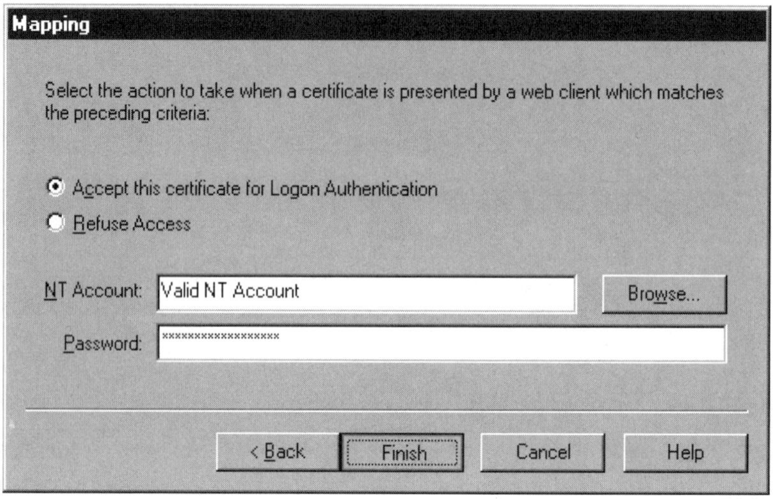

**Figure 15-16**  Select the action.

10. In the **Mapping** dialog box (Figure 15-16), select the appropriate action you want IIS to take when the match criteria are met. If you select **Accept this certificate for Logon Authentication,** enter a valid Windows NT account user name and password. Click **OK.**

11. In the **Confirm Password** dialog box, reenter the NT account password. Click **OK.**

## Summary

Certificate-based client authentication is based on information contained in a client certificate. Web sites and browsers enabled with SSL 3.0 can use this authentication method. In certificate-based authentication, clients are not required to enter a user name and password.

The information available in a certificate can be used both for authentication and authorization purposes. A Web server can use this information to map client certificates to user accounts and then use these mapped accounts to check access permission.

Certificate-based authentication can also be chosen as the preferred method for any environment, such as an on-line banking system, where clients can be required or are expected to have certificates.

# Part VI

# Microsoft Certificate Server

In Part VI, we present hands-on information about the concepts, formats, and security design ideas we discussed in earlier parts. These include custom X.509 extensions, local schemes for interacting with authentication databases, and locally designed protocols for authorizing of the issuance of certificates.[1]

Part VI devotes five chapters to describe the internal architecture of the Certificate Server, explore its interfaces, and discuss its potential for customization. In Chapter 16, we overview the internal components of the Certificate Server, seeking to understand the interface points that enable third-parties to take control, add value, and otherwise specialize the issuing system to local needs.

In Chapter 17, we show how to construct a policy module and a set of extension handlers. Corporate users can customize policy modules to make local decisions about how issuing occurs. We provide an example that shows how to construct such a module in Visual Basic.

In Chapter 18, we show how to construct an exit module. Exit modules enable the issuing system to integrate with other infrastructure components such as corporate directories and messaging systems. We provide an example that shows how to construct an exit module in Visual C++ and the Active Template Library.

In Chapter 19, we show how to construct an entry module. Entry modules enable different clients or their LRAs to interact with the issuing engine to submit requests and generally perform certificate management. In the Microsoft design, the entry module architecture allows for a site to host multiple issuers. Additionally, it enables transparent distributed networking of clients, LRAs, and CAs. We provide a simple entry module written as an ASP in VBScript that shows how to exploit the ability to switch requests between multiple issuers operating on multiple Certificate Servers.

---

1. We have used Microsoft Certificate Server as a learning tool to give you the building blocks of certificate issuing systems. See Chapter 8 for a discussion of other certificate servers and Chapters 9 and 10 for other methods to deploy digital certificates.

In Chapter 20, we examine the administration features offered by the Microsoft Certificate Server. Administration functions include revocation and managing queues of pending or rejected requests. We provide an example written in Java that interfaces to the engine, requests issuance of a CRL, and then multicasts the result to a large number of potential recipients.

# Chapter

## 16

# Microsoft Certificate Server— The Architecture

In Chapters 14 and 15 we used Microsoft Certificate Server to obtain server and client certificates. In this chapter, we will look at the Certificate Server from a programmer's standpoint. We will examine the architecture of the Certificate Server and focus on its programming interfaces. Because the Certificate Server design is based on the Component Object Model (COM), basic understanding of this technology is assumed in this chapter.

## Microsoft Certificate Server

Microsoft Certificate Server is a system service, running on an NT Server, that provides the following services:

- Receives certificate requests
- Processes certificate requests and issues certificates according to the security policy
- Delivers certificates
- Creates certificate revocation lists (CRLs)
- Logs all certificates and CRLs in a database for later auditing

Figure 16-1 shows the overall architecture of the Certificate Server and the lifecycle of a certificate request, which starts when the intermediary receives the request and ends when the Exit Module delivers the certificate.

As shown in Figure 16-1, there are six main components in the Certificate Server architecture: Intermediary, Server Engine, Policy Module, Extension Handlers, Exit Module, and Admin Tools. Except for the Server Engine, which is the core component, all the other modules can be replaced or customized. Let's look at what each one does.

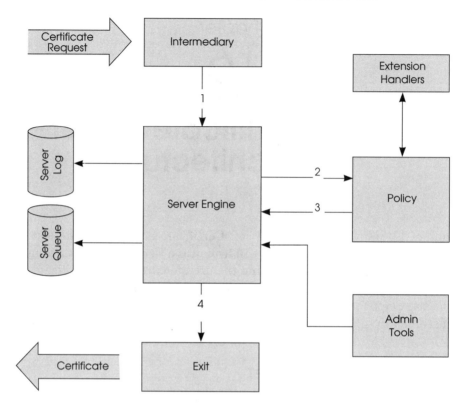

**Figure 16-1** Microsoft Certificate Server architecture.

## Intermediary

The **Intermediary** module receives certificate requests from clients and submits them to the Server Engine. Intermediaries are actually external COM applications that sit in between the certificate requesting programs and the Certificate Server and use DCOM to talk to the Server Engine. IIS, in this sense, is in an intermediary application because it provides the mechanism for requesting certificates from a browser using HTTP. Intermediary applications can be written to process certificate requests from other types of clients, such as an e-mail client, using different transport mechanisms. In Chapter 19, we will show how to write an intermediary application using Active Server Pages.

## Server Engine

The **Server Engine** module is the core component of the Certificate Server. It receives all requests from the intermediary applications and controls the flow of information between modules during the processing of a request. At each processing step, the Server Engine interacts with other modules using the interfaces displayed in Figure 16-2. The process ends with the generation of a certificate, the rejection of the request, or by making the request pending. We will explain this process in more detail later in this chapter.

The Server Engine uses the Server Log and Queue Databases to maintain status information and a log of all issued certificates and CRLs. The **Server Log** keeps a copy of all certificates and CRLs issued by the server. This information is kept so that the administrator can track, audit, and archive server activities. The **Certificate Administration Log Utility,** located at http://servername/CertSrv, provides administrative access to this database. The Server Engine also uses the Server Log for the following purposes:

- Storage of pending certificate revocations prior to publishing a CRL
- Storage of recent certificate requests in case of a problem, such as a delivery failure

The **Server Queue** maintains the status of a certificate request, such as receipt, parsing, authorization, and so on, as the server is processing the request. The **Certificate Administration Queue Utility,** also located at http://servername/CertSrv, provides administrative access to Server Queue databases.

## Policy Module

The **Policy Module** contains the rule-base that governs the issuance, renewal, and revocation of certificates. All certificate requests received by the Server Engine are forwarded to this module for validation. The Policy Module can also be used to set properties and extensions on the certificate based on supplemental information provided within a request.

Certificate Server's architecture supports only one Policy Module per server. It is possible and often necessary to customize and replace the default Policy Module. This can be achieved through the COM interfaces exported by the Server Engine. We will talk more about customizing the Policy Module in Chapter 17 when we write a sample policy module in Visual Basic.

The Policy Module supports DER encoding of three primitive data types used in certificate properties and extensions. These three default data types are String, Integer, and Date. To handle any other data types used by certificate extensions, external COM modules called **Extension Handlers** should be used. In these cases, the Policy Module should load the appropriate extension handler explicitly when needed. Chapter 17 explains extension handlers in more detail.

### Exit Module

The **Exit Module** may be used to publish issued certificates and CRLs. The Server Engine notifies the Exit Module, if one is installed on the server, whenever a certificate or CRL is generated.

The Certificate Server provides COM interfaces to write custom Exit Modules for different transports or custom delivery of issued certificates. For example, an LDAP Exit Module might be used to publish client certificates in a Directory Service. In Chapter 18 we will explain how to write your own Exit Module using Visual C++ and Active Template Library (ATL). Note that Certificate Server currently supports only one Exit Module, and it is not necessary to have an Exit Module for the Certificate Server to run.

### Admin Tools

IIS provides Web-based administration tools for accessing the data contained in the Server database. The **Certificate Log Utility** and the **Certificate Queue Utility,** located at http://servername/CertSrv, are examples of administrative tools that can be used to access the Server Log and the Server Queue, respectively. You can write your own administrative programs using the provided COM interfaces. More on this in Chapter 20.

# Certificate Server Programming

Certificate Server uses COM for communication between its different components as displayed in Figure 16-2. To customize the Certificate Server, you need to write your own COM components that implement some of the COM interfaces shown in this Figure and then plug them into the Server Engine. The Server Engine itself is the core of the architecture and cannot be replaced or customized. Before writing your own components, you need to know what these COM interfaces are and where and when they are used. Let's first see how the Certificate Server uses these interfaces by looking at the lifecycle of a certificate request.

## Lifecycle of a Certificate Request

Certificate Server goes through an initialization step when it starts up. During this step, it loads the Policy Module and the Exit Module, if one exists, and calls the ICertPolicy::Initialize and ICertExit::Initialize methods implemented by these modules. After a successful initialization, Certificate Server goes into a ready state. Initialization happens only once during the server start-up. Once the Certificate Server is in the ready state, it is prepared to accept and process certificate requests.

To send a certificate request, a client communicates with the intermediary using the mechanism defined by the intermediary. This can be, for example, Internet

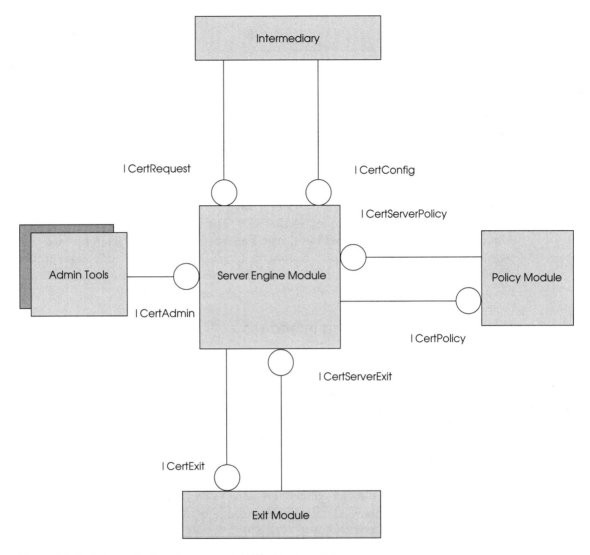

**Figure 16-2**  Microsoft Certificate Server COM interfaces.

Explorer (client) sending a request to IIS (intermediary). The intermediary then sends the certificate request to the Certificate Server using the ICertRequest::Submit method. To find the right Certificate Server, the intermediary should use the methods of the ICertConfig interface first, which we will explain later in this chapter.

When the Server Engine receives a certificate request, it notifies the Policy Module that a request has arrived by calling ICertPolicy::VerifyRequest. After examining the request, the Policy Module makes one of the following decisions:

- The certificate can be issued.
- The request should be denied.
- The request should be suspended.

If the request is suspended, an administrator must make the necessary changes to the request, if needed, and resubmit the request. Before returning from the ICertPolicy::VerifyRequest method, the Policy Module can examine and modify the certificate using the methods of ICertServerPolicy interface. If the Policy Module approves the issuance of the certificate, the Server Engine builds and signs the certificate after the VerifyRequest method returns.

When a certificate is issued, the Server Engine may call the Exit Module, if one exists, through the Notify method of the ICertExit interface, provided by the Exit Module. The Exit Module should indicate that it is interested in seeing issued certificates when its ICertExit::Initialize method is called by the Server Engine in the initialization phase. The Exit Module can examine and obtain the new certificate for publication by calling methods of the ICertServerExit interface.

## Exported versus Imported Interfaces

As you might have noticed, there are two different types of interfaces in the Certificate Server architecture: exported and imported. **Exported interfaces** are implemented by the Server Engine and used by other modules. **Imported interfaces** are implemented by the other modules and used by the Server Engine. As a programmer, your job is to implement imported interfaces of the modules you provide while making use of the available exported interfaces. Table 16-1 describes the exported interfaces and the modules that use these interfaces.

Note that all exported interfaces are implemented by in-process COM components (DLLs) and not the Server Engine executable (certsrv.exe) itself. This is a very flexible architecture that allows these components to reside on remote computers and communicate with any Server Engine using DCOM. We will see exactly how DCOM is used later in this chapter.

Table 16-2 shows the imported interfaces and the modules that are expected to implement them.

# DCOM and the Certificate Server

The Certificate Server's architecture uses DCOM for remote invocation of two of its exported interfaces, ICertRequest and ICertAdmin. The remote operation occurs beneath the surface whenever you use the configuration string, returned by the GetConfig method of the ICertConfig interface, in the methods of these two inter-

**Table 16-1** Certificate Server Exported COM Interfaces

| Interface | Used By | Exported By | Description |
|-----------|---------|-------------|-------------|
| ICertConfig | Intermediary and Admin programs | Certcli.dll | Get information on available Certificate Servers, etc. |
| ICertRequest | Intermediary | Certcli.dll | Send certificate requests and retrieve certificates, etc. |
| ICertServerPolicy | Policy Module | Certif.dll | Get and Set certificate properties and extensions, etc. |
| ICertServerExit | Exit Module | Certif.dll | Get certificate properties and extensions, etc. |
| ICertAdmin | Admin programs | Certadm.dll | Publish CRLs, get CRLs, resubmit a request, etc. |

**Table 16-2** Certificate Server Imported COM Interfaces

| Interface | Implemented By | Imported By | Description |
|-----------|----------------|-------------|-------------|
| ICertPolicy | Policy Module | Server Engine | Get notification on arrival of certificate requests, etc. |
| ICertExit | Exit Module | Server Engine | Get notification on issuance of certificates, etc. |

faces. To understand how this works, let's first look at the ICertConfig interface more closely and then see how it is used to call other methods remotely.

## Server Engine Configuration Interface

The **ICertConfig** interface is used by the intermediary and administrative programs to get information about installed Certificate Servers. It provides methods to get information about the default Certificate Server, available Certificate Servers, and the configuration fields of a Certificate Server.

Table 16-3 shows the methods provided by the ICertConfig interface.

When a Certificate Server is installed, its configuration information, including the information provided during the installation, is saved to a file in a shared folder specified during the installation as shown in Figure 16-3. One particularly important field is the configuration string. A **configuration string** is a Certificate Server hostname and a Certificate Server name separated by a slash.

**Table 16-3**   ICertConfig Methods

| Method | Description |
|--------|-------------|
| GetConfig | Gets the configuration string of the default Certificate Server. |
| GetField | Gets a field from the configuration information of the current Certificate Server. |
| Next | Points to the next available Certificate Server. |
| Reset | Resets the configuration query state to point at the specified Certificate Server. |

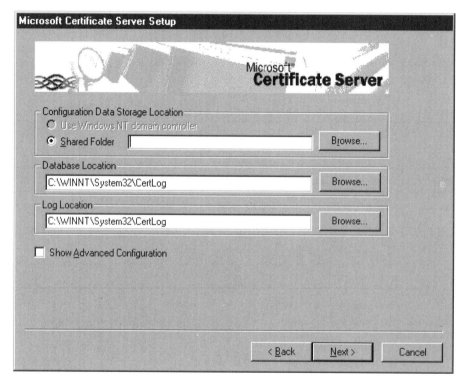

**Figure 16-3**   Certificate Server shared folder setup during installation.

Figure 16-4 shows the Certificate Server registry entries saved under the HKEY_LOCAL_MACHINE\SYSTEM\CurrentControlSet\CertSvc key. ICertConfig looks up the name of the shared folder saved in the Configuration Directory and then reads a data file in this shared folder to get the information on the installed Certificate Servers and their configurations. All Certificate Servers that use a common shared folder during their installations are considered to be part of the same **Certificate Server installation base**. A configuration string uniquely identifies a Certificate Server within an

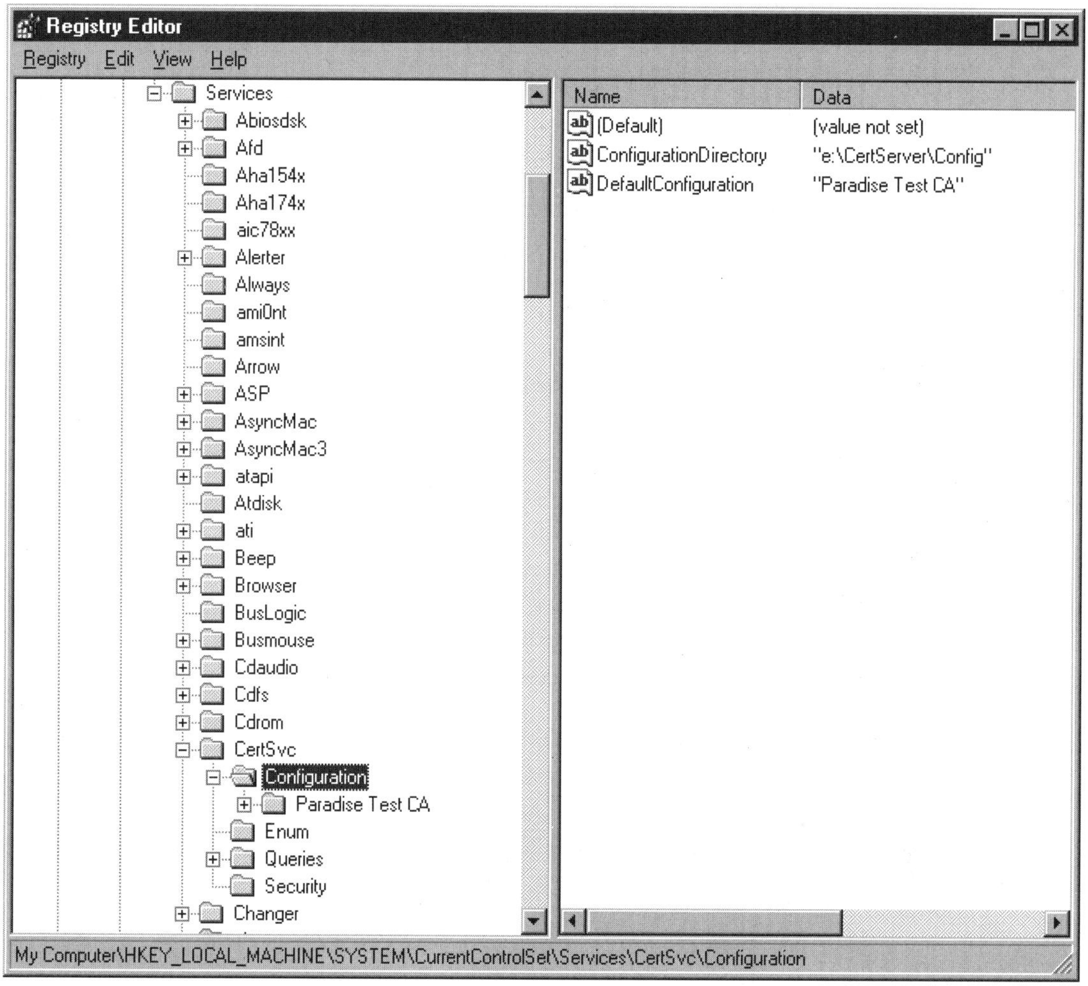

**Figure 16-4** Certificate Server Registry entries.

installation base. ICertConfig::GetConfig returns the configuration string of the default Certificate Server in an installation base, which is set during the installation of a Certificate Server.

Table 16-4 shows the configuration fields that are kept as part of the configuration information for each Certificate Server. Most of this information is provided during the installation of a Certificate Server. The installation program, however, creates the Config field using the provided **CA Name** field and the name of the host where the Certificate Server is running. The ICertConfig::GetField method can be used to retrieve the values of these fields.

**Table 16-4** Certificate Server Configuration Fields

| Field Name | Description |
|---|---|
| CA Name | Name of this Certificate Server. |
| OrgUnit | The unit name of the organization. |
| Organization | The name of the organization running this server. |
| Locality | Locality of the organization. |
| State | State where the company resides. |
| Country | Name of the country. |
| Config | Configuration string (*hostname / CA Name*). |
| ExchangeCertificate | Name of the file containing the key exchange certificate. |
| SignatureCertificate | Name of the file containing the signing certificate. |
| Comment | Descriptive information about the certificate server. |

As you have probably noticed in this chapter, and will see in coming chapters where we program the Certificate Server, we do not show the arguments and return values of the interface methods. You should refer to the Certificate Server documentation to learn more about the method prototypes in Visual Basic, Java, and C++ languages.

## Using DCOM to Connect to Remote Certificate Servers

It is now time to see how to use DCOM to remote some of the methods we discussed earlier and connect to remote Certificate Servers. The two interfaces that can use DCOM are ICertRequest and ICertAdmin. These two interfaces need to run remotely because it is necessary to be able to send certificate requests to any Certificate Server within an installation base and to administer different Certificate Servers within the installation base remotely.

To use DCOM, certificate server designers have added an extra argument to all methods that can be remoted. This extra argument is the configuration string of the target Certificate Server. You can get a configuration string in two ways depending on which Certificate Server you want to communicate with.

If you want to communicate with the default Certificate Server in an installation base, you can use the ICertConfig::GetConfig method, as shown in the following code segment, written in C:

```
#include "certsrv.h"
hr = CoCreateInstance(
        CLSID_CCertConfig,
        NULL,
        CLSCTX_INPROC_SERVER,
```

```
            IID_ICertConfig,
            (VOID **) &pCertConfig);
if (SUCCEEDED(hr)){
        BSTR configString;
        hr = pCertConfig->GetConfig(0, &configString);
        if (SUCCEEDED(hr)){
                // configString now points to the default
                // Certificate Server
        }
        // Handle error conditions
}
```

If you need to communicate to a Certificate Server other than the default one, you should iterate through all available Certificate Servers to find the one you are looking for and then get its configuration string. The following code segment, written in VBScript as part of an ASP application, shows how to do this:

```
Dim nextSvr, svrCommonName
Dim IcertConfig, configString
Set ICertConfig = _
        Server.CreateObject("CertificateAuthority.Config")
configString = ""
nxtSvr = ICertConfig.Next
Do while nextSvr <> -1
        svrCommonName = ICertConfig.GetField("CommonName")
        ' We assume we are looking for the Certificate Server that
        ' has Platinum in its common name!
        If InStr(svrCommonName, "Platinum") Then
                configString = ICertConfig.GetField("Config")
                Exit Do
        End If
        nextSvr = ICertConfig.Next
Loop
If configString <> "" Then
        ' configString now points to the Certificate Server
End If
```

Note that these two code segments use different ways to call the methods of the ICertConfig interface. The first example uses a direct COM interface, which is the preferred way to call COM interfaces in C or C++. The second example uses the IDispatch interface to call the methods of ICertConfig. This shows that ICertConfig is implemented as a dual interface. Actually, all interfaces exported by the Certificate Server are dual interfaces. This is the recommended way to implement COM interfaces.

When you use one of the methods of ICertRequest or ICertAdmin that take an argument pointing to a Certificate Server configuration string, the configuration string is first parsed by the method to get the name of the host running the Certificate Server. The host name is then used by the method to communicate with the Certificate Server running on the host using DCOM. All of this is transparent to users because these interfaces are implemented as in-process COM components running on the local host and the remote functionality is hidden in the implementation of these components, without requiring any extra work on behalf of the callers.

## Summary

The Microsoft Certificate Server has several modules that communicate with each other using COM. You can customize some of these modules, such as the Policy and the Exit Modules, by writing COM components that implement the required interfaces. You can write other modules, such as intermediary and admin programs, by simply using appropriate interfaces exported by the Certificate Server.

Certificate Servers that keep their configuration information in the same shared folder belong to a Certificate Server installation base. Two of the interfaces, ICertRequest and ICertAdmin, use DCOM internally to communicate with remote Certificate Servers within an installation base. These interfaces use the configuration string obtained from the ICertConfig methods to locate the remote Certificate Server. A configuration string is the Certificate Server hostname and the Certificate Server name separated by a slash. The details of using DCOM are taken care of in the components implementing these interfaces.

Chapter

# 17

# Programming Microsoft Certificate Server—The Policy Module and Extension Handlers

In Chapter 16, we looked at the Microsoft Certificate Server architecture and its programming interfaces in general. We saw that the Certificate Server is shipped with a default Policy Module. In a real deployment, however, you need to replace this module with one that you develop to enforce your own CA policy rules. In this chapter, we will show you how to write and plug in your own customized Policy Module. But first, we need to define some important technical terms that we will use repeatedly throughout the rest of this book.

## Attributes, Properties, and Extensions

**Certificate request properties** are name-value pairs within a certificate request that contain information about the subject of the certificate and his public key. Certificate request properties are stored in the Certificate Server database. They are read-only for the Policy and the Exit modules and may be used to construct a certificate.

**Certificate Request Attributes** are arbitrary name-value string pairs that can be passed to the Certificate Server with the certificate request or set using administrative tools. Certificate request attributes are also stored in the Certificate Server database and are read-only for Policy and Exit modules. These attributes are not placed in a generated certificate, but they can be used for private communication with the Policy or the Exit modules.

**Certificate properties** are standard name-value pairs that, among other things, contain information about the certificate subject and issuer. Certificate properties are generated by the Server Engine from the request and stored in the Certificate Server database. Some of the certificate properties are writable by the Policy Module. Examples of read-only properties are public-key and algorithm information. For example, the subject name and the NotBefore and NotAfter properties are writable. The Server Engine sets some of the certificate properties, such as the serial number, after the Policy Module validates a certificate request.

**Certificate extensions** are optional name-value pairs that can exist in an X.509 v3 certificate for customization purposes. Certificate extensions are generated by the Server Engine and can be set or modified by the Policy Module or administrative tools. An object ID (OID), a sequence of integers, specifies the name of an extension. For more information about certificate extensions refer to Chapter 3.

Certificate Server uses request properties and attributes to construct a certificate. The Policy Module can also use certificate request properties and attributes to set some of the certificate properties and create certificate extensions. As you will see, most of the Certificate Server COM interface methods used by the Policy and Exit modules deal with getting and setting these attributes, properties, and extensions.

## Policy Module Interfaces

The **ICertServerPolicy** is the interface implemented by the Server Engine to be used by the Policy Module. Using this interface, the Policy Module can enumerate certificate extensions, get and set certificate properties, get and set certificate extensions, etc. The Policy Module can perform all these operations while it is inside its VerifyRequest method. This method is called whenever the Server Engine receives a certificate request.

Table 17-1 shows the methods provided by the ICertServerPolicy interface.

To use the methods listed in Table 17-1, the Policy Module should first set the context of operations using the **SetContext** method, which takes a handle to the certificate request. The Server Engine provides this handle to the Policy Module when it calls the VerifyRequest method. The Policy Module can ask the Server Engine to add to or modify certificate properties by calling **SetCertificateProperty** and set certificate extensions by using the **SetCertificateExtension** method. Because the Policy Module can change certificate properties, certificate properties can be different from request properties.

The **ICertPolicy** is the interface that a Policy Module should implement to plug into the Server Engine. The Server Engine uses the methods of this interface to initialize the Policy Module and submit a notification to the module that a new certificate request has arrived for consideration. The Policy Module should then process the request and return to the server with a "request is OK," "request is denied," or "request is pending" status.

Table 17-2 shows the methods provided by the ICertPolicy interface.

**Table 17-1**   ICertServerPolicy Methods

| Method | Description |
|---|---|
| EnumerateAttributes | Returns the OID of the next attribute from the request. |
| EnumerateAttributesClose | Closes attribute enumeration operation. |
| EnumerateAttributesSetup | Sets up the attribute enumeration operation. |
| EnumerateExtensions | Returns the OID of the next extension from the certificate. |
| EnumerateExtensionsClose | Closes extension enumeration operation. |
| EnumerateExtensionsSetup | Sets up the extension enumeration operation. |
| GetCertificateExtension | Gets a specified certificate extension. |
| GetCertificateExtensionFlags | Gets the flags of the extension acquired by the last call to GetCertificateExtension. |
| GetCertificateProperty | Returns a named property of the certificate. |
| GetRequestAttribute | Returns a named attribute from the request. |
| GetRequestProperty | Returns a named property from the request. |
| SetCertificateExtension | Adds a new extension to the certificate. |
| SetCertificateProperty | Adds a named property to the certificate. |
| SetContext | Sets the context of all above operations. |

**Table 17-2**   ICertPolicy Methods

| Method | Description |
|---|---|
| GetDescription | Returns a description for the Policy Module. |
| Initialize | Called by the Server Engine to let the Policy Module initialize itself. |
| ShutDown | Called by the Server Engine before it is terminated. |
| VerifyRequest | Called by the Server Engine every time a new request arrives. |

# Writing Customized Policy Modules

Now that you have learned about the Policy Module interfaces, let's see how to write a customized Policy Module. The Policy Module, regardless of the programming language you choose, should be a COM DLL that implements the ICertPolicy interface. In this section, we will write a sample Policy Module in Visual Basic.

When you use Visual Basic (VB), the name of the VB project that produces this DLL should be **CertificateAuthority** and the name of the class that implements the ICertPolicy interface should be **Policy.** This is required because the Server Engine looks for a **CertificateAuthority.Policy** key in the registry when it wants to locate and load the Policy Module. To implement your Policy Module in VB 5.0, use the following steps:

1. Create a new ActiveX DLL project.

2. Select the **General** tab of the Project Properties dialog box, set the project name to CertificateAuthority, select the **Unattended Execution** option, and set the Start up Object to **None.**

3. Change the name of the class VB creates for you to **Policy,** and set its instancing to **MultiUse (5).**

4. Implement the four (public) methods of ICertPolicy interface in your Policy class.

5. Compile the ActiveX DLL and save it under any name you desire.

6. Stop the Certificate Authority service from the Services dialog box.

7. Register your Policy Module using the **regsvr32 *yourpolicy.dll*** command. (This step is not necessary if your Certificate Server is running on the same machine. VB registers your component as part of the compilation.)

8. Start the Certificate Authority service from the Services dialog box.

When Certificate Server restarts, it loads your Policy Module and calls the Initialize method. If the Certificate Server has any problems loading the Policy Module, it will not start and an event will be logged in the System Event Log. When your Policy Module is loaded, the Certificate Server will call the Policy Module's VerifyRequest method whenever a certificate request arrives.

For debugging purposes, you can start the Certificate Server from the command line using the certsrv –z command and then use dialog boxes and windows for debugging. When you have finished debugging, you need to remove all user-interface elements because the Certificate Server runs as a system service, and it should not use the Windows desktop to render any user interface windows.

## A Sample Policy Module

We are now ready to write our sample Policy Module. This sample Policy Module, written in Visual Basic, uses a dialog box to show all the information that can be obtained from a received certificate request using the ICertServerPolicy interface. It also uses a simple authentication policy that validates the subject name against a database. When you run the Certificate Server in the standalone mode, you see the content of the certificate request and the result of our simple user validation in a dialog box. You should then use the **Close** button to direct the Policy Module to issue the certificate (Figure 17-1). The purpose here is just to show the framework for a Policy Module and how to use the ICertServerPolicy interface methods. Because of the dialog box, you need to run the Certificate Server from the command line in standalone mode using the certsrv –z command. When you run Certificate Server as a system service, any modules loaded by the Server Engine should not use any user interface elements. Use dialog boxes and windows only when you are debugging your modules.

Our sample Policy Module implements the four methods of ICertPolicy. In the Initialize method, we set our global variables that point to the ICertServerPolicy and our private class that encapsulates a simple user validation routine:

```
Set CertServer = New CcertServerPolicy
Set usrAuth = New UserAuth
```

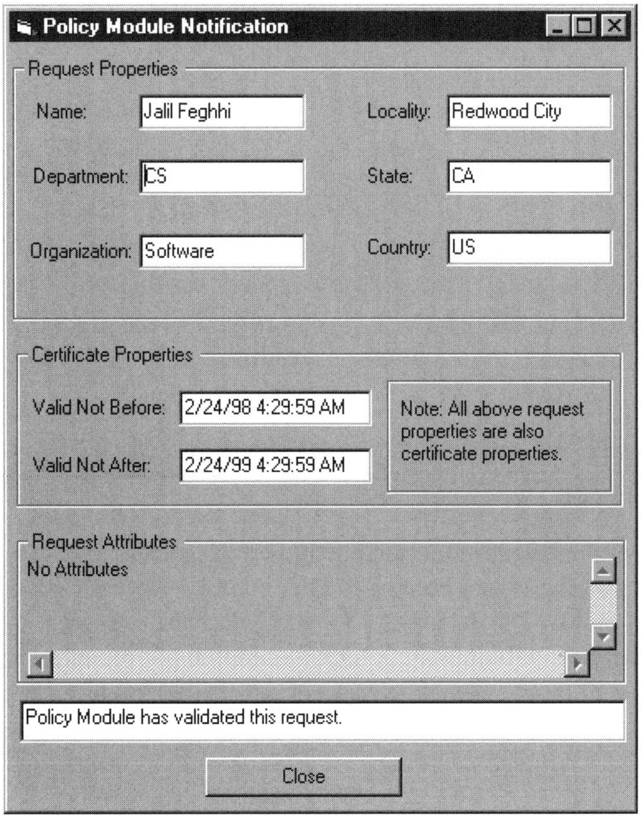

**Figure 17-1**  Sample Policy Module (debug mode).

CCertServerPolicy class is defined in certif.dll library, and you must reference this library in your VB project for this code to work. As part of our clean up in the ShutDown method, we set these global variables to nothing to let the system unload the components. In the third method, GetDescription, we just return a string containing the description of the module.

The heart of any Policy Module is the VerifyRequest method. In our sample, we first set the context of all operations to the context passed to the method:

```
CertServer.SetContext context
```

After setting the context, we can use all the methods of our CertServer object (ICertServerPolicy) to get any information we want about the certificate request or the under construction certificate to validate the request. For the request attributes, for example, we can get the value of each enumerated attribute using the GetRequestAttribute method:

```
CertServer.EnumerateAttributesSetup (0)

attrib = CertServer.EnumerateAttributes

count = 0

Do Until Len(attrib) = 0

count = count + 1

attribValue = CertServer.GetRequestAttribute(attrib)

'Process the attribute

Loop
```

To get certificate request properties, we can use the GetRequestProperty method as in the following code segment. Note that in this case, we need to specify the type of the property:

```
Str = CertServer.GetRequestProperty("Subject.OrgUnit", _
        PROPTYPE_STRING)
```

Because the Server Engine has partially constructed a certificate when it calls the VerifyRequest method of the Policy Module, all of the request properties can also be obtained from the certificate using the GetCertificateProperty method, which has the same syntax as GetRequestProperty. The only two properties that are not in the request and should be retrieved using GetCertificateProperty are the NotAfter and NotBefore properties:

```
NotBefore = CertServer.GetCertificateProperty("NotBefore", _
        PROPTYPE_DATE)
```

```
NotAfter = CertServer.GetCertificateProperty("NotAfter", _
        PROPTYPE_DATE)
```

The Policy Module uses ValidUser method of usrAuth object to validate the request in the VerifyRequest function as follows:

```
If (usrAuth.ValidUser(frmCert.txtName.Text)) Then
        frmCert.txtStatus.Text = _
            "Policy Module has validated this request."
    Else
        frmCert.txtStatus.Text = _
            "Policy Module does not accept this request: " & _
            "User is not validated."
End If
```

Listing 17-1 shows part of the source code for the sample Policy Module.

**Listing 17-1  Sample Policy Module Listing**

```
'To use this object, add a reference to CertIF 1.0 typelib
Dim CertServer As CCertServerPolicy
Dim usrAuth As UserAuth


''''''''''''''''''''''''''''''''''''''''''''''''''''''''''''''''''
' Initialize: Called by Certificate Server when it loads
'             our module.
'
' Do all one time module-level initialization here.
''''''''''''''''''''''''''''''''''''''''''''''''''''''''''''''''''
Public Sub Initialize(strConfig As String)
    Set CertServer = New CCertServerPolicy
    Set usrAuth = New UserAuth
End Sub


''''''''''''''''''''''''''''''''''''''''''''''''''''''''''''''''''
' ShutDown: Called by Certificate Server when it terminates.
```

```
'
' Do all necessary cleanup here.
''''''''''''''''''''''''''''''''''''''''''''''''''''''''''''''''
Public Sub ShutDown()
    MsgBox "Shutting down"
    Set CertServer = Nothing
    Set usrAuth = Nothing
End Sub
''''''''''''''''''''''''''''''''''''''''''''''''''''''''''''''''
' GetDescription: Called by Certificate Server to get the policy
'                 module description.
''''''''''''''''''''''''''''''''''''''''''''''''''''''''''''''''
Public Function GetDescription() As String
    GetDescription = "Chap 18 - Sample Custom Policy Module"
End Function


''''''''''''''''''''''''''''''''''''''''''''''''''''''''''''''''
' VerifyRequest: Called by Certificate Server for every
'                certificate request.
'
' In this function you can:
'   Check the certificate request properties and attributes.
'   Check the certificate properties.
'   Set certificate properties and extensions.
'   Have the certificate server to accept, deny, or make the
'   certificate pending.
''''''''''''''''''''''''''''''''''''''''''''''''''''''''''''''''
Public Function VerifyRequest(strConfig As String, _
                              context As Long, _
                              bNewRequest As Long, _
                              flags As Long) As Long


    Dim str As String
```

```
'Set the context of operations first
CertServer.SetContext context

CheckCertAttributes
CheckCertProperties

'Validate the user
If (usrAuth.ValidUser(frmCert.txtName.Text)) Then
     'Set any extensions you want here
     'We set a mandatory one here using a fictitious OID
     CertServer.SetCertificateExtension _
          "1.2.3.4.5.6.7.8.9" _
          , PROPTYPE_STRING, _
          EXTENSION_CRITICAL_FLAG, _
          "An extension that must exist"

     frmCert.txtStatus.Text = _
          "Policy Module has validated this request."

     VerifyRequest = VR_INSTANT_OK
Else
     frmCert.txtStatus.Text = _
          "Policy Module does not accept this request: " & _
          "User is not validated."

     VerifyRequest = VR_INSTANT_BAD
End If
'Certificate Server blocks here till you close the
'form. Need to be removed when done with debugging
frmCert.Show 1

Exit Function
CheckErr:
MsgBox "Error " & Err.Number & " - " & Err.Description
```

```
        VerifyRequest = VR_INSTANT_BAD
End Function
```

As for the policy rules that we are implementing in this sample module, we have put the logic into a separate class, UserAuth (Listing 17-2), to check the subject information against a user database. In our simple case, we just make sure that the name of the user exists in the database. In the initialization method of this class, we use an Active Data Object (ADO) component to open the database and get its Users table:

```
strSource = "DSN=UserBaseDSN"
Set rstUsers = New ADODB.Recordset
rstUsers.CursorType = adOpenStatic
rstUsers.CursorLocation = adUseClient
rstUsers.Open "Users", strSource, , , adCmdTable
```

To be able to access ADODB object, you need to reference the Microsoft ActiveX Data Object Library in your VB project. In this code segment, we have assumed that a system DSN already exists for the database. You can find the sample access database, userbase.mdb, on the companion CD-ROM. In the ValidUser method of this class, we just search through the User table to find the name of the user:

```
Do While (Not rstUsers.EOF)
        strName = rstUsers!userName
        ' Call method based on user's input.
        If UCase(userName) = UCase(strName) Then
            ValidUser = True
            Exit Do
        End If
        rstUsers.MoveNext
Loop
```

Listing 17-2 shows the VB class implementing our simple user authentication.

### Listing 17-2  A Simple User Authentication Class

```
'''''''''''''''''''''''''''''''''''''''''''''''''''''''''''''''''''''''''
' User Validation Module
```

```
'     This class assume a system DSN named UserBaseDSN has already
'     been created. This DSN points to a database with a table
'     named Users that contains a column named userName
' Note:
'     Remove all forms and dialog boxes when the Certificate
'     Server runs as a system service.
''''''''''''''''''''''''''''''''''''''''''''''''''''''''''''''''''''
Option Explicit
'To use this object, add a reference to Microsoft ActiveX Data
'Objects Library
Private rstUsers As ADODB.Recordset

Private strSource As String
''''''''''''''''''''''''''''''''''''''''''''''''''''''''''''''''''''
' ValidUser: Called to validate a user
''''''''''''''''''''''''''''''''''''''''''''''''''''''''''''''''''''
Public Function ValidUser(userName As String) As Boolean
    'On Error GoTo CheckErr
    Dim strName As String

    ValidUser = False
    rstUsers.MoveFirst
    Do While (Not rstUsers.EOF)
        strName = rstUsers!userName
        ' Call method based on user's input.
        If UCase(userName) = UCase(strName) Then
            ValidUser = True
            Exit Do
        End If
        rstUsers.MoveNext
    Loop
    Exit Function
'CheckErr:
    'MsgBox "Error " & Err.Number & " - " & _
```

```
    '                        Err.Description & "(" & Err.Source & ")"
End Function
'''''''''''''''''''''''''''''''''''''''''''''''''''''''''''''''''''''''''''
' Class_Initialize: Called when the object is built
'
' Do all one time object-level initialization here.
'''''''''''''''''''''''''''''''''''''''''''''''''''''''''''''''''''''''''''
Private Sub Class_Initialize()
    ' Open recordset from Authors table.
    strSource = "DSN=UserBaseDSN"

    Set rstUsers = New ADODB.Recordset
    rstUsers.CursorType = adOpenStatic
    ' Use client cursor to enable AbsolutePosition property.
    rstUsers.CursorLocation = adUseClient
    rstUsers.Open "Users", strSource, , , adCmdTable
    Exit Sub
End Sub
'''''''''''''''''''''''''''''''''''''''''''''''''''''''''''''''''''''''''''
' Class_Terminate: Called when the object is destroyed
'''''''''''''''''''''''''''''''''''''''''''''''''''''''''''''''''''''''''''
Private Sub Class_Terminate()
    On Error GoTo 0
    rstUsers.Close
End Sub
```

## Extension Handlers

A certificate is a collection of ASN.1 data types that is encoded using DER. Every data item that goes into a certificate, except for the extensions, has a predefined data type. Extensions, however, are arbitrary items, and they can have user-defined data types. Because everything needs to be DER encoded in a certificate, if you want to add extensions with a type that is not known to the Certificate Server, you need to encode the extension yourself before adding it to the certificate. The only data types that Certificate Server can handle are Date, Integer, and

String. Any other types need to be encoded explicitly before being passed to the ICertServerPolicy::SetCertificateExtensions method in the Policy Module.

Certificate Server includes a default extension handler, CertEnc.dll, that provides methods for encoding other common data types, such as BitString, AltName, and CRLDistInfo. This COM component has a number of interfaces, each providing an Encode method that returns a DER-encoded type. If you have data type that is not supported by this default extension handler, you have to write a custom extension handler. One way to do this is to write a COM in-process component that has an interface to encode your data type. You can then load this component in the Policy Module and use it to set your certificate extensions. Listing 17-3, written in Visual Basic, shows how to use the default extension handler to encode the SubjectAltName extension:

**Listing 17-3   Using the Extension Handler Provided by the Certificate Server**

```
' Reference CertEnc.dll library in your VB
' first project
Public Const CERT_ALT_NAME_RFC822_NAME As Long = 2
Public Const CERT_ALT_NAME_DNS_NAME As Long = 3
Public Const CERT_ALT_NAME_URL As Long = 7
Public Sub EncAltName()
    On Error GoTo CheckErr

    Dim altEnc As CCertEncodeAltName
    Dim encodedStr As String

    Set altEnc = New CCertEncodeAltName
    'We want to set three entries
    altEnc.Reset 3

    ' Set each entry
    altEnc.SetNameEntry 0, CERT_ALT_NAME_RFC822_NAME, _
"email@company.com"
    altEnc.SetNameEntry 1, CERT_ALT_NAME_DNS_NAME, _
"www.company.com"
    altEnc.SetNameEntry 2, CERT_ALT_NAME_URL, _
```

```
"http://www.company.com"
    'Do the encoding
    encodedStr = altEnc.Encode
    'For testing let's decode and see what we get
    altEnc.Decode encodedStr
    MsgBox altEnc.GetName(0) & "," & altEnc.GetName(1) & _
            "," & altEnc.GetName(2)
    Set bitEnc = Nothing
    Exit Sub
CheckErr:
    Set altEnc = Nothing
    ' Handle the error
End Sub
```

When you use DER-encoded types, you need to use the PROPTYPE_BINARY for the type of your extension in the SetCertificateExtension method. This tells the method that the value passed for the extension is already DER encoded.

## Summary

You can write a customized Policy Module by writing a COM in-process component that implements the ICertPolicy interface. In a customized Policy Module, you can deny a certificate request based on the information available in the request, accept and customize it by adding special extensions to the certificate under construction, or make it pending for further processing by an administrator.

Not all modules have write access to properties and extensions of a certificate. For example, a Policy Module has write access to some of the certificate properties and extensions. All request properties and attributes are read-only for all modules.

You should not use a user interface in your Policy Module. Because the Certificate Server runs as a system service, it does not have access to the Windows Desktop and cannot render windows or dialog boxes. For testing purposes, your module can have a user interface provided that you run the certificate server from the command line by using the certsrv –z command.

Chapter

# 18

# Programming Microsoft Certificate Server—The Exit Module

In a real-world deployment of any certificate server, you may want to be notified when certain events happen. For example, you may be interested in knowing when the certificate server issues or revokes a certificate or when it publishes a CRL. Microsoft Certificate Server's Exit Module can help in such situations. We continue our discussion of Microsoft Certificate Server programming with how to write and use a customized exit module.

## Certificate Server and the Exit Module

When the Certificate Server starts, it will load the Exit Module if there is one already installed on the system. The Certificate Server then notifies the Exit Module each time there is an event in which the Exit Module has expressed interest. Examples of such events are issuance of a new certificate, revocation of a certificate, and publishing of a new CRL. Using such event notifications, an Exit Module can respond by publishing issued certificates in a Directory Service or multicasting hot CRLs.

The **Exit Module** is a COM component of the Certificate Server architecture that implements the ICertExit interface. Here is a brief description of what happens when the Certificate Server wants to load the Exit Module at start-up:

1. The Server Engine, using COM APIs, looks up the registry for a component called CertificateAuthority.Exit. If one exists, it loads it. If not, it assumes there is no Exit Module and continues.

2. If an Exit Module is loaded, the Server Engine queries it for an ICertExit interface. If the query is successful, it calls the Initialize method of this interface.

3. In this method, the Exit Module should specify the events it wants to receive from the Certificate Server.

4. If the query is not successful, the Server Engine queries the loaded module for an Automation interface to use to call the Initialize method (via IDispatch::Invoke method of the Automation interface).

5. If this step also fails, the Server Engine assumes that no proper Exit Module is available and continues with its normal operation.

6. If the Server Engine could load the Exit Module and initialize it, it calls the Exit Module's Notify method (using ICertExit or IDispatch, as appropriate) whenever there is an event of interest to the Exit Module.

An Exit Module can use the ICertServerExit interface provided by the Certificate Server to get more information about the received events when the Server Engine calls its Notify method. Let's first look at the methods of ICertServerExit and ICertExit interfaces.

## The Exit Module Interfaces

**ICertServerExit** is the interface exported by the Server Engine to be used by an Exit Module. This interface provides methods for the Exit Module to get and enumerate elements of requests and issued certificates.

Table 18-1 shows the methods provided by the ICertServerExit interface.

To use these methods, the Exit Module must set the context of operations using the **SetContext** method, which takes a handle to the certificate request. The Server Engine provides this handle to the Exit Module when it calls the Notify method of the Exit Module. The Exit Module can use the methods to get further information about the issued or revoked certificate, the published CRL, and so on.

It is important to point out that most of the ICertServerExit methods shown in Table 18-1 are also available in the ICertServerPolicy interface. The only methods that are not provided by ICertServerExit are methods to set certificate properties and extensions. In most cases, when the Exit Module gets a notification, the certificate is already built and issued. For this reason, all the properties and extensions of a certificate are read-only for the Exit Module. Only the Policy Module and Admin Tools have write access to these properties and extensions.

The **ICertExit** interface, implemented by an Exit Module, is used by the Certificate Server to communicate with the Exit Module and notify it when interesting events occur. The Exit Module expresses interest in specific events when the Certificate Server calls the Initialize method of this interface. Table 18-2 shows the methods provided by this interface.

**Table 18.1** ICertServerExit Methods

| Method | Description |
|---|---|
| EnumerateAttributes | Returns the OID of the next attribute of the published certificate. |
| EnumerateAttributesClose | Closes attribute enumeration operation. |
| EnumerateAttributesSetup | Sets up attribute enumeration operation. |
| EnumerateExtensions | Returns the OID of the next extension of the published certificate. |
| EnumerateExtensionsClose | Closes extension enumeration operation. |
| EnumerateExtensionsSetup | Sets up extension enumeration operation. |
| GetCertificateExtension | Gets a specified certificate extension. |
| GetCertificateExtensionFlags | Gets the flags of the extension acquired by the last call to GetCertificateExtension. |
| GetCertificateProperty | Gets a specified property from the published certificate. |
| GetRequestAttribute | Gets a specified attribute from the published certificate request. |
| GetRequestProperty | Gets a specified property from the published certificate request. |
| SetContext | Sets the context of all the other operations. |

An Exit Module can express interest in any of the events listed in Table 18-3 by setting an event mask when the Certificate Server calls the Exit Module's Initialize method.

After an Exit Module receives an event in its Notify method, it usually uses the ICertServerExit interface exported by the Server Engine to communicate with the Server Engine and get more information about the received event. All this will become clearer when you write your own Exit Module in the next section.

# Writing Customized Exit Modules

As we will explain in Chapter 19, a certificate client application can use the GetCertificate method of the ICertRequest interface to retrieve a certificate after it

**Table 18-2**   ICertExit Methods

| Method | Description |
|---|---|
| GetDescription | Returns a textual description of the Exit Module. |
| Initialize | Called by the Server Engine once during initialization. |
| Notify | Called by the Server Engine to notify the Exit Module that an event of interest has occurred. |

sends a request to an intermediary. If there is a need, for example, to publish an issued certificate to a Directory Service or send a certificate to the applicant via e-mail, you should write and use a customized Exit Module to do so.

As with the Policy Module, you can write your own Exit Module in any programming language, including Visual Basic, Java, C, and C++. To write an Exit Module in Visual Basic, follow the steps described in the Writing Customized Policy Modules section of Chapter 17. The only difference is that the Exit Module should implement the methods of ICertExit interface in a public class named **Exit.** See the Certificate Server Programming Reference for more information on the parameters these methods take and their return values. Do not forget to register your module using the regsvr32 *yourmodule.dll* command. Visual Basic and Visual Studio do this for you by default when you compile your components.

**Table 18-3**   Event Masks Used by Exit Modules

| Name | Description |
|---|---|
| EXITEVENT_INVALID | Invalid event. |
| EXITEVENT_CERTISSUED | Certificate issued. |
| EXITEVENT_CERTPENDING | Certificate pending. |
| EXITEVENT_CERTDENIED | Certificate denied. |
| EXITEVENT_CERTREVOKED | Certificate revoked. |
| EXITEVENT_CERTRETRIEVEPENDING | Retrieval of pending certificate successful. |
| EXITEVENT_CRLISSUED | CRL issued. |
| EXITEVENT_SHUTDOWN | Certificate Server shutdown. |

In the next section, we will use Visual C++ and the Active Template Library (ATL) to develop a sample Exit Module. We show how an Exit Module registers itself to receive events and how it can use ICertServerExit interface methods to get more information about the received events. You can write your own Exit Module by modifying and rebuilding this project. Note that all the error handling is omitted from the code segments and listings shown in the following sections. The complete project files for our Exit Module are on the companion CD-Rom. To be able to compile this project, you need to install the latest version of Windows Platform SDK available at http://www.microsoft.com/msdn/sdk/.

## A Sample Exit Module

In our sample Exit Module, we use ATL 2.0 to create a dual-interfaced in-process COM object that implements the ICertExit interface. In the Initialize method of our object (CCertExit class), we first set a global pointer to the ICertServerExit interface:

```
hr = CoCreateInstance(

        CLSID_CCertServerExit,

        NULL,

        CLSCTX_INPROC_SERVER,

        IID_ICertServerExit,

        (VOID **) &pServer);
```

In this call to CoCreateInstance, we are asking COM to load a DLL implementation of the object by specifying CLSCTX_INPROC_SERVER for the class context. This is because ICertServerExit interface is implemented in certif.dll and not the Server Engine (certsrv.exe).

The main method of the Exit Module is the Notify function. In this method, your actions depend on the type of the event you receive. In our example, we have a switch statement that processes a certificate issuance event and prints the occurrence of any other events.

Listing 18-1 shows parts of the Exit.cpp file that contains the implementation of the ICertExit interface. Note that all printf statements are useful only when you run the Certificate Server from the command line in the standalone mode using the certsrv –z command. They should be removed or replaced with calls to log a message to the system log in the released version of the Exit Module.

**Listing 18-1** An Implementation of the ICertExit Interface in C++

```
/*
**_____
** CCertExit::Initialize
**_____
*/
STDMETHODIMP
CCertExit::Initialize(/* [in] */ BSTR const configStr,
                          /* [retval][out] */ LONG __RPC_FAR
*evtMask)
{
  HRESULT hr = S_OK;

  //
  // CLSID_CCertServerExit and IID_ICertServerExit
  // are defined in certif.h included with Platform SDK
  hr = CoCreateInstance(
          CLSID_CCertServerExit,
          NULL,
          CLSCTX_INPROC_SERVER,
          IID_ICertServerExit,
          (VOID **) &pServer);

  if (SUCCEEDED(hr)){
    *evtMask = ALL_EVENTS;
  }
  return hr;
}


/*
**_____
** CCertExit::Notify
**
```

```
**      Called by Server Engine when there is an event we are
**      interested in.
**_____
*/
STDMETHODIMP
CCertExit::Notify(/* [in] */ LONG event,
                  /* [in] */ LONG context)
{
  HRESULT hr = S_OK;
  char *str = "UNKNOWN EVENT!";

  switch (event){
  case EXITEVENT_CERTISSUED:
    str = "Certificate issued.";
    break;

  case EXITEVENT_CERTPENDING:
    str = "Certificate pending.";
    break;

  case EXITEVENT_CERTDENIED:
    str = "Certificate denied.";
    break;

  case EXITEVENT_CERTREVOKED:
    str = "Certificate revoked.";
    break;

  case EXITEVENT_CERTRETRIEVEPENDING:
    str = "Retrieve pending.";
    break;

  case EXITEVENT_CRLISSUED:
```

```
      str = "CRL issued";
      break;

    case EXITEVENT_SHUTDOWN:
      str = "Shut down";
      Terminate();
      break;
  }
  if (fDebugMode){
    printf("Exit::Notify received: %s\n", str);
  }

  if (EXITEVENT_CERTISSUED == event){
    hr = ProcessIssuedCert(context);
   }
  return(hr);
}


/*
**_____

** CCertExit::GetDescription
**_____

*/
STDMETHODIMP
CCertExit::GetDescription(
    /* [retval][out] */ BSTR *pstrDescription)
{
  HRESULT hr = S_OK;

  *pstrDescription = SysAllocString(myExitDescription);
  if (NULL == *pstrDescription){
    hr = E_OUTOFMEMORY;
  }
```

```
    return(hr);
}
```

We can use our ICertServerExit interface pointer (pServer) to get more information about the received events. To do that, we first set the context of all subsequent calls to the context passed to the Notify method:

```
pServer->SetContext(context)
```

If the event is for an issued certificate, we can enumerate the certificate extensions as in the following code segment:

```
BSTR extName = NULL;
LONG extFlags;
VARIANT varValue;
VariantInit(&varValue);
hr = pServer->EnumerateExtensionsSetup(0);
while (TRUE){
  hr = pServer->EnumerateExtensions(&extName);
  if (S_FALSE == hr){
    // End of extensions
    break;
  }
  hr = pServer->GetCertificateExtension(extName,
                                        PROPTYPE_BINARY,
                                        &varValue);
  // To do: got the extension OID. Process it!
  // Clear b/f reusing.
  VariantClear(&varValue);
}
```

You can modify this code, for example, to look for an e-mail extension and automate the process of sending the certificate to the customer using their e-mail address. It is also possible to get any certificate properties such as the serial number of an issued certificate:

```
VARIANT varValue;
BSTR strName = NULL;
VariantInit(&varValue);
strName = SysAllocString(wszPROPCERTIFICATESERIALNUMBER);
hr = pServer->GetCertificateProperty(strName,
                                      PROPTYPE_STRING,
                                      &varValue);
```

For example, one of the functions called by our ProcessIssuedCert function is PublishIssuedCert, which retrieves the issued certificate and publishes it to a Directory Service. Listing 18-2 shows how we can get a copy of the certificate using the GetCertificateProperty method.

**Listing 18-2** Retrieving an Issued Certificate

```
HRESULT PublishIssuedCert(ICertServerExit *pServer)
{
  HRESULT hr;
  VARIANT varValue;
  BSTR strName = NULL;

  VariantInit(&varValue);
  strName = SysAllocString(wszPROPRAWCERTIFICATE);
  hr = pServer->GetCertificateProperty(
              strName, PROPTYPE_BINARY,
              &varValue);
    // To do: Publish the Certificate, for example, to a
    // Directory Service here
     VariantClear(&varValue);
}
/*
**_____
** ProcessIssuedCert
**_____
*/
```

```
HRESULT ProcessIssuedCert(LONG context)
{
  HRESULT hr;
  //
  // Set the context of all other calls to this
  // certificate.
  hr = pServer->SetContext(context);
  hr = CheckIssuedCert(pServer);
  hr = PublishIssuedCert(pServer);
  return(hr);
}
```

After you build your Exit Module, don't forget to stop the Certificate Server, register your new Exit Module using regsvr32 myexil.dll, and then restart the Certificate Server.

## Summary

The Exit Module can be used for various reasons, such as publishing an issued certificate or CRL to a Directory Service and custom delivery of certificates. The Exit Module is basically a COM component that implements the ICertExit interface.

The Exit Module has read-only access to certificate properties and extensions and to request properties and attributes. Request attributes can be used as a means of private communication with the Exit Module. The current version of Certificate Server supports only one Exit Module, and it is possible to run the Certificate Server without having an Exit Module.

Chapter

# 19

# Programming Microsoft Certificate Server—Certificate Clients and Intermediaries

One of the important interfaces a certificate server needs to provide is the one a client application should use to communicate with the certificate server. In this chapter, we will look at one of the Microsoft Certificate Server components, which can be used to submit a certificate request, retrieve an issued certificate, and so on.

## Certificate Client and Intermediary

In the Microsoft Certificate Server architecture, three components are needed to request a certificate: the certificate client, the intermediary, and the Server Engine. These components interact in the following way:

1. The certificate client creates a certificate request and sends it to the intermediary.

2. The intermediary finds the correct configuration string by calling the GetConfig method of the ICertConfig interface exported by the Server Engine.

3. The intermediary sends the certificate request to the Certificate Server using the Submit method of the ICertRequest interface, which is also exported by the Server Engine.

4. The client retrieves the issued certificate using the GetCertificate method of the ICertRequest interface.

The **certificate client** is a standalone application that generates cryptographic keys, creates a certificate request, sends it to an intermediary for further processing, and receives the issued certificate. A certificate client usually runs on the client's machine.

The **intermediary** receives certificate requests from certificate clients, submits requests to the Server Engine, and retrieves and sends the issued certificates back to the certificate clients. The intermediary runs on the machine where the

Certificate Server resides, but it can communicate with and send the requests to any Certificate Server within an installation base. The third entity in this process is the Server Engine that creates and signs the certificate.

The Certificate Server architecture does not define the transport mechanism between the certificate client and the intermediary for sending certificate requests and receiving issued certificates. In fact, the reason for having two components to communicate with the Server Engine is to allow any transport mechanism to be used. Microsoft has already provided support for HTTP-based communication by its integration of IIS with the Certificate Server. Later in this chapter, we will see exactly how this is done when we write our own Web-based certificate client and intermediary applications using xenroll.dll, VBScript, and Active Server Pages. If you need to use other transport mechanisms, such as e-mail, you should provide your own client and intermediary.

The intermediary uses the ICertConfig and ICertRequest interfaces exported by the Server Engine to communicate with the Certificate Server. In Chapter 16, we described the ICertConfig interface and explained how it is used to remote some interfaces using DCOM. In our sample code in this chapter, we will see how to use this interface exactly to locate Certificate Servers and send certificate requests to a remote Certificate Server. But first, let's look at ICertRequest, the second interface used by the intermediary.

## Certificate Request Interface

Certificate Server exports the ICertRequest interface to be used by the intermediary. ICertRequest has methods for operations such as submitting a certificate request, checking the status of a submitted request, and retrieving an issued certificate. The root certificate of the Certificate Server can also be obtained using this interface.

Table 19-1 shows all the methods provided by the ICertRequest interface:

**Table 19-1**   ICertRequest Methods

| Method | Description |
|---|---|
| GetCACertificate | Returns the root certificate of the Certificate Server. |
| GetCertificate | Returns the certificate issued for the last submitted request. |
| GetDispositionMessage | Returns a message for the disposition of the last submitted request. |
| GetLastStatus | Returns the status code for the last submitted request. |
| GetRequesId | Returns the internal request number of the last submitted request. |
| RetrievePending | Attempts to retrieve a certificate from a pending request. |
| Submit | Submits a request to the Certificate Server. |

Note that there is no method in this interface to create a certificate request. As mentioned before, certificate client applications, not intermediaries, create certificate requests.

The Submit method is probably the most complicated method of the ICertRequest interface. Let's look at it and the GetCertificate method more closely. You can refer to the Certificate Server Programming Reference for information about the other methods.

ICertRequest::Submit method has the following signature (in C++ syntax):

```
#include <certsrv.h>
HRESULT Submit(LONG requestFlags,
BSTR const certRequest,
BSTR const requestAttributes,
BSTR const configString,
LONG *disposition);
```

Table 19-2 describes the arguments of this method.

The first argument, requestFlags, can be used to specify three different things: the encoding of the request, the format of the request, and whether the request is encrypted. For the request encoding type, one of the flags listed in Table 19-3 can be used.

**Table 19-2**  Submit Method Arguments

| Argument | Description |
|---|---|
| RequestFlags | Specifies the encoding and the format of the request and whether the request is encrypted. |
| CertRequest | Pointer to the string containing the certificate request. |
| RequestAttributes | Pointer to the string containing extra attributes for the request. |
| ConfigString | Pointer to the configuration string of a certificate server. It can specify a remote Certificate Server. |

**Table 19-3**  Request Encoding Flags

| Flag | Description |
|---|---|
| CR_IN_BASE64HEADER | BASE64 encoding with begin/end. |
| CR_IN_BASE64 | BASE64 encoding without begin/end. |
| CR_IN_BINARY | Binary (DER) encoding. |

The binary encoding is the standard ASN.1 DER encoding. A binary-encoded request can be further encoded in base64 so it can be transferred over transport mechanisms that do not support binary (8-bit) encoding. Microsoft's Certificate Enrollment Control, for example, generates a base64-encoded PKCS #10 request.

One of the flags listed in Table 19-4 can be used to specify the format of the request.

The PKCS #10 format is the de facto standard defined by RSA for certificate requests. Internet Explorer uses this format. Keygen is the format defined by Netscape, and it is used by Navigator. Certificate Server can process requests in both formats.

It is possible to encrypt the request using the exchange key of the Certificate Server. In this case, the Certificate Server will look at content as a PKCS #7–encrypted message. Use one of the flags listed in Table 19-5 to specify the encrypted content.

The RequestAttributes is a string that contains extra request attributes. An attribute is basically a name-value pair. RequestAttributes can contain attributes separated by newline character. A colon must be used to separate a name from its value. Certificate Server will ignore nonstandard attributes, but they can be used to set proprietary extensions in the Policy Module.

The disposition argument is a return value that specifies the disposition of the certificate request. A text message corresponding to the disposition value can be obtained by calling the GetDispositionMessage method. The disposition can be one of the values listed in Table 19-6.

The last two dispositions need some more explanation. The CR_DISP_ ISSUED_OUT_OF_BAND is used whenever a certificate is issued, but it is sent to the requestor via some other means, such as by e-mail or on a floppy disk. Because the Policy Module cannot currently specify such a case, you will never see this disposition. The CR_DISP_UNDER_SUBMISSION disposition is returned when the Policy Module makes the request pending for further processing by an administrator, to set specific extensions, and so on. If the administrator resubmits the certificate, it can be

**Table 19-4**  Request Format Flags

| Flag | Description |
|------|-------------|
| CR_IN_PKCS10 | PKCS #10 request. |
| CR_IN_KEYGEN | Keygen request. |

**Table 19-5**  Request Encryption Flags

| Flag | Description |
|------|-------------|
| CR_IN_ENCRYPTED_REQUEST | Request is encrypted. |
| CR_IN_ENCRYPTED_ATTRIBUTES | Attributes are encrypted. |

**Table 19-6** Request Disposition Codes

| Code | Description |
|---|---|
| CR_DISP_INCOMPLETE | Request did not complete. |
| CR_DISP_ERROR | Request has failed. Use the GetLastStatus method to get the error status code. |
| CR_DISP_DENIED | Request is denied. |
| CR_DISP_ISSUED | Certificate is issued and ready to be retrieved. |
| CR_DISP_ISSUED_OUT_OF_BAND | Certificate is issued separately. |
| CR_DISP_UNDER_SUBMISSION | Request is under submission. |

delivered to the client using the Exit Module. Alternatively, the client can use the RetrievePending method of the ICertRequest interface to obtain the certificate.

GetCertificate is the other method of the ICertRequest interface that we will be using in our sample code. This method has the following signature:

```
#include <certsrv.h>

HRESULT GetCertificate(LONG getFlags,

    BSTR *issuedCertificate);
```

The getFlags argument can be used to specify the encoding type and also whether you want the complete chain of certificates. Use one of the flags listed in Table 19-7 to specify the encoding type of the returned certificate.

To request that the complete certificate chain be included with the certificate, add the CR_OUT_CHAIN flag to the one you chose from Table 19-7.

The second argument, issuedCertificate, is a pointer to the issued certificate, and the complete certificate chain if requested, packaged in a PKCS #7 format. Note that the GetCertificate method returns the certificate issued in the last successful call to the submit method.

The Submit and GetCertificate methods both return an HRESULT value, which is the standard return type for COM methods. If the call is successful, the return value is S_OK.

# Writing Customized Certificate Clients and Intermediaries

Microsoft Certificate Server comes with a Web-based certificate client (ceenroll.asp) and an HTTP-based intermediary (ceaccept.asp). The Certificate Enrollment Tools page located at http://servername/CertSrv/CertEnroll/ uses ceenroll.asp to request a client authentication certificate. Ceenroll.asp sends the certificate request to ceaccept.asp, which

**Table 19-7**   Certificate Encoding Flags

| Flag | Description |
|------|-------------|
| CR_OUT_BASE64HEADER | BASE64 encoding with begin/end. |
| CR_OUT_BASE64 | BASE64 encoding without begin/end. |
| CR_OUT_BINARY | Binary (DER) encoding. |

submits the request to the default Certificate Server and sends the issued certificate back to the client's machine, where it can be installed.

Sometimes you may need to provide your own certificate client and intermediary; for example:

- You want to allow transport mechanisms other than HTTP, such as e-mail (SMTP).

- You need to enforce your own enrollment and certificate processing rules. For example, if you have different Certificate Servers for different certificate types, you can write an intermediary that communicates with the right Certificate Server using DCOM.

- You are a local registration authority (LRA), and you want to enforce your user authentication rules at the certificate client or intermediary level before sending the request to the Certificate Server (Refer to Chapter 10 for more information on LRAs).

Certificate Server does not define any interfaces for client applications. Intermediaries use ICertConfig and ICertRequest interfaces and can be written in any language that supports COM, such as Visual Basic, VBScript, Microsoft J++, and C++. Intermediaries do not need to be registered and are not loaded by the Server Engine. There are also no restrictions on the number of intermediaries.

## Sample Certificate Client and Intermediary

In this section, we provide two sample Web applications, a certificate client and an intermediary. In our certificate client we use the Certificate Enrollment Control (xenroll.dll) to create a certificate request, which we submit to our intermediary application via HTTP. You can find more information on the Certificate Enrollment Control in the Certificate Server documentation.

In our intermediary application, after we receive the certificate request, we first use the ICertConfig interface to find the right Certificate Server. We then use the

Submit method of the ICertRequest interface to send the request to the appropriate Certificate Server. Finally, we retrieve and install the issued certificate on the user's machine from within the browser. Both our applications are developed in VBScript and ASP using Microsoft Visual InterDev. Our main focus here is to show how to use ICertConfig and ICertRequest interfaces and how to send a request to a remote Certificate Server. As before, the whole example can be found on the companion CD-ROM. Let's look at the highlights of each application first.

## The Certificate Client

In our certificate client (CertEnroll.asp), we create a simple enrollment form that has four fields: subject's first name and last name, country, and the certificate class. We assume there are three different certificate classes: platinum, gold, and silver. Because there can be only one signature key per Certificate Server, we further assume we have three different Certificate Servers, one for each request type. Certification authorities usually sign different certificate types with different signature keys.

Figure 19-1 shows the enrollment form used by our client application and the certificate type field.

The client application uses ASP for server-side scripting. When the client downloads the page from his browser, all the scripts within <% and %> delimiters will be executed on the IIS server. In our server-side scripts, written in VBScript, we first determine the type and version of the browser using the BrowserType control provided by IIS:

```
Set BrowserCap = Server.CreateObject _
                              ("MSWC.BrowserType")
BrowserType = UCase(BrowserCap.browser)
BrowserVersion = BrowserCap.version
```

This control, which is created on the server, uses the information provided by the browser to determine the type and version of the browser. If the browser is the right type (Internet Explorer 4 in our sample code), we create the Certificate Enrollment Control using the OBJECT tag:

```
<% If ControlType + "XENROLL" Then %>
  <OBJECT
    classid="clsid:43F8F289-7A20-11D0-8F06-00C04FC295E1"
    id=ICertEnrollControl>
  </OBJECT>
<% End If %>
```

**Figure 19-1** Sample certificate enrollment form.

Note that this second control is created on the client's machine because it is not part of the server-side script. This means that the cryptographic keys are created on the client's machine, which is a common practice. The cryptographic keys are saved to a location defined in the Cryptographic Security Provider (CSP) used by the control. A CSP is a component that provides security services such as generating and storing keys, signing messages, and storing certificates. If you want, for example, to save the keys and the issued certificate on a smart card, you need to install a CSP capable of doing so. See the Certificate Enrollment Control documentation for more information.

One thing missing from the last code example is the CODEBASE field on the OBJECT tag. If the control is not available on the user's machine, the browser uses the value of this field to download the object from the server. We have not used this field here because the location of this control may vary. You need to provide this information for the controls you use in your client scripts.

When the user fills out the form and submits the request, we first make sure the data is valid. Then we build the subject's distinguished name (DN) from the provided data, and finally use our control to create the certificate request:

```
ICertEnrollControl.KeySpec = 1
reqPKCS10 = ICertEnrollControl.CreatePKCS10(DN, _
            "1.3.6.1.5.5.7.3.2")
```

We use AT_KEYEXCHANGE (1) for the KeySpec property. This value is used by the control to create a key pair that is good for both signing and encrypting. The OID "1.3.6.1.5.5.7.3.2" is for client authentication and will be used in the KeyUsage extension of the certificate. The created request is in PKCS #10 format and is kept in a hidden field of HTML form as in the following line of code to be retrieved by the intermediary after the data is being sent:

```
theForm.RequestData.value = reqPKCS10
```

In our client application, we also set the flags to be used in the submit call. Because the request we are sending is a PKCS #10 request encoded in base64, we use 257, which is CR_IN_PKCS10 (256) plus CR_IN_BASE64 (1). We also send the flag related to the encoding of the issued certificate to be used when our certificate is delivered. We would like the issued certificate to be base64-encoded and to receive the certificate chain, so we use 257, which is CR_OUT_CHAIN (256) plus CR_OUT_BASE64 (1). Both flags are sent to the server in hidden fields as follows:

```
theForm.SubmitFlag.value = 257
theForm.GetCertFlag.value = 257
```

Listing 19-1 shows the main part of our client application. The part that contains the description of the HTML form is not included in the listing.

**Listing 19-1** Sample Certificate Client Application

```
<%@ LANGUAGE=VBSCRIPT%>
<%Response.Expires=0%>
<HTML>
<HEAD>
<TITLE> Certificate Request Processing Page</TITLE>
<META HTTP-EQUIV="Cache-Control" CONTENT="no cache">
<META HTTP-EQUIV="Pragma" CONTENT="no cache">
<META HTTP-EQUIV="Expires" CONTENT="0">
<%
```

```
'
' CertEnroll.asp - Certificate Enrollment ASP file
'
'    This is a sample certificate client application
'    written in ASP. For simplicity, we only process
'    certificate requests from IE 4.0 browsers.
'

    Dim ControlType, BrowserType, BrowserVersion

ControlType = ""
BrowserType = ""
BrowserVersion = 0

Call InitASPEnv
%>

<% If ControlType = "XENROLL" Then %>
  <OBJECT
    classid="clsid:43F8F289-7A20-11D0-8F06-00C04FC295E1"
    id=ICertEnrollControl>
  </OBJECT>

<% End If %>

<%
  '
  ' InitServerEnv - Initialize ASP environment
  '
  Sub InitASPEnv()
    Dim BrowserCap
    '
    ' Use BrowserType control provided by ASP to
    ' get information on client's browser
```

```
    Set BrowserCap = Server.CreateObject _
                                ("MSWC.BrowserType")


    BrowserType = UCase(BrowserCap.browser)
        BrowserVersion = BrowserCap.version


    If InStr(BrowserType, "IE") Then
      If BrowserVersion >= 4 Then
        ControlType = "XENROLL"
      End If
    End If
  End Sub
%>


<SCRIPT LANGUAGE="VBSCRIPT">
<!--
Option Explicit

'
' SendRequest - Creates a PKCS10 request to be sent
'               to the ProcCertReq.asp
'
Sub SendRequest()
    Dim theForm
    Dim FirstName, LastName, Country, Email
    Dim CommonName,DN, reqPKCS10

    ' VBSCRIPT only supports this error handling
    ' Prevents runtime errors from stopping the
    ' script
    On Error Resume Next

    Set theForm = Document.frmRequest
```

```
' Read the values from the form
FirstName = theForm.FirstName.value
    LastName = theForm.LastName.value
Country = theForm.Country.value
Email = theForm.Email.value

If FirstName = "" or LastName = "" or _
    Country = "" or Email = "" or _
    theForm.CertClass.Value = "None" Then
        ' Dont send to server.
        MsgBox "Invalid Data! Please try again."
    Exit sub
End If
    CommonName = FirstName & " " & LastName

DN = ""
DN = DN & "C=" & Country & ";" _
        & "CN=" & CommonName & ";"
```

```
<% If ControlType = "XENROLL" Then %>
    DN = DN & "Email=" & Email & ";"
    '
    ' AT_KEYEXCHANGE (1) is good for both
    ' exchange and signature
    ICertEnrollControl.KeySpec = 1
    '
    ' "1.3.6.1.5.5.7.3.2" is for client authentication
    reqPKCS10 = ICertEnrollControl.CreatePKCS10(DN, _
            "1.3.6.1.5.5.7.3.2")
    theForm.RequestData.value = reqPKCS10

<% End If %>
```

```
      If err.number = 0 Then

         '

         ' CR_IN_PKCS10 (256) + CR_IN_BASE64 (1) for
         ' Submit method flags
         theForm.SubmitFlag.value = 257

         '

         ' CR_OUT_CHAIN (256) + CR_OUT_BASE64 (1)
         ' for GetCertificate method flags
         theForm.GetCertFlag.value = 257

         theForm.submit

      Else
         ' Dont send to server.
         MsgBox "Error - " & Err.number & Err.description
      End If
End Sub
-->
</SCRIPT>
</HEAD>
```

## Sample Intermediary

In our intermediary (ProcCertReq.asp), first we create the ICertConfig and ICert-Request objects on the server. Both objects provide an IDispatch (Automation) in-terface that can be used in environments such as VBScript that only support late binding:

```
Set ICertRequest = _
      Server.CreateObject("CertificateAuthority.Request")
Set ICertConfig   = _
      Server.CreateObject("CertificateAuthority.Config")
```

We then extract the submitted information using the Form collection of the Request object provided by ASP.  The most interesting field in our sample intermediary is the certificate class type:

```
CertClass       = Request.Form("CertClass")
```

The CertClass value is used to find a Certificate Server assigned to issue certificates of the specified class. To do this, we call the FindCertServer function:

```
ConfigString = FindCertServer(CertClass)
```

In this function, we use methods of ICertConfig to find the appropriate Certificate Server. We first go through the configuration fields of all the installed Certificate Servers. Note that we assume that the common name field of each Certificate Server contains the name of the certificate class it supports:

```
Do while nextSvr       <>-1
     svrCommonName = ICertConfig.GetField("CommonName")
```

If we find a match, we get the configuration string of the Certificate Server and return it in the FindCertServer variable:

```
    If InStr(svrCommonName, class) Then
      FindCertServer = ICertConfig.GetField("Config")
      Exit Do
    End If
```

If we don't find a match, we go to the next Certificate Server:

```
    nextSvr = ICertConfig.Next
```

The returned configuration string (ConfigString) is then used in the Submit method to send the request to the correct (possibly remote) Certificate Server:

```
Disposition = ICertRequest.Submit(SubmitFlag, _
                  reqPKCS10, ReqAttributes, ConfigString)
```

If the certificate is issued, we retrieve it using the flag specified by the client:

```
IssuedCert = ICertRequest.GetCertificate(GetCertFlag)
```

So far, all of this is happening on the server side. If everything goes fine, the intermediary sends a page to the client, together with the issued certificate and client-side script, to install the certificate on the client's machine. The Certificate Credential Control is once again created on the client and used to install the certificate:

```
ICertEnrollControl.AcceptPKCS7(certPKCS7)
```

Listing 19-2 shows the main part of our intermediary. The part containing the description of the HTML installation page is not included in this listing. Pay special attention to the ASPifyBinaryVar function, which we should use before sending a binary variable to the client via ASP.

**Listing 19-2** Sample Intermediary

```
<%@ LANGUAGE=VBSCRIPT%>
<%Response.Expires=0%>


<HTML>
<HEAD>
<TITLE> Certificate Request Processing Page</TITLE>
<META HTTP-EQUIV="Cache-Control" CONTENT="no cache">
<META HTTP-EQUIV="Pragma" CONTENT="no cache">
<META HTTP-EQUIV="Expires" CONTENT="0">


<%
    '
    ' Process a PKCS10 Client Authentication Certificate
    ' Request
    '
    On Error Resume Next

    Dim IssuedCert, Disposition, ErrorCode
    Dim ConfigString, reqPKCS10
    Dim SubmitFlag, GetCertFlag, ReqAttributes, ControlType
    Dim ICertRequest, ICertConfig
    Dim CertClass


    Call InitASPEnv

    reqPKCS10      = Request.Form("RequestData")
    SubmitFlag     = Request.Form("SubmitFlag")
    GetCertFlag    = Request.Form("GetCertFlag")
```

```
    ReqAttributes     = Request.Form("CertAttrib")
    ControlType  = Request.Form("ControlType")
    CertClass        = Request.Form("CertClass")


    ' We need to get the right Certificate Server based on
    ' the CertClass
    ConfigString = FindCertServer(CertClass)


    If ConfigString <> "" Then


      ' Found a Certificate Server
      Disposition = ICertRequest.Submit(SubmitFlag, _
                     reqPKCS10, ReqAttributes, ConfigString)
      If Disposition = 3 Then


        ' Get the issued certificate from the server
        IssuedCert = ICertRequest.GetCertificate(GetCertFlag)
      Else
        ErrorCode = ICertRequest.GetLastStatus()
      End If
      End If
%>
<%
'
' Initialize ASP Environment
'
Sub InitASPEnv()
  Set ICertRequest = _
Server.CreateObject("CertificateAuthority.Request")
  Set ICertConfig = _
      Server.CreateObject("CertificateAuthority.Config")
End Sub
```

```
'
' Find a Certificate Server that is assigned to process
' certificate requests of the specified class
'
Function FindCertServer(class)
   Dim nextSvr, svrCommonName

   FindCertServer = ""

   nxtSvr = ICertConfig.Next
   Do while nextSvr <> -1
      svrCommonName = ICertConfig.GetField("CommonName")
      If InStr(svrCommonName, class) Then
         FindCertServer = ICertConfig.GetField("Config")
         Exit Do
      End If
      nextSvr = ICertConfig.Next
   Loop
End Function


'
' Convert a binary variable to a sequence of outVars
' that can be sent to the client safely
'
Function ASPifyBinaryVar(inVar, outVar)
   Dim inVarLen, quoteChar, newLinePos
   Dim moreChars, startFrom, beginLinePos
   Dim initVar, wrappedOutVar

   ASPifyBinaryVar = ""
   quoteChar = chr(34)
   inVarLen = Len(inVar) - Len(vbNewLine)
```

```
      initVar = outVar & " = " & quoteChar & quoteChar
      wrappedOutVar = outVar & " = " & outVar & " & "


   moreChars = True
   startFrom = 1

   Do While (moreChars)
     beginLinePos = startFrom
     newLinePos = InStr(startFrom, inVar, vbNewLine)

     If newLinePos > 0 Then
       nxtLine = Mid(inVar, beginLinePos, _
                     newLinePos - beginLinePos)
       ASPifyBinaryVar = ASPifyBinaryVar & _
                     wrappedOutVar & quoteChar & _
                     nxtLine & quoteChar
       If newLinePos >= inVarLen Then
         moreChars = False
       End If
     Else
       moreChars = False
     End If

     ASPifyBinaryVar = ASPifyBinaryVar & vbNewLine
     startFrom = newLinePos + Len(vbNewLine)
   Loop
   ASPifyBinaryVar = initVar & vbNewLine & ASPifyBinaryVar
End Function
%>


<% If ControlType = "XENROLL" Then %>
   <OBJECT
      classid="clsid:43F8F289-7A20-11D0-8F06-00C04FC295E1"
```

```
            id=ICertEnrollControl>
    </OBJECT>
<% End If %>


<% If ControlType = "XENROLL" Then %>
<SCRIPT LANGUAGE="VBSCRIPT">
<!--
Option Explicit

Sub DownloadCert()
   Dim msg
   Dim certPKCS7

   On Error Resume Next

   <%=ASPifyBinaryVar(IssuedCert,"certPKCS7")%>

   <% If ControlType = "XENROLL" Then %>
     ICertEnrollControl.AcceptPKCS7(certPKCS7)
   <% End If %>

   If err.Number = 0 Then
     window.location = "success.htm"
   Else
     msg = "Error installing the certificate." & _
             vbNewLine & vbNewLine & "Error: " & Hex(err)
     MsgBox msg, 32, "<%=ControlType%>"
     window.location "failure.htm"
   End If
End Sub
-->
</SCRIPT>
<% End If %>
</HEAD>
```

## Summary

A certificate client and an intermediary are used hand in hand to create and submit a certificate request to a Certificate Server. Certificate clients are usually Web-based applications that create and send the request to an intermediary using HTTP protocol. Intermediaries can use the same transport to send the issued certificate back to the client. They can also use other mechanisms, such as e-mail, to send the issued certificate or a notification that the certificate is ready for download to the client later.

No interface is exported by the Certificate Server for certificate clients. Intermediaries, on the other hand, should use ICertConfig and ICertRequest interfaces to communicate with the Certificate Server. It is possible to use the methods of these interfaces to submit certificate requests to remote Certificate Servers.

There is no limitation on the number of intermediaries. Intermediaries do not need to be registered because the Certificate Server does not load them. The current version of Certificate Server supports only intermediaries that run on a Certificate Server, but this may change in the future.

# 20

# Programming Microsoft Certificate Server—Admin Programs

One of the responsibilities of a Certificate Server administrator is to revoke certificates, generate certificate revocation lists (CRLs), resubmit pending requests, and monitor certificate logs and queues. In this chapter, we will examine Microsoft Certificate Server's administration interface. In our sample Admin programs, written in Java, we will show how to multicast hot CRLs, revoke certificates, and get lists of issued certificates. Before we start, we should point out that the focus of this chapter is about *writing* Admin programs and not about issues or even the available tools for administration of Certificate Server. You need to refer to the Certificate Server documentation for this purpose.

## Certificate Server and Admin Programs

To carry out their day-to-day tasks, Certificate Server administrators need to use Admin programs to

- Generate CRLs from all revoked certificates
- Resubmit requests made pending by the Policy Module
- Set certificate extensions on pending requests
- Revoke certificates
- Deny certificate requests
- Examine the certificate server log and queue databases

**Admin programs** are standalone executables that use the ICertAdmin and ICertConfig interfaces to communicate with the Server Engine. Like intermediaries, Admin programs do not need to implement a COM interface, and there is no need to register them because the Server Engine does not load them. Because the ICertAdmin interface does not provide any methods to access the certificate server log and queue databases, some Admin programs need to be connected directly to these databases to monitor them.

Certificate Server is shipped with some basic Web-based Admin programs to view the log and queue databases and revoke certificates. You can access these tools from Certificate Server Tools Page at http://servername/CertSrv. Also, standalone programs such as CertUtil and CertReq can be used to do basic administrative tasks such as generating a CRL. You can get more information about using these programs by referring to the Certificate Server documentation.

## Administration Interface

**ICertAdmin** is the interface exported by the Server Engine that is used by Admin programs. This interface provides methods to revoke a certificate, publish a CRL, get a published CRL, resubmit a pending request, and so on.

Table 20-1 shows the methods provided by the ICertAdmin interface.

We will use some of these methods later in this chapter when we write our own Admin programs. Refer to Chapter 16 for information about the ICertConfig interface, which is also used by Admin programs.

**Table 20-1**   ICertAdmin Methods

| Method | Description |
|---|---|
| DenyRequest | Denies the specified certificate request. |
| GetCRL | Gets the current certificate revocation list. |
| GetRevocationReason | Returns a text string specifying the reason a certificate was revoked. |
| IsValidCertificate | Checks the validity of a certificate. |
| PublishCRL | Publishes a new certificate revocation list. |
| ResubmitRequest | Resubmits the specified request to the Policy Module for reconsideration. |
| RevokeCertificate | Revokes a certificate. |
| SetCertificateExtension | Adds a new extension to a certificate that is under construction. |
| SetRequestAttributes | Sets attributes in the specified request. |

# Writing Customized Admin Programs

To simplify things, we classify Admin programs into two different types. The first type of Admin programs uses the ICertAdmin and ICertConfig interfaces to communicate with the Server Engine and perform any of the operations supported by this interface. The second type of Admin programs gets connected to the databases maintained by the Server Engine for monitoring and auditing purposes. Of course, you can write Admin programs that use the ICertAdmin and ICertConfig interfaces and connect to the databases at the same time.

Writing Admin programs that use the ICertAdmin and ICertConfig interfaces is easy and similar to other components we have developed so far. All you need is to use ICertAdmin and ICertConfig interfaces to connect to the Server Engine and then call the methods of these interfaces. We saw how to do that in VB, C++, and VBScript when we wrote our customized Policy Module, Exit Module, and intermediary application. In the next section, we will see how to do the same thing using Java and the Microsoft JDK.

Writing Admin programs that connect to the Server Engine databases is easy once you learn more about the databases. All you need is to use your preferred method of accessing database tables and records. In the next section, we will use JDBC to do so.

The Server Engine uses an Access database, named certsrv.mdb by default, to maintain information on certificate requests, issued certificates, issued CRLs, and so on. The location of this database is specified during the installation of the Certificate Server. Table 20-2 lists the tables currently available.

You can get more information about these tables, their fields, and how they are related when you open them using Microsoft Access. We will see how to use some of these tables in the next section.

**Table 20-2**  Certificate Server Database Tables

| Table | Description |
|---|---|
| CertificateExtensions | Certificate extension information. |
| Certificates | Issued certificates. |
| CRLs | Issued certificate revocation lists. |
| Miscellaneous | Miscellaneous persistent data. |
| NameExtensions | Auxiliary name information. |
| Names | Names and subnames. |
| RequestAttributes | Extra attributes information. |
| Requests | Certificate request information. |

## A Sample Admin Program

In our sample Admin program we use Java and JDBC to create a simple tool that can be used to get the list of certificate requests, revoke an issued certificate, and publish, retrieve, and multicast a CRL. In the following sections, we look at the highlights of each class followed by the code listing for each class. You can find the whole example, which was developed using Visual J++ 1.1 and Java SDK 2.0, on the companion CD-ROM.

To be able to access a COM component from Java, you need to use Microsoft JDK 2.0 or later and the JActiveX command it provides. First, you need to create wrapper Java classes that describe the COM components using JActiveX and the /javatlb switch as follows:

```
JActiveX /javatlb certadm.dll
JActiveX /javatlb certif.dll
```

JActiveX creates Java files, one for each class, structure, enumeration, and interface described by the type library contained in each DLL. These files are put in a subdirectory named after the DLL in the TrustLib directory specified by the registry key HKEY_LOCAL_MACHINE\SOFTWARE\Microsoft\Java VM\TrustedLibsDirectory. On my NT server, for example, this command creates Java files in the \Winnts\Java\Trustlib\certadm and \Winnts\Java\Trustlib\certif directories. We import these wrapper Java files using the import keyword in our Admin program.

Listing 20-1 shows how we revoke a certificate in the Certificate class.

**Listing 20-1**   Revoking a Certificate in certificate.java

```
public void revoke(int reason, double rvktime)
{
    ICertConfig certConfig = (ICertConfig) new CCertConfig();
    String  configString = certConfig.GetConfig(0);


    ICertAdmin certadm = (ICertAdmin) new CCertAdmin();
    certadm.RevokeCertificate(configString, serialNum,
                              reason, rvktime);

}
```

We have also put all operations related to CRLs in our CRL Java class. One of the methods of this class is to multicast the latest CRL to an Internet multicast group. Listing 20-2 shows how it is done.

**Listing 20-2** Multicasting a CRL in CRL.java

```
public void multicast(String group, int port, int ttl) {
    InetAddress gaddr;
    ICertAdmin certadm = (ICertAdmin) new CCertAdmin();
    String crl = this.get();
    try {
        gaddr = InetAddress.getByName (group);
    }
    catch (Exception e) {
        adminCtxt.logMessage ("Error - Bad multicast addr:" + e);
        return;
    }
    try {
        byte[] buf = crl.getBytes();
        DatagramPacket pack = new
            DatagramPacket (buf, buf.length, gaddr, port);

        MulticastSocket msocket = new MulticastSocket();
        msocket.send (pack , (byte) ttl);
    }
    catch (Exception e){
        adminCtxt.logMessage ("Error - Could not multicast: "
            + e);
    }
}
```

You can find more information on multicasting using Java in [FEGH97].

Another interesting Java class in our sample Admin program is the CertBase class, which abstracts operations related to getting information from the Server Engine database. In this class, we use JDBC to connect to the certsrv.mdb database, join the Requests and Certificates tables, and read and display the RequestID, SerialNumber, DispositionMessage, and RevokedWhen fields. Listing 20-3 shows how to connect to the database in CertBase constructor.

**Listing 20-3**   Getting Connected to certsrv.mdb Using JDBC in CertBase.java

```java
public CertBase (AdminContext ctxt) throws Exception{
adminCtxt = ctxt;

    String url   = "JDBC:ODBC:CertSrv";
    String query =
      "SELECT Certificates.RequestID,SerialNumber " +
      " ,DispositionMessage, RevokedWhen FROM Certificates" +
      " INNER JOIN Requests ON Certificates.RequestID "+
      " = Requests.RequestID";
    try {
      // Load the jdbc-odbc bridge driver
      Class.forName ("com.ms.jdbc.odbc.JdbcOdbcDriver");


      DriverManager.setLogStream(null);


      // Attempt to connect to a driver.
      con = DriverManager.getConnection (
                  url, "", "");


      // Check for, and display any warnings generated
      // by the connect.
      checkForWarning (con.getWarnings ());
      // Get the DatabaseMetaData object and display
      // some information about the connection

      DatabaseMetaData dma = con.getMetaData ();


      // Create a Statement object so we can submit
```

```
      // SQL statements to the driver
      stmt = con.createStatement ();

      // Submit a query, creating a ResultSet object
      rs = stmt.executeQuery (query);
    }
    catch (SQLException ex) {
      logSQLException(ex);
      throw new Exception ("Get an SQL Exception");
    }
  }
```

To read all the requests from the joined table, we use the listRequests function that calls nextRequest, shown in Listing 20-4, repeatedly to iterate through the result set we created in the CertBase constructor.

**Listing 20-4**  Getting the Next Request in CertBase.java

```
public String nextRequest ()
    throws SQLException, NoSuchElementException
  {
    int i;
    String field;

    ResultSetMetaData rsmd = rs.getMetaData ();
    int numCols = rsmd.getColumnCount ();

    // Display data, fetching until end of the result set
    boolean more = rs.next ();
    if (more) {
      StringBuffer row = new StringBuffer(rowWidth);
      for (i = 1; i <= numCols; i++) {
       field = rs.getString(i);
       if (null == field) {
        field = " - ";
       }
```

```
        row.insert((i-1) * spacing, field);
      }
      return row.toString();
  }
  else{
    throw new NoSuchElementException(
      "No more certificate entry");
  }
}
```

When you run the sample program using the jview CertAdmin command, the user interface shown in Figure 20-1 will be displayed. You can get a list of all certificate requests by pressing the **Request Log** button. If you want to revoke a certificate, you should select one of the requests that represents an issued certificate and then click on the **Revoke Certificate** button. A CRL that contains revoked certificates can be generated and multicast using the **Publish New CRL** and **Multicast CRL** buttons, respectively. **Get CRL** retrieves and displays the last generated CRL in base64 format.

The user interface shown in Figure 20-1 is designed using the dialog resource editor available in Visual J++. This resource file is then processed by the Java Resource wizard to create an equivalent Java AWT class. You can find all of the project files on the companion CD-ROM. Like all other sample projects developed in this book, this project should be used only as a template when you write your own Admin programs.

## Summary

Admin programs are used to accomplish tasks such as generating CRLs, revoking certificates, resubmitting pending certificate requests, setting certificate extensions, and monitoring the operation of a Certificate Server. ICertAdmin and ICertConfig are the two COM interfaces you should use to write your own Admin programs. You can also write programs, that connect to the Server Engine database to get information about received requests or issued certificates. There is no need to register Admin programs, nor is there any limit on the number of such programs.

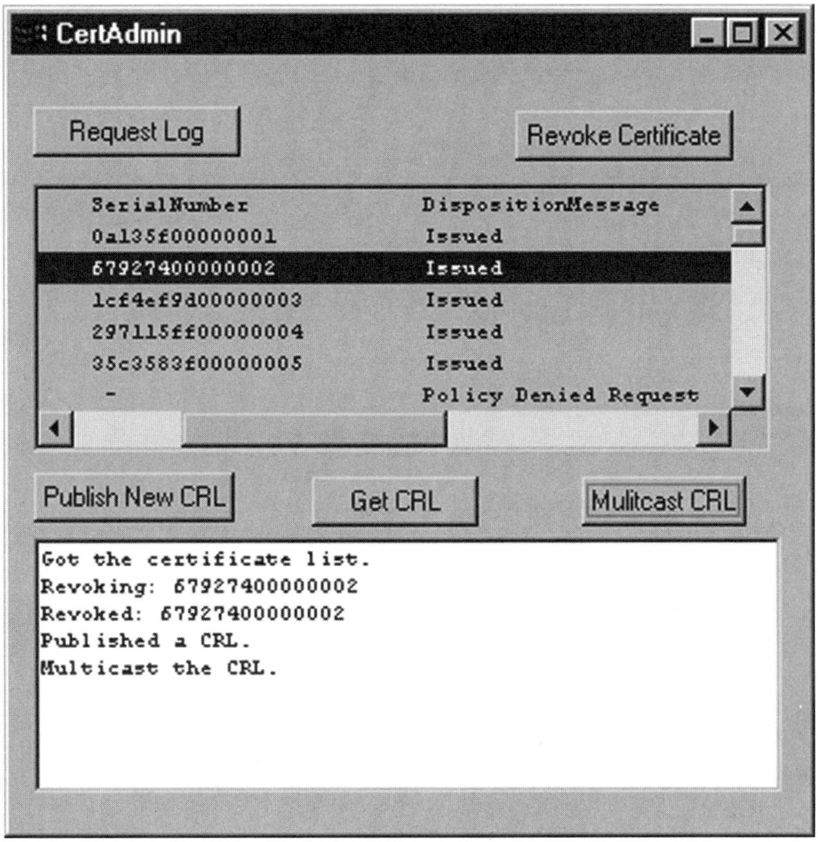

**Figure 20-1** Sample Admin program.

# Reference

[FEGH97]   Feghhi, J. *Web Developer's Guide to Java Beans*, Scottsdale, AZ: Coriolis Group, Inc., 1997.

# Appendix

# A

# Abstract Syntax Notation (ASN.1)

The following material is excerpted from "A Layman's Guide to a Subset of ASN.1, BER, and DER," an RSA Laboratories technical note. The Layman's Guide is a part of the RSA Data Security, Inc. Public-Key Cryptography Standards (PKCS) document series. We present this discussion for readers who may be unfamiliar with the notation system used to specify many of the security data objects used in the interworking standards featured in this book.

Abstract Syntax Notation One, abbreviated ASN.1, is a notation for describing abstract types and values.

In ASN.1, a type is a set of values. For some types, there are a finite number of values, and for other types there are an infinite number. A value of a given ASN.1 type is an element of the type's set. ASN.1 has four kinds of type: simple types, which are "atomic" and have no components; structured types, which have components; tagged types, which are derived from other types; and other types, which include the CHOICE type and the ANY type. Types and values can be given names with the ASN.1 assignment operator (::=), and those names can be used in defining other types and values.

Every ASN.1 type other than CHOICE and ANY has a tag, which consists of a class and a nonnegative tag number. ASN.1 types are abstractly the same if and only if their tag numbers are the same. In other words, the name of an ASN.1 type does not affect its abstract meaning; only the tag does. There are four classes of tag:

*Universal,* for types whose meaning is the same in all applications; these types are only defined in X.208.

*Application,* for types whose meaning is specific to an application, such as X.500 directory services; types in two different applications may have the same application-specific tag and different meanings.

*Private,* for types whose meaning is specific to a given enterprise.

*Context-specific,* for types whose meaning is specific to a given structured type; context-specific tags are used to distinguish between component types with the same underlying tag within the context of a given structured type, and component types in two different structured types may have the same tag and different meanings.

The types with universal tags are defined in X.208, which also gives the types' universal tag numbers. Types with other tags are defined in many places and are always obtained by implicit or explicit tagging (see Section 2.3). Table 1 lists some ASN.1 types and their universal-class tags.

ASN.1 types and values are expressed in a flexible, programming-language–like notation, with the following special rules:

- Layout is not significant; multiple spaces and line breaks can be considered as a single space.

- Comments are delimited by pairs of hyphens (--), or a pair of hyphens and a line break.

- Identifiers (names of values and fields) and type references (names of types) consist of upper- and lower-case letters, digits, hyphens, and spaces; identifiers begin with lower-case letters; type references begin with upper-case letters.

The following four subsections give an overview of simple types, structured types, implicitly and explicitly tagged types, and other types. [...]

2.1 Simple types

**Table A-1**   Some Types and Their Universal-Class Tags

| *Type* | *Tag number (decimal)* | *Tag number (hexadecimal)* |
|---|---|---|
| INTEGER | 2 | 02 |
| BIT STRING | 3 | 03 |
| OCTET STRING | 4 | 04 |
| NULL | 5 | 05 |
| OBJECT IDENTIFIER | 6 | 06 |
| SEQUENCE and SEQUENCE OF | 16 | 10 |
| SET and SET OF | 17 | 11 |
| PrintableString | 19 | 13 |
| T61String | 20 | 14 |
| IA5String | 22 | 16 |
| UTCTime | 23 | 17 |

Simple types are those not consisting of components; they are the "atomic" types. ASN.1 defines several; the types that are relevant to the PKCS standards are the following:

BIT STRING, an arbitrary string of bits (ones and zeroes).

IA5String, an arbitrary string of IA5 (ASCII) characters.

INTEGER, an arbitrary integer.

NULL, a null value.

OBJECT IDENTIFIER, an object identifier, which is a sequence of integer components that identify an object such as an algorithm or attribute type.

OCTET STRING, an arbitrary string of octets (eight-bit values).

PrintableString, an arbitrary string of printable characters.

T61String, an arbitrary string of T.61 (eight-bit) characters.

UTCTime, a "coordinated universal time" or Greenwich Mean Time (GMT) value.

Simple types fall into two categories: string types and non-string types. BIT STRING, IA5String, OCTET STRING, PrintableString, T61String, and UTCTime are string types.

String types can be viewed, for the purposes of encoding, as consisting of components, where the components are substrings. This view allows one to encode a value whose length is not known in advance (e.g., an octet string value input from a file stream) with a constructed, indefinite-length encoding [...].

The string types can be given size constraints limiting the length of values.

2.2 Structured types

Structured types are those consisting of components. ASN.1 defines four, all of which are relevant to the PKCS standards.

SEQUENCE, an ordered collection of one or more types.

SEQUENCE OF, an ordered collection of zero or more occurrences of a given type.

SET, an unordered collection of one or more types.

SET OF, an unordered collection of zero or more occurrences of a given type.

The structured types can have optional components, possibly with default values.

2.3 Implicitly and explicitly tagged types

Tagging is useful to distinguish types within an application; it is also commonly used to distinguish component types within a structured type. For instance, optional components of a SET or SEQUENCE type are typically given distinct context-specific tags to avoid ambiguity.

There are two ways to tag a type: implicitly and explicitly.

Implicitly tagged types are derived from other types by changing the tag of the underlying type. Implicit tagging is denoted by the ASN.1 keywords [*class number*] IMPLICIT […].

Explicitly tagged types are derived from other types by adding an outer tag to the underlying type. In effect, explicitly tagged types are structured types consisting of one component, the underlying type. Explicit tagging is denoted by the ASN.1 keywords [*class number*] EXPLICIT […].

The keyword [*class number*] alone is the same as explicit tagging, except when the "module" in which the ASN.1 type is defined has implicit tagging by default. ("Modules" are among the advanced features not described in this note.)

For purposes of encoding, an implicitly tagged type is considered the same as the underlying type, except that the tag is different. An explicitly tagged type is considered to be like a structured type with one component, the underlying type. Implicit tags result in shorter encodings, but explicit tags may be necessary to avoid ambiguity if the tag of the underlying type is indeterminate (e.g., the underlying type is CHOICE or ANY).

2.4 Other types

Other types in ASN.1 include the CHOICE and ANY types. The CHOICE type denotes a union of one or more alternatives; the ANY type denotes an arbitrary value of an arbitrary type, where the arbitrary type is possibly defined in the registration of an object identifier or integer value.

# Appendix

# B
—

# Structuring X.509 Certificates for Use with Microsoft Products

## An Introduction for Prospective Certificate Issuers

December 4, 1997
Microsoft Corporation
**Contents**

## *Abstract*

This document is intended for prospective certificate issuers, often referred to as Certificate Authorities (CAs), who wish to issue X.509 v3 certificates for use with Microsoft products. Certificates play a key role in public key cryptography, creating a binding between an entity's public key, their name, and other attributes. CAs provide a basis for managing trust relationships for public key technologies in a manner that is efficient and scalable. They do this by reducing the problem of secure key distribution to a large number of principals down to secure distribution of the keys of a small number of certificate issuers. Products from Microsoft, Netscape, and others rely on certificates for correct functioning. This document describes some of those products and the details of the certificates and certificate verification procedures that support them.

## Introduction

The following sections describe what certificates are and what technologies and applications they are used in, and make recommendations to CAs on the use of specific fields and extensions defined in X.509 v3 certificates.

### A Brief Introduction to Certificates

Prior to the 1970s published work on cryptography was based on secret key algorithms. Two parties were able to communicate privately and securely, but only once had they exchanged a secret key. In 1976 Whitfield Diffie and Martin Hellman invented public key cryptography and demonstrated that parties could communicate without a prearranged shared secret. Public key cryptography is based on a pair of keys, public and private, in which the public key may be freely distributed and the private key is only known to the owning entity. However, the problem of reliably distributing public keys still remained. In 1978, Kohnfelder showed that the key distribution problem may be reduced to the problem of reliably distributing a small number of public keys. These public keys belong to Certificate Authorities (CAs) or certificate issuers, and the certificates they issue validate the public keys of other entities.

All certificates use the technology of public-key–based digital signature to bind a public key to a principal. The principal may be identified in various ways, for instance, using an X.500 name space. The issuer digitally signs the certificate to validate the association of public key and principal, and any additional attributes.

The only standard for certificates in broad use today is ISO X.509 version 3. These certificates are represented as self-describing ASN.1 data structures. The core v1 fields contain basic information, such as the X.500 identity of the principal. Version 3 introduced the concept of extensions, which allow specification of arbitrary attributes as part of the Certificate. The IETF PKIX draft standards have defined a number of these extensions relevant to Internet applications. There is emerging support for these. In addition, RSA has developed a set of extensions and interpretations for use in S/MIME secure mail applications.

Additional resources may be found at:

- http://ietf.org/ids.by.wg/pkix.html (PKIX drafts)
- ftp://ietf.org/internet-drafts/draft-ietf-pkix-ipki-part1-06.txt (PKIX X.509 certificates)
- http://www.rsa.com/rsalabs/pubs/PKCS/ (PKCS)

- http://www.imc.org/draft-dusse-smime-cert/ (S/MIME)
- http://premium.microsoft.com/msdn/library/sdkdoc/intro_3a26.htm (cryptography introductory references)

Microsoft maintains a list of public CAs:

- http://www.microsoft.com/security/ca/ca.htm (list of public CAs)

### Technologies that Use Certificates

Specific Microsoft technologies that use X.509 v3 certificates are described below. For a general overview of Microsoft security technologies, *see also:*

http://www.microsoft.com/security (Microsoft Security Advisor)

### Server Authentication

Used to authenticate a server to a client using the TLS/SSL protocols. TLS stands for Transport Layer Security and is currently a *draft IETF spec,* which Microsoft intends to implement once ratified by the IETF. In both, the server transmits its certificate to the client as part of a protocol in which the server proves it owns the corresponding private key. *See also:*

http://www.microsoft.com/security/tech/csa/digserv.htm

### Client Authentication

Used to authenticate a client to a server using the TLS/SSL protocols. During the server authentication described above, the client also transmits its certificate to the server and proves it owns the corresponding private key. Typically the server will then map that certificate into a local user or into a set of access rights. *See also:*

http://www.microsoft.com/security/tech/misf3.htm

### Code Signing

Supports generation of digital signatures for executable content, such as applications, controls, DLLs, or self-extracting executables. This ensures the integrity of the data and allows the identity of the author to be determined. *See also:*

http://www.microsoft.com/workshop/prog/default.asp#sec

### Timestamping

Timestamping provides an assured means for determining when a specific action took place. Microsoft presently supports optional timestamping with Microsoft Authenticode to provide information as to when executable content was signed. This provides a means to determine if the content was signed while the signer's certificate was valid, even if the signer's certificate has subsequently expired or been revoked. It relies on a third-party timestamping service, which will typically be associated with a CA. *See also:*

http://www.rsa.com/pub/pkcs/ascii/pkcs-7.asc, section 9.2

http://www.rsa.com/pub/pkcs/ascii/pkcs-9.asc, section 6.5

### E-Mail

Microsoft has supported signed and encrypted e-mail based on public key technology in Exchange for some time. However, this was not generally interoperable with other products. S/MIME is emerging as a de facto standard for interoperable secure e-mail and is currently supported by Microsoft Outlook Express. *See also:*

http://www.rsa.com/smime/

### Disk Encryption

Public key technology has an important role in disk encryption products. We can use a public key to shroud the actual symmetric keys used for encryption/decryption. This provides efficient operation and ensures that only the owner of the private key will be able to decrypt the file. Taking advantage of this approach, one can create data recovery support, or encrypt files to multiple readers, by shrouding the encryption key using multiple public keys.

http://www.microsoft.com/ntserver/library/efs.exe

### Server Gated Cryptography

Server Gated Cryptography (SGC) defines a mechanism for negotiating strong cryptographic security for TLS/SSL sessions based on the presence of a special server-side certificate. Distribution of these certificates is controlled in accordance with an export license from the U.S. Department of Commerce. The SGC certificates are distinguished by a special extendedKeyUsage extension value as described later in this document. *See also:*

http://microsoft.com/industry/finserv/m_finserv/m_fordev_g.htm

## Microsoft Products that Use Certificates

### Microsoft Internet Explorer (Version 3.0 and higher)

Supports Server Authentication and Client Authentication. Also, supports download and signature verification of Authenticode signed packages, controls, and applets. Functionality may also be accessed via the Wininet SDK and the Java VM. Server Gated Crypto is supported. *See also:*

http://www.microsoft.com/security/ca/howto.htm

### Microsoft Internet Information Server

Supports Server Authentication, Client Authentication, Server Gated Crypto. *See also:*

http://www.microsoft.com/security/tech/csa/digserv.htm

### Microsoft Outlook Express

Supports S/MIME encrypted mail and is fully interoperable with other S/MIME products. *See also:*

http://www.microsoft.com/ie/ie40/oe/features-f.htm?/ie/ie40/oe/smime.htm

### Tools and Software Development Kits

Authenticode code signing, timestamping utilities. *See also:*

http://www.microsoft.com/msdn/sdk/inetsdk/help/inet1320-f.htm

### Microsoft Encrypted File System (EFS)

This feature to be released with Microsoft Windows NT 5.0 was announced at a recent Professional Developers Conference. *See also:*

http://premium.microsoft.com/msdn/library/sdkdoc/fsys_1fou.htm

## *Certificate Fields and Extensions Used by Microsoft Products*

This section describes the X509 v3 certificate fields and extensions examined by Microsoft products and makes recommendations as to their appropriate usage. This is not a complete list of fields and extensions available to certificate issuers, rather it is a snapshot of fields and extensions that are currently examined and how they are interpreted.

## *Certificate Purpose and Policy*

### Key Usage
**Extension:**
KeyUsage (OID 2.5.29.15).
**References:**

ftp://ietf.org/internet-drafts/draft-ietf-pkix-ipki-part1-06.txt

http://www.imc.org/draft-dusse-smime-cert

**Discussion:**
KeyUsage, ExtendedKeyUsage, and BasicConstraints act together to delimit the uses for which the certificate is designed and enable applications to disallow the use of the certificate in inappropriate contexts. Defined key usages are listed below. Key usage is a bit string, and therefore multiple usages may be defined for a given certificate. Typical combinations of usages are also listed below, by application. **Note:** PKIX recommends that this extension be marked critical if used.

### Key Usages

- digitalSignature
- nonRepudiation
- keyEncipherment
- dataEncipherment
- keyAgreement
- keyCertSign
- cRLSign
- encipherOnly
- decipherOnly

## Typical Key Configurations by Application

- Encryption keys - keyEncipherment | dataEncipherment

- Signature keys - digitalSignature | nonRepudiation

- Server Authentication - digitalSignature | nonRepudiation | keyEncipherment

- Client Authentication - digitalSignature | nonRepudiation | keyAgreement (for Diffie Hellman)

- Certificate Issuers - keyCertSign | cRLSign

## Microsoft Recommendation:

This extension should be used if the purpose of the certificate is known. If the extension is absent, Microsoft applications will assume the certificate is valid for all usages. If the extension is present, Microsoft products will interpret the extension in the same way whether marked critical or not. If the extension is present, the actual usage must conform to the specified usage. The only Microsoft application that currently enforces KeyUsage is Microsoft Outlook.

## Extended Key Usage
## Extension:
ExtKeyUsageSyntax (OID 2.5.29.37).
## Reference:

ftp://ietf.org/internet-drafts/draft-ietf-pkix-ipki-part1-06.txt

## Discussion:
KeyUsage, ExtendedKeyUsage, and BasicConstraints act together to delimit the uses for which the certificate is designed and enable applications to disallow the use of the certificate in inappropriate contexts.

This extension may be marked critical or noncritical. If noncritical multiple usages may be listed the certificate should be considered valid for any of the usages listed. This extension should be marked critical if the certificate is to be used for only one of the purposes listed below. This extension is verified by applications accessing the certificate. The application must decide whether to require the usage to be explicitly listed and whether it must be marked critical.

In Microsoft verification software, the user or administrator has the option to restrict ExtendedKeyUsage further than the certificate itself allows. This would be done by editing local attributes attached to the certificate (discussed further below).

A list of PKIX defined usages and common Microsoft defined usages is given below.

*Current Public Defined Usages:*

```
1.3.6.1.5.5.7.3.1 - Server Authentication
1.3.6.1.5.5.7.3.2 - Client Authentication
1.3.6.1.5.5.7.3.3 - Code Signing
1.3.6.1.5.5.7.3.4 - Email
1.3.6.1.5.5.7.3.5 - IPSec End System
1.3.6.1.5.5.7.3.6 - IPSec Tunnel
1.3.6.1.5.5.7.3.7 - IPSec User
1.3.6.1.5.5.7.3.8 - Timestamping
```

*Current Private Defined Usages:*

```
1.3.6.1.4.1.311.2.1.21 - Individual Code Signing (use with
 1.3.6.1.5.5.7.3.3)
1.3.6.1.4.1.311.2.1.22 - Commercial Code Signing (use with
 1.3.6.1.5.5.7.3.3)
1.3.6.1.4.1.311.10.3.1 - Certificate Trust List Signing
1.3.6.1.4.1.311.10.3.3 - Microsoft SGC (Server Gated Crypto)
1.3.6.1.4.1.311.10.3.4 - Microsoft Encrypted File System (EFS descrip
 tion above)
2.16.840.1.113730.4.1 - Netscape SGC (Server Gated Crypto)
```

**Microsoft Recommendation:**

Microsoft verification interprets Extended Key Usage as follows. If the extension is not present, the certificate is considered to be valid for any usage (this supports backward compatibility with certificates that did not use this extension). Otherwise, the interpretation depends on the usage. It is recommended that this extension not be marked critical at this time. At the current time:

- Authenticode requires that Code Signing be the unique usage specified.
- SGC operation requires the SGC usage be specified.
- Timestamping requires that timestamping usage be specified.

Supplementary to the ExtendedKeyUsage extension within the certificate, Microsoft supports user settable properties on certificates corresponding to each ExtendedKeyUsage. The purpose of these properties is to allow the user to have more granular control of verification policy on the local machine. Typically the user would set these properties to restrict the usages for CA certificates on their computer. For instance, from the Internet Explorer 4.0 Certificate Management User Interface, the user may un-check a CA certificate in a list of CA certificates otherwise trusted for a given usage. Note that the user may only further restrict usages and cannot render a certificate valid for usages that are not supported by the certificate itself. These user settings do not affect the certificate itself, only its interpretation on the particular computer where the properties are set.

A given certificate is valid only for the intersection of key usages of all the certificates in the chain to its root (as determined by both the ExtendedKeyUsage extension contained explicitly within those certificates and the corresponding user settable properties). In other words, to be valid for a particular usage, the end-entity certificate and all certificates in the chain must all be valid for that usage.

## Basic Constraints
**Extension:**
BasicConstraints (OID 2.5.29.19).
**References:**

ftp://ietf.org/internet-drafts/draft-ietf-pkix-ipki-part1-06.txt

http://www.imc.org/draft-dusse-smime-cert

**Discussion:**
Defines whether the certificate is for an issuer or end-entity certificate. If specified and the certificate exists in an inappropriate place in the certificate chain, verification fails (so that an end entity may not issue certificates). May also be used to specify a maximum certificate chain length. If the maximum chain length is specified and the chain length is exceeded, verification fails. PKIX requires that this extension be used and be marked critical for issuer certificates.

**Microsoft Recommendation:**
It is recommended that this extension be used in all certificates, to enable the verification software to detect whether issuer and subject certificates are being used in the correct context.

## Certification Practice Statement and Policies
**Extension:**
CertificatePolicies (OID 2.5.29.32).
**References:**

ftp://ietf.org/internet-drafts/draft-ietf-pkix-ipki-part1-06.txt

http://www.imc.org/draft-dusse-smime-cert

**Discussion:**

Provides a description either in the form of text or a URL of the issuer's practice or issuance policy. It allows a URL to the issuer's Certificate Practice Statement, or direct embedding of issuer policy information, such as a UserNotice in text form within the certificate.

**Microsoft Recommendation:**

It is recommended that this extension be included in all certificates, since it defines what reliance the verifier may place on the certificate.

**Names**
**Serial Number**
**Field:**

CertificateSerialNumber.

**Reference:**

ftp://ietf.org/internet-drafts/draft-ietf-pkix-ipki-part1-06.txt

**Discussion:**

The combination of issuer name and certificate serial number should uniquely identify the given certificate. Therefore, among certificates from a single issuer, each should have a unique serial number.

**Microsoft Recommendation:**

This extension should always be used, and the serial number should be unique among certificates from a given issuer. The combination of issuer and serial number is used in several ways. It enables checking of the certificate against certificate revocation lists (CRLs). For issuer certificates, it enables building unique certificate chains (see AuthorityKeyIdentifier).

**Subject Name**
**Field:**

SubjectName.

**References:**

ftp://ietf.org/internet-drafts/draft-ietf-pkix-ipki-part1-06.txt

http://www.imc.org/draft-dusse-smime-cert

**Discussion:**

This is an X.500 name associated with the subject of the certificate.

**Microsoft Recommendation:**

For issuer certificates, it is recommended that the SubjectName always be used. The SubjectName in the issuer's certificate should match the issuer name in the

AuthorityKeyIdentifier of all certificates issued, since this enables the building of unique certificate chains (see AuthorityKeyIdentifier).

For Server Authentication, the Common Name attribute of the certificate SubjectName is checked against the URL requested in the connection. If the name does not match the URL, an appropriate action is taken, such as querying the user. Microsoft does not support wildcarding for server names.

## Name Constraints
**Extension:**
NameConstraints (OID 2.5.29.30).
**Reference:**

ftp://ietf.org/internet-drafts/draft-ietf-pkix-ipki-part1-06.txt

**Discussion:**
This extension may serve to enhance the ability of root or high-level CAs to create sub-CAs. When present, it limits the name space for which a CA may issue certificates.
**Microsoft Recommendation:**
This extension is not interpreted by Microsoft products at the current time.

## Subject Alternate Name
**Extension:**
SubjectAltName (OID 2.5.29.17).
**References:**

ftp://ietf.org/internet-drafts/draft-ietf-pkix-ipki-part1-06.txt

http://www.imc.org/draft-dusse-smime-cert

**Discussion:**
This field is used for non-X.500 names. It may be used in addition to the SubjectName or as a replacement for it.

E-mail addresses may be encoded either in the SubjectAltName or in the SubjectName or both. They may be encoded in the SubjectName by using the EmailAddress attribute defined in the *PKCS-9 specification*. SMIME receivers are required to be able to read an e-mail address from either the SubjectAltName or the SubjectName.

Naming forms that are supported include those listed below, and private naming forms may be added.

- **E-mail** (SMTP as defined in RFC-822)

- **DNS**
- **X.400**
- **Directory**
- **EDI**
- **URI**
- **IP Address**

**Microsoft Recommendation:**
This extension should be used whenever X.500 is insufficient to capture the name-space of subjects. At the present time, no Microsoft products require the use of SubjectAltName. All Microsoft products that support S/MIME are capable of reading e-mail names from this extension or from the SubjectName, as required. Future versions of Microsoft Exchange Server will issue certificates with X.500 names that do not contain the EmailAddress attribute and will place the SMTP address in the SubjectAltName extension.

**Issuer Name**
**Field:**
IssuerName.
**Reference:**

ftp://ietf.org/internet-drafts/draft-ietf-pkix-ipki-part1-06.txt

**Discussion:**
The Issuer name should be explicitly included in any certificate in order to help build the chain of parents and uniquely identify the parent. Use the IssuerName for X.500 names.
**Microsoft Recommendation:**
The IssuerName or IssuerAltName may be used by applications for filtering or qualifying certificates, for instance, in the TLS/SSL protocols. Microsoft recommends that the AuthorityKeyIdentifier be used rather than IssuerName or IssuerAltName for the purpose of building certificate chains (see AuthorityKeyIdentifier).

**Issuer Alternate Name**
**Extension:**
IssuerAltName (OID 2.5.29.18).
**Reference:**

ftp://ietf.org/internet-drafts/draft-ietf-pkix-ipki-part1-06.txt

**Discussion:**
This extension provides the ability for certificate issuers to have non-X.500 names.
**Microsoft Recommendation:**
The IssuerName or IssuerAltName may be used by applications for filtering or qualifying certificates, for instance, in the TLS/SSL protocols. Microsoft recommends that AuthorityKeyIdentifier be used rather than IssuerName or IssuerAltName for the purpose of building certificate chains (see AuthorityKeyIdentifier).

**Certificate Chains**
**Authority Key Identifier**
**Extension:**
AuthorityKeyIdentifier (OID 2.5.29.35).
**Reference:**

ftp://ietf.org/internet-drafts/draft-ietf-pkix-ipki-part1-06.txt

**Discussion:**
This extension is used to identify the signer of a given certificate. PKIX supports two forms of identification, one specifying the CA key used to sign the given certificate (keyIdentifier), and the other specifying the actual CA certificate used to sign the given certificate (the combination of authorityCertIssuer and authorityCertSerialNumber). PKIX recommends specification of the signing key, whereas Microsoft recommends specification of the actual CA certificate, in order to guarantee a unique certificate chain. It has been suggested that CAs may want to specify the key only as a method for changing the semantics of previously issued subject certificates (by reissuing new CA certificates under the same key). However, this implies that the semantics of those subject certificates may not be easily determined. Without a unique certificate chain, some aspects of the meaning of a given certificate may depend on which version or versions of the issuer certificate happen to be available in the local context, and may therefore not be well defined.
**Microsoft Recommendation:**
It is recommended that this extension be present in every certificate and that authorityCertIssuer and authorityCertSerialNumber be specified. This enables building a unique certificate chain, which is accomplished by matching the SubjectName and CertificateSerialNumber in the issuer's certificate with the authorityCertIssuer and authorityCertSerialNumber in the AuthorityKeyIdentifier of the subject certificate.

**Access Location**
**Extension:**
AuthorityInfoAccessSyntax (OID 1.3.6.15.5.7.1.2).

**Reference:**

> ftp://ietf.org/internet-drafts/draft-ietf-pkix-ipki-part1-06.txt

**Discussion:**
Describes a way of accessing certificates required to build a certificate chain. Generally not the preferred method of distributing parent certificates—they will typically be distributed along with the certificate in question or explicitly installed as trusted. If parent certificates cannot be located in any other way, the verifier will attempt to use this extension. However, this method has the potential of being low performance and may fail if a network connection cannot be established. It is therefore advisable for the issuer to bundle its certificate and the certificates of its parents along with the subject certificate, and applications should be prepared for the chain of certificates rather than just the subject certificate.

**Microsoft Recommendation:**
It is recommended that this extension be used and that there be a distribution point for issuer certificates to cover circumstances where the subject certificate may become separated from the rest of its certificate chain.

**Dates and Status**
**Validity**
**Field:**
Validity.
**References:**

> ftp://ietf.org/internet-drafts/draft-ietf-pkix-ipki-part1-06.txt

**Discussion:**
Validity period is encoded as UTCTime values for NotBefore and NotAfter.

**Microsoft Recommendation:**
It is recommended that issuers not issue certificates with expirations after their own certificate expires. The certificate may fail to verify if its validity period is not nested within the validity periods of all of its parents. Microsoft makes no specific recommendation as to the duration of CA or end-entity certificates.

**CRL Distribution Points**
**Extension:**
CRLDistributionPoints (OID 2.5.29.31).
**References:**

> ftp://ietf.org/internet-drafts/draft-ietf-pkix-ipki-part1-06.txt

> ftp://ietf.org/internet-drafts/draft-ietf-pkix-ipki-part1-06.txt (CRL structure)

**Discussion:**
Certificate Revocation Lists (CRL) provide a method for distributing information on the validity status of certificates. CRLs are generally issued on a periodic basis, and their validity periods are noted in the CRL itself, so that the verification system may refresh if appropriate.

**Microsoft Recommendation:**
It is recommended that this extension be present so the verifier knows where to obtain CRLs issued by the CA. Both versions 1 and 2 CRLs will be supported by Microsoft products.

**Note:** The URL may be used for various access protocols. Currently HTTP is supported, and LDAP will be supported in future releases of Microsoft products for connecting to directory services.

**OnLine Certificate Status**
**Extension:**
AuthorityInfoAccessSyntax (OID 1.3.6.15.5.7.1.2)
**Reference:**

> ftp://ietf.org/internet-drafts/draft-ietf-pkix-ipki-part1-06.txt

**Discussion:**
Online Certificate status provides an alternative to CRLs. However, online verification typically requires a network connection for each verification and, therefore, has associated performance and availability concerns.

**Microsoft Recommendation:**
Microsoft does not currently support on-line revocation checking within its products. On-line checking may be useful in certain situations; however, for most applications the advantages are outweighed by scalability, availability, and performance problems.

**Cryptography**
**Signature**
**Fields:**
Signature, AlgorithmIdentifier (external and internal to TBSCertificate).
**References:**

> ftp://ietf.org/internet-drafts/draft-ietf-pkix-ipki-part1-06.txt
>
> http://www.imc.org/draft-dusse-smime-cert

**Discussion:**
Actual signature and algorithm used by the issuer to sign this certificate. The signature is a hash of the remainder of the certificate, the TBSCertificate ("to be signed" certificate) that contains all the rest of the certificate information. The

AlgorithmIdentifier is repeated twice: once outside the TBSCertificate so that processing may begin, and again inside the TBSCertificate for verification.

**Microsoft Recommendation:**

Microsoft products only support the RSA algorithms for use with public key certificates at the current time. This will be expanded in future products to support other public-key algorithms, such as DSA, via CryptoAPI.

For consistency with other PKCS forms that do not carry the corresponding repeat of the AlgorithmIdentifier, Microsoft does not currently verify that the AlgorithmIdentifier inside the TBSCertificate is correct.

**Subject Public Key**

**Field:**

SubjectPublicKeyInfo.

**Reference:**

ftp://ietf.org/internet-drafts/draft-ietf-pkix-ipki-part1-06.txt

**Discussion:**

Public key and algorithm associated with the subject in this certificate.

**Microsoft Recommendation:**

The subject public key is a basic ingredient of any certificate. Microsoft products only support the RSA algorithm for use with public key certificates at the current time. This will be expanded in future products to support other public-key algorithms, such as DSA and Diffie-Hellman, via CryptoAPI.

**Certificate Extensions Not Currently Used by Microsoft Products**

**Policy Mappings**

**Extension:**

PolicyMappings (OID 2.5.29.33).

**Reference:**

ftp://ietf.org/internet-drafts/draft-ietf-pkix-ipki-part1-06.txt

**Discussion:**

This extension applies to issuer certificates and allows issuers to identify their issuance policies with those of other issuers. It is most likely to become useful in the context of cross-certification.

**Microsoft Recommendation:**

This extension is not utilized by Microsoft products at the current time.

**Policy Constraints**

**Extension:**

PolicyConstraints (OID 2.5.29.34).

**Reference:**

ftp://ietf.org/internet-drafts/draft-ietf-pkix-ipki-part1-06.txt

**Discussion:**
This extension applies to issuer certificates. It may be used to place certain limitations on issuer policies.

**Microsoft Recommendation:**
This extension is not interpreted by Microsoft products at the current time, and its use is not recommended. If marked critical, verification will fail.

**PrivateKeyUsagePeriod**
**Extension:**
IssuerAltName (OID 2.5.29.16).
**Reference:**

ftp://ietf.org/internet-drafts/draft-ietf-pkix-ipki-part1-06.txt

**Discussion:**
PKIX recommends against the use of this extension.

**Microsoft Recommendation:**
This extension is not utilized by Microsoft products at the current time, and its use is not recommended. If marked critical, verification will fail.

**Subject Key Identifier**
**Extension:**
SubjectKeyIdentifier (OID 2.5.29.14).
**Reference:**

ftp://ietf.org/internet-drafts/draft-ietf-pkix-ipki-part1-06.txt

**Discussion:**
This extension if used contains the hash of the subject key. It may be used in conjunction with the form of Authority Key Identifier in which the issuer's public key is specified via a hash. In this case the verifier is saved the expense of computing a hash and need only compare the issuer's Subject Key Identifier and the subject's Authority Key Identifier (which must be identical).

**Microsoft Recommendation:**
Microsoft recommends the issuer and serial number method of specifying parent certificates, not comparison of keys, because the issuer may have multiple certificates against a given key. *See also* Authority Key Identifier.

**Subject Directory Attributes**
**Extension:**
PolicyMappings (OID 2.5.29.9).
**Reference:**

ftp://ietf.org/internet-drafts/draft-ietf-pkix-ipki-part1-06.txt

**Microsoft Recommendation:**
This extension is not utilized by Microsoft products at the current time, and its use is not recommended.

*We welcome your feedback. Please address comments and questions to Secure@microsoft.com.*
**Note:** The information contained in this document represents the current view of Microsoft Corporation on the issues discussed as of the date of publication. Because Microsoft must respond to changing market conditions, it should not be interpreted to be a commitment on the part of Microsoft, and Microsoft cannot guarantee the accuracy of any information presented after the date of publication. This document is for informational purposes only. Microsoft makes no warranties, express or implied, in this document. *© 1997 Microsoft Corporation. All rights reserved. Used with permission.*

# Appendix
## C
##

# Quick Summary of VeriSign's Certification Practice Statement[1]

## VeriSign's Certification Practice Statement

Quick Summary of Important CPS Rights and Obligations
Please see the text of the CPS for details. This summary is incomplete. Many other important issues are discussed in the CPS.

1. This Certification Practice Statement controls the provision and use of VeriSign's public certification services [§ 1.1, § 2.1]—including certificate application [§ 4], application validation [§ 5], certificate issuance [§ 6], acceptance [§ 7], use [§ 8], and suspension and revocation [§ 9].

2. You (the user) acknowledge that (i) you have been advised to receive proper training in the use of public key techniques prior to applying for a certificate and that (ii) documentation, training, and education about digital signatures, certificates, PKI, and the PCS are available from VeriSign [§ 1.6].

3. VeriSign offers different classes of certificates [§ 2.2]. You must decide which class(es) of certificate are right for your needs.

4. Before submitting a certificate application [§ 4.2], you must generate a key pair [§§ 2.3.3, 4.1] and keep the private key secure from compromise in a trustworthy manner[§ 4.1.1]. Your software system should provide this functionality.

5. You must accept [§ 7.1] a certificate before communicating it to others, or otherwise inducing their use of it. By accepting a certificate, you make certain important representations [§ 7.2].

6. If you are the recipient of a digital signature or certificate, you are responsible for deciding whether to rely on it. Before doing so, VeriSign recommends that you check the VeriSign repository to confirm that the certificate is valid and not

---

1. See http://www.verisign.com/repository/summary.html for the online copy of this document.

revoked, or suspended and then use the certificate to verify [§ 8.1] that the digital signature was created during the operational period of the certificate by the private key corresponding to the public key listed in the certificate, and that the message associated with the digital signature has not been altered.

7. You agree to notify [§ 12.10] the applicable issuing authority upon compromise of your private key.

8. This Certification Practice Statement provides various warranties made by VeriSign and the issuing authorities [§ 11.3]. VeriSign also has a refund policy [§ 11.1]. Otherwise, warranties are disclaimed and liability is limited by VeriSign and issuing authorities [§§ 11.2 and 11.3].

9. The NetSure Protection Plan, on its effective date, will provide enhanced warranty protection to subscribers of VeriSign-issued certificates who obtain certificates after the effective date. Relying parties can obtain the benefits of the Netsure Protection Plan by purchasing a certificate at VeriSign's Digital ID Center at https://digitalid.verisign.com/enroll.html. The NetSure Protection Plan alters the limitations of liability applicable to subscribers who obtain certificates on or after the effective date. For more information, see the NetSure Protection Plan at https://www.verisign.com/repository/netsure and the NetSure Protection Plan FAQ at https://www.verisign.com/repository/netsure_faq.

10. The Certification Practice Statement contains various miscellaneous provisions [§ 12], requires compliance with applicable export regulations [§ 12.2], and prohibits infringement [§ 12.14].

Appendix

# D
——

# VeriSign's Perspective on OnSite LRA Service versus Certificate Servers[1]

| VeriSign OnSite | Do-It-Yourself Products |
|---|---|
| Easy to use | Requires hardware/software maintenance, including database and network operations |
| No extensive training required | High level of prior technical knowledge, as well as extensive training, required |
| Less expensive | Can cost up to 10 times as much for total solution |
| No additional hardware or software | Requires purchase of server and software |
| Easily distributed | Centralized, secure server facility required |
| Grows to fit your needs | Lacks interoperability, scalability |
| Leading PKI, certificate infrastructure expertise | Requires extensive training on behalf of user |

**Figure D-1** VeriSign's comparison of OnSite service with certification products.

---

1. See http://www.verisign.com/onsite/index.html.

# Index

# CD-ROM Warranty